W9-BAC-509

The ACP Group and the EU Development Partnership

Annita Montoute • Kudrat Virk
Editors

The ACP Group and the EU Development Partnership

Beyond the North-South Debate

Editors
Annita Montoute
Institute of International Relations
The University of the West Indies
St Augustine, Trinidad and Tobago

Kudrat Virk
Centre for Conflict Resolution
Cape Town, South Africa

ISBN 978-3-319-45491-7   ISBN 978-3-319-45492-4   (eBook)
DOI 10.1007/978-3-319-45492-4

Library of Congress Control Number: 2016954264

© Centre for Conflict Resolution 2017
This work is subject to copyright. All rights are solely and exclusively licensed by the Publisher, whether the whole or part of the material is concerned, specifically the rights of translation, reprinting, reuse of illustrations, recitation, broadcasting, reproduction on microfilms or in any other physical way, and transmission or information storage and retrieval, electronic adaptation, computer software, or by similar or dissimilar methodology now known or hereafter developed.
The use of general descriptive names, registered names, trademarks, service marks, etc. in this publication does not imply, even in the absence of a specific statement, that such names are exempt from the relevant protective laws and regulations and therefore free for general use. The publisher, the authors and the editors are safe to assume that the advice and information in this book are believed to be true and accurate at the date of publication. Neither the publisher nor the authors or the editors give a warranty, express or implied, with respect to the material contained herein or for any errors or omissions that may have been made.

Cover design by Samantha Johnson

Printed on acid-free paper

This Palgrave Macmillan imprint is published by Springer Nature
The registered company is Springer International Publishing AG
The registered company address is: Gewerbestrasse 11, 6330 Cham, Switzerland

This book is dedicated to the memory of Norman Girvan (1941–2014), Professor Emeritus of the University of the West Indies and Secretary-General of the Association of Caribbean States from 2000 to 2004, and of Kaye Whiteman (1936–2014), senior Information Official at the European Commission between 1973 and 1982 and Editor of West Africa *from 1982 to 1999, both committed to African, Caribbean, and Pacific solidarity, and both giants in their fields.*

Contents

LIST OF FIGURES

LIST OF TABLES

Acknowledgements

For four decades the development partnership between the African, Caribbean, and Pacific (ACP) group and the European Union (EU) has withstood the test of time, and endured as one of the most comprehensive of its kind. But now it faces a key juncture in its history, as power diffuses and traditional paradigms break down with the rise of new powers in the global South. Against the backdrop of an evolving global order, both the ACP and the EU are engaged in critical conversations on the future of their joint endeavour beyond 2020. This book seeks to ensure that more African, Caribbean, and Pacific voices are heard in these debates and discussions, which affect their own countries and regions, their individual lives, and their shared aspirations for a sustainable future and a more just world for the ACP's one billion citizens. First and foremost, we would like, therefore, to thank the contributing authors to this volume—mainly from the ACP, but also beyond—for bringing their voices to the conversation, for their dedication and perseverance, as well as for their immense patience with, and willingness to respond to, the seemingly endless demands of a protracted editing process.

This project was initiated by the Centre for Conflict Resolution (CCR) in Cape Town, South Africa, with a view to assessing the ACP-EU partnership and assisting the efforts of the ACP Secretariat and Ambassadorial Working Group on Future Perspectives, in particular, to chart a new direction for their organisation. Our debt to CCR for its initiative, as well as sponsorship and support for the book that has arisen from it, is immense. We would like to thank, in particular, Adekeye Adebajo, the Executive Director of CCR, for his invaluable guidance and untiring commitment to bringing the project to fruition. Our journey to this point has been long and hard, and we are grateful to several members of the Centre's family for their indispensable support, especially Jill Kronenberg and Liliane Limenyande, who ably lent administrative support to the project. We would like further to acknowledge the main funders of CCR's Africa Programme over the past four years—the governments of Denmark, Finland, the Netherlands, Norway, and Sweden. This book is an integral part of the Centre's efforts to bridge the North-South gap in knowledge production. We owe considerable thanks as well to Jason Cook for his meticulous copy-editing of the manuscript.

A special word of thanks must go to the late Norman Girvan and the late Kaye Whiteman, whose work has inspired our thinking about ACP-EU relations and development cooperation in general. Girvan was committed to the principles of justice and equity, which he felt must form the basis of the ACP-EU partnership, and he further saw regional integration as a tool for building ACP unity. Whiteman's knowledge of African politics and history was immense, and his commitment to improving the prospects of the continent, which he covered for much of his life as a journalist and writer, was boundless. Both Girvan and Whiteman were strong advocates of ACP solidarity. This volume is, in part, in honour of their commitment and celebrates their lives, work, and legacies.

Finally, it has been a pleasure to work with Anca Pusca, Anne Schult, and their colleagues at Palgrave Macmillan. We hope that this book will help in shaping the debates on the historic partnership between the ACP group and the EU, and inspire interest among a young generation of scholars in Africa, the Caribbean, and the Pacific, in particular, to grapple with the hard questions that it raises in a time of tremendous change.

Annita Montoute and Kudrat Virk
May 2016

List of Abbreviations

AASM	Associated African States and Madagascar
ACE	Architects Council of Europe
ACP	African, Caribbean, and Pacific
ACPP	Africa Conflict Prevention Pool
ACS	Association of Caribbean States
ADB	Asian Development Bank
AEC	African Economic Community
AfDB	African Development Bank
AfT	Aid for Trade
AGA	African Governance Architecture
ALBA	Bolivarian Alliance for the Peoples of Our America
AMIF	Asylum, Migration, and Integration Fund
AMIS	African Union Mission in Sudan
AMISOM	African Union Mission in Somalia
APF	African Peace Facility
APSA	African Peace and Security Architecture
ARI	Africa Research Institute
ASF	African Standby Force
ATN	African Trade Network
AU	African Union
AUSP	African Union Support Programme
B&S	Business and Strategies Europe and Linpico
BBC	British Broadcasting Corporation
BLNS	Botswana, Lesotho, Namibia, and Swaziland
BPST	British Peace Support Team
BRICS	Brazil, Russia, India, China, and South Africa

BRIDGES-LAC   Building Relationships and Improving Dialogues Geared Towards Erasmus Mundus Goals—Latin America and Caribbean
CACM   Central American Common Market
CAFRA   Caribbean Association for Feminist Research and Action
CAFTA-DR   Central America-Dominican Republic Free Trade Agreement
CAP   Common Agricultural Policy
CAR   Central African Republic
CARICOM   Caribbean Community
CARIFORUM   Forum of the Caribbean Group of ACP States
CCR   Centre for Conflict Resolution
CDE   Centre for the Development of Enterprise
CELAC   Community of Latin American and Caribbean States
CEWS   Continental Early Warning System
CFA   *Communauté Financière Africaine*
CFC   Common Fund for Commodities
CFSP   Common Foreign and Security Policy
CHARM   Customs Heads of Administration Regional Meeting
CIA   Central Intelligence Agency
CIGI   Centre for International Governance Innovation
CII   Confederation of Indian Industry
CIVETS   Colombia, Indonesia, Vietnam, Egypt, Turkey, and South Africa
CNDP   *Congrès National pour la Défense du Peuple*
CNPC   China National Petroleum Corporation
COMESA   Common Market for Eastern and Southern Africa
COMPAS   Centre on Migration, Policy, and Society (University of Oxford)
CONCORD   European NGO Confederation for Relief and Development
CPA   Cotonou Partnership Agreement
CPDC   Caribbean Policy Development Centre
CPLP   Lusophone Development Cooperation Organisation
CRIP   Caribbean Regional Indicative Programme
CRNM   Caribbean Regional Negotiating Machinery
CSME   CARICOM Single Market and Economy
DCI   Development Cooperation Instrument
DFID   Department for International Development (Britain)
DG DEVCO   Directorate-General for International Cooperation and Development (EU)
DG EXPO   Directorate-General for External Policies (EU)
DIE   German Development Institute

DIRCO	Department of International Relations and Cooperation (South Africa)
DRC	Democratic Republic of the Congo
DTI	Department of Trade and Industry (South Africa)
DW	*Deutsche Welle*
EAC	East African Community
EAEC	European Atomic Energy Community
EBA	Everything But Arms
ECCAS	Economic Community of Central African States
ECDPM	European Centre for Development Policy Management
ECLAC	Economic Commission for Latin America and the Caribbean (UN)
ECOPAS	European Consortium for Pacific Studies
ECOWAS	Economic Community of West African States
ECUs	European currency units
EDF	European Development Fund
EEAS	European External Action Service
EEC	European Economic Community
EEZ	exclusive economic zone
EIB	European Investment Bank
ENAEE	European Network for the Accreditation of Engineering Education
EPA	economic partnership agreement
EPC	European Policy Centre
EPG	Eminent Persons Group (ACP)
ESA	Eastern and Southern Africa
ESDP	European Security and Defence Policy
ESfO	European Society for Oceanists
EU	European Union
EUFOR	EU force
EU-LAC	EU, Latin America, and the Caribbean
EUPOL	EU police mission
EUSEC	EU Security Sector Reform Mission
FAO	Food and Agriculture Organisation
FAQ	frequently asked questions
FARDC	*Forces Armées de la République Démocratique du Congo*
FDI	foreign direct investment
FICs	Forum Island Countries
FITUN	Federation of Independent Trade Unions and NGOs
FOCAC	Forum on China-Africa Cooperation
FOCAL	Canadian Foundation for the Americas
FOMUC	*Force Multinationale en Centrafrique*

FRIDE	*Fundación par las Relaciones Internacionales y el Diálogo Exterior*
FTA	free trade agreement
FTAA	Free Trade Area of the Americas
G-8	Group of Eight
G-20	Group of 20
G-77	Group of 77
G-90	Group of 90
GAERC	General Affairs and External Relations Council (EU)
GAM	Global Approach to Migration
GAMM	Global Approach to Migration and Mobility
GATS	General Agreement on Trade in Services
GATT	General Agreement on Tariffs and Trade
GDP	gross domestic product
GEPA	Ghana Export Promotion Authority
Glopolis	Prague Global Policy Institute
GMG	Global Migration Group
GMOD	Global Migrants Origins Database (University of Sussex)
GNI	gross national income
GSP	Generalised System of Preferences
IADB	Inter-American Development Bank
IAFS	India-Africa Forum Summit
IBSA	India, Brazil, and South Africa
ICC	International Criminal Court
ICT	information and communications technology
ICTSD	International Centre for Trade and Sustainable Development
IDEA	International Institute for Democracy and Electoral Assistance
IDM	International Dialogue on Migration
IDPs	internally displaced persons
IDS	Institute of Development Studies (University of Sussex)
IEA	International Energy Agency
IEMF	EU Interim Emergency Multinational Force
IFAD	International Fund for Agricultural Development
IFIs	international financial institutions
IGAD	Intergovernmental Authority on Development
IISD	International Institute for Sustainable Development
ILO	International Labour Organisation
IMC	International Marketing Council of South Africa
IMF	International Monetary Fund

IOB	Operations Evaluation Department (Dutch Ministry of Foreign Affairs)
IOM	International Organisation for Migration
IPR	intellectual property [rights]
IROCC	Inter-Regional Organisations Coordinating Committee
ITC	International Trade Centre
JAES	Joint Africa-EU Strategy
JCEUS	Joint Caribbean-EU Strategy
JETRO	Japan External Trade Organisation
LDC	least-developed country
LGBTI	lesbian, gay, bisexual, transgender, and intersex
LSE	London School of Economics and Political Science
MCES	Micronesian Chief Executives' Summit
MDGs	Millennium Development Goals
MFLM	Multilateral Framework on Labour Migration (ILO)
MFN	most-favoured-nation
MGI	McKinsey Global Institute
MICOPAX	Mission for the Consolidation of Peace in the Central African Republic
MINURCAT	United Nations Mission in the Central African Republic and Chad
MISCA	African-led International Support Mission to the Central African Republic
MONUC	United Nations Organisation Mission in the DRC
MSG	Melanesian Spearhead Group
MTS	ACP Multilateral Trading System programme
NAFTA	North American Free Trade Agreement
NAM	Non-Aligned Movement
NATO	North Atlantic Treaty Organisation
NAVFOR	naval force (EU)
NDB	New Development Bank (BRICS)
NEPAD	New Partnership for Africa's Development
NGOs	non-governmental organisations
NIC	National Intelligence Council (US)
NIEO	New International Economic Order
NIPs	National Indicative Programmes
OAS	Organisation of American States
OAU	Organisation of African Unity
OBREAL	*Observatorio de las Relaciones Unión Europea—América Latina*
OCO	Oceania Customs Organisation

OCTs	overseas countries and territories
ODA	official development assistance
ODI	Overseas Development Institute
OECD	Organisation for Economic Cooperation and Development
OECS	Organisation of Eastern Caribbean States
OIF	*Organisation International de la Francophonie*
ORs	outermost regions
OVL	Oil and Natural Gas Corporation Videsh (India)
OWTU	Oil Workers Trade Union (Trinidad and Tobago)
PACER	Pacific Agreement on Closer Economic Relations
PACE-SD	Pacific Centre for Environment and Sustainable Development (University of the South Pacific)
PAHO	Pan-American Health Organisation
PFL	Pacific Forum Line
PICTA	Pacific Island Countries Trade Agreement
PIDF	Pacific Islands Development Forum
PIF	Pacific Islands Forum
PINA	Pacific Islands News Association
PiPP	Pacific Institute of Public Policy
PLG	Polynesian Leaders Group
PSIDS	Pacific Small Islands Development Forum
R2P	responsibility to protect
RECAMP	*Renforcement des Capacités Africaines de Maintien de la Paix*
RECs	regional economic communities
RIP	Regional Indicative Programme
RMI	Raw Materials Initiative
SAC	Sugar Association of the Caribbean
SACU	Southern African Customs Union
SADC	Southern African Development Community
SAIIA	South African Institute of International Affairs
SAIS	School of Advanced International Studies (Johns Hopkins University)
SAPs	structural adjustment programmes
SDGs	Sustainable Development Goals
SHIRBRIG	UN Standby High-Readiness Brigade
SIPRI	Stockholm International Peace Research Institute
SIS	Smaller Island States (Pacific Islands Forum)
SMEs	small and medium enterprises
SPARTECA	South Pacific Regional Trade and Economic Cooperation Agreement
SPF	South Pacific Forum

SSR	security sector reform
STABEX	*Système de Stabilisation des Recettes d'Exportation*
SVEs	small and vulnerable economies
SWOT	strengths, weaknesses, opportunities, and threats
SYSMIN	*Système de Développement du Potentiel Minier*
TDCA	Trade, Development, and Cooperation Agreement (South Africa)
TGA	trade-in-goods agreement
TIS	trade-in-services
TMSA	TradeMark Southern Africa
UEMOA	*Union Économique et Monétaire Ouest Africaine*
UK	United Kingdom
UN	United Nations
UN DESA	United Nations Department of Economic and Social Affairs
UNAMID	African Union-United Nations Hybrid Operation in Darfur
UNASUR	Union of South American States
UNCTAD	United Nations Conference on Trade and Development
UNDP	United Nations Development Programme
UNECA	United Nations Economic Commission for Africa
UNESCAP	United Nations Economic and Social Commission for Asia and the Pacific
UNHCR	United Nations High Commissioner for Refugees
UNITAF	Unified Task Force
UNOGBIS	United Nations Peacebuilding Support Office in Guinea-Bissau
UNOSOM	United Nations Operation in Somalia
US	United States
UWI	The University of the West Indies
VENRO	*Verband Entwicklungspolitik Deutscher Nichtregierungsorganisationen*
V-Flex	Vulnerability Flex
WFP	World Food Programme
WINAD	Women Institute for Alternative Development (Trinidad and Tobago)
WIRSPA	West Indies Rum and Spirits Producers Association
WITS	World Integrated Trade Solution
WTO	World Trade Organisation

PART I

Historical Foundations of the ACP-EU Relationship

CHAPTER 1

Introduction

Annita Montoute

Four decades on from the establishment of the African, Caribbean, and
Pacific (ACP) group of states in 1975, the future of its historic development partnership with the European Union (EU) has become fragile
and uncertain. Since 2000, the Cotonou Partnership Agreement has provided the overarching framework for trade, aid, and political cooperation
between the 79-member ACP group and the 28-strong EU.[1] This volume, which explores the evolution and future prospects of the ACP-EU
relationship, is particularly timely, with the end of the 20-year Cotonou
Agreement approaching in 2020 and both sides engaged in deliberating
the way forward for the partnership. The third and final five-yearly review
of Cotonou in 2015 has since been called off—testimony to the fragile
foundations of the ACP's long-time engagement with the EU. With much
of the analysis on the ACP-EU relationship led, or conducted, by scholars
and institutions outside the African, Caribbean, and Pacific regions, this
edited collection—with essays contributed mainly by ACP academics and
policymakers—seeks to ensure that more non-European voices contribute
to critical debates on the ACP's post-2020 future as a group and on its
engagement with the EU.[2] The endeavour is vital with the very existence

A. Montoute (✉)
Institute of International Relations, The University of the West Indies (UWI),
St Augustine, Trinidad and Tobago

© The Author(s) 2017
A. Montoute, K. Virk (eds.), *The ACP Group and the EU*
Development Partnership, DOI 10.1007/978-3-319-45492-4_1

of the ACP group arguably at stake, given the importance of cooperation with the EU as the raison d'être for its creation.

While many in the African, Caribbean, and Pacific regions, as well as in Europe, believe that the ACP-EU relationship remains important for both sides, there is consensus that its nature is destined to change due to various factors, as assessed in a chapter by the current Guyanese ACP Secretary-General, Patrick Gomes. These include an evolving international order characterised by: the rise of new economic powers such as China, Brazil, and India in the global South; the shifting priorities of both the ACP group and the EU against this backdrop; the debated impact of the ACP-EU relationship on development and regional integration in the ACP; the continued asymmetries in political and economic power between the two sides; and the growing role of political issues (such as human rights, "good governance", and the rule of law) in the relationship.

Both sides—the ACP since 2010 and the EU since 2011—have been engaged in formal processes of reflection on the future of their relationship as they at the same time deliberated on the post-2015 sustainable development agenda. Since their launch in September 2015, the new Sustainable Development Goals (SDGs) have been adopted by the ACP as the broad framework to inform the future direction of ACP-EU relations after 2020. This is understandable given the fact that 39 out of the 48 least-developed countries (LDCs), as defined by the United Nations (UN) in 2014, are members of the ACP group, with the EU committed—including through its engagement with the group—to UN-set goals for the eradication of world poverty.

Historically, developing countries have held that industrialised countries have an obligation to contribute to reversing the patterns of under-development engineered by past imperialism. Given the origins of ACP-EU cooperation as a means for European powers to maintain formal ties with their former colonies (see Whiteman in this volume), there was a general predisposition at the outset to view the relationship through a neo-colonial lens. Early analyses of the relationship tended to subscribe to theories of dependency,[3] and to explain ACP development—or rather its lack thereof—in terms of the unequal relations between the six regions of the group—West, Central, East, and Southern Africa; the Caribbean; and the Pacific—and Europe. Ghanaian scholar Samuel Asante, for example, argued in 1981 that the Lomé regime—the predecessor to Cotonou—was an instrument of dependence and exploitation.[4]

Dependency theory is useful for understanding how structural inequality between the industrialised North and the global South has impacted on the latter's development. However, as Canadian scholar John Ravenhill noted in 1985, it does not explain several aspects of the ACP group's engagement with the EU. These include the ACP's reasons for entering into the relationship with Brussels in the first place; the way the African, Caribbean, and Pacific countries themselves sought to frame the relationship; and their failure eventually to attain their desired objectives.[5] Instead, Ravenhill proposed a different model for understanding the ACP-EU relationship in the context of the Lomé regime (1975–2000), which he termed "collective clientelism"—"a relationship in which a group of weak states combine in an effort to exploit the special ties that link them to a more powerful state or group of states".[6] More specifically, Ravenhill argued that the ACP group signed up to the Lomé Convention to secure material benefits from Europe without having to reciprocate.

Other works on the ACP-EU relationship have drawn from liberal approaches that stress the growth of interdependence among states, and viewed the Lomé Convention as an indicator of increasing equality between the ACP and the EU. Drawing on theories of international cooperation, British scholar William Brown argued in 2002, for example, that the Lomé Conventions, as well as Cotonou, epitomised instances of international cooperation among states for mutual interest, and as such, should be understood within the broader context of the evolution of North-South relations.[7] A few scholars and analysts have also used realist approaches to explain the provision of EU aid to the ACP group, identifying European self-interest as the main motivation for it.[8] In an article published in *African Affairs* in 1998, Gorm Olsen, for example, argued that Europe had prioritised its security interests over the promotion of human rights and democracy as conditions for providing aid to African countries.[9]

On the whole, these analyses of the ACP-EU relationship have gone beyond the technical approaches that have otherwise tended to be taken by the EU,[10] as well as by some ACP trade negotiators. This volume, with its diverse group of contributors, not only includes practitioner perspectives (see, for example, Carim, Gonzales, and Katjavivi), but also steps outside the narrow confines of technical discussions and seeks to understand the strategic contours of the ACP-EU relationship (see, for example, Gomes, Virk, and Whiteman). The discussion in individual chapters is located within the broad framework of key geo-strategic, political, and economic shifts since the late 1980s through the 2000s—including the creation of the World Trade Organisation (WTO) and the rise of new economic powers, in particular Brazil, Russia, India, China, and South Africa (the BRICS bloc)[11]—that have impacted the interests, options, and priorities of both the ACP group and the EU.

All in all, the context of the ACP-EU relationship has changed radically since it was originally conceived, and even more so since the signing of the Cotonou Agreement in 2000. Discourses on the international division of labour, although they must be articulated, can no longer be confined within the framework of traditional divisions between the industrialised North and the global South. The world has become increasingly multipolar, particularly since the turn of the twenty-first century, with the ongoing shift of power from its previous concentration in the North to the East and the South. These dynamics have been reflected in the evolution of the ACP-EU relationship, and as such will inevitably inform the construction of the post-Cotonou framework.

HISTORICAL CONTEXT: EVOLUTION OF THE ACP-EU RELATIONSHIP

Kaye Whiteman, a former British *fonctionnaire* at the EU Commission in Brussels between 1973 and 1982, recounts in his rich historical chapter in this volume that the foundations of the ACP-EU relationship were laid in the 1957 Treaty of Rome establishing the European Economic Community (EEC), which provided for an association with the overseas territories of the signatories. This association was given concrete form by the Yaoundé Convention of 1963 (renewed in 1969) between the EEC and 18 former European colonies in Africa, with financial support provided by the second and third iterations of the European Development Fund (EDF). The EDF was launched in 1959 as the main instrument for providing European aid to the overseas territories. Britain's entry into the EEC in 1973 led to the transformation of the association into a more open and inclusive framework for cooperation that incorporated former British colonies in Africa, the Caribbean, and the Pacific.[12] The first Lomé Convention was signed in February 1975 by the nine-member EEC and 46 ACP countries, with the latter giving formal expression to their unity as a negotiating bloc later in the same year. The Georgetown Agreement of 1975 established the ACP group of states with its main aim being "to negotiate and implement, together, cooperation agreements with the European Community".[13]

Lomé I—accompanied by the third EDF—did not represent a radical departure from the Yaoundé Conventions, but instead included important changes that accommodated shifts in the international environment and Britain's accession to the EEC in 1973.[14] First, Lomé replaced the reciprocal trade preferences that had obtained under Yaoundé with trade non-reciprocity for almost all ACP exports into the European common market. Second, it introduced separate trading protocols on sugar, bananas, and beef and veal.[15] These commodity protocols reflected Britain's desire to bring its special preferences for bananas and sugar under the EU umbrella. Third, Lomé I created STABEX (*Système de Stabilisation des Recettes d'Exportation*), a funding mechanism for the stabilisation of earnings from agricultural exports in case of price fluctuations.

The Lomé Convention was subsequently renewed three times: in 1980 and 1985 for five-year periods and then in 1990 for a ten-year period, with support provided by the fourth, fifth, and sixth iterations of the EDF respectively. Lomé II established SYSMIN (*Système de Développement du Potentiel Minier*)—an equivalent to STABEX for the mineral sector—while Lomé III emphasised rural development and food self-sufficiency. The latter also introduced the idea of policy dialogue between the two sides, with Lomé IV going further by including policy conditionalities for European aid to ACP countries and respect for human rights as a fundamental clause.

The evolution of the ACP-EU relationship, as evidenced by the transition from the Lomé regime to Cotonou in 2000, reflected broader shifts in the global political economy and in development thinking in the 1980s and 1990s. The end of the Cold War by 1990 was seen by many as a triumph of global capitalism.[16] Neo-liberal thought, embodied in the set of policy prescriptions known as the Washington Consensus, gained influence in development policymaking in Western-dominated multinational institutions, in particular the International Monetary Fund (IMF) and the World Bank. During the debt crisis of the 1980s, as developing countries turned to these institutions and Western donors for loans, they were forced through policy conditionalities to adopt neo-liberal prescriptions based on free-market economics. With the conclusion of the Uruguay Round of trade negotiations, the WTO was established in 1995, replacing the General Agreement on Tariffs and Trade (GATT). The WTO was premised on a philosophy of reciprocity and non-discrimination in trade, and it "locked" developing countries yet further into the dominant neo-liberal paradigm. In particular, the GATT waiver that had been granted for non-reciprocity in ACP-EU trade under the Lomé Conventions came under increasing pressure. The Lomé trade provisions were eventually declared to be WTO-incompatible in 1997. This was subsequently used by Brussels as the basis for future ACP-EU trade negotiations. The result was the Cotonou Agreement of 2000.

Although funding aspects remained intact, there was a fundamental shift in the trade component of the ACP-EU relationship under Cotonou. This new agreement—negotiated between 1998 and 2000—was seen as a framework to "help the ACP countries adjust and integrate into the multilateral trading system".[17] New economic partnership agreements (EPAs) based on trade reciprocity were the centrepiece of the neo-liberal turn under Cotonou. The EU further insisted that the EPAs should be negotiated on a regional basis rather than with the ACP as a whole. This not only marked a significant change from Lomé, but also roused the ACP's suspicions of a European intention to break up the ACP group. The EU's political and economic advantages over the ACP, however, hindered the latter's ability and willingness to resist European demands. Cotonou furthermore linked "good governance" with sustainable development, which placed the responsibility for development on the shoulders of ACP members while shifting the focus away from structural economic constraints, inequities in global trade, and EU trade policies (in particular, agricultural subsidies of about €55 billion a year in 2013)[18] as development inhibitors.

In addition to the concern that Lomé's non-reciprocity-based trade regime contravened the GATT/WTO principle of non-discrimination, several other reasons were cited by Brussels for its demise. These included the poor results of ACP-EU development cooperation under Lomé,[19] and the "outdated" nature of Lomé-type preferences as a means to boost ACP trade performance,[20] with the exception of certain sectors such as textiles, clothing, fisheries, and commodities including sugar, beef, and veal. The importance of the EU's preferential regime for the ACP was also seen to have been undermined by the reduction of European trade barriers within the multilateral trade framework and by the establishment of preferential arrangements with third countries (for example, South Africa—see Carim in this volume).[21] However, changing national interest–based calculations in a new and still-evolving geo-political context after the end of the Cold War were arguably the main drivers behind the EU's preference for a reciprocal trade regime for the ACP. The analysis and recommendations contained in the EU Commission's 2006 communication "Global Europe: Competing in the World" articulate a trade policy agenda aimed at opening new markets for EU exports, removing restrictions to access resources (raw materials), and expanding the agenda to include new areas, in particular "intellectual property (IPR), services, investment, public procurement and competition", to facilitate "new market access for EU businesses".[22]

Main Issues in the ACP-EU Relationship

Shifting Strategies and Interests

Since the turn of the twenty-first century, ongoing tectonic shifts in the global political and economic order, as well as internal developments in the ACP and the EU, have together forced both sides to reassess their priorities, strategies, and historical relationships.[23] The gradual enlargement of the EU since the end of the Cold War has shaped European attitudes and policy towards the ACP countries, with many newer member states favouring the strengthening of relations with Asia and the use of (scarce) financial resources for development in the wider EU neighbourhood (as opposed to the ACP regions).[24] Efforts to make the EU more democratic, transparent, and efficient have also played a role. In this regard, the Lisbon Treaty of 2007 was of particular significance for ACP-EU relations, because it changed the way that Brussels engaged with its international partners. Notably, the ACP group is not mentioned in the Lisbon Treaty, as it had been in the Treaty of Maastricht of 1992. There is furthermore no "ACP unit within the EEAS [European External Action Service] and the internal structure of the Commission's new Directorate-General for EuropeAid Development and Cooperation".[25] Instead, ACP matters are dealt with mainly by the Africa directorate (one of five geographic directorates in the EEAS). In the Directorate-General for International Cooperation and Development (DG DEVCO), Africa and ACP matters are addressed by two geographic directorates: East and Southern Africa and ACP Coordination, as well as West and Central Africa.[26] This structure is indicative not only of the EU's preference for a regional approach to its international engagements (see Gomes in this volume), but also of the prominence of Africa in its relations with the ACP.

In terms of gross domestic product (GDP), sub-Saharan Africa's growth rate averaged 5.6 per cent between 2000 and 2012.[27] This growth surge was attributable in large part to the continent's abundant natural resources, high commodity prices, and rising trade with new and emerging markets such as China and India. Other drivers included a decline in conflict, improved governance, lower levels of external debt, higher consumption levels, increased foreign direct investment (FDI), and technological changes.[28] These developments have made Africa more attractive to its traditional and new partners, and have increased the continent's leverage and confidence in its external relations. At the same time, however, these developments have also stolen some of the spotlight from the rest of the ACP group. This has been reflected in the greater interest shown by the EU towards Africa, compared to the Caribbean and Pacific regions.

The rise of emerging economies in the global South has been one of the most significant developments in the global arena since the signing of the Cotonou Agreement in 2000. How the ACP and the EU have engaged, and will continue to do so, with these rising economies, has implications for the future of their four-decade relationship.[29] The EU's 2006 "Global Europe" strategy acknowledges the importance of the BRICS countries to the global economy, and the need to have a strategy towards China in particular. Since the 1990s, Europe has sought to use "strategic partnerships"—a term formally introduced in 2003—as a foreign policy tool for strengthening relations not only with its traditional partners, but also with new and rising powers, with a view towards both meeting its domestic needs and boosting its position as a global actor. Seven out of the EU's ten strategic partnerships are with new or (re-)emerging powers: Brazil, China, India, Mexico, Russia, South Africa, and South Korea.

Similar to Europe, the ACP is increasingly engaging with the BRICS countries and other emerging economies in more systematic ways. To some extent, the five BRICS countries have an advantage over Europe in the ACP regions—they do not have a history of colonial domination in Africa, the Caribbean, or the Pacific. Not unlike Europe, the ACP is seeking to boost economic growth and achieve sustainable development through its engagement with these new actors. China, Brazil, and India, in particular, have actively pursued relations with ACP countries in their quest for raw materials and greater investment and trade opportunities, and consequently have challenged traditional US and European economic dominance in the African, Caribbean, and Pacific regions. For its part, the ACP too has actively sought out, and welcomed, the BRICS in view of the opportunities that they can provide for access to exclusive economic groupings such as the Group of 20 (G-20). The emerging economies also provide: alternative models for the ACP to promote economic growth and to reduce poverty; an alternative source of funding on more favourable terms than those offered by Europe; and opportunities for expanded and diversified trade, investment, development aid, and technical assistance.[30] Proposals for strengthening relations between the ACP and the BRICS bloc range from those that favour retaining the ACP's relationship with the EU, while pursuing new partnerships with the five-member bloc of emerging economies, to others that favour more robust South-South cooperation (see Gomes and Virk in this volume on the dynamics between the ACP, the EU, and the BRICS).

The Nature and Role of Development in the ACP-EU Relationship

In principle, African, Caribbean, and Pacific development is central to the ACP-EU relationship. The EU's 1996 green paper on the relationship contended that the ACP did not experience significant increases in trade performance and diversification, nor economic growth, under Lomé's preferential trade regime.[31] For example, ACP exports to the EU rose modestly at best from 10.5 billion European currency units (ECUs) in 1976 to 18.6 billion ECUs in 1994, with commodities continuing to constitute over 80 per cent of total ACP exports.[32] However, the green paper also identified individual cases—such as Botswana, Côte d'Ivoire, Mauritius, Zimbabwe, and Jamaica—that benefited from the Lomé protocols and diversified away from traditional exports. As Nigerian scholar T. Ademola Oyejide has similarly pointed out, preferences were beneficial in some respects. For example, the sugar, and beef and veal protocols contributed significantly to the GDP of Mauritius and Botswana respectively, while countries such as Kenya, Mauritius, and Zimbabwe were able to diversify into non-traditional sectors (for instance, clothing and processed fish). Oyejide suggests that there was nothing inherently wrong with the Lomé trade preferences, but rather that the conditions under which they were implemented contributed to the ACP's poor economic performance. The positive impact of Lomé was inhibited by "restrictions" such as "ceilings, quotas and non-tariff barriers ... and rigid rules of origin".[33] Be that as it may, the EU, by rejecting the Lomé model and subscribing to the free market–based principles of the WTO, has conformed to—even reinforced—the shift towards neo-liberalism in development policy discourse, based on the assumption that economic liberalisation leads to development.[34]

As of September 2015, the Caribbean was the only ACP region to have signed and begun implementing an economic partnership agreement with the EU. Another three EPA negotiation processes had been concluded in Africa—with West Africa in February 2014, the Southern African Development Community (SADC) EPA group in July 2014, and the East African Community (EAC) in October 2014—though only the SADC-EU EPA had been signed by June 2016.[35] It is thus not possible to assess the performance of ACP-EU trade under a reciprocity-based trade regime. That said, historical analyses can provide a starting point for discussion. South Korean scholar Ha Joon Chang, for example, has illustrated that while industrialised countries have preached neo-liberal policies to developing countries as the path to development, they themselves followed a contrary route—they pursued protectionist policies and embraced state intervention to "climb the ladder" of development, and only opened up their markets once their industries had become competitive. Furthermore, strong and effective institutions emerged as an outcome of, rather than a requirement for, development.[36] This suggests that despite the prevailing "consensus", free trade and institution-building—as promoted by the EPAs—may not be *the* answer to the ACP development challenge.

Moreover, as the EPA negotiations have shown, the ACP and the EU have differing perspectives on development (see Carim, Akokpari, and Katjavivi in this volume). In keeping with the dominant neo-liberal consensus, the EU's approach—as reflected in the Cotonou Agreement—has been that development is attained primarily "through trade liberalisation and the creation of the right policy framework to attract investment".[37] The ACP approach to development, on the other hand, has emphasised accompanying development enablers. In the context of the EPA negotiations, this has taken the form of arguments in favour of the provision of development finance—in addition to the resources typically provided under the EDF—to reduce supply-side constraints in ACP countries and to address their adjustment costs, through legally binding provisions.[38] However, due mainly to the political and economic asymmetries that exist between the two sides, the EU position has tended to prevail. Cotonou furthermore strengthens the emphasis on policy conditionality, and thereby expands the notion of ACP development to include non-economic issues. The agreement provides for the discontinuation of development assistance as a last resort should ACP countries contravene its provisions on human rights, rule of law, and democracy and "good governance".

Critical evaluations of the economic partnership agreement between the Forum of the Caribbean Group of ACP States (CARIFORUM) and the EU, signed in 2008, indicate that the EPA is, for the most part, not designed to deliver development. The substance of the agreement negates its rhetoric and that of the Cotonou Agreement about developmental objectives,[39] although it has had some benefits such as encouraging the development of sanitary and phytosanitary standards and increasing awareness of new market opportunities (see Gonzales in this volume). Furthermore, the EPA framework violates a key ingredient of sustainable development models: "development from below"—the idea that development strategy is driven by national priorities. Instead, the EPAs have been informed by the development ideology of Western-dominated international institutions, which have forced weaker developing countries into accepting their norms, which in turn has left very little space for autonomous policy development by these countries. South Africa, though, may be an exception. Compared to Tshwane's (Pretoria) previous stand-alone Trade, Development, and Cooperation Agreement (TDCA) of 1999, the SADC-EU EPA provides—as Xavier Carim points out in his chapter in this volume—greater policy space for South Africa in certain respects (such as export taxes).

Non-state actors, civil society in particular, could play an important role in facilitating "development from below" in ACP-EU trade and development cooperation, but only if their autonomy and independence are nurtured. However, the potential of civil society has been stifled by the dynamics that govern funding of non-state actors within the framework of ACP-EU cooperation, as well as by the largely state-centric reality of the relationship. Unlike governmental actors, which the ACP co-funds with the EU, non-state actors—even in cases of intra-ACP cooperation—have tended to be funded by the EU rather than by the collective ACP.[40] In addition, more European civil society organisations than their ACP counterparts have benefited from this funding.[41] As critics have noted: "ACP-EU cooperation has remained a rather closed shop, managed in a highly centralised and bureaucratic manner".[42] The ACP has also historically relied for its research on non-ACP think tanks. In this regard, the absence of any mention of a role for civil society in ACP development—except on women's issues—in the 2016 Port Moresby Declaration of the Eighth Summit of ACP Heads of State and Government is noteworthy.[43]

The Impact of the ACP-EU Partnership on ACP Regional Integration

From the outset, support for ACP regional cooperation has been an important aspect of the ACP-EU relationship. The impact of the Lomé Conventions (1975–2000) on regional cooperation and integration in Africa, the Caribbean, and the Pacific, however, was uneven with varied degrees of success across regions and sub-regions.[44] Furthermore, in the 1980s, the usefulness of "closed regionalism" based on trade protectionism came to be increasingly questioned, and by the 1990s was viewed as a hindrance to globalisation processes. Instead, the notion of "open regionalism" gained greater acceptance. This held that regional integration schemes could serve as building blocks for an open and liberal multilateral trading system under the newly created WTO, if they were "open"—that is, non-discriminatory towards outsiders and based on liberalisation of "substantially all trade".[45]

These developments informed the configuration of the EPAs between the ACP and the EU. Notably, the Cotonou Agreement places little to no emphasis on regional cooperation in historical, social, and cultural areas that have helped in shaping the decades-long regional integration efforts in the ACP.[46] Not surprisingly, progress towards the EPAs has been beset with problems related to the state-of-play in ACP regional integration. As Guyanese scholar Havelock Brewster has noted, it is ironic that the economic partnership agreements aver to promoting regional integration, yet "the very process of concluding the EPAs has proven to be one of the most internally divisive occurrences in the history of ACP integration movements, creating the emergence of different versions of, and defections from, the EPA by individual States within integration groupings".[47]

In Africa, with only three (of five) EPA negotiating processes concluded—one of the agreements signed and the signature processes for the other two agreements yet to be completed—the impact of the EPAs on the continent's efforts to increase intra-regional trade and value-added exports, and to set its own regional integration and development priorities, is fiercely debated, with the adequacy of development finance for regional integration under the proposed new agreements questioned in equal measure (see Katjavivi in this volume). The lack of alignment between EPA negotiating configurations and Africa's regional economic communities (RECs) has also threatened to exacerbate the existing challenge of overlapping memberships, with the problem particularly acute in Southern

Africa, where the 15 members of SADC are split across four separate EPA groupings (see Carim in this volume). In the case of the Caribbean, its EPA with the EU—as Norman Girvan and I suggest in this volume—could subvert the region's own vision of a Caribbean Community Single Market and Economy (CSME), although as Anthony Gonzales suggests in his chapter, the implementation of the EPA also has the potential to add much-needed momentum to the regional integration efforts of the Caribbean Community (CARICOM). In the Pacific, meanwhile, the notion that an EPA with Brussels might support its region-building efforts has been called into question by the EU's abandonment of a regional approach to fisheries—a key sector in the region—in favour of bilateral agreements (see Tavola in this volume).

Arguably, the EU's strategy of addressing non-trade issues (such as migration) outside of the ACP framework, through regional organisations and processes, has further complicated African, Caribbean, and Pacific regional cooperation and integration efforts. In Africa, in particular, Europe has engaged in parallel diplomacy with the African Union (AU) on political, and peace and security issues. This shift towards a regional approach on the part of the EU has also been apparent in its establishment of joint strategies with individual ACP regions—Africa in 2005, and the Caribbean and the Pacific in 2006 respectively (see Gomes in this volume). Taken together with the negotiation of separate economic partnership agreements with different regions, as opposed to the ACP as a whole, these developments may have damaged any remaining hope—however illusive—of ACP-wide integration.

The Challenge of Asymmetries Between the ACP and the EU

The manner in which the ACP and the EU have structured their relations, given the asymmetry in power between them, has been shaped by broader developments in economic thought and policy. The idea that developing countries did not have to extend reciprocal trade preferences to industrialised trade partners gained traction during the 1960s and 1970s in the United Nations Conference on Trade and Development (UNCTAD), as newly independent countries in the global South used their numerical leverage to fight for acknowledgement of their disadvantaged position in world trade.[48] This thinking was reflected in Lomé's non-reciprocal trade regime. Asymmetric treatment for developing countries was formally incorporated into GATT in 1979, though it had provided an informal and non-binding basis for trade with developing countries since 1971.[49] Preferential treatment under GATT supported an inward-looking strategy of development, and developing countries were allowed certain exemptions from GATT rules (for example, for infant industry protection) that allowed them to pursue import substitution strategies. In subsequent years, however, there was a shift in development thinking that emphasised "export-led growth" over "import-substituting industrialisation".[50]

The WTO maintained this shift towards export-led growth, with an emphasis on "free trade" for the achievement of economic development and integration into the international economy. In particular, the rules of the multilateral trading system do not allow for trade preferences to be extended to one country, or trading partner, if the same preferences are also not offered to others. This applies even to small and vulnerable economies (SVEs), as demonstrated by the case of the Lomé banana protocol. In 1997, the WTO ruled that the EU's banana import regime under Lomé was discriminatory, with devastating consequences for the economies of the small banana-producing Caribbean Windward Islands (see Girvan and Montoute in this volume).

The WTO provides for special and differential treatment for developing countries (such as longer timeframes to implement agreements), as well as for additional concessions (for example, non-prohibition of the use of export subsidies) for least-developed countries. But these provisions are largely non-binding, and the nature and extent of the concession to be made are at the discretion of the industrialised countries. This has made the inclusion of substantial provisions on special and differential treatment for the ACP in the EPAs a matter for tricky negotiations. The CARIFORUM-EU EPA—the first, and so far only, such agreement to be implemented between an ACP region and the EU—includes provisions for special and differential treatment for the Caribbean countries in several areas (such as lower tariff cuts and longer transition periods).[51] However, it is worth noting that the transition periods accorded by the EU to its Caribbean ACP partners do not compare to the centuries of protectionism enjoyed by European countries in their development and industrialisation trajectory.[52] As Girvan and I explain in this volume, the agreement— in particular, its most-favoured-nation (MFN) clause—is a hindrance to the development of South-South cooperation, in particular through the expansion of Caribbean trade with new and emerging economies such as the BRICS bloc. Under the EPA with the EU, CARIFORUM countries must provide the same treatment to the EU as they do to any major economy with which they enter a trading relationship.[53]

The economic strength of the EU dwarfs the individual GDP of the seven EPA negotiating regions (see Fig. 1.1). As Ghanaian scholar John Akokpari argues in this volume, the vast disparities in economic size inevitably translate into differences in political power and negotiating strength, which gives Europe a distinct advantage over the ACP. Therefore, gains from the economic and political aspects of the relationship have tended disproportionately to favour the EU. The situation is further exacerbated by the donor-recipient relationship between the two sides that derives from the development assistance provided by Brussels to the ACP through the European Development Fund. The ACP's recognition in the 2016 Port Moresby Declaration of "the need to count primarily on [its] own efforts and strengths, as well as the need for diversified partnerships … to achieve a level of social and economic development", while acknowledging the benefits of its partnership with the EU, is thus a positive step towards addressing the asymmetry between the two sides.[54]

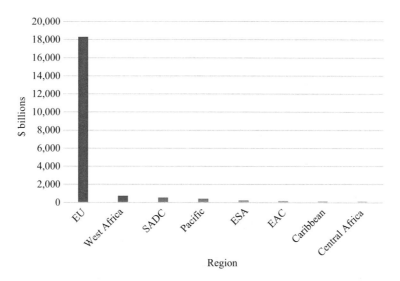

Fig. 1.1   GDP of the EU and the seven EPA negotiating regions, 2014. *Source*: Author's calculations based on World Bank statistics, http://data.worldbank. org/, and United Nations Statistics Division, *World Statistics Pocketbook*, https:// data.un.org/ (accessed 7 August 2015). *Note*: The data for Niue is for 2012

The EU used the rules of the WTO to push for the inclusion of reciprocal trade agreements with the ACP that are likely to deepen existing asymmetries between the two sides. These rules were largely shaped by powerful players such as the EU in the first place (see Girvan and Montoute in this volume). Europe has thus been able to use its more dominant position to impose its neo-liberal thinking and artificial regional divisions on the ACP, and in the process has threatened to dismantle over four decades of African, Caribbean, and Pacific solidarity while weakening the leverage that the 79-member ACP had in its numbers.

This does not, however, completely absolve the ACP of its responsibility to deliver the benefits of development to its own constituents, nor does it entirely strip the grouping of its agency. Over the span of four decades, the group has had limited success in forging intra-ACP cooperation, especially in the area of trade. The intra-ACP academic mobility scheme in the field of higher education is a positive example. The hard reality, though, is that the partnership between the 79 African, Caribbean, and Pacific countries has been more conducive to facilitating relations between the ACP and the EU than relations among themselves. Even so, the ACP group could have been more proactive and used existing processes under the ACP-EU framework for advancing greater cooperation among the ACP regions.

Political Issues in the ACP-EU Relationship

While the first Lomé Convention of 1975 focused squarely on economic issues, by the time Lomé IV was signed in 1989, this had changed, with political issues having gradually crept into the agreements. Negotiated against the backdrop of an evolving human rights regime towards the end of the Cold War, Lomé IV marked an important break from the past in that Article 5 of the convention deemed respect for human rights to be an inextricable part of the development process. It also included "democratic principles and the rule of law" as "essential elements of the Convention",[55] identifying them—along with human rights—as conditionalities for EU funding. The Cotonou Agreement of 2000 further expanded and deepened the emphasis on these political issues. It introduced "good governance" as another "fundamental element" of the relationship. The agreement also provided for "flexible" processes—"formal or informal" and at different levels—for discussion of non-traditional issues for cooperation such as the arms trade, military spending, drugs, organised crime, child labour, migration, climate change, and gender. On the one hand, this expansion of the ACP-EU relationship beyond economic issues illustrates a maturing of the partnership. It also indicates an acknowledgement of an expanded understanding of development as a multi-dimensional process that cannot be detached from social and political considerations. On the other hand, there is evidence to indicate that "the suspension of aid is not an effective tool for promoting or restoring breaches of the 'essential' or 'fundamental' elements [of the partnership] in ACP states".[56] The imposition of conditionalities neither strengthens the partnership nor necessarily promotes the well-being of the ACP's more than 900 million citizens.

Article 8 of the Cotonou Agreement also carves out a role for civil society in the African, Caribbean, and Pacific regions in the area of political dialogue. This represents a radical shift from the Lomé era. Although the participation of non-state actors under Lomé IV was mainly felt to be important for the successful implementation of projects, civil society participation is identified in Cotonou as being "fundamental" to the various dimensions of the partnership, including the political dialogue. However, the extent to which such participation has taken place, as well as the impact it has had, on political issues in the ACP-EU partnership—for example, in the area of human rights—is uncertain. This is due to the fact that political dialogue processes have not been well documented, mainly because of "the secretive nature of these processes. Public information on many 'how' dimensions (with specific reference to human rights concerns) related to Article 8 is scarcely available".[57] Where information exists—as in EU reports on human rights and democracy, for example—the implementation or the impact of political processes has tended not to be the main focus. There are a few cases, though, in which ACP countries have unsuccessfully opposed EU funding of civil society political projects, such as those related to gay rights in Cameroon.[58] This example illustrates the lack of consensus between the ACP and the EU on certain political issues.

Cotonou further provides for participation by regional organisations in the political dialogue. Concern has arisen, however, that the ACP-EU framework is being sidelined, with regional organisations taking its place as the preferred forum for addressing issues related to peace and security, democracy, human rights, and migration. This has been seen most clearly in Africa. For example, "European and African continental bodies now lead the political dialogue on the delicate issues of migration and mobility". Peace and security issues are handled by the "African Union (AU Peace and Security Council, Africa Peace and Security Architecture), the Regional Economic Communities and … the Africa-EU Partnership (JAES, summits)",[59] while democracy, "good governance", and human rights "are more systematically dealt with in the African Governance Architecture (AGA) and the EU-AU dialogue mechanisms". For some, this is an indication that the ACP-EU relationship "has lost traction, political clout and bargaining power".[60] Although the Caribbean and the Pacific have received less attention, the EU has devised similar processes in these regions. The Joint Caribbean-EU Partnership Strategy of 2012, for example, addresses issues such as crime and security. Brussels has also engaged in discussions with Caribbean countries on political issues such as human rights, peace and security, migration, drugs, and terrorism through the Community of Latin American and Caribbean States (CELAC). Although the EU does not have a similar comprehensive partnership with the Pacific, the EU-Pacific strategy of 2006 has provided for a policy dialogue on issues such as global security and the environment.

On the whole, the EU has attached greater priority to the political pillar of Cotonou. For the ACP, however, the trade and economic component of the partnership has ranked far higher on its agenda for cooperation with Europe. Indeed, it would be fair to say that the EPAs, in particular, have been the defining feature of the ACP-EU partnership since 2000 from African, Caribbean, and Pacific perspectives. In addition, graduation from grant-based funding and the threat of losing the EDF have further gained in significance for the ACP since the EU's adoption of its 2011 *Agenda for Change*,[61] which highlights the principle of differentiation as a basis for targeting the EU's resources, and emphasises development support for least-developed countries. This book provides a comprehensive survey of the various dimensions of the ACP-EU relationship, and as such covers two issues, in particular, under the political pillar that have been key for the ACP—security and migration (see Adebajo, Knoll, and Nurse and Ruggeri in this volume)—while acknowledging the place of the political dialogue in Africa-EU relations (see Akokpari in this volume). All in all, though, this volume—in keeping with the importance it attaches to the inclusion of ACP perspectives in debates on the current and future prospects of development cooperation with Europe—places greater emphasis on the trade and economic dimensions of this relationship. Furthermore, the actual and potential impact of the trade and development pillars of Cotonou has, albeit arguably, greater significance for the ACP's more than 900 million citizens. The consequences of the EPAs, in particular, on ACP policy space, regional integration efforts, and livelihoods, as well as the potential socio-economic impact of graduation from EU grant-based funding, could be game-changing for the ACP.

Outline of the Book

In Chapter 2, British analyst Kaye Whiteman examines the political history of the ACP-EU relationship, including the "virtues" of the relationship in the Lomé era and the dramatic shift to Cotonou, as well as the lessons that the ACP's and the EU's shared past provides for taking the partnership forward. Drawing on his wealth of personal experience as a Eurocrat in Brussels between 1973 and 1982, Whiteman identifies the struggles and triumphs of the ACP and the EU since the foundation of their relationship through the 1957 Treaty of Rome, and focuses in particular on what he calls the "spirit of Lomé"—a sense of solidarity, cooperation, and collective action. While acknowledging a need to re-think the ACP-EU relationship against the backdrop of ongoing changes in the global political and economic order, Whiteman argues that the ACP-EU partnership continues to be a more appropriate and relevant framework than that provided by regional strategic partnerships for addressing the challenges faced by African, Caribbean, and Pacific countries. These countries came together under the "chance circumstances of history", and for Whiteman, they could do the same once again now, given "a real common interest" in overcoming the shared challenge of their future relationship with the EU.

Chapters 3, 4, and 5 provide a systematic examination of the EU's relationship with Africa, the Caribbean, and the Pacific individually, while assessing region-building efforts and the impact of Cotonou on these efforts in all three regions. In Chapter 3, Ghanaian scholar John Akokpari argues that political and economic asymmetries between the EU and Africa have resulted in negative consequences for the continent, with Europe largely having reaped the benefits of their encounter. For Akokpari, the EU's regional approach to the EPAs represents continuity, with the economic partnership agreements having been, or being, negotiated at the expense of Africa's own regional integration endeavours.

In Chapter 4, Jamaican scholar Norman Girvan and I provide the Caribbean story of the ACP-EU relationship. We argue that, despite the challenges of Lomé, the Caribbean benefited from the agreement's preferential trade regime. However, the CARIFORUM-EU economic partnership agreement mandated by Cotonou has marked a dramatic shift in the Caribbean-EU relationship, which has had a negative impact on the relationship itself, as well as on Caribbean regional integration and development prospects. We further argue that the antidote to the EPA lies in the fortification of regional integration processes that can then facilitate a strengthened re-engagement with the EU and do so in solidarity with the ACP.

In Chapter 5, Fiji's Kaliopate Tavola focuses on the Pacific, a region defined by its unique and fragmented geography. Tavola assesses the lack of momentum in EU-Pacific relations and the weaknesses of Pacific regional integration, despite years of European support. In so doing, he looks at both internal and external factors that have constrained the development of Pacific regionalism. Key internal challenges that the Pacific faces include: the vast economic and political disparities between Pacific ACP countries; the dominance of Australia and New Zealand in the region; and a lack of leadership and political will to deepen Pacific regionalism. In this respect, for Tavola, the burden of responsibility for the failures of Pacific regional integration lies in large part within the region itself. At the same time, the EU's support through the ACP framework for the Pacific's region-building efforts has not met regional expectations, with Europe's relationship with the Pacific ACP lacking impetus. Tavola argues in favour of deepening Pacific regionalism to achieve development, supported by a re-vitalised EU-Pacific ACP framework and by an economic partnership agreement that takes into account the peculiar features and needs of the Pacific region.

With the extended negotiations for a regional EU-Pacific EPA still ongoing, the Caribbean continues to be the only ACP region to have signed and begun implementing an economic partnership agreement; though negotiations have been concluded for three EPAs with SADC, West Africa, and the EAC. In Chapter 6, Namibia's speaker of parliament and former ambassador to the EU, Peter Katjavivi, provides an African perspective on the economic partnership agreements. The chapter details African concerns—ranging from those related to technical issues such as rules of origin, to broader matters such as policy flexibility—in the EPA negotiations, and discusses the negative implications of the agreements for African development and regional integration. Katjavivi argues that the different approaches taken by Africa and the EU to the EPA negotiations, particularly on the development component in the agreements, have been a key challenge. He is further critical of the EPA processes for their failure to take into account major development challenges including those related to globalisation, climate change, and poverty eradication. For Katjavivi, as for Akokpari, the economic partnership agreements seem primarily to be about furthering the EU's commercial interests in Africa, while being in contravention of Brussels's stated concern with the promotion of development in the ACP regions and globally.

In Chapter 7, South Africa's ambassador to the WTO, Xavier Carim, focuses in-depth on the anatomy of the negotiating process in the SADC-EPA group, from a South African perspective. In so doing, he highlights the challenges that arose from the differences in approach taken by the EU and South Africa to the EPA negotiations, as well as the key developments that contributed to the successful conclusion of the process. The SADC-EU EPA process was particularly complicated for three reasons: one, South Africa's stand-alone TDCA with Europe and the latter's insistence on treating the former differently from the rest of the sub-region; two, Southern Africa's regional arrangements, including SADC but also the Southern African Customs Union (SACU); and three, the 15-member SADC being split across four EPA negotiating groups. Carim argues that South Africa's participation in the process throughout was driven by a need to ensure that the agreement should serve the sub-region, as well as Africa's development and region-building agendas. At the same time, Carim also notes the potential of the agreement—as well as variations across the five African EPAs—to still undermine these.

In Chapter 8, Trinidadian scholar Anthony Gonzales examines the challenges that the Caribbean has experienced in implementing its economic partnership agreement—signed in 2008—and assesses its impact on the region's trade and development prospects, as well as its regional integration schemes. The chapter further identifies lessons—based on the Caribbean's experience—for African and Pacific countries that are still negotiating or finalising EPAs with the EU. Gonzales argues that the Caribbean agreement has had some beneficial impacts, despite the slow pace of implementation and the problems that have arisen in the process. The former include: the expansion of some non-traditional agricultural exports; the creation of new contacts in the EU market; and an increase in awareness of the need for policy reforms and development in new trade-related areas such as competition. Gonzales further urges the Caribbean ACP countries to, among other things, focus on increasing their competitiveness, developing new export sectors, and implementing regional integration schemes in order to realise more fully the potential benefits of the EPA. For the rest of the ACP, the Caribbean experience shows the importance of timely and adequate mobilisation of resources, and of understanding the "symbiotic relationship between negotiation and implementation".

Chapters 9, 10, and 11 focus on three political issues that have gained prominence in the ACP-EU relationship. The Africa-EU security relationship—in particular, the EU's performance in promoting peace and security on the continent—is the focus of Nigerian scholar Adekeye Adebajo in Chapter 9. The chapter provides a historical account of the security role played by European powers in Africa, highlighting the differences in approach taken by Britain, France, and Germany, before turning to an assessment of the EU's evolving present-day military role on the continent. Drawing on case studies of recent European interventions in the Democratic Republic of the Congo (DRC), and Chad and the Central African Republic (CAR), Adebajo questions the effectiveness of the EU's security operations on the continent. Despite the EU's increasingly sophisticated security architecture, Adebajo argues that the EU has been more concerned with maintaining its position as a net provider of security globally than with achieving genuine and sustainable peace in Africa. He further argues that the EU could play a more effective security role in Africa by: providing support for the strengthening of Africa's regional bodies; strengthening the UN's peacekeeping capacity by placing European troops under its umbrella; supporting more effective burden-sharing between the UN and African organisations; and continuing to support efforts to reform and democratise the UN Security Council for greater African representation.

In Chapter 10, German analyst Anna Knoll examines migration in the ACP-EU relationship in the context of an evolving global debate on the links between migration and development. Knoll outlines the major patterns of global migration, while highlighting those most relevant to the ACP-EU relationship. The chapter examines the differences in the perspectives of the ACP and the EU on South-South migration and North-South migration, and reflects on the treatment of migration in the future of the ACP-EU relationship. Knoll argues that although understanding of the links between migration and development has increased in both the EU and the ACP since 2000, this was not reflected in the 2010 revision of the Cotonou Agreement, with continued tensions between the two sides over migration management and the rights of migrants. She further argues that migration and mobility have brought both opportunities and challenges for the ACP and the EU, and that they promise to be a "defining feature of future development dynamics in both regions". There is thus a need for the ACP as well as the EU to improve their understanding of the migration-development nexus, with a view to realising its beneficial effects. For Knoll, the EU needs to move beyond security-focused migration and better integrate the development aspects of migration into its relationship with the ACP, while the ACP for its part needs to pay greater attention to inter-regional cooperation for the management of intra-ACP migrant flows.

In Chapter 11, Trinidadian academic Keith Nurse and Italian scholar Ramona Ruggeri complement Knoll's essay by examining the links between diasporas and development, and the role of diaspora relations in the ACP-EU partnership. Not unlike Knoll, Nurse and Ruggeri argue that in light of development and demographic challenges faced by the ACP and the EU respectively, both regions stand to benefit from strengthening their dialogue and partnership on migration, diaspora relations, and related issues. They focus on the economic aspects of ACP-EU diaspora relations, in particular, and argue for a "strategic approach" to addressing the challenges posed by brain drain and labour mobility. Nurse and Ruggeri further argue for greater understanding of, and support for, diasporic economic flows, especially with respect to remittances and diasporic trade, which offer innovative avenues to address the development gap in ACP economies and the labour gap in the EU. In this respect, the chapters by both Knoll, and Nurse and Ruggeri put forward the case for less restrictive migration policies, greater respect for migrant rights, and improved data and analyses on migration and diasporic communities.

In Chapter 12, Guyanese scholar-diplomat Patrick Gomes is concerned with the future perspectives of the ACP group, as well as the prospects of its relationship with the EU. Gomes shares Kaye Whiteman's view that the ACP group can build on its past experiences, while forging ahead in a way that takes into account key global trends as well as their impact on both the EU and the ACP. Gomes examines in greater detail the evolving global context and its implications for the prospects of the ACP-EU relationship. Gomes also provides a detailed account of the ongoing process of reflection on the ACP's post-Cotonou future within the group. He goes further than Whiteman in arguing that this process needs to include consideration not only of the future of the ACP's relationship with Europe, but also of the 79-member ACP group itself. Gomes charts the different perspectives that have been put forward, but at the same time favours strengthening intra-ACP cooperation, and doing so in a way that builds on the ACP's experiences with Europe and seeks greater engagement with the new and emerging economies of the global South.

Gomes thus lays the foundation for Indian scholar Kudrat Virk's discussion in Chapter 13 on the dynamics of relations between ACP countries and the BRICS economies, in particular China, India, and Brazil. Virk charts the relevance and presence of these emerging powers in the ACP regions. While acknowledging the opportunities that the rise of the BRICS has brought for African, Caribbean, and Pacific countries—in particular, as an alternative source of trade and aid, as well as information and knowledge of development, to the EU—Virk also cautions against an uncritical acceptance of the motivations and interests of the BRICS in pursuing greater engagement with Africa in particular and the ACP more generally. She argues in favour of a more balanced and strategic approach by African, Caribbean, and Pacific countries towards these new players— one that uses intra-BRICS competition and rivalry to diversify ACP economies and achieve their development objectives; builds new partnerships without undermining the ACP group's development cooperation with the EU; and bases itself on lessons of the past.

In sum, four key themes emerge from the essays in this volume. First, the continued relevance for the ACP of its development partnership with the EU, as one among a diverse set of new and emerging relationships in response to changes in the global political economy. Second, the importance of regional integration both to ACP development and in the ACP-EU relationship. Third, the challenges posed by asymmetries between the two sides. And fourth, the differences in the respective approaches of the ACP and EU to development in the African, Caribbean, and Pacific regions. The future—or lack thereof—of the ACP-EU relationship beyond 2020 will be informed by how these issues are addressed and resolved.

Notes

1. In a national referendum, held in June 2016, Britain voted to leave the European Union (EU). Official negotiations were yet to begin at the time of writing, but as and when Britain leaves the Union, the membership of the EU will be reduced to 27.
2. *See* Centre for Conflict Resolution (CCR), *The African, Caribbean, and Pacific (ACP) Group and the European Union (EU)*, seminar report, Cape Town, South Africa, January 2014, http://www.ccr.org.za.

3. For a critical overview of this literature, *see* John Ravenhill, *Collective Clientelism: The Lomé Conventions and North-South Relations* (New York: Columbia University Press, 1985).

4. Samuel K.B. Asante, "The Lomé Convention: Towards Perpetuation of Dependence or Promotion of Interdependence?", *Third World Quarterly* 3, no. 4 (October 1981), pp. 671–672.

5. Ravenhill, *Collective Clientelism*. *See also* William Brown, *The European Union and Africa: The Restructuring of North-South Relations* (London: Tauris, 2002).

6. *See* Ravenhill, *Collective Clientelism*, p. 22.

7. Brown, *The European Union and Africa*, pp. 5–8. *See also* Isebill V. Gruhn, "The Lomé Convention: Inching Towards Interdependence", *International Organization* 30, no. 2 (Spring 1976), pp. 241–262.

8. *See* Brown, *The European Union and Africa*, p. 11.

9. Gorm Rye Olsen, "Europe and the Promotion of Democracy in Post Cold War Africa: How Serious Is Europe and for What Reason?", *African Affairs* 97, no. 388 (1998), p. 366.

10. Brown, *The European Union and Africa*, p. 4.

11. CCR, *South Africa and the BRICS: Progress, Problems, and Prospects*, seminar report, Tshwane (Pretoria), South Africa, November 2014, http://www.ccr.org.za.

12. *See* Kaye Whiteman, "The Rise and Fall of Eurafrique: From the Berlin Conference of 1884–1885 to the Tripoli EU-Africa Summit of 2010", in Adekeye Adebajo and Kaye Whiteman (eds.), *The EU and Africa: From Eurafrique to Afro-Europa* (London: Hurst; New York: Columbia University Press; and Johannesburg: Wits University Press, 2012), pp. 23–43, esp. pp. 31–33.

13. ACP Secretariat, "FAQ [Frequently Asked Questions]", http://www.acp.int/node/7 (accessed 21 September 2015).

14. Ravenhill, *Collective Clientelism*, p. 47.

15. Arvind Panagariya, "EU Preferential Trade Policies and Developing Countries", 27 August 2002, p. 7, http://www.columbia.edu/~ap2231/Policy%20Papers/Mathew-WE.pdf (accessed 7 August 2015).

16. Jonathan R. Macey and Geoffrey P. Miller, "The End of History and the New World Order: The Triumph of Capitalism and the Competition Between Liberalism and Democracy", Faculty

Scholarship Series Paper no. 1645, 1992, http://digitalcommons.law.yale.edu/fss_papers/1645 (accessed 20 July 2015).

17. Matthew McQueen, "ACP-EU Trade Cooperation After 2000: An Assessment of Reciprocal Preferences", *Journal of Modern African Studies* 36, no. 4 (1998), p. 671. *See also* Matthew McQueen, Christine Phillips, David Hallam, and Allan Swinbank, *ACP-EU Trade and Aid Co-operation: Post-Lomé IV* (London: Commonwealth Secretariat, 1998); and Konrad von Moltke, *Implications of the Cotonou Agreement for Sustainable Development in the ACP Countries and Beyond* (Manitoba: International Institute for Sustainable Development [IISD], 2004).

18. European Commission, "CAP Expenditure in the Total EU Expenditure", CAP Post-2013: Key Graphs & Figures, March 2015, http://ec.europa.eu/agriculture/cap-post-2013/graphs/graph1_en.pdf (accessed 10 December 2015).

19. European Commission, "Green Paper on Relations Between the European Union and the ACP Countries on the Eve of the 21st Century: Challenges and Options for a New Partnership", Brussels, Belgium, 20 November 1996, pp. 22–24.

20. Henri-Bernard Solignac-Lecomte, "Effectiveness of Developing Country Participation in ACP-EU Negotiations", working paper (London: Overseas Development Institute [ODI], October 2001), p. 13.

21. Solignac-Lecomte, "Effectiveness of Developing Country Participation", p. 13.

22. European Commission, "Global Europe: Competing in the World—A Contribution to the EU's Growth and Jobs Strategy", p. 7, http://trade.ec.europa.eu/doclib/docs/2006/october/tradoc_130376.pdf (accessed 29 July 2015).

23. *See* James Mackie, Bruce Byiers, Sonia Niznik, and Geert Laporte (eds.), *Global Changes, Emerging Players, and Evolving ACP-EU Relations: Towards a Common Agenda for Action?*, Policy and Management Report no. 19 (Maastricht: European Centre for Development Policy Management [ECDPM], 2011).

24. Geert Laporte, "What Future for the ACP and the Cotonou Agreement? Preparing for the Next Steps in the Debate", Briefing Note no. 34 (Maastricht: ECDPM, April 2012), p. 3.

25. "Resolution on the Impact of the Treaty of Lisbon on the ACP-EU Partnership", adopted by the ACP-EU Joint Parliamentary Assembly, Lomé, Togo, 23 November 2011, p. 2.
26. European Commission, Directorate-General for International Cooperation and Development (DG DEVCO), "Organisational Structure of DG DEVCO", https://ec.europa.eu/europeaid/organisational-structure-dg-devco_en (accessed 20 September 2015).
27. African Development Bank, *Africa Development Report 2012: Towards Green Growth in Africa* (Tunis-Belvedere: African Development Bank Group, 2012), p. 6.
28. African Development Bank, *Africa Development Report 2012*, pp. 7–8.
29. *See* Mackie et al., "Global Changes, Emerging Players, and Evolving ACP-EU Relations".
30. *See* Mackie et al., "Global Changes, Emerging Players, and Evolving ACP-EU Relations".
31. European Commission, "Green Paper on Relations Between the European Union and the ACP Countries", pp. 17–18.
32. European Commission, "Green Paper on Relations Between the European Union and the ACP Countries", pp. 18, 90.
33. T. Ademola Oyejide, "Costs and Benefits of 'Special and Differential Treatment' in GATT/WTO: An African Perspective", in Ademola Oyejide and William Lyakurwa (eds.), *Africa and the World Trading System*, vol. 1, *Selected Issues of the Doha Agenda* (Trenton and Asmara, N.J.: Africa World Press, 2005), pp. 196–197.
34. von Moltke, *Implications of the Cotonou Agreement for Sustainable Development*, p. 2.
35. European Commission, "Overview of EPA Negotiations", updated September 2015, http://trade.ec.europa.eu/doclib/docs/2009/september/tradoc_144912.pdf (accessed 6 December 2015).
36. Ha Joon Chang, *Kicking Away the Ladder: Development Strategy in Historical Perspective* (London: Anthem, 2002).
37. Sanoussi Bilal and Corinna Braun-Munzinger, "EPA Negotiations and Regional Integration in Africa: Building or Stumbling Blocks?", *Trade Policy Review* 3 (2010), p. 89.
38. *See* Norman Girvan, "Implications of the Cariforum-EC EPA", 2008, http://www.normangirvan.info/wp-content/uploads/2008/01/girvanimplicationsepa10jan.pdf (accessed 10 August

2015); and Bilal and Braun-Munzinger, "EPA Negotiations and Regional Integration in Africa", p. 89.

39. *See* Havelock Brewster, "The Anti-Development Dimension of the European Community's Economic Partnership Agreement for the Caribbean", paper presented at the Commonwealth Secretariat High-Level Technical Meeting "EPAs: The Way Forward for the ACP", Cape Town, 7–8 April 2008, http://www.normangirvan. info/the-anti-development-dimension-of-the-european-communitys-economic-partnership-agreement-for-caribbean-havelock-brewster (accessed 2 July 2015).

40. Niels Keijzer, Mark Furness, Christine Hackenesch, and Svea Koch, *Towards a New Partnership Between the European Union and the African, Caribbean, and Pacific Countries After 2020* (Bonn: German Development Institute, 2015), p. 12.

41. European NGO Confederation for Relief and Development (CONCORD), "Intra-ACP Funds", CONCORD Cotonou Working Group Briefing Paper, ACP-EU Joint Parliamentary Assembly, 21st Session, Budapest, 16–18 May 2011, p. 2.

42. Jean Bossuyt, Niels Keijzer, Alfonso Medinilla, and Marc De Tollenaere, *The Future of ACP-EU Relations: A Political Economy Analysis*, ECDPM Policy Management Report no. 21 (Maastricht: ECDPM, 2016), p. xiv, emphasis in original removed.

43. *See* Port Moresby Declaration, ACP/28/005/16 Final, Eighth Summit of ACP Heads of State and Government, "Repositioning the ACP Group to Respond to the Challenges of Sustainable Development", Port Moresby, Papua New Guinea, 31 May–1 June 2016.

44. ACP-EU Joint Assembly Working Group on Regional Cooperation in the ACP Countries, "Report on Regional Cooperation in the ACP Countries", ACP-EU 2484/B/99/fin, 30 March 1999, http://www.europarl.europa.eu/intcoop/ acp/94_01/020_00_01_en.htm (accessed 10 August 2015).

45. For a discussion of globalisation and regionalisms, *see* Helen E.S. Nesadurai, *Globalisation, Domestic Politics, and Regionalism* (New York: Routledge, 2004).

46. *See* Daniel H. Levine and Dawn Nagar (eds.), *Region-Building in Africa: Political and Economic Challenges* (New York: Palgrave Macmillan, 2016); Chris Saunders, Gwinyayi A. Dzinesa, and Dawn Nagar (eds.), *Region-Building in Southern Africa: Progress,*

Problems, and Prospects (London and New York: Zed, 2012); Adebajo and Whiteman, *The EU and Africa.*

47. Brewster, "The Anti-Development Dimension", p. 18.

48. Robert Read, "The Generalised System of Preferences and Special and Differential Treatment for Developing Countries in the GATT and WTO", in William A. Kerr and James D. Gaisford (eds.), *Handbook on International Trade Policy* (Cheltenham: Edward Elgar, 2007), pp. 459–460.

49. Read, "The Generalised System of Preferences and Special and Differential Treatment", p. 465.

50. Read, "The Generalised System of Preferences and Special and Differential Treatment", pp. 458, 465, 468.

51. Caribbean Regional Negotiating Machinery (CRNM), "Special and Differential Treatment Provisions in the CARIFORUM-EC Economic Partnership Agreement", Caribbean Regional Negotiating EPA Brief, 2008, p. 3.

52. *See* Chang, *Kicking Away the Ladder.*

53. CRNM, "Special and Differential Treatment Provisions", p. 3.

54. Port Moresby Declaration, preambular para. E.

55. European Commission, "The Cotonou Agreement", http:// ec.europa.eu/development/body/cotonou/lome_history_en. htm (accessed 10 August 2015).

56. Andris Zimelis, "Conditionality and the EU-ACP Partnership: A Misguided Approach to Development?", *Australian Journal of Political Science* 46, no. 3 (September 2011), p. 402.

57. Jean Bossuyt, Camilla Rocca, and Brecht Lein, "Political Dialogue on Human Rights Under Article 8 of the Cotonou Agreement", Brussels, March 2014, p. 5, http://www.europarl.europa.eu/ meetdocs/2009_2014/documents/deve/dv/study_political_ dialogue_/study_political_dialogue_en.pdf (accessed 24 April 2016).

58. Bossuyt, Rocca, and Lein, "Political Dialogue on Human Rights", p. 16.

59. Geert Laporte, "The Challenges of Global Governance and the Emerging World Order: What Role for the ACP-EU Partnership?", Brussels, 6 June 2014, p. 3, http://ecdpm.org/wp-content/ uploads/ACP-DAY-06.06.2014-presentation-Geert-Laporte.pdf (accessed 10 August 2015).

60. Laporte, "The Challenges of Global Governance and the Emerging World Order", p. 4.

61. European Commission, "Increasing the Impact of EU Development Policy: An Agenda for Change", Communication from the Commission to the European Parliament, the Council, the European Economic and Social Committee, and the Committee of the Regions, COM (2011) 637 Final, Brussels, 13 October 2011, https://ec.europa.eu/europeaid/communication-commission-european-parliament-council-european-economic-and-social-committee-and_en (accessed 5 May 2016).

CHAPTER 2

A History of the ACP-EU Relationship: The Origins and Spirit of Lomé

Kaye Whiteman[†]

The formal relationship between the African, Caribbean, and Pacific (ACP) group of states and the European Union (EU) dates back to the signing of the first Lomé Convention in February 1975. The signatories at the time were the nine-member European Economic Community (EEC)—now the EU—and 46 African, Caribbean, and Pacific countries. The ACP group was officially established by the Georgetown Agreement later in 1975, although its members had been negotiating together since 1973.[1] The signing of Lomé was thus a pivotal experience in the ACP-EU relationship, serving as a marker against which the subsequent evolution of the partnership has been judged.

The main aim of this chapter is to examine the origins of Europe's relations with the ACP and the nature of Lomé against the backdrop of Britain's entry into the EEC in 1973. I explore the historical circumstances that threw together the African, Caribbean, and Pacific countries and resulted in the formation of the ACP group. I seek partly to unravel some of the myths that have developed around this period, but also to take the opportunity to re-emphasise some of the virtues of the ACP-EU relationship. With this purpose in mind, the narrative concentrates on the political history of the ACP-EU relationship, which is otherwise often

[†]Author was deceased at the time of publication.

K. Whiteman (✉)
Nigeria, Africa

© The Author(s) 2017
A. Montoute, K. Virk (eds.), *The ACP Group and the EU
Development Partnership*, DOI 10.1007/978-3-319-45492-4_2

buried in the economic, social, and developmental aspects of the partnership. I suggest that the origins and nature of Lomé contain lessons for the contemporary relationship between the ACP and the EU, which has expanded in the twenty-first century to cover a widening range of issues, particularly security and migration, and since 2007 has come to be surrounded—rather uncomfortably—in controversy over economic partnership agreements (EPAs).

From Yaoundé to Lomé

The origins of the formal relationship between the EU and the African, Caribbean, and Pacific regions go back to the very creation of the European Economic Community by the 1957 Treaty of Rome. In particular, Part IV of the treaty envisaged an association of the overseas territories of Belgium, France, the Netherlands, and Italy (four of the six Rome signatories, with the other two being Germany and Luxembourg), with provision for a European Development Fund (EDF). The vast majority of these overseas territories were in Africa, with 15 administered by France, two by Belgium, and one by Italy in 1956.[2] As decolonisation gathered pace in Africa from 1960 onwards, European powers sought to preserve their economic ties with, and provide for, almost all the designated associated states. In 1963, the Yaoundé Convention was signed with 18 newly independent African countries, together known as the Associated African States and Madagascar (AASM).[3]

While all six EEC countries subscribed to Yaoundé, this trade and aid agreement was driven primarily by the French, who had insisted on accommodating overseas territories in the Rome Treaty in the first place, though Belgium had also been a strong advocate. The Germans and the Dutch were inclined to become involved in what in the early 1960s was only beginning to be called "overseas development", while standing back from what appeared to be a "neo-colonial" initiative, but other political imperatives prevailed.

For the then newly established EEC, the building of new structures was part of the European experiment. The European Development Fund was launched in 1959, and the creation of a system for the EDF in Africa was left to a powerful former French colonial servant, Jacques Ferrandi,[4] who directed the fund from 1960 to 1975. Ferrandi established a network of delegations in Africa—based essentially on French administrative practices—that was built to survive. The trade arrangements of the 1963

Yaoundé Convention (re-negotiated in 1969 as Yaoundé II) created a free trade area founded on the principle of reciprocity.

Yaoundé was criticised elsewhere in Africa for its neo-colonialism, especially by the radical governments of Kwame Nkrumah in Ghana and Sekou Touré in Guinea.[5] At the same time, under pressure from the Germans and the Dutch, the English-speaking East African Community (EAC)—comprising Kenya, Uganda, and Tanzania—together with Nigeria, contrived to sign their own association agreements with Europe, although in Nigeria's case its agreement in 1966 was never ratified because of the civil war of 1967–1970. These association agreements had extremely limited trade provisions and no aid provisions, as the French were determined to keep their own former colonial territories in a privileged position in the relationship.

Omar Bongo, president of Gabon from 1967 to 2009, was one of the most privileged leaders of what later came to be called *Françafrique*.[6] In an interview published as a book in 1994, Bongo recalled that he had once asked France's General Charles de Gaulle why he had been so reticent about the entry of Britain into the EEC.[7] According to Bongo, de Gaulle had replied: "It is because of you others, the francophone Africans. For you, in this affair of the European Community, everything happens *pro rata* because of demography, so when you see the giants, Nigeria, Tanzania, Kenya beside Gabon, one must be vigilant." Bongo's own comment was: "*Voilà*. It was his style of government, always watching over the francophone African countries."[8]

It would be absurd to suggest that British entry into the EEC was blocked because of the francophone African countries. De Gaulle principally felt that Britain would be a Trojan horse for the Americans in the EEC. Even so, France's sub-Saharan African territories were the last element of its former colonial empire. The French were determined to retain close ties with these territories after independence, and their relationship with Brussels was an essential part of the Gallic strategy. This was why Paris had gone so far as to threaten not to sign the Rome Treaty unless it contained a provision of association for overseas territories.

One wishes that Bongo had asked de Gaulle's successor, Georges Pompidou, why he changed his mind about British entry into the EEC, because it had important implications for Africa. Pompidou had a less dramatic approach to politics and was susceptible to the arguments of the Germans in particular, who were keen to see Britain become a member of the EEC. He also was said to have listened to the case being made by

Senegalese president Léopold Senghor (a fellow student of Pompidou in Paris at the Lycée Louis-le-Grand) for bringing the British in to facilitate regional integration in West Africa. The diaries of Jacques Foccart, an adviser on African affairs to both de Gaulle and Pompidou, include a passage—dated 5 September 1972—in which Senghor tells Foccart that *les anglais*,[9] supported by the Americans, are mounting a campaign against *la francophonie*. Foccart records that Senghor believed the Nigerians wanted a common market that was "uniquely African", but which Senghor felt was "unrealisable", and that he planned to say as much to Nigerian leader General Yakubu Gowon. This contradicts neither Senghor's view of Europe and Africa as "symbiotic", nor his views on the need for West African integration. One has to bear in mind that Senghor was well known for always being adept at telling his audience what he thought they wanted to hear.[10]

Pompidou's basic agreement with Britain's prime minister, Edward Heath, on British entry into the EEC, came at a summit in May 1971. Previous negotiations begun in 1961 had been rejected and then, when resumed in 1967, had stalled. When Heath came to power in May 1970, he was determined to pursue them with greater success. At the conclusion of the British EEC membership negotiations early in 1972, a compromise on the "association" was spelled out and, after multiple twists and turns, led to the birth of the ACP group. Protocol 22 of Britain's Treaty of Accession,[11] which came into force in January 1973, provided independent countries in Africa, the West Indies, the Indian Ocean, and the Pacific with three options for "ordering their relations with the Community" in the spirit of the 1963 Declaration of Intent by the EEC Council of Ministers: (1) taking part in the next Yaoundé Convention; (2) having one or more special conventions of association on the basis of Article 238 of the Rome Treaty, which permits third-party association involving "reciprocal rights and obligations"; and (3) concluding a simple trade agreement.

These terms aroused suspicions on the part of the group of countries that came to be known as the "associables"[12] (as opposed to the "associates" already in the Yaoundé system). These countries were rightly concerned about the eventual loss of both the system of Commonwealth Preferences and the Commonwealth Sugar Agreement, from which they benefited (see also Girvan and Montoute in this volume). This despite the fact that Protocol 22 stated that the accession treaty would "have as its firm purpose"[13] the "safeguarding of the interests" of those countries that featured in the protocol (the "associables"), which meant that there was an understanding that they would be looked after. Meanwhile, the members of both the old Commonwealth (Canada, Australia, and New Zealand) and the Asian Commonwealth (including India, Pakistan, Bangladesh, Sri Lanka, Malaysia, and Singapore) were more or less left to fend for themselves.

There was a body of opinion among some in the European Commission, as well as several Yaoundé associates such as Niger's president, Hamani Diori, that would have preferred separate negotiations for "associates" and "associables". These associates were concerned, above all, with preserving their existing privileges, known as the *acquis*, but their concerns were beaten off by a concerted diplomatic offensive to change the terms of reference. Also, there were others who were more ready to bow to the inevitable. The aforesaid diplomatic campaign involved "associables" from Africa and the Caribbean, as well as European Commission officials, including notably the new French Development Commissioner, Claude Cheysson. Cheysson was an unconventional trouble-shooter appointed in April 1973 to replace the more classic French diplomat, Jean-François Deniau, who had also been the European Commission official in charge of the negotiations for British entry into the EEC. Deniau, before returning to the French government, had produced a report[14] on the implications of enlargement for what was initially called "cooperation" but that had begun to open the way to what eventually came after. In particular, the Deniau report presaged flexibility on the question of reciprocity. This point was underlined by Dieter Frisch, a European Commission official who later became Director-General for Development, in a detailed and informative paper that he wrote in 2008 reflecting on 50 years of development policy.[15]

Cheysson was bilingual and had previously served as Executive Secretary of the Commission for Technical Cooperation in Africa, a joint Franco-British institution. He had been based in Nigeria, and was suspected in the Quai d'Orsay of being an anglophile. Indeed, Foccart in his diaries describes Cheysson on several occasions as being out of control, having gone over completely to *les anglais*.[16] An invaluable ally for Cheysson in his efforts to strike a new deal was Maurice Foley,[17] a pro-European Labour Party stalwart who had been a minister in the British Foreign Office in Harold Wilson's second administration. Foley, being pro-European, had been brought into the European Commission at the moment of British entry to be Deputy Director-General for Development, and was the most senior British recruit on the development side. Foley had good contacts in Africa, especially among the liberation movements, but also in Nigeria, where he had been a committed supporter of the federal cause in the last year of the civil war that ended in January 1970. High-level diplomatic initiatives were undertaken in Africa, using the forum of the Organisation of African Unity (OAU). As a result, the OAU's tenth anniversary summit, in May 1973, passed a now almost forgotten Economic Charter, which included a vital endorsement for collective African negotiations.[18]

One key concern for the "associables" was that the privileges that had been contained in the system of Commonwealth Preferences and the Commonwealth Sugar Agreement should be maintained for themselves. This meant, effectively, abandoning the principle of reciprocity that had been enshrined in Yaoundé, and that some hard-liners in the European Commission were anxious to preserve. Here the instrument of the Commonwealth proved useful. Armed with the OAU Economic Charter mentioned earlier, the Nigerian delegation—led by General Yakubu Gowon—to the Commonwealth Summit in Ottawa, Canada, in August 1973, sought the Commonwealth's support on this issue. In his speech in Ottawa, Gowon was forthright on the subject when he observed: "We must of necessity trade with Europe and the rest of the world. But we also want the world to know that it is fiction to speak of a free trade area between developed and developing countries."[19] The statement was a clarion call against the principle of reciprocity that the "associables" continued to stress. It was widely reported that there had been pressure from the United States (US) government to end the reciprocal free trade area, which Washington found exclusive. It was only towards the end of the 18 months of negotiations that began in 1973 that the vital concession was made, granting non-reciprocity and clearing the way for the signing of the first Lomé Convention between African, Caribbean, and Pacific countries, and the European Economic Community, in February 1975.[20]

LOMÉ AND THE BIRTH OF THE ACP

The African, Caribbean, and Pacific countries met together for the first time in an ad hoc ministerial meeting in Lagos, Nigeria, in July 1973, before going on to another meeting in Brussels, and agreed to negotiate together. The spokesman for the Caribbean group was Shridath Ramphal, foreign minister of Guyana, who said in Lagos that "we interpret the statements made [by the EEC] to mean that in its approach to the negotiations the community is not hidebound by existing stereotypes", but above all rejected the idea that "the talks should proceed on the concept of a free trade area."[21]

At the formal opening of negotiations in the grand surroundings of Egmont Palace in Brussels in October 1973, Ramphal (supported by the Pacific group) requested the Nigerian trade minister, Wenike Briggs, to act as spokesman for all three country groups. This symbolic collective act was one of the key moments in the formation of the ACP group, because from then on, throughout the negotiations, there was one spokesperson for the African, Caribbean, and Pacific countries, although at the signing of the convention in Lomé, Togo, each region of the ACP made a speech. Ramphal spoke for the Caribbean, but his words could be taken as an inspirational founding text for the whole nascent ACP group. He said that the negotiations had been "testimony to an even more ample fulfilment of the ambition for unity dimly perceived and cautiously advanced at the start ... I venture to suggest that the reality, tested as it has been in these negotiations, is of immense importance, not merely for the strength it brings to our group of states ... but for the new dimension it contributes to the efforts of our generation to evolve the structures of an interdependent world society."[22]

Ramphal was a key figure in the formation of the ACP as an independent group. The idea for such a group had already been germinating in his mind, not long after he became foreign minister of Guyana, when the foreign ministers of the Non-Aligned Movement (NAM) met in Georgetown in August 1972. The entry of Britain into the EEC was by then almost a certainty, and the implications for Commonwealth countries were far-reaching, so he made contact with a number of key representatives from Africa and the Caribbean, in particular, to raise the possibility of a common front. He would later write: "To say the seeds of the Lomé Convention were sown on the lawns of the Prime Minister's residence in Georgetown is perhaps hyperbole—but there is more than a grain of truth in it."[23]

There were many other innovative details in the first Lomé Convention, including STABEX (*Système de Stabilisation des Recettes d'Exportation*)— a scheme for the stabilisation of export earnings, created in response to developing-country complaints at deterioration in their terms of trade, and which was especially valuable for countries dependent on the export of one or two agricultural commodities. The Convention's chapters on regional cooperation and industrial cooperation were also innovative. Lomé I further involved a political narrative that Cheysson was particularly skilful at developing. For example, although the convention excluded Asia and Latin America, it was put forward as a model of the New International

Economic Order (NIEO), which had been promoted in the wake of the 1973 oil price crisis. Lomé I was also promoted as a legally binding contract between "equals" (as had been Yaoundé, in fact) and as an example of the fashionable idea of global interdependence.

Notably, the word "partnership" was used in the context of Lomé, while "association" was quietly dropped, as was the notion of *Eurafrique*, which had been part of the political superstructure of Yaoundé. The convention was proclaimed as politically neutral, which permitted it to be opened up to Marxist countries such as Ethiopia, Angola, and Mozambique, as well as liberal capitalist economies like Côte d'Ivoire and Kenya. This had some propaganda value in the cut and thrust of the Cold War, but after 1990, especially as human rights provisions began to be included in the texts, became much less of a positive advertisement, and was quietly dropped.

On the ACP side, the successful conclusion of the negotiations came from the solidarity of the group, in which the obvious potential for conflict and divergence was overcome by strategic diplomacy between key members of the group, especially among the ambassadors in Brussels who bore the brunt of the tensions of the negotiations with the EU, most of which took place in the antiseptic atmosphere of the Manhattan Centre just by the Gare du Nord in Brussels. This strategic diplomacy cut cross the three country groups. For example, Nigeria's ambassador, Olu Sanu, had close ties with his counterpart from Dahomey (now Benin), Gratien Pognon, with their ability to communicate with each other in a shared language—Yoruba—helping to forge their relationship. The network established by Ramphal and others with connections in Africa also left a lasting impact. Although the Pacific diplomats often felt themselves outsiders, they still were very keen to benefit from the strength of the group, an attraction that has since survived all the tensions of the past four decades. The connection between Africa and the Caribbean, in particular, was a living incarnation of Ali Mazrui's concept of the political strength of the "black Atlantic".[24] A greater awareness of this solidarity may help to understand why the ACP has survived despite serious attempts to undermine its coherence from the European side.

Just over three months after the signing of Lomé, African, Caribbean, and Pacific countries met in June 1975 in Georgetown, Guyana, to formally establish the ACP as a grouping. The Lomé negotiations had initially received support from the Coordinating Secretariat of the AASM, which had been set up under Yaoundé. However, after Georgetown, an ACP Secretariat was established in Brussels that became operational by 1976.

Initially funded by the ACP member states themselves, the secretariat soon found that arrears from some countries necessitated a request for at least 50 per cent of its budget to come from the European Development Fund. This has since encouraged a damaging feeling of dependence among African, Caribbean, and Pacific countries, while encouraging European paternalism.

The Georgetown concordat was based very much on the success of collective negotiation. This was the sentiment that gave rise to the "spirit of Lomé", which persuaded those who had felt that it was still based on a neo-colonial compromise into believing that it was an experience worth pursuing. It was portrayed as an example of what Tanzanian president Julius Nyerere called "the trade union of the poor". Scholar John Ravenhill, in a definitive book based on material collected in Brussels in the late 1970s, called it more cynically but realistically "collective clientelism".[25]

THE LIFE OF LOMÉ

Although Lomé had remarkable innovations, and the abandonment of reciprocity substantially altered the overarching paradigm, the mind-set that had been built into the Yaoundé system continued in the ACP-EU relationship. Marxist political scientist Guy Martin was of the opinion that Lomé essentially preserved the neo-colonial characteristics of Yaoundé, only more effectively because all of sub-Saharan Africa was now involved.[26] In a paper in a 1981 volume published by the London-based Overseas Development Institute (ODI),[27] Adrian Hewitt—one of the more balanced commentators on EU development matters—put it differently. He recorded many of the positive advantages of Lomé, but also noted: "[B]ecause the ACP Group was brought into existence primarily to receive special favours from the EEC—favours denied to the rest of the Third World—and because the selection and specification of the group was carried out by the EEC, the ACP are clearly a creature of the community ... it would not be the first time that a dominant member of a business partnership selected his prospective associates."

One has to remember that the then new Lomé Convention existed alongside an evolving European development policy that had been highlighted in a fresco put forward by Cheysson in 1974.[28] Over the next 25 years, European funds allocated to development (for a long time the second largest total after the Common Agricultural Policy [CAP]) became increasingly global, as Europe's relations developed in Asia and Latin

America, although none of the other agreements had the special contractual nature and intimacy of Lomé. The initial involvement of the OAU, and by the 1980s all of the front-line states of Southern Africa, translated into an increasingly positive influence on European views of, and policies towards, the South African apartheid regime. Once Lomé was signed, from my own worm's eye view in the European Commission, it seemed that the South African embassy in Brussels found itself increasingly on the defensive.

The signing of the first Lomé Convention in the Togolese capital in 1975 had been surrounded with almost beatific euphoria, enhanced by the long ordeal of the negotiations during which on several occasions it had looked as if accord was beyond the protagonists' grasp. The proclamation of Lomé's pioneering role in relations between industrialised and developing countries featured in all the speeches; and for those in the European Commission whose job it was to market the new treaty, there was excellent raw material. In the general ambiance of the early 1970s—before the era of the oil shock—there was a belief that a New International Economic Order was leading the way to a new concept of North-South dialogue. The turbulence generated by these ideas all but faded by the end of the decade, with the second post-Iran oil crisis in 1979. As the world entered the 1980s, there was an irrevocable change of mood that moved away from concessions and dialogue and into the tough world of free market economics.

In any case, the Lomé honeymoon did not last long, as the ACP countries gradually came to realise the realities of the unequal nature and inadequacy of their partnership with Europe, and often came to feel patronised and dismissed. Although the negotiations for Lomé I had been tense and difficult, there had still been a measure of élan, and a feeling among the ACP countries that the strength of their ties, combined with the uncertain international situation, gave them real negotiating muscle. The positive input provided by the Caribbean diplomats in discussing sugar had often been an inspiration. In contrast, the negotiations for Lomé II were conducted with less grace. When certain ACP ambassadors, and on occasion ministers, appeared too argumentative, their governments were openly pressured, even at heads-of-state level, to bring them into line. Furthermore, one of the main new features in Lomé II was SYSMIN (*Système de Développement du Potentiel Minier*), a system for guaranteeing the price of minerals (similar to STABEX). This was included only in the EEC's interest, owing to Europe's fears over risk to the supply of minerals from Africa in the aftermath of the 1978 Shaba affair, in which an invasion from former Katanga gendarmes into Zaire's mineral-rich province of Shaba had triggered a Franco-Belgian military intervention.

The inequality between the ACP and the EU became more telling in the 1980s as the global economic situation worsened, and Africa experienced what Nigerian scholar Adebayo Adedeji has referred to on many occasions as Africa's "lost decade".[29] The truth that independence did not mean easy prosperity was seriously brought home by the structural adjustment policies—harsh and inappropriate medicine for the continued agonies of under-development—imposed by the World Bank and the International Monetary Fund (IMF) on developing countries. For African countries in particular, the economic turmoil and increased dependence undermined their negotiating position, especially as European Development Fund resources became ever more valuable to them in their period of crisis. Whereas Lomé I had shown the ACP's negotiating muscle, this now became increasingly hard to mobilise.

In his 1984 book,[30] Ravenhill spells out with clarity the main elements of disillusion. According to him, the ACP's "collective clientelism"—a term he coined—led to many shortcomings. It had, for example, failed to guarantee the tariff advantages that ACP states enjoyed over third parties in the EEC, or to guarantee the ACP share of the European market; and had not provided protection against the patron (the EEC) engaging in behaviour detrimental to the interests of the clients (the ACP states). Ravenhill questions "a contractual relationship in which the clients' rights were unequivocally identified"; in other words, the "equal partnership" was not jointly managed. Most of these points could be applied to the situation that obtained through the 1980s and 1990s up to the signing of the Cotonou Partnership Agreement in 2000, and almost certainly beyond, although a range of new, more potent grievances have intruded since Cotonou.

The bureaucracy of the EEC, and in many cases the difficulty of aid absorption in some ACP countries (such as Benin, Rwanda, and Chad), imposed ever more powerful delays on the disbursement of EDF resources. It somehow seemed that as the Lomé Conventions grew in size and pagination, so morale declined. Because of the difficulties of achieving satisfactory outcomes in the negotiations, and what was called "Lomé fatigue", it was decided in 1989 that the Lomé Convention's life should be extended for ten years with a mid-term review after five, mainly to renew the EDF. The same issues animated the framework of the Cotonou

Agreement, which was later signed for 20 years with similar revision provisions. There was thus already an atmosphere of frustration and deepening disillusionment on both sides that presaged a serious shake-up.

In this context, the main source of comfort and reassurance for the ACP was the (relative) permanence of the EDF—it was always there. The tensest moment in every negotiation with Europe, going right back to Yaoundé, came in the discussion of the EDF amount, although it sometimes looked like a case of supplicants seeing how much they could get out of benefactors. Elsewhere I have referred to the "morose crisis" of 1995, when "it was only French willingness to put up more funds that ensured that the deal for the new EDF went through", which despite constant nudging and speculation has remained outside the EU budget.[31]

From Lomé to Cotonou

The Cotonou Agreement, signed in June 2000, was vaunted at the time as a normalisation and rationalisation of a relationship that Europe felt had got out of hand.[32] A European Commission green paper,[33] issued in 1996, tried to put ACP-EU relations in the twenty-first century "in the context of the EU's worldwide relations with developing countries" and in the context of its own development policy, which had been officially enshrined in a legal EU instrument for the first time in the Maastricht Treaty of 1991. The green paper stressed the broader context provided by the birth of the World Trade Organisation (WTO), whose tougher, more free-trade-oriented options hardened the EU's advocacy of a return to reciprocity. The green paper also indirectly mooted the possible break-up of the ACP as a group. Both of these features found their way into the eventual agreement, the latter in the form of the economic partnership agreements that were essentially to be negotiated with six (later seven) regional groupings over a seven-year period by 2007. The Caribbean and the Pacific were easy to define, and in Africa, West Africa and Central Africa likewise, but in Eastern and Southern Africa the complexity of overlapping groupings led to substantial difficulties, not helped by the fact that South Africa, although accepted as a member of the ACP, had a separate accord with the EU (see Carim in this volume). The eventual African EPA negotiating groups were an example of the propensity in Brussels for bureaucratic dictation, and as the EPA deadline approached, the EU's approach came to seem more and more like "divide and rule", however much the Europeans pleaded good intentions (see Akokpari, and Katjavivi in this volume.)

In the context of its time, certain aspects of Cotonou were probably unavoidable. The final agreement was a simplification of over-elaborate drafts, and the jettisoning of the chapters on industrial and cultural cooperation did not mean that the ideas contained in them had been thrown out. The loss of STABEX and SYSMIN also did not provoke much concern. Cotonou was still, however, enough of a radical departure from the Lomé regime to provoke serious criticism. The most articulate was from Austrian academic Kunibert Raffer, who argued in 2001 that Cotonou was undoing Lomé's concept of partnership, and was "a decisive step in restoring the situation the EEC had originally wanted when negotiating the first Lomé Convention". He referred, in particular, to the vexed issue of non-reciprocity. Lomé's progressive aspects had been agreed, Raffer said, "in a period of anxiety, catching up with the neo-liberal zeitgeist". The EU, he noted, had now turned into a "normal donor", although a donor with "more than normal leverage" with the ACP group, and with "joint institutions to keep up the appearance of partnership".[34] Raffer's critique was echoed by Guyana's Carl Greenidge, ACP Deputy Secretary-General from 1992 to 2000, in an essay on the subject titled "Return to Colonialism?" in which he blamed the potentially colonial relationship between the ACP and the EU on the structure of global economic relations.[35]

What accounted then for some of the difficulties that the ACP faced in Cotonou? Some have mentioned failures in leadership on the ACP side. While the importance of personalities at the ACP Secretariat fed into the challenge, institutional difficulties were equally present. Apart from the complexities of relations with the European institutions, on the ACP side there were problems that arose from the imbalance of powers between the Committee of Ambassadors and the Secretariat. Some of the ambassadors developed considerable expertise in the complexities of their dossiers, which meant that their advice tended to be taken wholesale by their home governments, where there was all too often little awareness of the mysterious nuances of the EU's workings. It also meant they frequently liked to keep a restraining hand on the ACP Secretariat.

On the European side, there had been a steady growth in the powers of the Council vis-à-vis the Commission, which had always tended in the past to see itself (sometimes unjustifiably) as unofficial intermediary between the European member states and the ACP, although the European Commissioner for Development and ACP Countries himself, João de Deus Pinheiro, in his introduction to the 1996 green paper, pronounced the post-colonial period as "drawing to an end".[36] In discussions in Brussels in July 2010, especially in the Council, I found officials all too ready to brand Lomé as a colonial relic. The focus instead was on the Africa-EU strategic partnership, especially its security aspects, and the whole ACP experience was discounted as marginal.

Two personalities on the European side had an impact on the debate over the economic partnership agreements, in particular. This was the "good cop, bad cop" double act in the European Commission of the blandly persuasive Louis Michel (from Belgium), the Commissioner for Development and Humanitarian Aid, and Britain's Peter Mandelson, the Trade Commissioner. Mandelson's uncomplimentary description of the two largest ACP member states, Nigeria and South Africa, as "elephants in the room",[37] and his spurious charge that the protests against the EPAs had been stirred up by development-focused non-governmental organisations (NGOs), were both unhelpful provocations, while ignoring the real problems of the ACP.

The other institution heavily implicated in the Lomé relationship was the European Parliament, through the ACP-EU Joint Assembly. This had its roots in the former joint parliamentary "association", which had been labelled as *Eurafricaine* (at a period when the relationship under French influence was described as *Eurafrique*),[38] and in Lomé's early years never really seemed to be pulling its weight, in part because of the relative powerlessness of the parliament in the European configuration. With its powers reinforced by the Treaty of Maastricht (1991) and Treaty of Nice (2001), the European Parliament has since played a more significant role in ACP-EU affairs, showing that it can be of real assistance to the ACP. The culmination of this was the speech, widely praised by many in the ACP, made by the then co-president of the ACP-EU Joint Parliamentary Assembly, Glenys Kinnock, at the ACP Summit in Accra in October 2008.[39] In this she was deeply critical of the whole EPA process, citing the *Financial Times*'s characterisation of the interim EPAs as a "tangled cats [*sic*] cradle, if not a mangled dog's breakfast". From the outset, Kinnock said, the European Commission "approached EPAs as if they were conventional free trade agreements focusing on market openings rather than tools for development … several years later there is still the relentless repetition of the mantra of reciprocity—as if that were a word which automatically denotes fairness. It only denotes fairness when the reciprocity is between equals". It is clearly too late to turn back the clock to Lomé, but the message from her speech helped place the EPAs in perspective.

On a positive note, the challenge that the EPA process has presented to the ACP may have been an agent for restoring a measure of power into its negotiating positions. At the height of tension over the EPAs, the resolution of the ACP Council of Ministers of December 2007[40] contained such a forceful attack on mercantilism that one felt that the "spirit of Lomé"—against all other evidence—still carried on.

In the late 1990s, given the difficulties the ACP faced, one could have imagined the Caribbean and the Pacific going their separate ways. However, both Shridath Ramphal and Edwin Carrington, Secretary-General of the Caribbean Community (CARICOM) between 1992 and 2010 after 15 years at the ACP Secretariat (including five as Secretary-General), have observed that the Caribbean interest (although with its own specificity) still needed the reinforcement of African backing, especially with South Africa in the ACP.[41] The inclusion of the Dominican Republic and Cuba in the ACP also gave Spain a stronger interest in keeping the ACP-EU relationship afloat. Meanwhile, the addition of Haiti reinforced the group's special vocation as a supporter of island states. This has been one of the main attractions for the Pacific, which has otherwise appeared to be a little on the outside of the ACP group, while remaining passionately attached to it, perhaps because it gave the Pacific countries an extra voice in the international arena.

An additional irritant in the ACP-EU relationship more than a decade since Cotonou has been the growth of a parallel European policy on Africa in the form of an Africa-EU strategic partnership, with the first Africa-EU summit held in Cairo, Egypt, in April 2000 (see Akokpari in this volume). This has given the impression of dysfunctionality. For example, Article 11 of Cotonou makes a link between security and development, which has been reinforced in the statutory revisions of the agreement in 2005 and 2010. Yet, since the formation of the African Union (AU) in 2002, Europe and Africa have engaged directly—outside the formal framework of the ACP-EU relationship—on security issues. Direct links have been established with the strengthened EU Council of Ministers, in terms of both funding for the AU Commission and development of peace operations under the aegis of the African Union, first in Darfur in 2006 and then in Somalia since 2007 (see Adebajo in this volume). The ACP was not involved in the development of AU-EU relations, even though the funds made available for Europe's security cooperation with Africa came from the EDF, an essential element of Cotonou.

The second Africa-EU summit, held in Lisbon, Portugal, in December 2007, duly adopted a Joint Africa-EU Strategy (JAES) and an action plan,[42] but took place in a sour atmosphere. Ironically, it coincided with the December 2007 deadline for the conclusion of the EPA process. A number of critical speeches were made, including by Senegalese president Abdoulaye Wade and South Africa's Thabo Mbeki.[43] The joint strategy thus did not start well and has proved difficult to implement. The unfortunate choice of Tripoli as the venue for the December 2010 Africa-EU summit only added to its credibility challenge, as it came not long before the events of the Arab Spring overtook Libya and led to the fall of Muammar Qaddafi in October 2011. There has also been a certain lack of will to implement the strategic partnership, as well as a lack of substance, compared with the necessity of coping with the complex if often difficult issues raised by trade and aid that are central to the ACP-EU relationship.

CONCLUDING REFLECTIONS

Is it possible to see the "spirit of Lomé" of the mid-1970s still living on? Having been involved in the Lomé process and having had a ringside view of the long negotiating sessions for both Lomé I and II, I can say that it existed. The trans-national solidarity on the ACP side in negotiation, and the willingness on the European side to open real new doors, made it worthwhile, despite Europe's shameless willingness to go four times to a signing ceremony in the capital city of one of Africa's more squalid dictatorships. Times have changed dramatically since the mid-1970s, however, and it now seems almost irrelevant to talk of "the end of the post-colonial era".

If the chance circumstances of history brought the African, Caribbean, and Pacific regions together, then a real common interest, in face of the challenges they are confronted with in Brussels, can still bind them together. For Africa, apart from increasingly distinct security questions, Cotonou still offers greater prospects of dealing with critical issues than does its strategic partnership with the EU. The changed balance of global economic power, especially with the rise of new powers in Asia and Latin America (see Virk in this volume), is reason for both the ACP and Europe to reconsider their relationship. Africa, in particular, now has a global stance very different from its posture during the doldrums of the 1980s.

Even if, upon the expiry of the Cotonou Agreement in 2020, the ACP-EU relationship finally pulls apart, it can be said that the partnership has played a genuinely historic role and framed some of the most crucial encounters between Africa and Europe—that it has contained elements of a model for inter-state relations in this changed world.

NOTES

1. Centre for Conflict Resolution (CCR), *The African, Caribbean, and Pacific (ACP) Group and the European Union (EU)*, seminar report, Cape Town, South Africa, January 2014, p. 9, http://www.ccr.org.za (accessed 11 June 2015).

2. The 15 French-administered overseas territories were Chad, Côte d'Ivoire, Dahomey, the French Congo, Gabon, Guinea, Madagascar, Mauritania, Niger, Oubangui-Chari, Senegal, Soudan, Upper Volta, and two United Nations (UN) Trust Territories— Cameroon and Togo. The two Belgian-administered territories were the Belgian Congo and Rwanda-Urundi (the latter as a UN Trust Territory), while Italy administered Somalia.

3. They were Benin (Dahomey), Burkina Faso (Upper Volta), Burundi, Cameroon, the Central African Republic (CAR), Chad, Congo-Brazzaville, Côte d'Ivoire, the Democratic Republic of the Congo (DRC), Gabon, Madagascar, Mali, Mauritania, Niger, Rwanda, Senegal, Somalia, and Togo.

4. "*Jacques Ferrandi, un Inconditionnel de l'Eurafrique*", obituary, *Le Monde*, 3 December 2004, p. 14.

5. William Zartman, *The Politics of Trade Negotiations Between Africa and the EEC* (Princeton: Princeton University Press, 1971), pp. 18–23.

6. The term *Françafrique* was originally coined by Felix Houphouët-Boigny to describe favourably the closeness of the relationship, but it later became a term of criticism for the cronyism the relationship involved. *See* François-Xavier Verschave, *La Françafrique* (Paris: Stock, 1998).

7. Britain is used as a synonym for the United Kingdom (UK) in this context.

8. Omar Bongo and Christian Casteran, *Omar Bongo, les Confidences d'un Africain: Entretiens avec Christian Casteran* (Paris: Albin Michel, 1994), p. 90.

9. Curiously, there is not one reference throughout the diaries to *les Britanniques*. Charles de Gaulle's statement of 14 January 1963, vetoing British membership, also refers throughout to "England". *See* Charles de Gaulle, *Discours et Messages 1962–5*, vol. 5 (Paris: Plon, 1970).

10. Jacques Foccart, *La France Pompidolienne: Journal de l'Elysée IV, 1971–2* (Paris: Fayard/Jeune Afrique, 2000).
11. "Treaty Concerning the Accession of the Kingdom of Denmark, the Republic of Ireland, and the United Kingdom of Great Britain and Northern Ireland to the EEC [European Economic Community] and the EAEC [European Atomic Energy Community]", Brussels, Belgium, 22 January 1972.
12. They were Barbados, Botswana, Fiji, Gambia, Ghana, Guyana, Jamaica, Kenya, Lesotho, Malawi, Mauritius, Nigeria, Sierra Leone, Swaziland, Tonga, Trinidad and Tobago, Uganda, Western Samoa, and Zambia. The Bahamas and Grenada gained independence in 1973 and 1974, respectively, and subsequently became "associables" before the signing of Lomé.
13. Uwe Kitzinger, *Diplomacy and Persuasion: How Britain Joined the Common Market* (London: Thames and Hudson, 1973), pp. 133–134. Kitzinger records difficult discussion on the translation of the French phrase *aura au coeur*, literally "have at heart", which was considered too opaque, so what was agreed was a more acceptable diplomatic formula.
14. EU Commission, "Renewal and Enlargement of the Association of the AASM and Certain Commonwealth Developing Countries", COM (73) 500 final, memorandum of the Commission to the Council, 4 April 1973, *Supplement to the Bulletin of the European Communities*.
15. Dieter Frisch, *The European Union's Development Policy: A Personal View of 50 Years of International Cooperation*, Policy Management Report no. 15 (Maastricht: European Centre for Development Policy Management, 2008).
16. Jacques Foccart, *La Fin du Gaullisme: Journal de l'Elysée V, 1973–4* (Paris: Fayard/Jeune Afrique, 2001).
17. Kaye Whiteman, "Maurice Foley", obituary, *The Guardian*, 22 February 2002, p. 43.
18. Organisation of African Unity (OAU), "Declaration on Cooperation, Development, and Economic Independence", AHG/Res.69, adopted at the 19th Ordinary Session of the OAU Assembly of Heads of State and Government, Addis Ababa, Ethiopia, 28 May 1973.
19. Quoted in Kaye Whiteman, "Ramphal and the Lomé Convention", in Richard Bourne (ed.), *Shridath Ramphal: The Commonwealth*

and the World: Essays in Honour of His 80th Birthday (London: Hansib 2008), p. 160.

20. The 46 African, Caribbean, and Pacific countries that signed the first Lomé Convention were the Bahamas, Barbados, Benin, Botswana, Burkina Faso, Burundi, Cameroon, the Central African Republic, Chad, Congo-Brazzaville, Côte d'Ivoire, the Democratic Republic of the Congo, Equatorial Guinea, Ethiopia, Fiji, Gabon, Gambia, Ghana, Grenada, Guinea, Guinea-Bissau, Guyana, Jamaica, Kenya, Lesotho, Liberia, Madagascar, Malawi, Mali, Mauritania, Mauritius, Niger, Nigeria, Rwanda, Senegal, Sierra Leone, Somalia, Sudan, Swaziland, Tanzania, Togo, Tonga, Trinidad and Tobago, Uganda, Western Samoa, and Zambia.

21. Whiteman, "Ramphal and the Lomé Convention", pp. 159–160.

22. Whiteman, "Ramphal and the Lomé Convention", p. 161.

23. Sonny Ramphal, "Remembering to Score: A Retrospective", http://silvertorch.com/sonny-ramphal-1.html (accessed 19 June 2015).

24. Ali Mazrui, "The Black Atlantic from Othello to Obama: In Search of a Post-Racial Society", in Adekeye Adebajo and Kaye Whiteman (eds.), *The EU and Africa: From Eurafrique to Afro-Europa* (Johannesburg: Wits University Press; and London: Hurst, 2012), pp. 419–440.

25. John Ravenhill, *Collective Clientelism: The Lomé Convention and North-South Relations* (New York: Columbia University Press, 1984).

26. Guy Martin, "Africa and the Ideology of Eurafrica: Neo-Colonialism or Pan-Africanism", *Journal of Modern African Studies* 2, no. 2 (1982), pp. 221–258.

27. Adrian Hewitt, "The Lomé Conventions: Myth and Substance of the 'Partnership of Equals'", in Margaret Cornell (ed.), *Europe and Africa: Issues in Post-Colonial Relations* (London: Overseas Development Institute, 1981), pp. 21–42.

28. European Commission, "Development Aid: Fresco of Community Action Tomorrow", Brussels, *Supplement to the Bulletin of the European Communities*, 1974.

29. This term was coined by Adebayo Adedeji, Executive Secretary of the United Nations Economic Commission for Africa (UNECA) from 1975 to 1991.

30. Ravenhill, *Collective Clientelism*, p. 309.

31. Kaye Whiteman, "Africa, the ACP, and Europe: The Lessons of 25 Years", *Development Policy Review* 16, no. 1 (1998), p. 33.
32. It had been planned to sign the agreement in Fiji, with the distance symbolising a new start, but because of a political crisis it was moved to Cotonou, capital of Benin, which was arguably too close to the by now shunned Lomé for comfort.
33. European Commission, "Green Paper on Relations Between the European Union and the ACP Countries on the Eve of the 21st Century: Challenges and Options for a New Partnership", Brussels, 20 November 1996.
34. Kunibert Raffer, "Cotonou: Slowly Undoing Lomé's Concept of Partnership", Discussion Paper no. 23 (Manchester: Development Studies Association, European Development Study Group, 2001).
35. Carl B. Greenidge, "Return to Colonialism? The New Orientation of European Development Assistance", in Marjorie Lister (ed.), *New Perspectives on European Union Development Cooperation* (Boulder, CO, and Oxford: Westview, 1999), p. 103.
36. Verband   Entwicklungspolitik   Deutscher Nichtregierungsorganisationen (VENRO), "The Future of the EU-ACP Cooperation", working paper (Bonn, Germany, 13 February 1998), http://www.venro.org/fileadmin/Publikationen/ arbeitspapiere/arbeitspapier_01_en.pdf (accessed 19 June 2015).
37. Kaye Whiteman, "The Rise and Fall of Eurafrique", in Adebajo and Whiteman, *The EU and Africa*, p. 41.
38. Whiteman, "The Rise and Fall of Eurafrique", pp. 23–44.
39. Glenys Kinnock, speech at the sixth ACP Summit, Accra, Ghana, 2 October 2008, http://www.eesc.europa.eu/resources/docs/ eesc-2008-37-en.pdf (accessed 18 June 2015).
40. ACP Council of Ministers, "Declaration of the ACP Council of Ministers at Its 86th Session Expressing Serious Concern on the Status of the Negotiations of the Economic Partnership Agreements", ACP/25/013/07, Brussels, 13 December 2007.
41. In private conversations with the author, 2008–2009.
42. Available at http://www.consilium.europa.eu/uedocs/cms_data/ docs/pressdata/en/er/97496.pdf (accessed 12 June 2015).
43. Stephen Castle, "Trade Deals Stymied at Lisbon Meeting", *New York Times*, 10 December 2007.

PART II

An Anatomy of the ACP-EU Relationship

CHAPTER 3

The EU and Africa: The Political Economy of an Asymmetrical Partnership

John Akokpari

The relationship between Africa and the European Union (EU) is steeped in history, with origins that date back to the colonial era. The contemporary record of this relationship can be traced through the framework agreements governing the broader partnership between the African, Caribbean, and Pacific (ACP) group of states and the EU. Prior to the creation of the ACP in 1975, Europe's relations with Africa were institutionalised in the Yaoundé Agreements of 1963 and 1969, which were subsequently replaced by the Lomé Conventions, which then provided the basis for ACP-EU development cooperation until the signing of the Cotonou Partnership Agreement of 2000. From Yaoundé and Lomé to Cotonou, each phase of the relationship has had its peculiar characteristics, but a fundamental asymmetry between the two sides—Africa and the EU—has been an underlying constant. Beyond the ACP-EU partnership, since 2000, regular Africa-EU summits have provided a parallel process through which the continent's relationship with Europe has further developed.

African countries have been largely driven by a desire for greater trade, investment, and development aid in their relationship with Europe, while the EU—in an era of greater competition from new and emerging powers

J. Akokpari (✉)
Department of Political Studies, University of Cape Town (UCT),
Cape Town, South Africa

© The Author(s) 2017
A. Montoute, K. Virk (eds.), *The ACP Group and the EU Development Partnership*, DOI 10.1007/978-3-319-45492-4_3

such as China and India (see Virk in this volume)—has sought to forge closer ties with Africa in order to secure market access and preserve its traditional spheres of influence on the continent. Since 2002, Africa-EU relations have been dominated, in particular, by protracted negotiations for economic partnership agreements (EPAs) mandated by the Cotonou Agreement of 2000. Although the EU Commission has promoted the EPAs as a means to accelerate Africa's development and integration into the global economy, African countries have, by and large, expressed greater scepticism about the potential benefits of the agreements (see Katjavivi in this volume). Furthermore, over the past decade, Europe has gradually seemed to move away from the transcontinental ACP framework and towards Africa's regional organisations, in particular the African Union (AU), as its preferred framework for dealing with issues affecting the continent.

This chapter surveys Africa-EU relations over the past decade. In so doing, I suggest that while African countries derive important trade and aid benefits from their multi-faceted partnership with Europe, this has remained an asymmetrical relationship that places constraints on Africa's regional integration and development efforts. The chapter begins with an overview of the Africa-EU trade and economic relationship under Lomé and Cotonou, before taking a more in-depth look at the African EPA negotiating processes. This is followed by discussion on the EU's development assistance to Africa, as well as its newer partnership with the continent under the framework of Africa-EU summits and the Joint Africa-EU Strategy (JAES) of 2007. The chapter concludes with a brief reflection on the way forward for Africa-EU relations.

Africa-EU Trade: From Lomé to Cotonou

Signed in June 2000, the Cotonou Agreement currently provides the overarching framework for trade, aid, and development cooperation between the 28-member EU and the 79-member ACP group of states.[1] Prior to Cotonou, the ACP-EU relationship had been governed by the Lomé regime, one based on the principle of trade non-reciprocity (see Whiteman in this volume). Generally speaking, the impact of the development partnership on Africa under Lomé was mixed. For the ACP countries, and especially African countries, the trade regime was beneficial in terms of providing them with preferential access to the European market for primary commodities. At the same time, however, trade relations were skewed in favour of the EU, which used Africa as a market for its industrial products.

With the end of the Cold War by 1990 and Africa's marginalisation in the decade that followed, Africa-EU trade plummeted to a low. Sub-Saharan Africa's share in the EU's external trade decreased from 3.2 per cent in 1985 to less than 1.4 per cent in 2006. This owed in large part to Africa's declining importance for Britain and France, both former colonial powers that remained the continent's most important trading partners in the EU. Between 1985 and 2006, Britain's trade with sub-Saharan Africa decreased from 3.7 per cent to 2.3 per cent of its total, while France's dwindled from 5.2 per cent to 2 per cent of the country's total.[2] Furthermore, trade between Africa and the EU continued to be asymmetrical, and skewed in favour of the latter. While in 2007 the EU accounted for 75 per cent of sub-Saharan Africa's trade, the latter remained "an increasingly marginal market for both EU exports and imports".[3]

The Cotonou Agreement was, in principle, more ambitious in promoting development and balanced trade between Africa and the EU than the Lomé Conventions had been. The main objectives of Cotonou, as set out in Article 19 of the agreement, include "poverty reduction and ultimately its eradication; sustainable development; and progressive integration of the ACP countries into the world economy". Article 20 of the agreement identifies the achievement of economic growth, and job and employment creation; the development of the private sector; and the promotion of regional integration as important aims.[4] Cotonou further calls for the negotiation of economic partnership agreements to replace Lomé's non-reciprocity-based trade regime. These agreements were promoted as "instruments for development"[5] that would assist ACP countries in attaining economic growth and attracting foreign investments, while instituting new trade arrangements compatible with the free-market-based rules of the World Trade Organisation (WTO) and making ACP economies more competitive globally. The EPAs were thus heavily informed by a neo-liberal paradigm, and through them the EU has aimed for comprehensive liberalisation involving not just trade in commodities, but also new areas such as services, investment, government procurement, intellectual property, and competition.[6]

African countries, meanwhile, viewed the EPAs as a potential means to sustain and expand their access into the European common market—particularly agricultural products—in an increasingly globalised international economic system, in which Africa otherwise remained on the margins.

Intra-regional trade in Africa also remained low, making access to external markets vitally important. According to *The Economist*, intra-regional trade in Africa was a mere 12 per cent in 2013 compared to 60 per cent in Europe and Asia, and 40 per cent in North America in the same year.[7]

AFRICA-EU ECONOMIC PARTNERSHIP AGREEMENTS

For the negotiations towards the Cotonou-mandated EPAs, ACP countries are divided into seven regional groupings: West Africa, Central Africa, Eastern and Southern Africa (ESA), the East African Community (EAC), the Southern African Development Community (SADC) EPA group, the Caribbean, and the Pacific. In keeping with Articles 35(2) and 37(3) of the Cotonou Agreement, each regional grouping has negotiated separately for an EPA with the European Union. These negotiations began in September 2002, and were to have been completed by December 2007, with implementation of the negotiated agreements in January 2008. However, by the 2007 deadline, the Caribbean was the only regional grouping to have concluded negotiations for an economic partnership agreement with the EU (see Girvan and Montoute, and Gonzales in this volume). In the Pacific, an interim EPA was concluded (signed in 2009) with only two countries—Fiji and Papua New Guinea (see Tavola in this volume). In Africa, only 14 countries—Côte d'Ivoire and Ghana in West Africa; Cameroon in Central Africa; Comoros, Madagascar, Mauritius, Seychelles, Zambia, and Zimbabwe in Eastern and Southern Africa; and Botswana, Lesotho, Mozambique, Namibia, and Swaziland in the SADC group—had concluded interim agreements by the 2007 deadline.[8] These interim EPAs were intended to ensure continued access to the European market, while the final agreements were still being negotiated. Several African countries (for example, Angola, Namibia, and South Africa), however, were by then wary of the EPAs because of the potential negative impacts of the agreements on their national economies (see Katjavivi in this volume).[9]

Despite the concerns expressed by African countries, the EU continued to push its liberalisation agenda and compelled the EPA negotiations to conclusion. In September 2011, the European Commission issued a fresh deadline, threatening to withdraw preferential market access for countries that failed to ratify the interim EPAs they had previously signed by January 2014 (later extended to October 2014 by the European Parliament). This placed enormous, and even unnecessary, pressure on the EPA negotiating processes (see Carim in this volume). It further directly affected countries, which were at the time also dealing with significant domestic opposition to the EPAs. In Ghana, for example, the government faced stiff resistance from labour and wider civil society groups—including the Economic Justice Network, comprising Ghana's Trade Union Congress and Christian Council—to the economic partnership agreement between West Africa and the EU.[10] If Ghana were to sign the final EPA, it stood to lose an estimated $300 million in tariff revenue annually,[11] as well as the use of tariffs as a policy option to protect the country's local industries.[12] However, without the EPA, the country risked losing its preferential access to the European common market, with the EU being its biggest trading partner: the EU market accounted for about 38 per cent of agricultural goods exports from Ghana between 2012 and 2013. Furthermore, according to the Ghana Export Promotion Authority (GEPA), the value of the country's agricultural exports to the EU increased to $955 million in 2014 from $768 million in 2013. During the same period, the value of Ghana's agricultural exports to other developed countries plummeted by 28.6 per cent, from $258.6 million in 2013 to $184.7 million in 2014.[13]

In the months leading up to the EU-imposed deadline of October 2014, a number of inconclusive sub-regional and continental meetings were held in an attempt to craft common African positions on the EPAs. Overall, there was little to no consensus on the EPAs in any of the negotiating regions in Africa. The fact that the EU was negotiating the partnership agreements with regional groupings, rather than with individual countries, created a dilemma for those countries, in particular, that had been forced by circumstances to hesitantly accept interim EPAs in the first place. The intra-regional divisions were manifest clearly at a continental-level meeting in Addis Ababa, Ethiopia, in mid-2014. To craft a common position on the EPAs, African ministers of trade and industry met in an extraordinary session at the AU's headquarters in Addis Ababa in April 2014. Not surprisingly, the discussions were heated, but also inconclusive, with sharp disagreements over the long-term benefits of the agreements.[14] The April 2014 meeting thus failed in articulating a common African stance.

As of September 2015, three EPA negotiation processes had been concluded in Africa—West Africa in February 2014, the SADC EPA group in July 2014, and the East African Community in October 2014.[15] The SADC-EU EPA was signed in June 2016, with the signature processes ongoing for the agreements with West Africa and the EAC. Throughout the tortuous negotiations, it was clear that Africa lacked the leverage either to jettison the idea of the agreements or to negotiate them on its terms. African countries, predominantly agricultural exporting states, needed the EU. Thus, despite initial opposition, the EPA processes have continued in Africa, although the status of the agreements has continued to vary across the negotiating regions.[16]

AFRICAN OPPOSITION TO THE ECONOMIC PARTNERSHIP AGREEMENTS

African opposition to the economic partnership agreements with the EU is based on the perceived overall negative impact of the EPAs on the development prospects of the continent. A key objective of the partnership agreements, as identified in the Cotonou Agreement of 2000, is to help Africa's developmental efforts. However, critics maintain that the EPAs will exacerbate, rather than ameliorate, the continent's developmental challenges, and inhibit its regional integration efforts. Regional integration, in particular, has been seen as an alternative pathway to Africa's development in an era of globalisation.[17] The Abuja Treaty of 1991 captures the continent's vision for regional integration, while providing a roadmap for it that identifies "Africa's regional economic communities [RECs] as building blocks for the creation of an African Economic Community (AEC) by 2028".[18]

However, the EPA negotiating groupings in Africa do not all conform to the continent's five traditional geographic regions, as recognised by the AU: Central, Eastern, North, Southern, and West Africa. For example, Mauritania in North Africa is included in the EPA for West Africa. Meanwhile, Tanzania, Madagascar, Mauritius, Seychelles, Zimbabwe, and the Democratic Republic of the Congo (DRC)—six SADC countries—have not been included in the SADC EPA group, but are split across three different negotiating regions: the EAC, Eastern and Southern Africa, and Central Africa. This has made it challenging for the 15-member SADC to take a common position on the partnership agreements. (See Carim in this volume.) The EPAs thus risk further fragmenting a continent that is already contending with multiple and overlapping memberships in regional blocs, and compounding its regional integration challenges.[19] In the words of one concerned observer: "how do you create a custom union, a common market and a single monetary union if your member states have different trade arrangements with third parties?"[20] Not surprisingly, some have gone so far as to decry the EPAs as a "divide and conquer" tactic by

Europe to dominate Africa's trade,[21] in a manner reminiscent of the colonial divide and rule policy.

There is also concern that the EPAs will undermine industrialisation in Africa by encouraging the production of mainly agricultural goods, while perpetuating the asymmetrical nature of Africa-EU trade relations.[22] The raw-material-based and largely rain-fed agricultural economies, bequeathed by colonialism to Africa, have not yet witnessed a fundamental transformation, and the EPAs may make any such change more difficult. According to American scholar Mary Farrell, for example, the pressure to liberalise trade would prevent African countries "from extending protection to domestic infant industries against foreign competition, [would] make it more difficult to maintain public services under national ownership, and [would] restrict the opportunity to pursue industrial diversification strategies as part of a comprehensive program for economic development".[23] In addition, increased exports of industrial and manufactured products from the EU under the EPAs would be likely to undermine the emergence of new industries in Africa, while potentially suffocating the continent's few existing industries, which continue to lack competitiveness. The influx of Chinese imports, for example, has decimated the leather and textile industries in Kenya, Lesotho, Swaziland, and Zambia, causing massive job losses (see Virk in this volume).[24]

Meanwhile, African agricultural producers continue to be at a disadvantage due to EU subsidies to European farmers. Without access to similar subsidies, African farmers produce at higher costs, which reduces their competitiveness on the European and international markets. According to one study, published by the London-based Overseas Development Institute (ODI), EU subsidies to the cotton sector accounted for a 38 per cent loss in income for farmers in West and Central Africa during the 2003–2004 fiscal year.[25] The EU's agricultural subsidies thus undermine agricultural development in Africa. The liberalisation of Africa's agricultural market under the EPAs provides a further advantage to EU farmers, while creating the potential for decline in revenue to African producers. The lack of assistance from international financial institutions (IFIs) to African farmers makes a bad situation worse for the continent. In the words of the president of the African Development Bank (AfDB) and Nigeria's former minister of agriculture and rural development, Akinwumi Adesina: "[T]oday the small farmers in developing countries are not being supported ... The critical issue is that international development institutions and multilateral finance institutions have pursued policies of abandonment over the last 20/30 years and what we need today are policies of support for farmers."[26]

More generally, the power asymmetry between Africa and Europe places the former at a disadvantage in the distribution of the gains and losses of international free trade. As Swedish economist and sociologist Gunnar Myrdal noted back in 1970, "international [free] trade will generally tend to breed inequality and will do so more strongly when substantial inequalities are already established".[27] Or, as Frenchman Henri-Bernard Solignac-Lecomte—based at the Organisation for Economic Cooperation and Development (OECD) Development Centre—put it more recently in 2000: "[W]hile the multilateral system is based on rules applicable to all members, an FTA [free trade agreement] rests on a power relationship that permits the dominant partner, especially within a preferential North-South agreement, to influence the process of liberalisation of the other party as a function of its own interests."[28] Scepticism about the benefits for Africa—the weaker party in the EPAs—thus seems reasonable, particularly given the existing asymmetries in the Africa-EU trade relationship and the continent's overall dependence on Europe.

Determining the fiscal impact of the EPAs is difficult and complex. According to one estimate, African countries could lose between 10 and 30 per cent in import revenues under the EPAs.[29] The reduced revenue could, in turn, severely compromise African countries' ability to combat poverty through social interventions, or lead to greater indebtedness for governments already struggling to deliver essential services to their citizens. In this respect, although the alleviation of poverty is a key objective of the Cotonou Agreement, it is unclear how the EPAs will impact on the attainment of this goal. The partnership agreements are based on neo-liberal market principles, similar to those that underpinned the structural adjustment programmes (SAPs) once imposed by the International Monetary Fund (IMF) and the World Bank on African countries; and there is concern that they could have a similar impact, taking the continent backwards. These programmes entailed policy conditionalities, including tariff liberalisation and reductions in social spending (for example, on education and health), and contributed to what has been called the "lost decade" of the 1980s.[30]

Beyond the substantive content of the EPAs, the deadlines set by the European Commission for the conclusion of negotiations have been an additional source of contention between African countries and the EU (see Carim in this volume). These deadlines have not taken into account the prevailing conditions on the ground in Africa. In particular, the deadlines have not factored in the time required by African countries to create the necessary environment for large-scale liberalisation. The EU's lack of inclination to accommodate the views of African countries in setting deadlines re-echoes the idea of a partnership between unequals.

THE ROLE OF DEVELOPMENT ASSISTANCE IN AFRICA-EU RELATIONS

Historically, the European Union has been a major provider of development aid to Africa. The European Development Fund (EDF) is the major source of EU aid to Africa, although funding under the EDF has tended to decline since the end of the Cold War. In 1988–1989, African countries constituted 12 out of the 15 largest recipients of EU official development assistance (ODA) from the EDF worldwide. Twenty years on, in 2008–2009, only six African countries were among EU's top 15 aid recipients, with Eastern European and Latin American countries now constituting the majority.[31] However, despite the growing presence of China since the last decade, the EU remains the largest aid donor to Africa. In 2013, for example, the EU multilateral donation to Africa amounted to $5,973 million, representing 33 per cent of all multilateral disbursements to the continent.[32]

European aid to Africa takes various forms and includes assistance provided to individual African countries and for regional projects on the continent. In addition, individual EU member states provide various forms of bilateral assistance to African countries. The leading EU bilateral donors to Africa have been France, Britain, and Germany.[33] Between 2010 and 2013, France provided an average of $3,979 million, representing 13 per cent of total net bilateral disbursement to Africa; and Britain provided $3,592 million, representing 12 per cent; while Germany provided $2,885 million, representing 8 per cent.[34] The top three areas receiving EU support are the social, economic, and production sectors. Between 2010 and 2012, the social sector, comprising education, health, water, sanitation, social infrastructure, and services, received 40 per cent of total EU disbursement. This was followed by the economic sector (transport and communications, energy, and banking) at 20 per cent, while production (agriculture, forestry, and fishing; mining and construction; and trade and tourism) received 10 per cent of total EU assistance to Africa.[35]

Notably, the EU provided €55 million—disbursed between 2007 and 2011—for an African Union Support Programme (AUSP) with the objective of strengthening the AU Commission's role as a "motor of the [regional] integration process" and of supporting a "deepening of the partnership between the AU and the EU".[36] In this context, it is worth noting that in 2013, more than 50 per cent of the AU's operating budget of $277 million was funded by the EU, the United States (US), and China, with the remainder funded almost entirely by five AU members— Algeria, Egypt, Libya, Nigeria, and South Africa.[37] The EU further provided development assistance worth €40 million in 2011 over a four-year period until 2015 for three project areas—agriculture, environment, and climate change. Among the other areas that have benefited from the EDF since 2011 are infrastructure (€10 million), and science and technology (€14 million).

On the face of it, the EU is philanthropic in assisting in Africa's developmental efforts. In some ways, EU assistance to Africa is consistent with the broader Brussels objectives as articulated in the Cotonou Agreement, namely to alleviate poverty and promote development. The objectives of Cotonou were also consistent in assisting Africa to meet the United Nations' (UN) Millennium Development Goals (MDGs).[38] Indeed, the much-publicised 2005 Paris Declaration on Aid Effectiveness and the subsequent 2008 Accra Agenda for Action contained policies that would help maximise the positive impact of development assistance on recipient countries and accelerate Africa's development and poverty reduction. Two issues stand out in the Paris Declaration that are relevant in discussing EU development assistance to Africa: "coordination" on the part of donors and "ownership" on the part of recipients. Donor coordination was premised on the need for the EU to effectively coordinate and manage multilateral and bilateral aid to avoid the creation of "aid orphan" and "aid darling" countries. Recipient ownership, which is more pertinent to the current discussion, on the other hand, involves the crafting of measures that would make African governments feel a sense of ownership of disbursed aid. Thus, ownership involves "a significant transfer of power over resources from donors to recipients".[39] Ownership entails soliciting recipients' input in the aid policies that target them.

In practice, however, the EU aid regime has followed the old and familiar pattern of asymmetrical relations between donors and recipients. This is seen, among other ways, in the process and criteria for allocating aid. Historically, the EU has not been keen on relinquishing control of decisions relating to aid. Even in the aftermath of the Paris Declaration and the Accra Agenda, ownership and control over aid policies still remain largely under the control of the EU.[40] For certain, the recipient ownership principle has neither displaced nor replaced subtle conditionalities that, as will be shown in the next section, continue to attend EU aid. Some observers have been critical of the criteria used by the EU to allocate aid. While the dominant objective of the EU aid to ACP countries is to target poverty, the criteria did not necessarily target poor and needy countries. In Africa, aid darlings, including Burkina Faso, Ghana, Mozambique, Rwanda, Tanzania, Uganda, and Zambia, enjoy favouritism in EU fund allocation, while aid orphans—countries generally overlooked, including Burundi, the Central African Republic (CAR), Chad, and Guinea Bissau—remain starved.[41] Paradoxically, the aid orphans are among the poorest and neediest countries in Africa. The bureaucratic procedures involved in the EU in aid allocation have not helped in the speedy delivery of aid.[42]

Proposals to allocate aid to African countries are preceded by the preparation of a draft country strategic paper. Prepared by EU delegations in collaboration with recipient governments and local actors, these papers outline recipients' needs as well as EU interventions and time frames for implementation. In effect, country strategic papers provide the guiding frameworks for EU development assistance. However, critics have noted that in practice the country strategic papers capture the interests of donors represented by EU delegations, rather than the interests of recipients. Civil society organisations, for example, have noted the fact that in the transport sector the EU's support has tended to target "main structuring roads rather than roads in and leading to rural areas that would have greater impact on rural poverty".[43] Indeed, it is even observed that most of sub-Saharan Africa's country strategic papers for ACP countries are prepared without the input of recipient governments.[44] In short, EU development aid to Africa has more often tended to serve the particular interests of donors, notwithstanding the ever-present rhetoric on "partnership". Indeed, in light of the unequal control of development aid policies, one observer has questioned "the appropriateness of using the term 'partnership' rather than, for instance, a principal-agent relationship".[45]

POLITICAL ASPECTS OF THE AFRICA-EU RELATIONSHIP

The EU's financial assistance to Africa extends beyond trade to include aid in the areas of peace and security, governance, and democracy. Brussels, for example, has provided support for the African Peace and Security Architecture (APSA). An African Peace Facility (APF) was established in

2004. An initial amount of €300 million was allocated for the 2008–2010 period for capacity-building in support of AU peace operations, with the EU committing to further support for another three years. The initial deployment of 7,500 African troops to the AU Mission in Sudan (AMIS), established in May 2004, was funded largely by the EU, which committed €242 million in its support.[46] AMIS was subsequently transformed into the African Union/United Nations Hybrid Operation in Darfur (UNAMID) in July 2007 (and thereafter financed by the UN).[47] Despite some initial hesitance, the EU similarly supported the AU Mission in Somalia (AMISOM)—established by the AU Peace and Security Council in January 2007—with €35 million in 2007. The EU released another €20 million in December 2008 and a further €20 million in April 2009.[48] By 2011, total EU support for AMISOM under the APF totalled €208 million.[49]

In addition, the Mission for the Consolidation of Peace in the Central African Republic (MICOPAX)—established in July 2008 and led by the Economic Community of Central African States (ECCAS)—was supported by the EU with more than €225 million between 2008 and 2013.[50] In December 2013, MICOPAX was transformed into the AU-led International Support Mission to the Central African Republic (MISCA), which continued to enjoy the support of the EU. Brussels has also been involved in post-conflict reconstruction efforts in Côte d'Ivoire, collaborating with the Ivorian ministry of justice and other stakeholders in reforming the justice sector,[51] and remains one of the key sources of funding for the AU's peace and security efforts on the continent. (See Adebajo in this volume.)

Issues related to democratic governance in Africa have also featured prominently in EU-Africa relations. Aid and investment conditionality has been one of the main methods that Brussels has used to promote democracy on the continent.[52] Such conditionality, including the threat to withdraw and the actual withdrawal of aid, has been used to induce political reforms related to respect for human rights, liberalisation of political spaces, and holding of multi-party elections across Africa in countries such as Ghana and Kenya.[53] Less intrusively, the EU has sought to promote democracy in Africa through monitoring and providing financial support for elections on the continent. Since 2000, the EU has sent observer teams to monitor elections in various sub-Saharan African countries including Ghana, Tanzania, and Nigeria.[54] In February 2015, the EU pledged 10.3 billion Tanzanian shillings to electoral support in Eastern Africa between

2015 and 2018, including polls in Burundi in May 2015 and Tanzania in September 2015.[55]

In addition to incentives, the EU has also used sanctions against African countries to pursue its objective of promoting and protecting human rights. In February 2002, for example, the EU imposed economic sanctions on Zimbabwe, including a travel ban on President Robert Mugabe and other key Zimbabwean political and military figures over alleged human rights violations in the country, although in October 2015 most officials originally placed under the sanctions were de-listed, leaving only Robert Mugabe, his wife (Grace Mugabe), and the country's defence industries in the sanctions regime.[56]

Since 2000, the drive to forge a closer Africa-EU partnership, spanning a range of areas from regional integration to democratic governance, has taken the form of a series of summits between the two sides. Between 2000 and 2015, four Africa-EU summits were held. The first summit was held in Cairo, Egypt, in April 2000 and marked the beginning of a political dialogue between the EU and Africa. The joint Cairo declaration called for increased cooperation between the two regions; greater assistance from the EU to help promote human rights and democracy in Africa; and support for African efforts to resolve and manage conflicts on the continent.[57] The summit led to the EU's adoption of a comprehensive programme of strategic partnership—dubbed "The EU and Africa: Towards a Strategic Partnership"—in April 2005, with the main objective of assisting Africa in achieving the MDGs by 2015 and in promoting peace and security.

The second Africa-EU summit, held in Lisbon, Portugal, in December 2007, served as a follow-up to the Cairo meeting. The Lisbon summit took place in a shroud of controversy, with African leaders threatening a mass boycott over a potential European refusal to temporarily lift the travel ban on Zimbabwe's Robert Mugabe and permit his participation at the summit. In the end, the EU prioritised its partnership with Africa over Mugabe's human rights record and thus allowed the Zimbabwean leader to attend the joint Africa-EU meeting.[58] The Lisbon summit sought, among other things, to assess the progress made in promoting the strategic partnership between the two regions since the Cairo summit. Importantly, the summit produced the Joint Africa-EU Strategy, which called on the EU "to move away from a traditional relationship and forge a real partnership characterised by equality and the pursuit of common objectives".[59] The first JAES action plan (2008–2010) identified eight partnership themes, with the EU pledging to assist Africa in these areas: peace and security; democratic governance and human rights; trade and regional integration; the MDGs; energy; climate change; migration, mobility, and employment; and science, information society, and space.[60]

The third Africa-EU summit was held in Tripoli, Libya, in November 2010. In addition to re-affirming the commitments made at the previous two joint meetings—in particular, to the 2007 Joint Africa-EU Strategy as the basis for strengthening cooperation—the Tripoli summit adopted the second JAES action plan, covering 2011–2013, which focused broadly on peace and security in Africa.[61] At the Tripoli summit, African and European leaders committed themselves to jointly addressing key challenges, including: climate change; energy; HIV/AIDS; the MDGs; gender equality; and migration and employment in Africa. The Tripoli declaration further highlighted the importance of concluding the Cotonou-mandated economic partnership agreements, while emphasising the role of the private sector in driving African growth and development. Importantly, the EU re-affirmed its commitment to meeting the UN target of providing 0.7 per cent of its gross national income (GNI) for ODA overall. This promise, first made in 1970, has not been fulfilled in its entirety. At the Tripoli summit, the EU pledged to make more than €50 billion of ODA available to support its partnership programmes with Africa between 2011 and 2014.

The fourth Africa-EU summit was held in Brussels, Belgium, under the theme "Investing in People, Prosperity, and Peace", in April 2014.[62] Beyond re-affirming the commitments made at previous summits, the Brussels meeting sought to focus on four additional key areas: democracy and "good governance"; human development; sustainable inclusive development and growth, and continental integration; and global emerging issues, especially climate change.

In general, this series of joint summits between Africa and Europe has helped to deepen cooperation between the two regions in various areas including trade, peace and security, governance and democracy, and the environment. However, these summits have, at the same time, also helped to highlight the asymmetry in the partnership between the two regions. Successive summit communiqués have seen the EU commit to assisting Africa to achieve particular objectives, and not the other way round, underscoring the continent's dependence on Europe. In general, relations lacking mutual dependence are inherently asymmetrical and benefit the strong more than the weak. South African scholar Garth le Pere could not have been more apt in arguing that:

Brussels's rhetorical commitment to "partnership" has rung hollow when viewed within the context of the dialectic between expectation and capacities: both sides have seen demands colliding with the ability to meet them. However, the balance has swung decidedly in Brussels's favour, since the cooperation frameworks have served more to entrench and maintain particular EU interests than to promote trade and development in Africa.[63]

While EU-Africa relations remain intact despite the inherent asymmetry, a major disagreement is simmering between the two partners over the recognition of lesbian, gay, bisexual, transgender, and intersex (LGBTI) rights. With the exception of Swaziland, all African countries have, at least in theory, embraced democratic reforms, which are considered necessary for development. However, a recent more contentious conditionality is the pressure exerted by the EU and especially Britain on African countries to recognise LGBTI rights. This is a potential sticking point, as a majority of African states remain opposed to recognising LGBTI rights. For example, in response to British prime minister David Cameron's threat in 2011 of withholding development assistance if African governments failed to decriminalise same-sex relations, John Nagenda, a Ugandan presidential advisor, told the British Broadcasting Corporation (BBC) in October 2011 that "Uganda is, if you remember, a sovereign state and we are tired of being given these lectures by people ... If they must take their money, so be it".[64] Similarly, former Ghanaian president John Evans Atta-Mills said his country would rather go hungry than accept development aid made contingent on the recognition of gay rights. In his words:

> While we acknowledge all the financial assistance and all the aid which has been given to us by our development partners, we will not accept any aid with "strings attached" if that aid will not inure to our interests, or [if] the implementation—or the utilization—of that aid-with-strings-attached would rather worsen our plight as a nation, or destroy the very society that we want to use the money to improve.[65]

With homosexuality considered un-African and inimical to African cultural practices, many African states have outlawed it. Only South Africa, among the more than 50 countries in Africa, officially recognises the LGBTI community. Gambia, Nigeria, Uganda, Zimbabwe, and the predominantly Muslim North African countries have strict laws that impose long prison terms on individuals found to be engaging in same-sex relations. While Africa-EU relations may not be seriously threatened by the disagreement over the rights of LGBTI communities, since both parties have much to gain in the partnership outside this disagreement over human rights, it is nonetheless apparent that the issue of gay rights in aid repatriation will remain a sticking point in the foreseeable future. Yet the insistence by Europe for Africa to recognise gay rights is another manifestation of the asymmetry in the partnership between the two regions—a situation in which the EU, the dominant partner, seeks to set the conditions and agenda of the partnership.

Concluding Reflections

Since 2000, most African economies have been growing at a fairly rapid pace. By mid-2015 six of the 13 fastest-growing economies in the world were in Africa.[66] With expanding opportunities for trade and investment, the resource-rich continent has become an arena for a "new scramble" among competing powers—traditional actors such as the EU, as well as new and emerging powers like China, India, and Brazil (see Virk in this volume).[67] Against this backdrop, Brussels has sought to preserve and consolidate its trade and economic relationship with Africa through the EPAs mandated by Cotonou, while continuing to be a vital source of development assistance to a continent that, despite its recent growth surge, continues to face major governance, security, and development challenges. For their part, African countries have continued to need preferential access to the EU market—in particular, for agricultural products—and continued to be dependent upon financial and development support from Europe to progress towards achieving the MDGs, to build the continent's governance and security architectures, and to progress towards greater regional integration. The negotiating processes for the EPAs have been protracted and marred by discord and disagreement among African countries, and highlighted the continent's pliability and vulnerability.

Africa-EU relations have a long history, and since 2000 they have been re-moulded into a strategic partnership outside the ACP-EU framework. The partnership has been laudable in terms of broadening relations beyond trade and aid to include governance, peace, security, and climate change. However, these areas cannot be entirely divorced from the EPA framework under Cotonou, given the Africa-EU partnership and the ACP-EU framework's shared emphasis on African development. The EPAs, though symbiotic in appearance, are skewed in favour of the EU and will likely deepen the asymmetrical nature of its relations with Africa.

By and large, the agreements offer few opportunities for African countries to diversify away from the production of primary agricultural products—the commodities for which the EU is prepared to open up its common market. While the Africa-EU partnership is certain to continue to grow, it is a matter of debate if this skewed relationship will ultimately turn out to be one of equals.

NOTES

1. In a national referendum, held in June 2016, Britain voted to leave the European Union (EU). Official negotiations were yet to begin at the time of writing, but as and when Britain leaves the Union, the membership of the EU will be reduced to 27.
2. Denis M. Tull, "China in Africa: European Perceptions and Responses to the Chinese Challenge", Working Paper in African Studies, (Washington, D.C.: Johns Hopkins University, School of Advanced International Studies [SAIS], 2008), pp. 3–4.
3. John Kotsopoulos "The EU and Africa: Coming Together at Last?", policy brief, European Policy Centre (EPC), Brussels, July 2007, http://www.isn.ethz.ch/Digital-Library/Publications/Detail/?ots591=0c54e3b3-1e9c-be1e-2c24-a6a8c7060233&lng=en&id=44084 (accessed 20 September 2014). *See also* Ernst Stetter, "Five Reasons Why Africa Really Matters to the World", *Europe's World*, 1 June 2009, http://europesworld.org/2009/06/01/five-reasons-why-africa-really-matters-to-the-world/#.VSJZpuEpoah (accessed 10 February 2015).
4. "Second Revision of the Cotonou Agreement—Agreed Consolidated Text, 11 March 2010", Brussels, 19 March 2010, arts. 19–20, http://ec.europa.eu/development/icenter/repository/second_revision_cotonou_agreement_20100311.pdf (accessed 3 November 2014).
5. Marc Maes, "EPAs, the EU, and ACP—An Uneven Partnership", *Equal Times*, 1 October 2014, http://www.equaltimes.org/epas-the-eu-and-acp-an-uneven?lang=en#.VGsSD8nDuzE (accessed 13 October 2014).
6. Maes, "EPAs, the EU, and ACP.
7. "Intra-African Trade: The Road Less Travelled", *The Economist*, 17 April 2013, http://www.economist.com/blogs/baobab/2013/04/intra-african-trade (accessed 5 December 2015).

8. European Commission, "Fact Sheet on the Interim Economic Partnership Agreements: An Overview of the Interim Agreements", January 2009, http://trade.ec.europa.eu/doclib/docs/2009/january/tradoc_142188.pdf (accessed 6 December 2015).

9. Gumisai Mutume, "New EU Trade Deals Divide Africa", United Nations (UN), *Africa Renewal*, http://www.un.org/en/africarenewal/newrels/new-trade-pact-08.html (accessed 10 March 2015).

10. "Civil Society Groups Intensify Opposition to EPAs", *Myjoyonline* via *GhanaWeb*, 24 March 2014, http://www.ghanaweb.com/GhanaHomePage/NewsArchive/artikel.php?ID=304135 (accessed 10 October 2014).

11. "Civil Society Groups Intensify Opposition to EPAs".

12. Sylvester Bagooro, "West Africa and Europe Trade: Who Will Benefit More?", *Al Jazeera*, 22 June 2014, http://www.aljazeera.com/indepth/opinion/2014/06/west-africa-europe-trade-agree-2014621155835409177.html (accessed 9 June 2015).

13. Eugene Davis, "EU Issues 322 Red Flags ... over Substandard Goods", *B&FT Online*, 10 July 2015. http://thebftonline.com/business/economy/14590/EU-issues-322-red-flags-%E2%80%A6over-substandard-goods.html (accessed 6 December 2015).

14. "African Trade Ministers Split on EPA Path Forward As October Deadline Looms", *Bridges Africa*, 7 May 2014, http://www.ictsd.org/bridges-news/bridges-africa/news/african-trade-ministers-split-on-epa-path-forward-as-october (accessed 10 January 2015).

15. European Commission, "Overview of EPA Negotiations", updated September 2015, http://trade.ec.europa.eu/doclib/docs/2009/september/tradoc_144912.pdf (accessed 6 December 2015).

16. Thomas Lazzeri, "EU Wants to Force ACP Countries to Sign EPAs", *Africa Europe Faith and Justice Network (AEFJN)*, 2014, http://www.aefjn.org/index.php/352/articles/european-commission-wants-to-force-acp-countries-to-sign-epas.html (accessed 10 March 2015). *See also* "Declaration on the Economic Partnership Agreements (EPAs)", 25 October 2013, http://ti.au.int/en/documents/declaration-economic-partnership-agreements-epas (accessed 10 December 2015).

17. *See for example* World Bank, *Accelerated Development in Sub-Saharan Africa: An Agenda for Action* (Washington, D.C.: World Bank, 1981), p. 2; and Samuel K.B. Asante, *Regionalism and*

Africa's Development: Expectations, Reality, and Challenges (London: Macmillan, 1997).

18. Centre for Conflict Resolution (CCR), *Region-Building and Regional Integration in Africa*, policy research seminar report, Cape Town, South Africa, October 2014, p. 10, http://www.ccr. org.za (accessed 10 June 2015).

19. Richard Gibb, "Post Lomé: The European Union and the South", *Third World Quarterly* 21, no. 3 (2000), p. 476. *See also* Christopher Stevens, "Economic Partnership Agreements and Africa: Losing Friends and Failing to Influence", in Maurizio Carbone (ed.), *The European Union in Africa: Incoherent Policies, Asymmetrical Partnership, Declining Relevance?* (Manchester: Manchester University Press, 2013), p. 178.

20. Tarah N. Shaanika, "EPAs Are Bad for Africa", *TradeMark Southern Africa (TMSA)*, 25 April 2011, http://www.trade-marksa.org/print/news/epas-are-bad-africa (accessed 10 September 2014).

21. Stephen McDonald, Stephen Lande, and Dennis Matanda, "Why Economic Partnership Agreements Undermine Africa's Regional Integration" (Washington, D.C.: Wilson Center, April 2013), p. iv, http://www.wilsoncenter.org/sites/default/files/EPA%20 Article.pdf (accessed 10 October 2014).

22. Paul Goodison, "The Future of Africa's Trade with Europe: 'New' EU Trade Policy", *Review of African Political Economy* 34, no. 111 (March 2007), p. 149.

23. Cited in Asteris Huliaras, "EU-African Relations: Dealing with the Challenges of the Future", research paper, (Brussels: Centre for European Studies, 2009), p. 29.

24. John Akokpari, "The Political Economy of Chinese Capital in Sub-Saharan Africa: Implications for Governance", *Global Development Studies* 6, nos. 3–4 (2011), p. 72.

25. Ian Gillson, Colin Poulton, Kelvin Balcombe, and Sheila Page, "Understanding the Impact of Cotton Subsidies on Developing Countries", working paper (London: Overseas Development Institute [ODI], May 2004), p. 63, http://www.odi.org.uk/ resources/details.asp?id=3608&title=cotton-subsidies-development (accessed 17 February 2015).

26. Cited in Charles Mutasa, "A Critique of the EU's Common Agricultural Policy", in Adekeye Adebajo and Kaye Whiteman

(eds.), *The EU and Africa: From Eurafrique to Afro-Europa* (London: Hurst, 2012), p. 247.

27. Gunnar Myrdal, *The Challenge of World Poverty* (New York: Vintage, 1970), p. 279.

28. Henri-Bernard Solignac-Lecomte, *The Multilateral Aspects of the ACP-EU Partnership Agreement* (London: Commonwealth Secretariat, 2000), p. 52.

29. Matthew McQueen, "After Lomé IV: ACP-EU Trade Preferences in the 21st Century", *Intereconomics* 34, no. 5 (September/October 1999), p. 228.

30. CCR, *Region-Building and Regional Integration in Africa*, pp. 9–10.

31. Jonathan Glennie, "The Role of Aid to Middle-Income Countries: A Contribution to Evolving EU Development Policy", Working Paper no. 331 (London: ODI, 2011), pp. 9, 28. The 12 African countries among the top 15 recipients of ODA from the EU were Côte d'Ivoire, Ethiopia, Cameroon, Mozambique, Kenya, Egypt, Sudan, the Democratic Republic of the Congo (DRC), Tanzania, Senegal, Malawi, and Chad. By 2008–2009, however, the number had plummeted to six—Ethiopia, Morocco, Sudan, the DRC, Egypt, and Uganda.

32. Organisation for Economic Cooperation and Development (OECD), *Development Aid at a Glance: Statistics by Region—Africa* (Paris, 2015), p. 6.

33. Britain is used synonymously with the United Kingdom (UK) in this volume.

34. OECD, *Development Aid at a Glance*, p. 4.

35. OECD, *Development Aid at a Glance*, p. 10.

36. Delegation of the European Union to the African Union (AU), "Development Cooperation", http://eeas.europa.eu/delegations/african_union/eu_african_union/development_cooperation/index_en.htm (accessed 28 March 2015).

37. *See* "The African Union: Half a Century On", *The Economist*, 29 May 2013, http://www.economist.com/blogs/baobab/2013/05/african-union-0 (accessed 10 December 2015).

38. Maurizio Carbone, "Foreign Aid, Donor Coordination, and Recipient Ownership in EU-Africa Relations", in Carbone, *The European Union in Africa*, p. 125.

39. Carbone, "Foreign Aid, Donor Coordination, and Recipient Ownership", p. 124.
40. Rachel Heyman, "From Rome to Accra via Kigali: 'Aid Effectiveness' in Rwanda", *Development Policy Review* 27 (2009), p. 593.
41. Carbone, "Foreign Aid, Donor Coordination, and Recipient Ownership", p. 126.
42. Carlos Santiso, "Reforming European Foreign Aid: Development Cooperation as an Element of Foreign Policy", *European Foreign Policy Review* 7, no. 4 (2002), pp. 401–422.
43. Walter Eberlei and Denise Auclair, *The EU's Footprint in the South: Does European Community Development Cooperation Make a Difference for the Poor?* (Brussels: Coopération Internationale pour la Développement et la Solidarité [CIDSE], 2007), p. 5.
44. Carbone, "Foreign Aid, Donor Coordination, and Recipient Ownership", p. 128.
45. Stephen Kingah, "The Revised Cotonou Agreement Between the European Union and the African, Caribbean, and Pacific States: Innovations on Security, Political Dialogue, Transparency, Money, and Social Responsibility", *Journal of African Law* 50, no. 1 (2006), p. 68.
46. Garth le Pere, "AU-EU Security and Governance Cooperation", in Adebajo and Whiteman, *The EU and Africa*, p. 262.
47. *See* United Nations, "UNAMID Facts and Figures", http://www.un.org/en/peacekeeping/missions/unamid/facts.shtml (accessed 20 March 2015).
48. Gorm Rye Olsen, "The African Union and Regional Security: International Support to the 'African Solutions' Approach", paper presented at the Third Global International Studies Conference, Porto, Portugal, 17–20 August 2011, http://rucforsk.ruc.dk/site/en/publications/the-african-union-and-regional-security-international-support-to-the-african-solutions-approach%2887f1351f-3f30-401b-8b52-0cc99b51f827%29.html (accessed 14 February 2015).
49. *See* "EU Allocates €65.9 Million to Support Peacekeeping in Somalia", 28 March 2011, http://eu-un.europa.eu/articles/en/article_10876_en.htm (accessed 10 December 2015).

50. European Commission, "Fact Sheet—Central African Republic", Brussels, 16 December 2013, http://europa.eu/rapid/press-release_MEMO-13-1162_en.htm (accessed 9 February 2015).

51. UN Security Council, "Thirtieth Progress Report of the Secretary-General on the United Nations Operation in Côte d'Ivoire", UN doc. S/2012/506, 29 June 2012, http://www.un.org/ga/search/view_doc.asp?symbol=S/2012/506 (accessed 25 January 2015).

52. le Pere, "AU-EU Security and Governance Cooperation", p. 274.

53. Elena Fierro, *The EU's Approach to Human Rights Conditionality in Practice* (The Hague: Nijhoff, 2003), p. 94. *See also* Joseph Siegle, "Effective Aid Strategies to Support Democracy in Africa", paper presented at the conference "Africa Beyond Aid", Brussels, 24–26 June 2007, http://www.isn.ethz.ch/Digital-Library/Publications/Detail/?lang=en&id=105506 (accessed 10 December 2015).

54. *See* Ubale Musa/im, "EU Observers Commend Nigerian Elections", *Deutsche Welle (DW)*, 30 March 2015, http://www.dw.de/eu-observers-commend-nigerian-elections/a-18350209 (accessed 31 March 2015).

55. Marc Nkwame, "Tanzania: EU Pledges 10.3 Billion—in Support of Elections", *Tanzania Daily News* (Dar es Salaam), 20 February 2015, http://allafrica.com/stories/201502131524.html (accessed 24 March 2015).

56. Michael O'Kane, "EU Updates Zimbabwe, Yemen, Guinea, and Moldova Sanctions Regimes", *European Sanctions: Law and Practice*, 28 October 2015, http://europeansanctions.com/category/zimbabwe (accessed 10 December 2015).

57. South African Department of International Relations and Cooperation (DIRCO), "Cairo Declaration: Africa-Europe Summit Under the Aegis of the OAU and the EU", 3–4 April 2000, http://www.dfa.gov.za/foreign/Multilateral/africa/treaties/cairodec.htm (accessed 20 October 2014).

58. "Mugabe Invited to Lisbon Summit Despite Ban", *The Guardian*, 2 July 2007, http://www.theguardian.com/world/2007/jul/02/zimbabwe.eu (accessed 12 December 2015).

59. EU, *The Africa-European Union Strategic Partnership: Meeting Current and Future Challenges Together* (Luxembourg: Publications Office of the European Union 2011), p. 20.

60. EU, *The Africa-European Union Strategic Partnership*, p. 134.

61. *See* Third Africa-EU Summit, *Tripoli Declaration*, 29–30 November 2010, http://eu-un.europa.eu/articles/en/article_10445_en.htm (accessed 23 December 2015).
62. Africa-EU Partnership, "4th EU-Africa Summit (2014)", http://www.africa-eu-partnership.org/4th-africa-eu-summit (accessed 10 February 2015).
63. le Pere, "AU-EU Security and Governance Cooperation", p. 259.
64. "Uganda Fury at David Cameron Aid Threat over Gay Rights", *BBC News*, 31 October 2011, http://www.bbc.com/news/world-africa-15524013 (accessed 20 April 2016).
65. Quoted in Peter Baklinski, "'Let Them Cut Off Aid': African Countries Revolt Against UK Threat to Cut Aid over Homosexuality", 8 November 2011, https://www.lifesitenews.com/news/let-them-cut-off-aid-african-countries-revolt-against-uk-threat-to-cut-aid (accessed 15 April 2016).
66. These countries are Ethiopia, the DRC, Côte d'Ivoire, Mozambique, Tanzania, and Rwanda. *See* Elena Holodny, "The 13 Fastest-Growing Economies in the World", *Business Insider*, 12 July 2015, http://www.businessinsider.com/world-bank-fast-growing-global-economies-2015-6 (accessed 10 December 2015).
67. Harry Stephan, Michael Power, Angus Hervey, and Raymond Fonseca, *The Scramble for Africa in the 21st Century: A View from the South* (Cape Town: Renaissance Press, 2006), pp. 26–27.

CHAPTER 4

The EU and the Caribbean:
The Necessity of Unity

Norman Girvan[†] *and Annita Montoute*

The contemporary Caribbean is a divided region, a consequence of over 500 years of European colonisation, imperial rivalries, revolutionary upheavals, and independence struggles. The region comprises 16 independent countries[1]—all members of the African, Caribbean, and Pacific (ACP) group of states—and 17 dependent territories, divided among Dutch, English, French, and Spanish speakers. The Caribbean ACP countries together make up the Forum of the Caribbean Group of ACP States (CARIFORUM) and, with the one exception of Cuba, are parties to the Cotonou Partnership Agreement of 2000 and to an economic partnership agreement (EPA) signed with the European Union (EU) in 2008. Of the dependent territories in the region, four are outermost regions and 13 are overseas territories (see Tables 4.1 and 4.2). Europe's connections with the Caribbean, therefore, encompass direct political administration and

---

†Author was deceased at the time of publication.

N. Girvan
The University of the West Indies (UWI)
St AugustineTrinidad and Tobago

A. Montoute (✉)
Institute of International Relations, The University of the West Indies (UWI),
St Augustine, Trinidad and Tobago

© The Author(s) 2017   79
A. Montoute, K. Virk (eds.), *The ACP Group and the EU*
Development Partnership, DOI 10.1007/978-3-319-45492-4_4

Table 4.1   A Caribbean divided

Grouping	Number of states/ territories (2015)	Population (2012) (in thousands)
Caribbean	**35**	**44,100**
Independent states	**16**	**38,747**
African Caribbean and Pacific (ACP) Group of States	16	38,747
Forum of the Caribbean Group of ACP States (CARIFORUM)	15	27,476
Caribbean Community (CARICOM)	14	17,199
Dependent territories	**19**	**5,353**
European Union outermost regions	4	1,110
European Union overseas countries and territories	13	521[a]
Non–European Union (US-dependent territories)	2	3,722

Source: Authors' calculations based on Worldstatinfo, http://en.worldstat.info/Central_America_and_the_Caribbean/Anguilla; Statistics Netherlands, *Statistical Yearbook of the Netherlands 2012*, http://www.cbs.nl/en-GB/menu/publicaties/boeken/statistisch-jaarboek/archief/2014/statistical-yearbook-of-the-netherlands-2014-pub.htm; United Nations Statistics Division, *World Statistics Pocketbook*, http://unstats.un.org/unsd/pocketbook (accessed 9 July 2015); Central Intelligence Agency (CIA), *The World Factbook*, https://www.cia.gov/library/publications/the-world-factbook/geos/tb.html (accessed 1 May 2016)

[a]The estimates for Anguilla and Montserrat and Saint-Barthélemy included here are for 2011 and 2015 respectively

trade and development aid, as well as long-standing historical ties that are reflected in the region's languages, legal and political institutions, and various cultural forms. However, the region is changing. Caribbean states have forged their own institutions of regional integration and are building closer ties with their Latin American neighbours. This dynamism provides the context in which the Caribbean-EU relationship will continue to unfold.

In this chapter, we argue that the negotiations for the CARIFORUM-EU economic partnership agreement signalled a dramatic shift in the nature of Europe's relations with the Caribbean, one with several negative implications for the relationship as well as for Caribbean development. We further argue that the Caribbean needs to strengthen its region-building and regional integration efforts, and to re-strategise and re-define the terms of its engagement with the EU for a more meaningful relationship and for the achievement of sustainable development in the region. This requires that the Caribbean engages with the ACP group. We begin with a brief

Table 4.2 EU Caribbean OCTs and ORs

EU Caribbean overseas countries and territories[a]	Population (2014)
Netherlands-affiliated	
Aruba	103,889
Bonaire	19,899
Curaçao	164,463
Saba	1,846
Sint Eustatius	4,020
Sint Maarten	46,914
United Kingdom–affiliated	
Anguilla	16,086
Bermuda	69,839
British Virgin Islands	32,860
Cayman Islands	59,967
Montserrat[b]	5,215
Turks and Caicos Islands	49,070
French-affiliated	
Saint-Barthélemy	7,237[c]
EU Caribbean outermost regions[d]	
French Guiana	261,729
Guadeloupe	470,168
Martinique	405,688
St Martin	31,530
Non-EU Caribbean dependent territories	
United States	
Puerto Rico	3,620,897
US Virgin Islands	104,170
Total	**5,475,487**

Source: European Commission, "ORs and OCTs", http://ec.europa.eu/regional_policy/sources/doc-conf/epa/doc/ruptom_en.pdf (accessed 7 June 2015); World Population Review, http://worldpopula-tionreview.com (accessed 7 July 2015); Central Intelligence Agency (CIA), *The World Factbook*, https://www.cia.gov/library/publications/the-world-factbook (accessed 7 July 2015); and European Commission, "Saint-Barthélemy", https://ec.europa.eu/europeaid/countries/saint-barthelemy_en (accessed 1 June 2016)

[a]According to Articles 182–188 of the European Community Treaty, overseas countries and territories are not part of the European Union, even though they are part of their member state of reference. Because they do not belong to the European Union, European Community law does not apply to them, except for the association regime based on Part IV of the European Community Treaty, "Association of the Overseas Countries and Territories"

[b]Montserrat is a member of the Caribbean Community

[c]2015 estimate

[d]According to Article 299(2) of the European Community Treaty, "the overseas regions constitute an integral part of the European Union … and, as a consequence", European Community law applies to them fully

discussion of the origins of CARIFORUM as the Caribbean's regional interlocutor with the EU, and trace the shift from Lomé to Cotonou as the framework for ACP-EU engagement. We then provide an overview of trends in Caribbean-EU relations in the years leading up to the CARIFORUM-EU EPA negotiations, and next turn to the factors that contributed to the signing of a comprehensive economic partnership agreement and its implications for the Caribbean. Based on this analysis, we reflect on the future of Caribbean-EU and Caribbean-ACP relations, and also outline a Caribbean perspective on the broader ACP-EU relationship.

From CARICOM to CARIFORUM

Established in 1992, the Forum of the Caribbean Group of ACP States is a somewhat disparate collection of countries. The origins of the group lie more in the evolution of the EU's Caribbean policy than in a regionally driven integration agenda. In 1975, the Caribbean Commonwealth countries[2] played a key role in the formation of the ACP group and in the negotiation of the Lomé Convention (see Whiteman in this volume). The main concern of the Caribbean Commonwealth, at the time, was to ensure that the one-way trade privileges granted by Britain to its former colonies[3]—as part of a system of imperial and colonial preferences since the 1930s and 1940s—would be preserved after British entry into the European Economic Community (EEC). These trade preferences provided significant support to the Caribbean sugar and banana industries, which in turn were major sources of employment in the region. The direct results of the Caribbean Commonwealth's trade diplomacy included the Lomé Convention's Sugar Protocol; the EU's banana import regime; and the special arrangements governing rum and rice, introduced in 1975.

Except for Suriname, a former Dutch colony that joined the Lomé Convention in 1979, the Caribbean beneficiaries of trade preferences and aid under the first three Lomé Conventions were all former British colonial territories that had joined together to form the Caribbean Community (CARICOM) and its common market in 1973. Under Lomé IV (1990–2000), the Caribbean was reconfigured in conformity with the expansion and economic consolidation of the EU, as well as the latter's evolving strategic interest in the Caribbean region and its need to deal with a single regional interlocutor. The Dominican Republic and Haiti—two new Caribbean ACP countries—were included in Lomé IV.[4] With neither country a member of CARICOM,[5] a new regional forum—the Forum of the Caribbean Group of ACP States—was established in 1992 to conduct consultations and negotiations with the EU. But CARIFORUM has remained a loose grouping without institutional form,[6] juridical personality, or integration project, formed solely for the purpose of negotiating trade and aid arrangements with Europe. Suriname's later accession to CARICOM in 1995 and Haiti's in 2002 were to some extent logical corollaries of the EU-inspired creation of CARIFORUM. Membership in CARIFORUM provided an impetus, while facilitating dialogue, for both countries to accede to CARICOM—a tighter regional integration arrangement within the wider framework provided by the Caribbean Forum, the latter comprising CARICOM plus non-CARICOM Caribbean ACP states.

The case for inclusion of the Dominican Republic in CARICOM has always been problematic from the latter's point of view. The size and level of industrial development of the Dominican Republic represent a perceived threat to the ability of local producers in the rest of the Caribbean to compete with Dominican exports. In 2013, the gross domestic product (GDP) of the Dominican Republic was $61.2 billion,[7] compared to CARICOM's $65.6 billion.[8] CARICOM governments also fear the loss of fiscal revenues from customs duties. Furthermore, there are concerns about the extent of the Dominican commitment to the Caribbean region, with the country having joined the Central American Common Market (CACM) first as an associate member in 2004 and then as a full member in 2013, and having signed a free trade agreement (FTA) with Central America and the United States (US) in August 2004 (CAFTA-DR). As a result, applications by the Dominican Republic to join CARICOM have so far been unsuccessful, and a CARICOM–Dominican Republic free trade agreement—signed in August 1998—is reported to have encountered significant implementation challenges.[9] In this context, the participation of the Dominican Republic in the Caribbean EPA has—as discussed later—posed a significant challenge to CARICOM's regional integration agenda.

FROM LOMÉ TO COTONOU

At first glance, the Lomé regime appears to have been an ideal model for a development-supportive partnership between the industrialised North and the global South. It featured non-reciprocity of market access, special regimes for key commodities, commodity price stabilisation,[10] and the linking of trade and finance through contractual commitments for the delivery of development aid.[11] CARICOM countries benefited from both the trade and the aid aspects of Lomé. The commodity protocols were significant in supporting export earnings and employment in the Caribbean region. The expansion of banana exports, in particular, stimulated growth in several smaller Caribbean economies (such as St Lucia, Dominica, and St Vincent and the Grenadines), and helped alleviate poverty in rural areas. Under the Lomé regime, banana exports accounted for over 70 per cent of all export earnings from the EU in the case of St Lucia and Dominica, and for between 40 and 70 per cent in the case of St Vincent and the Grenadines.[12]

However, the non-reciprocal preferential access to the EU market granted under Lomé was not accompanied by a significant expansion and diversification of Caribbean exports. Only five ACP member states[13]— with Jamaica the only Caribbean country in this cohort—experienced growth of their exports to the EU at an equivalent or higher rate than that of other developing countries, or saw any significant export diversification.[14] On the contrary, the market share of the Caribbean ACP dropped from 0.5 to 0.3 per cent of total EU imports over the period 1976–1992 (see Table 4.3).[15] Later, during negotiations for Cotonou, this disappointing performance became the basis for the argument that non-reciprocity should be abandoned because it was not working or was having a perverse effect on Caribbean trade.[16] The counter-argument, though, was that export diversification was hindered by non-tariff barriers, including rules of origin and technical barriers to trade, and by the absence of targeted supply-side measures to boost export capabilities in non-traditional products. Still, aid flows assumed importance in the 1980s, as a result of the economic difficulties affecting several Caribbean countries,[17] with the Caribbean receiving 1.79 billion European currency units (ECUs) from the European Development Fund (EDF) between 1976 and 1995.[18]

The key development-supportive features of Lomé eventually became casualties of the changed ideological climate and the shifting international balance of forces in the 1980s and 1990s. Neo-liberal economic thinking came to the fore in the industrialised North, and was embodied in the Washington Consensus, featuring liberalisation, deregulation, and privatisation as the new mantra for economic reform and growth. The Third World debt crisis of the 1980s turned scores of developing countries into supplicants to the International Monetary Fund (IMF), the World Bank, and Western donors. Meanwhile, with the end of the Cold War and the

Table 4.3 Trends in trade between the European Union and developing countries, 1976–1992

EU Imports (€ billions)

	1976	1980	1985	1990	1992	Percentage Change, 1976–1992
ACP Caribbean[a]	0.8	1.6	1.6	1.4	1.5	87.5
Asia	6.7	16	26	509	66.4	891
Latin America	8.3	13.7	25.8	25.7	24.8	198.8
Mediterranean	9.6	16.4	32.3	29.8	30.3	215.6
All developing countries	70.7	114.3	128.9	143.8	145.6	105.9
Extra–European Community	157.7	269.9	399.7	461.5	487.6	209.2
World	308.6	518.9	828.2	1,127.6	1,207.8	291.4

Source: Michael Davenport, Adrian Hewitt, and Antonique Koning, *Europe's Preferred Partners? The Lomé Countries in World Trade* (London: Overseas Development Institute, 1995), p. 81, cited in Peter Clegg, "Renegotiating Lomé: The Future of the EU-ACP Caribbean Relationship", Discussion Paper no. 7 (Manchester: Development Studies Association, European Development Policy Study Group, October 1999), p. 3

[a]Exports of the 15 CARIFORUM states that were contracting parties to the Lomé Convention in 1992, although in earlier years some of them did not benefit from the trade provisions

collapse of the Soviet Union, the EEC transformed into the EU in 1993. The Uruguay Round of the General Agreement on Tariffs and Trade (GATT) concluded with the establishment in 1995 of the World Trade Organisation (WTO), with a new dispensation that emphasised reciprocity, non-discrimination, and the expansion of global trade rules into areas hitherto the preserve of domestic policy, such as services, investment, intellectual property, and government procurement. In other words, development was to be delivered by giving free rein to market forces and by guaranteeing a friendly and stable climate for investors.

The EU's banana import regime was the first major fallout of the newly created WTO's free market dispensation. The regime had already been the subject of two disputes under the GATT, in 1993 and 1994. In both cases, GATT panels found that the trade provisions of the Lomé Convention were incompatible with GATT rules. The GATT challenges were brought by five Latin American countries—Columbia, Costa Rica, Guatemala, Nicaragua, and Venezuela—and contended that the EU's banana import regime was discriminatory. In 1996, Ecuador, Guatemala,

Honduras, Mexico, and the US lodged a complaint against the EU's banana import regime in the WTO, which ruled in 1997 largely in their favour. Subsequently, EU preferences for bananas were gradually eroded in a long drawn-out battle, with the dispute ending only in 2012. This gradual dismantling of the EU's banana import regime has since had devastating consequences for Caribbean banana exporters. The value of banana exports from the Windward Islands—Dominica, Grenada, St Lucia, and St Vincent and the Grenadines—fell from $140 million in 1990 to below $40 million in 2008, or from more than 14 per cent to approximately 1.4 per cent of GDP.[19] Just as significant, the WTO's free-trade-based regime was thereafter invoked by European officials as the framework for ACP-EU trade negotiations.

The joint challenge of the EU banana import regime by the United States and the Latin American countries symbolised US support of corporate interests in the banana sector and served to consolidate the neoliberal orientation of the trade component of the Cotonou Agreement. The banana trade is monopolised by large US transnational corporations, the largest ones being Dole, Chiquita Brands, and Del Monte. The real reason for the US challenge of the EU banana import regime in 1996 can be traced to significant political funding provided by banana transnationals. This powerful economic incentive led the US to threaten four Latin American countries (Ecuador, Guatemala, Honduras, and Mexico) with sanctions if they failed to support the US position.[20] Although it would have also been in the interest of local elites to support Washington's position, the latter's behaviour may be partly explained by the impunity with which the US as the hegemonic power in the region has acted historically in the hemisphere, and in the Caribbean in particular. Caribbean banana-producing states were mere bystanders and marginalised in a legal move that threatened them disproportionately relative to the US and the EU, as well as threatening the Caribbean's very existence. In sum, the US played a significant role in invoking the legal basis against preferences and solidifying the WTO's neo-liberal philosophy. This, in turn, contributed to the weakening of the position of the Caribbean and the wider ACP group within the framework of Cotonou and in the EPA negotiations with the EU.

Through the Cotonou Agreement of 2000, the EU imposed an architecture that was detrimental to ACP interests in several respects. Although development financing was retained, this was de-linked from the trade provisions, which were instead to be contained in economic partnership agreements signed with six (later seven) separate ACP regions. Development was further equated to trade and investment liberalisation. The EPAs were to be negotiated under Article XXIV of GATT, which required liberalisation of "substantially all trade" among the partners, generally interpreted to mean 90 per cent of total trade. As the EPA negotiations unfolded, it became clear that the European Commission's negotiating mandate also called for inclusion of the so-called Singapore issues—investment, competition policy, public procurement (transparency), and trade facilitation—in the agreements, notwithstanding the fact that these were a contentious matter in the WTO itself and were eventually rejected at the Cancún WTO ministerial conference in September 2003.[21]

The Cotonou Agreement also resulted in a significant diminution of the Caribbean's bargaining power vis-à-vis the EU, on several counts. Detached from the rest of the ACP, the Caribbean's negotiating leverage was considerably reduced. With Haiti the only least-developed country (LDC) among them, the Caribbean states were unable to access the provisions of the Everything But Arms (EBA) initiative as an alternative to negotiating an EPA with the EU. Furthermore, the inclusion of a non-CARICOM member—the Dominican Republic—in the Caribbean EPA group meant that the Caribbean Community's negotiations would, in effect, have to proceed simultaneously on two parallel tracks.

The role of the US in contributing to the subversion of Caribbean development is not restricted to the EU preferential banana regime. Among the notorious cases is the contestation by the US of development policies inherent in Cuba's socialism since 1959 and Jamaica's democratic socialism model in the 1970s, under Michael Manley. Another case of interest is the leadership role the US played in the failed Free Trade Area of the Americas (FTAA) negotiations, launched in 1998. The FTAA aimed to establish a free trade agreement among countries of the Western Hemisphere, except Cuba. If the FTAA project had been successful it would have expanded a North American Free Trade Agreement (NAFTA)-type arrangement—that is, free trade among unequal players—to the entire hemisphere. The FTAA would have further locked the Caribbean into neo-liberal trade policies, expanded the web of trade deals in which the Caribbean was engaged, and driven the direction of the Caribbean's development agenda and its internal integration project. In fact, the 1992 recommendation of the Independent West Indian Commission[22] to deepen and widen the regional integration process was given impetus, not by internal, but rather external developments such as the FTAA process and the deepening of European integration.

Trends in the EU-Caribbean Relationship

The EU-Caribbean relationship is best seen as a multi-layered process, with overlapping and divergent interests on the Caribbean side, represented by various groupings and states. First, there is CARICOM comprising 13 countries (Haiti being the exception) with commodity-exporting sectors that have been the beneficiaries of preferential trading arrangements with the EU in the past. Of these, 12 are also members of the CARICOM Single Market and Economy (CSME). Second, there is Haiti, a member of CARICOM that is—unlike the rest of the group—an LDC qualifying for special financial assistance and not significantly dependent on trade preferences. Third, there is the Dominican Republic, with a newcomer's interest in gaining market access to Europe. We could also mention fourth, Cuba, which is a member of the ACP group but not a signatory to the Cotonou Agreement; as well as a fifth grouping, the Caribbean outermost regions and overseas territories of Europe, which have their own particular relations with the EU. In this chapter, we focus mainly on the "inner core" of the 13 CARICOM countries (that is, CARICOM excluding Haiti, and also naturally excluding the Dominican Republic, which is not a member).

For this inner-core group, its relationship with the European Union over the past two decades has been marked by a series of disappointments and a perception of broken promises. This has been accompanied by a harsh realisation of the Caribbean's marginalisation in a post-Cold-War, post-WTO world, with an awareness of the huge asymmetry in bargaining power between the two regions a constant theme. A number of episodes attest to the changing nature of the relationship:

- The perceived failure of the EU to adequately protect ACP interests in the negotiation of the WTO agreements during the Uruguay Round (1986–1994), and the resulting devastation—as mentioned earlier—of Caribbean banana-exporting economies.[23]
- The imposition of a negotiating architecture that substantially weakened Caribbean bargaining power in trade talks while imposing a "forced marriage" between CARICOM and the Dominican Republic through the creation of CARIFORUM in 1992.

- The unilateral decision by the EU in 2001 to grant duty-free market access through the Everything But Arms initiative to non-ACP LDCs in a manner that could be prejudicial to ACP exporters.
- The absence of additional EU aid commitments to take account of the adjustment costs of a Cotonou-mandated economic partnership agreement to the economies of CARICOM's inner-core group.
- The imposition of an agenda and deadline in the EPA negotiations tailored to the EU's interests that made a mockery of the ideal of "partnership".
- The failure to provide an alternative to the EPA consistent with Article 36(4) of Cotonou, thereby leaving Caribbean countries with no option but to conclude an EPA on EU terms.[24]
- The unilateral abrogation of the ACP-EU Sugar Protocol of 1975 in a manner detrimental to Caribbean (and ACP) interests.[25]
- The EU's failure to deliver on promises in its Aid for Trade[26] programme made at the conclusion of the Caribbean EPA negotiations in December 2007.
- The negotiation of trade agreements with non-ACP countries, which have had the effect of further eroding the value of trade preferences represented by duty-free market access for the Caribbean ACP countries in Europe.

EU officials have tended to justify these episodes on the basis of WTO law, EU policy, or factors beyond their control. This is somewhat disingenuous, as the EU itself had a strong hand in the crafting of the WTO agreements, and there is some degree of latitude in the interpretation of WTO law. In other words, what was legally possible in the negotiations was itself conditioned by EU policies and trade diplomacy. For example, in the negotiation of the WTO agreements, the EU was careful to insulate its domestic agricultural subsidies from the requirements to liberalise, yet left the agreements to be formulated in a way that exposed the Lomé non-reciprocal preferences to legal action. The waiver then granted by the WTO until December 2007, allowing the Lomé trade regime to remain in place temporarily, was used to pressure ACP countries to sign EPAs before the presumed deadline, even though there were differing interpretations of the requirements of WTO law on this subject.[27] In the Caribbean negotiations, EU officials also asserted that the EU's Generalised System of Preferences (GSP) was the only alternative to the EPA. However, this was a previously made policy decision that could itself have been altered.[28]

It is unclear whether Caribbean governments actually believed the EU's assurances, or accepted them as a negotiating tactic—given the power asymmetry in their relations—with the intention of trying to hold the EU to its word at a later date. If the former, this could be due to a somewhat naive trust in the "good faith" of Europeans—an example of a persistent colonial mentality. In any case, the pattern is a sobering reminder that EU officials will always put EU interests first; that assurances of special treatment and protestations of support for development are part of the rhetoric of trade diplomacy; and that the Caribbean should always seek to fortify its negotiating position by forging a united position within itself, building its international alliances, and seeking out all available options.

The EU has been more consistent towards the ACP—at least until now—in the provision of development assistance. Since 1975, the EU has provided bilateral grant funding to the ACP group of states through the European Development Fund. However, since the publication in 2011 of the EU's *Agenda for Change*, the future of the EDF has become vulnerable in the context of: the general uncertainty surrounding the future of ACP-EU relations in the run-up to Cotonou's expiry in 2020; the persistence of the Eurozone crisis; and, most importantly, the EU's history of broken promises to the ACP in the area of trade. As of 2015, the EU had not identified any ACP member in its list of 19 countries to be graduated from bilateral aid. If the EU does apply its criteria for graduation—differentiating upper-middle-income countries and countries representing more than 1 per cent of the world's GDP—to the ACP, the Caribbean will be disproportionately affected due to the high number of high- and upper-middle-income countries in the region, relative to the rest of the ACP.[29]

In terms of the political dialogue under Article 8 of Cotonou, as in the case of Africa (see Akokpari in this volume), the EU has shown a growing interest for engaging with the Caribbean on political issues in regional configurations, outside the ACP framework. Political dialogue on issues related to crime and security, human rights, democratic principles, the rule of law, "good governance", and migration has taken place with CARIFORUM under the umbrellas of the Joint Caribbean-EU Strategy, the EU's strategic partnership with the Community of Latin American and Caribbean States (CELAC), and specialised meetings.[30]

The EU-CARIFORUM Economic Partnership Agreement

The Caribbean was the only ACP region to have concluded negotiations for an economic partnership agreement with the EU by the initial deadline of December 2007, and in May 2015 remained the only region to have concluded and signed a "comprehensive" EPA.[31] The Southern African Development Community (SADC) EPA group concluded its negotiations for a regional agreement in July 2014, with the agreement signed in June 2016. West Africa closed negotiations of a goods and development cooperation agreement in February 2014, while the East African Community (EAC) also concluded negotiations for a regional EPA in October 2014. Meanwhile, the Eastern and Southern Africa (ESA) and Central Africa groups, as well as the Pacific, were in June 2016 still negotiating their regional deals. (See Carim, Katjavivi, and Tavola in this volume.) The Caribbean Regional Negotiating Machinery (CRNM) (now the Office of Trade Negotiations) was established in 1997 to coordinate CARICOM's external trade negotiations, and agreed to negotiate a full EPA with the EU in 2007 ahead of the rest of the ACP. The CRNM did so in the belief that this would help the region secure valuable benefits,[32] including greater access to markets in services,[33] privileged access to the EU's Aid for Trade programme, and duty-free and quota-free access for CARIFORUM exports to EU markets, while entrenching policy reform that would attract greater foreign investment (see Gonzales in this volume).

Despite opposition to the EPA from several segments of civil society and academia, the negotiations were concluded and the agreement signed in October 2008,[34] for several reasons. First, Caribbean leaders feared the imposition of high EU tariffs on CARICOM exports, which would have resulted in severe economic losses, with the value of ACP Caribbean goods exports to the EU totalling €24.68 billion between 2004 and 2008 (for CARICOM's EU export and import percentages, see Table 4.4).[35] Second, it was a strategy to continue receiving EU development assistance. Soon after the EPA was signed, agreements were concluded in November 2008 for the use of the tenth European Development Fund (2008–2013), of which 44 per cent was set aside for EPA implementation and accompanying measures.[36] ACP governments are also eligible under national programmes to receive funding for a number of focal areas, including direct budgetary support as in the case of Jamaica under the tenth EDF.[37] This made them vulnerable to EU pressure, as illustrated

Table 4.4   Trends in CARICOM-EU trade, 1991–2004

	1991–1995	1996–2000	2001–2004	Average
CARICOM exports to the EU (percentage of total CARICOM exports)	26.72	24.3	21.78	23.55
CARICOM imports from EU (percentage of total CARICOM imports)	12.28	9.78	10.04	10.43

Source: Pérez Caldentey, *Export Promotion Policies in CARICOM: Main Issues, Effects, and Implications* (Santiago, Chile: United Nations Economic Commission for Latin America and the Caribbean, Division of International Trade and Integration, 2005)

by the key role that Jamaica played in Caribbean decision-making on the EPA. Third, CARICOM members feared that if they delayed signing the EPA, the Dominican Republic would conclude a separate agreement with the EU, placing the country in a more advantageous position in terms of access to the European common market. Additionally, there were internal differences between the larger and smaller CARICOM countries, with the former (such as Jamaica) favouring further liberalisation and a full EPA, while the latter (for example, St Lucia) wanted to find a way of keeping their remaining preferences for banana exports. Fourth and finally, Caribbean governments—acting on the advice of negotiators—did not heed the arguments of civil society to re-open the talks, for fear that they would end up with a less favourable agreement. To some extent, the negotiations were completed to avoid embarrassing those who had aggressively defended the agreement. Officials who advised and influenced CARICOM leaders would have lost face if they had not gone through with the agreement.[38]

All these factors came into play in explaining the kind of EPA that the Caribbean signed up to. Given that Haiti is the only least-developed country in CARIFORUM, the option of exporting to the EU under the EBA initiative was not available to the group. Payment of GSP or most-favoured-nation (MFN) tariffs was presented as the only alternative, and this would have put Caribbean exporters at a severe disadvantage. Some CARIFORUM countries (such as Barbados and Bahamas) also had an interest in exporting non-traditional services (such as entertainment and cultural services) to the EU, and European officials used this as leverage for the inclusion of investment and trade-related measures as the quid pro quo for providing enhanced access to selected service sectors. The origins of the Caribbean EPA's problematic aspects thus lie in the overall architecture of the agreement as well as in specific provisions.

Flawed Negotiations

On the Caribbean side, the negotiations for the EPA were widely seen to have had significant shortcomings: one, they were characterised by limited stakeholder participation; and two, public understanding of the content and implications of the agreement was poor. While negotiators pointed to ample provisions for consultations with the private sector and other civil society groups, we argue that their actual participation and influence in the negotiations was varied and uneven. For example, at the regional level, civil society was represented by the Caribbean Policy Development Centre (CPDC), which represents diverse civil society groups, and trade unions were represented by the Caribbean Congress of Labour. However, at the national level—in Trinidad and Tobago, for example—non-governmental organisations (NGOs), particularly women's groups (such as the Women Institute for Alternative Development [WINAD] in Trinidad and Tobago, and other women's organisations under the umbrella of the Caribbean Association for Feminist Research and Action [CAFRA]), participated more actively and had a more comprehensive understanding of the implications of the agreement in comparison with trade unions. With the exception of Trinidad and Tobago's Oil Workers Trade Union (OWTU), which collaborated with NGOs through the Federation of Independent Trade Unions and NGOs (FITUN), trade union involvement was meagre—unlike women's organisations, trade unions were less active in progressive global networks and debates, and their interests were restricted to traditional labour concerns. Similarly, within the private sector, groups in the traditional and more established sectors of rum and sugar (for example, the West Indies Rum and Spirits Producers Association [WIRSPA] and the Sugar Association of the Caribbean [SAC]) played a more active role.

The nature of the information that these non-state actors provided accounted for the level of access and influence that they were allowed in the EPA negotiating process. The private sector, in particular the rum sector, was able to provide negotiators with specific information related to tariff lines, safeguard measures, and non-tariff barriers. This type of information was deemed to be more relevant to the negotiations than were the political arguments being raised by civil society groups. In other words, the neo-liberal philosophy that underpinned the negotiations gave the information provided by the private sector greater legitimacy over that of civil society.[39] Once the negotiated text was agreed, demands by civil society to delay the signing of the agreement, in order to permit greater public scrutiny, were opposed, with officials citing negotiating deadlines and the risk of losing "first mover" advantages for their refusal to concede.

Absence of an Effective Development Dimension

The lack of a genuine development dimension in the Caribbean EPA has been one of the major criticisms of the agreement.[40] Notably, CARICOM's own development vision, related to the implementation of its economic integration agenda, has been sidelined.[41] In effect, the EPA relies on market forces and private investment for the delivery of its development objectives, while failing to address the fundamental development challenges facing the region and failing to provide funding on the scale required to meet the adjustment costs of implementation.[42] Regional economists have noted the absence of targeted supply-side measures such as firm-level financial and technical support.[43] The numerous references in the EPA text to development cooperation are neither targeted nor quantified nor time bound, and hence they are largely meaningless in operational terms. Meanwhile, cooperation measures in areas of interest to EU firms—for example, customs administration, trade facilitation, and intellectual property—are spelled out in considerable detail. Furthermore, financing for the implementation of the EPA constitutes, in effect, a re-shuffling of funds provided under the tenth EDF under Cotonou. Much of the funds allocated for this purpose in the regional and national programmes also appear to cover mainly the holding of workshops, seminars, and committee meetings, and technical assistance for the drafting of laws and regulations required by the agreement. Caribbean governments appear to have set store by EU promises in the latter's Aid for Trade programme, but these have failed to materialise.[44] (See also Gonzales in this volume.)

Surrender of Policy Space

New-generation free trade agreements are typically WTO-plus, which puts tremendous pressure on the national and financial resources of developing countries. The expanded scope of these agreements beyond WTO requirements places severe limitations on the ability of governments to pursue autonomous development policy. Hence, the WTO-plus scope of the Caribbean EPA implies a significant diminution of national policy space. The agreement spells out detailed, mostly time-bound obligations for CARIFORUM governments in trade administration, services, investment, government procurement, and intellectual property. There is a built-in agenda calling for further negotiations on services liberalisation and on competition policy and electronic commerce. Specific provisions that diminish policy space include: the requirements for national treatment for EU goods and services, and EU suppliers and investor firms; the restrictions on infant-industry protection; the prohibitions on local content requirements and on export taxes; and the most-favoured-nation and regional preference clauses.[45]

Impact on Regional Integration

Strengthening regional integration is one of the EU's declared objectives for the economic partnership agreements. However, it is one of the most problematic aspects of the Caribbean EPA. To begin with, the CARIFORUM group of states has no legal standing as a Caribbean integration body. Yet Article 233 of the EPA lists the Caribbean parties to the agreement as the "CARIFORUM states acting collectively"; and further: "Where individual action is provided for or required to exercise the rights or comply with the obligations … reference is made to the 'Signatory CARIFORUM States'." In effect, each individual CARIFORUM country will be legally accountable to the EU for carrying out its EPA obligations.

Meanwhile, the Caribbean Community, which has an established juridical personality and integration programme, is not a juridical party to the EPA. The arrangement, by its very nature, thus seems designed to bypass CARICOM rather than to strengthen it, while depriving individual CARICOM countries of the juridical protection of the Caribbean Community in their dealings with the EU, in particular the European Commission. The EPA has also introduced major complications for CARICOM's own economic integration scheme—the CARICOM Single Market and Economy. EPA obligations cover several subject areas (for example, public procurement and intellectual property) that have been contemplated for inclusion in the CSME, but that have not yet been negotiated and legally established within CARICOM. The EPA provisions have, in large part, pre-empted the CSME regulatory regimes in these areas. Furthermore, CARICOM had envisaged the CSME as a platform for wider engagement with international markets. Yet it seems likely that the EPA will lead to the sidelining of the CSME and its eventual elimination as an economic integration scheme in any meaningful sense. Since 2007, CSME implementation has been at a virtual standstill, and in May 2011, CARICOM leaders officially put the project "on pause".[46] Although this decision was subsequently rescinded, the underlying situation remains the same, and the 2015 deadline for the completion of the CSME has not been met. (See also Gonzales in this volume.)

Finally, CARICOM has a free trade agreement with the Dominican Republic that does not cover services, investment, and other trade-related areas. The EPA's regional preference clause requires all CARIFORUM states to grant each other the same privileges that they give to the EU. CARICOM countries will therefore have to liberalise trade, services, and investment with the Dominican Republic to the same degree as with the EU. The possible extension of the CARICOM–Dominican Republic FTA has therefore, in large measure, been pre-empted by the EPA.

Onerous Implementation

Implementation of the EPA by CARIFORUM has varied from one member country to another, but the process has, generally speaking, been slow (see Gonzales in this volume). The legality of EPA implementation has furthermore been questioned in cases where the agreement has not been ratified or has not come into force.[47] Although all CARICOM countries have been working towards EPA implementation since 2008, as of August 2014 only seven of the 15 CARICOM member states had ratified the agreement.[48] A regional CARIFORUM implementation unit has been established, but this merely monitors implementation and has no legal or executive authority over member states. Challenges related to EPA implementation include financial constraints as well as the absence of supporting infrastructure such as competition authorities, especially in the smaller Organisation of Eastern Caribbean States (OECS) countries.

By 2012, at least seven Caribbean countries had reportedly failed to implement the first round of tariff cuts, scheduled for 2011, due to their need for customs revenues. Five of the seven subsequently implemented the scheduled reductions, bringing the number of compliant states to 12, of which ten have since implemented the second round of cuts scheduled for 2013.[49] At the second meeting of the Joint CARIFORUM-EU Council, held in October 2012, major differences emerged between the two sides on several issues, including the tariff liberalisation schedules for automobiles, auto parts, and paper products.[50] These remained unresolved in 2014, though an informal working group had been set up to address the matter of vehicles and auto parts.[51]

Small Caribbean exporters have complained about continued difficulties in accessing the EU market. A widespread perception remains among Caribbean stakeholders that the EU's Aid for Trade promises to the region have not been fulfilled.[52] Preference erosion for Caribbean exports has taken place as the EU has negotiated free trade agreements with other regions (such as Central America).[53] Mutual recognition agreements, a requirement for accessing EU services markets, also continue to be lacking. Meanwhile, civil society participation in implementation was delayed until 2014, due to CARIFORUM's indecision on the composition of its side of the Joint CARIFORUM-EU Consultative Committee.

In short, the EPA remains a contentious issue in the Caribbean, with problematic features, onerous implementation obligations, and questionable benefits.

THE FUTURE OF CARIBBEAN-EU RELATIONS

A healthy, development-supportive relationship between the Caribbean and the EU would rest on three pillars. The first would be a principle of genuine partnership based on sovereign equality and the right of each country and region to determine its own path to development. This would also take into account the huge asymmetries in size and levels of development between the two regions. The second pillar would comprise a clearly defined strategic agenda by, and for, the Caribbean—one of sustainable human development for the region and of supportive strategic international engagements, including relations with traditional partners such as the EU and the ACP, as well as with emerging players in the global South, in particular Brazil, Russia, India, China, and South Africa of the BRICS bloc (see Virk in this volume), and new Latin American configurations (for example, CELAC). The third pillar would be an appropriate set of political and institutional arrangements among Caribbean states enabling the region to provide a coherent, united front in dealings with the EU.

However, this raises a question: Which "Caribbean"? CARIFORUM does not include the most populous Caribbean country—Cuba—and lacks a juridical and institutional personality. We take the view that CARICOM would be the most logical point of departure—it is the established and premier integration grouping in the region, containing 14 of 16 Caribbean states. But CARICOM suffers from a number of shortcomings that need to be addressed, including an incomplete integration agenda, a poor implementation record, severe institutional inadequacies, and a tendency towards incoherence among its members in their foreign policy positions and external economic alignments. Also, the non-CARICOM Caribbean includes the region's two most populous states—Cuba and the Dominican Republic—as well as a large number of non-independent territories with which the Caribbean Community shares common interests in environmental, economic, security, and cultural matters. This means that the existing network of Caribbean cooperative relations in various spheres would need to be further developed as well. The strategic objective should be to increase the collective resilience of Caribbean states to enhance their autonomy of action in international fora. As the EU is a major player in the Caribbean through its overseas countries and territories, CARICOM should leverage this in its engagement with the EU, in particular to achieve the aforesaid objective.

In 2012, a Joint Caribbean-EU Strategy (JCEUS) was endorsed. This strategy covers a wide range of subjects of interest to the Caribbean,[54] while identifying the funding instruments for them.[55] It is argued that the strategy will open new opportunities for Caribbean countries in trade, investment, and inter-regional cooperation, particularly with newer EU members that do not have historical ties to the region.[56] The joint strategy can serve as a framework for CARIFORUM-EU engagement on non-trade and trade-related issues and also, looking ahead, as a possible basis for continued engagement in the post-2020 era, when grant funding may end. Indeed, the strategy may become even more relevant to the EU as a complement to the CARIFORUM-EU EPA if the Cotonou Agreement is not renewed, or is replaced with a new framework, when it expires in 2020. The EU's objective through the joint strategy is to leverage the EPA and existing funding envelopes to maintain its Caribbean foothold and to secure support among CARIFORUM states in multilateral and other fora, particularly in view of the growing influence of the BRICS countries (see Virk in this volume). For the Caribbean, the problem with the joint strategy arises from the weaknesses noted earlier: CARIFORUM's indeterminate status and its lack of a clearly articulated regional strategy for development, integration, and international engagement. Failure to address these shortcomings risks further institutionalisation of an EU-driven agenda and process in the region.

The joint-strategy process could also further undermine the ACP and serve as another step in the "regionalisation" of EU-ACP relations.

CARIBBEAN-ACP RELATIONS

CARICOM needs to prioritise healing its relationship with the ACP group, which has been fractured as a result of the EPA negotiations. These relations are likely to continue to be strained as a result of EU proposals for differentiation and graduation that will further fragment its development cooperation with the ACP on the basis of countries' per capita income levels. CARICOM's interest lies in securing ACP support for its case for continued special treatment on the basis of the smallness and vulnerability of individual countries. Both CARICOM and CARIFORUM will also need ACP support in resolving their differences with the EU over the implementation of the Caribbean EPA—differences that are bound to multiply in the future as the full implications of the agreement become manifest. The basis for a durable Caribbean-ACP alliance, however, would need to be an all-ACP agreement that identifies guidelines for the building of its future trade relationship with Europe, and that responds to the ACP's own development objectives and its articulation of the role of external trade relationships in achieving these objectives.

In 2011, a report by the Maastricht-based European Centre for Development Policy Management (ECDPM)[57] identified four scenarios for the future of the ACP: one, that it should diversify its relationship beyond the EU to other partners such as the BRICS countries, the US, and Canada; two, that it should operate as three separate regions—Africa, the Caribbean, and the Pacific—with the ACP serving as an umbrella framework; three, that it should expand its membership to incorporate groups with similar interests, including LDCs and small vulnerable economies (SVEs); and four, that it should expand its membership to include North African countries. There is also the view that the ACP should move beyond development assistance as the central feature of its relationship with the EU, for example, by establishing its own ACP development fund with contributions from the EU and other donors, or by modelling itself on the Commonwealth or *Organisation International de la Francophonie* (OIF) (see Gomes in this volume). However, such options can be meaningfully considered only in the context of an overarching strategy for ACP development and international engagement. For example, there is the question of overlap with other bodies of which ACP countries are

Table 4.5 Caribbean states: Population, GDP per capita, and selected affiliations

Country	Population (2012), in thousands (estimated)	GDP per capita 2012 (US$)	Affiliations
Cuba	11,271	6301	ACP, ALBA, CELAC
Dominican Republic	10,277	5731	ACP, CARIFORUM, CELAC
CARICOM			
Antigua and Barbuda	89	13,207	ACP, CARIFORUM, CARICOM, ALBA, CELAC
Bahamas	372	21,624	ACP, CARIFORUM, CARICOM, CELAC
Barbados	283	16,004	ACP, CARIFORUM, CARICOM, CELAC
Belize	324	4796	ACP, CARIFORUM, CARICOM, CELAC
Dominica	72	6958	ACP, CARIFORUM, CARICOM, ALBA, CELAC
Grenada	105	7418	ACP, CARIFORUM, CARICOM, ALBA, CELAC
Guyana	795	3585	ACP, CARIFORUM, CARICOM, CELAC, UNASUR
Haiti	10,174	707	ACP, CARIFORUM, CARICOM, CELAC
Jamaica	2769	5343	ACP, CARIFORUM, CARICOM, CELAC
St Kitts and Nevis	54	14,268	ACP, CARIFORUM, CARICOM, ALBA, CELAC
St Lucia	181	7289	ACP, CARIFORUM, CARICOM, ALBA, CELAC
St Vincent and the Grenadines	109	6349	ACP, CARIFORUM, CARICOM, ALBA, CELAC
Suriname	535	9377	ACP, CARIFORUM, CARICOM, CELAC, UNASUR
Trinidad and Tobago	1337	17,365	ACP, CARIFORUM, CARICOM, CELAC
Total	**38,747**	–	

Source: United Nations Statistics Division, *World Statistics Pocketbook*, https://data.un.org/ (accessed 9 July 2015)

(continued)

Table 4.5 (continued)

ACP African, Caribbean, and Pacific Group of States; *ALBA* Bolivarian Alliance for the Peoples of Our America; *CARICOM* Caribbean Community; *CARIFORUM* Forum of the Caribbean Group of ACP States; *CELAC* Community of Latin American and Caribbean States; *UNASUR* Union of South American States

also members, such as the Group of 77 (G-77), the African Union (AU), CARICOM,[58] and the Pacific Islands Forum (PIF). The ACP will need to have a well-defined strategy to identify the best option for the group going forward.

Continental regionalisation projects are likely to continue to act as an alternative pulling force for both the Caribbean and Africa, with developments in the Pacific pointing to a movement towards greater sub-regionalism (see Tavola in this volume). Increasingly, CARICOM countries are being drawn into a network of Latin American alliances in the form of the Community of Latin American and Caribbean States, the Union of South American States (UNASUR), and the Bolivarian Alliance for the Peoples of Our America (ALBA) (see Table 4.5). African ACP countries, meanwhile, are participating in region-building and regional integration processes through the AU and the continent's regional economic communities (RECs). The EU also has for some time been engaged in regionalising its relations with Latin America and Africa through its summits with the Latin America and the Caribbean (EU-LAC) and its summits with the AU. (On EU-Africa relations, see Akokpari, Carim, and Katjavivi in this volume.) Taking the long view, the general thrust of EU strategic policy seems to be the phasing out of the ACP as a significant interlocutor, and its possible disbandment as a development partner after the expiry of the Cotonou Agreement in 2020. This is consistent with the ongoing restructuring of the EU's regional and global relationships in the post-Lomé, post–Lisbon Treaty era. Notably, however, this view is not shared by Caribbean ambassadors in Brussels, who believe that there are strong geopolitical and geo-economic reasons for the EU to continue to engage with the ACP and for the ACP to continue to engage as a bloc with the EU.

A CARIBBEAN PERSPECTIVE ON THE FUTURE OF ACP-EU RELATIONS

In 2013, the German Development Institute (DIE) and the European Centre for Development Policy Management produced a study on the future of ACP-EU relations, based on interviews with key ACP and EU stakeholders.[59] Among those interviewed were a small group of Caribbean ambassadors in Brussels.[60] These viewpoints from the Caribbean indicate a mutual interest in the EU-ACP relationship, and a mutual belief in the value in continuing it. Some hold the view that the absence of the mention of the ACP group in the Lisbon Treaty of 2009 is not an indication of the EU's dwindling interest in the ACP, with one interviewee contending that it not unusual for the name of a third party to be excluded from a constitution. Several reasons were put forward by the Caribbean ambassadors to explain the EU's interest in the ACP. Historically, many EU countries have benefited from the ACP group. Newer EU member states have also gained indirectly from the ACP, because the former have benefited from the wealth of Western European states. In the case of the Caribbean in particular, the EU has a direct interest because of Europe's overseas territories and outermost regions. Furthermore, the ACP's 79 member countries constitute a significant voting share at the UN General Assembly, making the group a valuable source of diplomatic support. The EU's comparative advantage in development cooperation also has been predominantly based on its experiences with the ACP within the context of the Lomé and Cotonou Agreements. This has, in turn, enabled the EU to gain leverage as a leading development actor on the global stage, and to learn and build on these experiences in other areas of development cooperation. For example, the EU's European Neighbourhood Policy uses a budget support system that is based upon its experiences with the ACP.

On the Caribbean side, it is felt that the EU continues to be a valuable partner, for many reasons. The European Union remains an important international player with significant influence globally, and could act as a counterweight to the BRICS and the US in the Caribbean. The EU could therefore leverage influence on behalf of the ACP in relation to other partners. The interviewees also indicated that the ACP values the EU's exercise of soft power globally, and further that the EU remains important as a market for ACP goods and services.

In terms of the ACP's future engagement with the EU, the Caribbean ambassadors in Brussels see the ACP as a bloc as being more powerful than the African, Caribbean, and Pacific regions individually when negotiating and defining relations with Europe. It is also easier for the EU to engage with the ACP as a bloc than with separate countries or regions. In particular, the existence of the ACP group allows the EU to deal with the multitude of interests, some overlapping, that exist among its 79 members under one framework, while facilitating coalition formation on common issues in international fora. There is a feeling that the EU's strategic and political influence in Africa, the Caribbean, and the Pacific would weaken if it were no longer executed through the framework of the ACP.

Finally, it is felt that while the nature of their relationship might change, the ACP's link with the EU will likely remain in one form or the other. The ACP countries, for their part, need to find common ground on issues of mutual concern, such as global public goods, migration, and climate change, on which the group could speak with one voice in multilateral settings. Diversifying the ACP's relations with the BRICS, while maintaining a strong link with the EU, is cited as a viable scenario. At the same time, there is a sense of caution about pursuing relations with the BRICS, which need to be supported by further research, with careful consideration given to defining the modus operandi of any new relationship (see Virk in this volume).

Concluding Reflections

Many challenges to Caribbean regional integration have stemmed from the EU's decision to impose CARIFORUM as its preferred Caribbean interlocutor under the Cotonou framework. There remain a diversity of interests among Caribbean states, and several key developments have soured Caribbean-EU relations over time, including most recently the negotiations for the CARIFORUM-EU EPA and the agreement's negative implications for the prospects of achieving sustainable development in the Caribbean. Despite some progress, challenges continue to bedevil implementation of the EPA since it was signed in 2008. As of May 2014, ratification of the agreement stood at only 50 per cent, and thus the benefits to regional integration remain unfulfilled promises. Disappointment reigns in terms of access by CARIFORUM service providers to the EU market. Implementation has continued to be constrained by resource challenges, with the functioning of joint institutions remaining inadequate in terms of providing support for the agreement.[61] (See Gonzales in this volume.) But a genuine and more meaningful partnership between the EU and the Caribbean can be built, one within the framework of the ACP. This needs to be premised on the development of a clear strategy by the Caribbean, for the Caribbean, and on the rationalisation of the Caribbean regional integration project.

Notes

1. They are Antigua and Barbuda, Bahamas, Barbados, Belize, Cuba, Dominica, the Dominican Republic, Grenada, Guyana, Haiti, Jamaica, St Kitts and Nevis, St Lucia, St Vincent and the Grenadines, Suriname, and Trinidad and Tobago.
2. These Caribbean Commonwealth countries were Antigua and Barbuda, Bahamas, Barbados, Belize, Dominica, Grenada, Guyana, Jamaica, St Lucia, St Kitts and Nevis, St Vincent and the Grenadines, and Trinidad and Tobago.
3. Lorand Bartels, "The Trade and Development Policy of the European Union", *European Journal of International Law* 18, no. 4 (2007), p. 733.
4. Spain joined the European Economic Community (EEC) in 1986, and Spanish trade and investment interests in the Caribbean, notably tourism, were among the drivers for the proposed inclusion of the Dominican Republic and Cuba in Lomé IV. Cuba's accession was aborted as a result of political differences with the European Union (EU). In 2000, Cuba was admitted to the African, Caribbean, and Pacific (ACP) group, becoming the only ACP member country not to be a party to the Cotonou Partnership Agreement of 2000.
5. Haiti was not a member of the Caribbean Community (CARICOM) when the Forum of the Caribbean Group of ACP States (CARIFORUM) was established in 1992, joining CARICOM only later in 2002. The Dominican Republic is, to date, not a member of CARICOM.
6. The CARIFORUM Secretariat is located in the CARICOM Secretariat in Georgetown, Guyana, where an Assistant Secretary-General has responsibility for CARIFORUM matters. The Secretary-General of CARICOM also serves as the Secretary-General of CARIFORUM, although the arrangement has been the source of ongoing controversy between the Dominican Republic and CARICOM.
7. World Bank, *World Development Indicators 2015*, http://wdi.worldbank.org/table/4.2 (accessed 6 July 2015).
8. CARICOM Secretariat, National Accounts, Statistics of CARICOM Member States, Regional Statistics, http://www.caricomstats.

org/Files/Databases/National_Accounts/Summary/Current.pdf (accessed 6 July 2015).

9. 23rd Inter-Sessional Meeting of the Conference of Heads of Government of the Caribbean Community, Paramaribo, Suriname, 8–9 March 2012.

10. STABEX (*Système de Stabilisation des Recettes d'Exportation*), set up by Lomé II, and SYSMIN (*Système de Développement du Potentiel Minier*), later set up by Lomé III, were compensatory financing schemes for export income shortfalls due to price instability affecting agricultural and mineral export commodities respectively.

11. This was handled through the European Development Fund (EDF), which was replenished in each cycle of the Lomé Convention.

12. Peter Clegg, "Renegotiating Lomé: The Future of the EU-ACP Caribbean Relationship", Discussion Paper no. 7 (Southampton: Development Studies Association, European Development Policy Study Group, October 1997), p. 5, http://www.business.mmu.ac.uk/edpsg (accessed 10 May 2015).

13. The five ACP countries were Jamaica, Botswana, Côte d'Ivoire, Mauritius, and Zimbabwe.

14. European Commission, "Green Paper on Relations Between the European Union and ACP Countries on the Eve of the 21st Century: Challenges and Options for a New Partnership", Brussels, Belgium, November 1996, pp. 17–18.

15. Michael Davenport, Adrian Hewitt, and Antonique Koning, *Europe's Preferred Partners? The Lomé Countries in World Trade* (London: Overseas Development Institute, 1995), p. 5.

16. The "perverse effect" was said by some economists to be the result of incentivising continued specialisation in commodity exports.

17. Clegg, "Renegotiating Lomé", p. 2.

18. European Commission, *The Caribbean and the European Union* (Luxembourg: Office for Official Publications of the European Communities, 1995), p. 3.

19. Montfort Mlachila, Paul Cashin, and Cleary Haines, "Caribbean Bananas: The Macroeconomic Impact of Trade Preference Erosion", International Monetary Fund (IMF) Working Paper, March 2010, p. 15, http://www.imf.org/external/pubs/ft/wp/2010/wp1059.pdf (accessed 10 May 2015).

20. *See* European Commission, "EC Fact Sheet on Caribbean Bananas and the WTO", Memo no. 97/28, Brussels, 18 March 1997, http://europa.eu/rapid/press-release_MEMO-97-28_en.htm?locale=en (accessed 3 May 2015).

21. *See* European Commission, "Green Paper on Relations Between the European Union and ACP Countries", for an explanation of how globalisation impacted the EU's policy agenda.

22. *Time for Action: The Report of the Independent West Indian Commission* (Bridgetown, 1992).

23. After 1994, a series of World Trade Organisation (WTO) rulings effectively dismantled EU preferences for ACP bananas, leading to a severe contraction of the industry in the smaller Caribbean islands. The dispute was formally ended in November 2012.

24. Article 37(6) of the Cotonou Partnership Agreement contains an EU undertaking to examine alternative possibilities for non-least-developed countries that do not wish to conclude an economic partnership agreement, in order to provide them "with a new frame-work for trade which is equivalent to their existing situation and in conformity with WTO rules". In the event, the EU determined that the only alternative for the Caribbean was to export to the European market under the Generalised System of Preferences (GSP), which would have resulted in significant tariffs on Caribbean exports.

25. Under the Sugar Protocol of 1975, the EU committed to import-ing 1.3 million tons annually of ACP sugar at guaranteed prices. In 2009, the EU unilaterally abrogated the protocol as part of the reform of its Common Agricultural Policy (CAP).

26. Aid for Trade is an initiative developed by the WTO in 2005 in which assistance is provided to developing countries and least-developed countries for overcoming supply-side capacity con-straints and poor trade-related infrastructure in order to enable them to participate more effectively in, and benefit from, global trade. The Aid for Trade initiative has been embraced by the EU in its trade relations with developing countries. The European Commission defines Aid for Trade as "assistance provided to sup-port partner countries' efforts to develop and expand their trade as leverage for growth and poverty reduction". European Commission, "Aid for Trade", http://ec.europa.eu/trade/pol-icy/countries-and-regions/development/aid-for-trade (accessed 13 May 2015).

27. Bartels, "The Trade and Development Policy of the European Union", pp. 715–756.

28. *See for example* Christopher Stevens, Jane Kennan, and Mareike Meyn, *The Costs to the ACP of Exporting to the EU Under the GSP* (London: Overseas Development Institute, March 2007).

29. *See* Niels Keijzer, Florian Krätke, Brecht Lein, Jeske van Seters, and Annita Montoute, "Differentiation in ACP-EU Cooperation Implications of the EU's Agenda for Change for the 11th EDF and Beyond", Discussion Paper no. 134 (Maastricht: European Centre for Development Policy Management [ECDPM], October 2014), http://ecdpm.org/wp-content/uploads/2013/10/DP-134-ACP-EU-Cooperation-Implications-EU-Agenda-Change-11-EDF-2012.pdf (accessed 26 April 2016).

30. European Parliament, "Fact Sheets on the European Union", http://www.europarl.europa.eu/atyourservice/en/displayFtu.html?ftuId=FTU_6.6.2.html (accessed 4 May 2016).

31. The CARIFORUM-EU EPA covers goods, services, investment, and trade-related issues. Negotiations were concluded in December 2007, and the agreement was signed in October 2008 by 14 CARIFORUM countries, with Haiti signing later, in December 2009.

32. Caribbean Regional Negotiating Machinery (CRNM), "CRNM Briefing Note for the JPA", 27 September 2007, pp. 3, 6, http://www.normangirvan.info/wp-content/uploads/2009/04/crnm-briefing-note-to-jpa-ass-sept07.pdf (accessed 17 May 2015).

33. CRNM, "What's in the EPA for the Private Sector?" Private Sector Trade Note, 19 December 2007, pp. 1, 5, http://www.norman-girvan.info/whats-in-the-epa-for-the-private-sector-crnm (accessed 17 May 2015).

34. Haiti, as also mentioned earlier, signed the agreement in December 2009.

35. European Commission, "European Union, Trade in Goods with ACP—Caribbean Countries", Brussels, 10 April 2015, p. 4, http://trade.ec.europa.eu/doclib/docs/2006/september/tradoc_113476.pdf (accessed 12 May 2015).

36. European Commission, "European Community–Caribbean Region: Regional Strategy Paper and Regional Indicative Programme, 2008–2013", Strasbourg, France, 15 November 2008, p. 41, http://eulacfoundation.org/sites/eulacfoundation.

org/files/pdf/EUROPEAN%20COMMUNITY%20_%20CARIB
BEAN%20REGION%20%20REGIONAL%20STRATEGY%20
PAPER.pdf (accessed 17 May 2015).

37. European Commission, "Jamaica-European Community Country
Strategy Paper and National Indicative Programme for the Period
2008–2013", Strasbourg, 15 November 2008, pp. 43–44, http://
ec.europa.eu/europeaid/sites/devco/files/csp-nip-
jamaica-2008-2013_en.pdf (accessed 17 May 2015).

38. Norman Girvan, "Social Movements Confront Neoliberalism:
Reflections on a Caribbean Experience", *Globalizations* 9, no. 6
(2012), p. 759.

39. *See for example* Annita Montoute, "Civil Society Participation in
Trade Negotiations: A Caribbean Case Study", PhD dissertation,
University of the West Indies, St Augustine, Trinidad and Tobago,
2009.

40. Havelock Brewster, "The Anti-Development Dimension of the
European Community's Economic Partnership Agreement for the
Caribbean", paper presented at the Commonwealth Secretariat
High-Level Technical Meeting *EPAs: The Way Forward for the
ACP*, Cape Town, South Africa, 7–8 April 2008, http://www.
normangirvan.info/the-anti-development-dimension-of-the-
european-communitys-economic-partnership-agreement-for-
caribbean-havelock-brewster (accessed 2 July 2015).

41. Norman Girvan, "Implications of the Cariforum-EC EPA", 2008,
http://da-academy.org/girvanimplicationsepa10jan.pdf (accessed
17 May 2015).

42. Chris Milner estimated the adjustment costs for CARIFORUM
economies at €924 million. The regional allocation for EPA implementation under the tenth EDF is a mere €33 million, with mod-
est allocations made in the national programmes. Also, it is
important to note that "EPA implementation" does not necessarily
refer to economic adjustment costs. Chris Milner, "An Assessment
of the Overall Implementation and Adjustment Costs for the ACP
Countries of Economic Partnerships with the EU", Report to the
Commonwealth Secretariat, London, England, October 2005,
p.   47,   http://www.normangirvan.info/wp-content/
uploads/2008/07/milner-epa-adjustment-study-oct2005.pdf
(accessed 17 May 2015).

43. Brewster, "The Anti-Development Dimension", p. 2.

44. Errol Humphrey, "Implementing the Economic Partnership Agreement: Challenges and Bottlenecks in the CARIFORUM Region", Discussion Paper no. 117 (Maastricht, Netherlands: ECDPM, June 2011), p. 8, http://ecdpm.org/wp-content/uploads/2013/11/DP-117-Economic-Partnership-Agreement--Challenges-CARIFORUM-Region-2011.pdf (accessed 17 May 2015).
45. Girvan, "Implications of the Cariforum-EC EPA".
46. "Is There Any Hope for CARICOM?" *Guyana Chronicle Online*, 14 March 2012, http://guyanachronicle.com/is-there-any-hope-for-caricom (accessed 13 May 2015).
47. Joyce van Genderen-Naar, "The CARIFORUM-EU EPA Five Years Later", presentation to the ACP-EU Joint Parliamentary Assembly, Paramaribo, Suriname, 27 November 2012, p. 7, http://www.normangirvan.info/wp-content/uploads/2012/12/NAR-Development-Content-of-CF-EPA-Nov-12.pdf (accessed 17 May 2015).
48. They included the Dominican Republic (2008), Antigua and Barbuda (2008), Dominica (2009), Belize (2011), Guyana (2012), St Lucia (2012), and St Vincent and the Grenadines (2012). Business and Strategies (B&S) Europe and Linpico, *Monitoring the Implementation & Results of the CARIFORUM-EU EPA Agreement*, Final Report, September 2014, p. 8, http://trade.ec.europa.eu/doclib/docs/2014/october/tradoc_152824.pdf (accessed 17 May 2015).
49. B&S Europe and Linpico, *Monitoring the Implementation & Results*, p. 35.
50. CARIFORUM officials argued that the agreed ten-year moratorium on the duties to be applied to imports of automobiles and auto parts was not reflected in the tariff liberalisation schedules in Annex XXX of the EPA. European Commission officials, on the other hand, argued that any such errors could be corrected only by an amendment to the agreement and that this would involve a lengthy and time-consuming process. Van Genderen-Naar, "The CARIFORUM-EU EPA Five Years Later", pp. 7, 10.
51. B&S Europe and Linpico, *Monitoring the Implementation & Results*, p. 35.
52. Humphrey, "Implementing the Economic Partnership Agreement", p. 8.

53. Van Genderen-Naar, "The CARIFORUM-EU EPA Five Years Later", pp. 9, 13.
54. These include regional integration and cooperation in the wider Caribbean; reconstruction and institutional support to Haiti; climate change and natural disasters; crime and security; and joint action in bi-regional and multilateral fora and on global issues.
55. The relevant funding instruments include the European Development Fund, the Development Cooperation Instrument (DCI), and the Instrument for Stability and the Thematic Programmes, as well as instruments provided by EU financial institutions such as the European Investment Bank (EIB); these are complemented with further contributions by EU member states, Caribbean financial instruments, and CARIFORUM member states.
56. Annita Montoute, Quinnelle Kangalee, and Zhara Allyene, "The Joint Caribbean EU Strategy: Reflections and Analysis", workshop report, Institute of International Relations, University of the West Indies, St Augustine, 15 April 2011, p. 3, http://www.ecdpm. org/Web_ECDPM/Web/Content/Download.nsf/0/2838EC6 BFD50A367C125788F00302F19/$FILE/Report%20work-shop%20FINAL.pdf (accessed 17 May 2015).
57. James Mackie, Bruce Byiers, Sonia Niznik, and Geert Laporte (eds.), *Global Changes, Emerging Players, and Evolving ACP-EU Relations: Towards a Common Agenda for Action?* ECDPM 25th Anniversary Seminar, Policy and Management Report no. 19 (Maastricht: ECDPM, 2011), http://www.ecdpm.org/pmr/19 (accessed 30 June 2015).
58. Mackie et al., *Global Changes*, pp. 35, 39.
59. Mario Negre, Niels Keijzer, Brecht Lein, and Nicola Tissi, "Towards Renewal or Oblivion? Prospects for Post–2020 Cooperation Between the European Union and the Africa, Caribbean, and Pacific Group", Discussion Paper no. 9 (Bonn and Maastricht: German Development Institute [DIE] and ECDPM, 2013), http://ecdpm.org/wp-content/uploads/2013/10/DP-9-Post-2020-Cooperation-EU-Africa-Caribbean-Pacific.pdf (accessed 17 May 2015).
60. This summary has been extracted from interview data collected by the authors, on behalf of the ECDPM for Negre et al., "Towards Renewal or Oblivion?".
61. B&S Europe and Linpico, *Monitoring the Implementation & Results*, p. 12.

CHAPTER 5

The EU and the Pacific: A Tale of Unfulfilled Expectations

Kaliopate Tavola

Pacific regionalism remains a work in progress, characterised by institutions that have fallen short of expectations and that need to be strengthened significantly in order to achieve the full benefits of integration in the region. In a joint review of Pacific regionalism, conducted in 2005, the Asian Development Bank (ADB) and the Commonwealth Secretariat outlined three types of regional institutions: regional cooperation, regional provision of services, and regional market integration.[1] The review defined "regional market integration" as the reduction of trade barriers between countries in the region, contrasting it with the broader concept of "regional integration", which includes not only the removal of such barriers but also the creation of shared institutions such as central banks and regulatory bodies (regional provision of services) for facilitating the free movement of goods, services, and people. The joint report also showed that, historically, "many regions (including the Pacific) have often opted for regional institutions and approaches that, despite high costs, did not yield the necessary offsetting benefits".[2] The ADB and Commonwealth Secretariat review further argued that "given the Pacific's unique characteristics, only by moving to 'deeper' forms of regionalism—increased regional provision of services and regional market integration—will the

K. Tavola (✉)
Fiji's Minister for Foreign Affairs and External Trade, Suva, Fiji

© The Author(s) 2017
A. Montoute, K. Virk (eds.), *The ACP Group and the EU Development Partnership*, DOI 10.1007/978-3-319-45492-4_5

[Pacific Islands] Forum [PIF] create the necessary pool of benefits needed to make regional institutions sustainable and beneficial to its members".[3] Yet, a decade later, regional integration has not moved beyond a free trade area (FTA) in most of the African, Caribbean, and Pacific (ACP) regions, with the Pacific, in particular, continuing to be "highly fragmented due to the composition of the region, including both rich economies (Australia and New Zealand) and tiny, least developed island states".[4]

Since the Lomé Convention of 1975, regional integration has been a key element in the relationship between the Pacific ACP states and the European Union (EU).[5] (See Whiteman in this volume on the history of the ACP-EU relationship.) While neither Lomé I nor Lomé II (the latter signed in 1979) specifically mentioned regional integration, both conventions included provisions for assistance for regional and inter-regional (ACP) cooperation.[6] The term "regional integration" made its first appearance in Lomé III (negotiated by 1984) in the context of articles related to industrial development and regional cooperation.[7] The Lomé IV Convention of 1989 shifted the focus to the development of services that could stimulate regional integration,[8] and featured the contribution of structural adjustment resources to encourage the process.[9] The Cotonou Agreement of 2000 placed further emphasis on a range of issues including the need for regional and sub-regional integration processes to facilitate the integration of ACP economies into the global economy, highlighting especially: the role of trade and the private sector in this regard; the contributory role of the Joint ACP-EU Parliamentary Assembly; the development of capacities for regional economic integration; the building of economic and trade cooperation on regional integration initiatives; the need for economic partnership agreements (EPAs) to take regional integration processes into account; and structural adjustment support to encourage these processes.[10]

Over a span of four decades, European trade, economic, and development cooperation under the Lomé Conventions and the Cotonou Agreement has sought to supplement the resources and efforts of the Pacific ACP states towards achieving regional integration. However, the objectives of EU cooperation have remained largely unmet, with rhetoric failing to match reality on the ground. In recent years, cooperation between the Pacific and the EU has been characterised by a general air of malaise, as evidenced by protracted EU-Pacific economic partnership agreement negotiations that have lacked momentum and creativity, with a final agreement yet to be concluded and the EU proposing a three-year suspension of the talks. In this regard, the EPA process has been symptomatic of the overall vitality, or rather lack thereof, of relations between the EU and the Pacific ACP states.

Based on a critical examination of challenges in the Pacific region, I argue in this chapter—in agreement with the ADB and the Commonwealth Secretariat—that regional integration in the Pacific must be deepened to achieve its benefits for the island developing countries, and supported by better implementation and targeted initiatives within the EU-Pacific ACP framework. The chapter also reflects on the future of Pacific regionalism, while offering recommendations to re-energise and redirect the future of EU-Pacific relations.

The Challenges of Pacific Regional Integration

Geography and Composition of the Region

The fragmented geography of the Pacific island countries—in particular their wide dispersion and isolation, and large distances to external markets—has been a serious challenge to the region's integration efforts. Kiribati, for example, has a total land area of just over 700 square kilometres, but the island country has an exclusive economic zone (EEZ) area of more than 3.5 million square kilometres. This is the largest EEZ area among the Pacific island countries, yet it represents only 17.8 per cent of their total EEZ area.[11] Equally, the smallness of the Pacific island countries has posed a number of problems typically associated with such size, including: limited human and financial resources, resulting, in turn, in high costs for economic and social services; lack of institutional memory due to quick staff turn-over, especially in the sub-regional Smaller Island States (SIS) group;[12] poor infrastructure; weak absorptive capacity; and lack of commercial and trade prospects for many of the island states.[13] As the ADB–Commonwealth Secretariat report concluded in 2005, international case studies showed that "groupings of purely small states often do not create the net benefits needed" from regional cooperation and market integration.[14]

Yet Pacific leaders, as well as the overall ACP-EU cooperation framework of the Lomé Conventions, failed to respond effectively and creatively to the unique challenges of geography for integration efforts in the region. On the contrary, these geographic and size-related problems have tended to be understated and undervalued, and consequently have not been fully factored into regional planning and activities in the Pacific. The region's Smaller Island States—Niue, for example—have at times questioned the benefits accruing to them from the Pacific Islands Forum's programmes, including the Regional Indicative Programme (RIP) under first the Lomé Conventions and then the Cotonou Agreement. In this regard, Pacific leaders failed to identify Pacific regional integration as a special case that could serve as a developmental model and a guide for the other ACP regions. More recently, though, in 2012 at the United Nations Economic and Social Commission for Asia and the Pacific (UNESCAP), Pacific leaders successfully argued that the region's small island developing states should be given special consideration by the international community.[15] The outcome document of the Rio+20 United Nations (UN) Conference on Sustainable Development, held in June 2012, contained several outcomes that were particularly relevant for the Pacific region, and reaffirmed the "special case" for small island developing states.[16]

An appreciation of the specific challenges of regional integration in the Pacific demands the application of more unconventional economic principles and methods (such as subsidisation of regional projects). The membership of Australia and New Zealand—both major donors—in the 16-member Pacific Islands Forum,[17] the main body for regional cooperation, has further complicated the region's efforts in this regard, with the two countries' economic ideas and preferences often differing from those of the rest. For example, in 2004 a transportation study[18] that sought, among other things, to re-orient and re-vamp the operations of the Pacific Forum Line (PFL)—a shipping line established in 1978—recommended subsidisation of its operations to enable the PFL to service all routes (economic and non-economic). At the same time, the study also cautioned against hasty attempts to broaden the PFL's sphere of operation. But the subsidisation proposal was never implemented, with donor views prevailing over those of Pacific leaders. Instead, further capitalisation through a loan from the European Investment Bank (EIB) was pursued, with the PFL subsequently focusing only on a few key routes. As a member of the Organisation for Economic Cooperation and Development (OECD), the EU is seen by many in the region to be a custodian of the Washington Consensus and to be sympathetic to the economic preferences of fellow OECD members Australia and New Zealand, and therefore unlikely to consider policy options that deviate from traditional mainstream economic theories and practices.

Political Dynamics in the Region: The Role of Australia and New Zealand

The membership of Australia and New Zealand in the Pacific Islands Forum is an idiosyncrasy. In 1971, newly independent Pacific states—specifically the Cook Islands, Fiji, Nauru, and Western Samoa (now Samoa) and Tonga—sought to form their own regional grouping, apart from the metropolitan powers in the then South Pacific Commission, including Australia, New Zealand, Britain, France, and the United States (US). However, the Pacific states then reversed course and invited Australia and New Zealand to join them in their new grouping. In a brief note in a 2005 report, Tony Hughes, former governor of the central bank of the Solomon Islands, observed that there was hesitation on the part of the Pacific leaders in inviting Australia and New Zealand to join the proposed new group, but also observed that Canberra and Wellington had gone to great lengths to ensure that both countries became founding members of the new grouping—the South Pacific Forum (SPF), rechristened the Pacific Islands Forum in 2000.[19] An increasing number of regional commentators now believe that the inclusion of Australia and New Zealand in the PIF at the forum's founding was a mistake.[20] This view has since been reaffirmed by the undue dominance of the two industrialised countries in regional decision-making.

Moreover, Canberra and Wellington's membership in the PIF has served to magnify the existing inequality and divisions among the Pacific ACP states. For example, Papua New Guinea has an area of 462,000 square kilometres, while Nauru occupies a mere 21 square kilometres, compared to Australia's 7.7 million square kilometres and New Zealand's 270,000 square kilometres. Population size among the Pacific island countries ranges from over 7 million in Papua New Guinea (2012) to 1,625 in Niue (2006). This stands in contrast to Australia's population of 21.4 million (2008) and New Zealand's population of 4.3 million (2008). Developmental status and per capita gross domestic product (GDP) similarly vary markedly in the Pacific ACP region. The PIF includes: two industrialised countries, Australia and New Zealand (both OECD members); seven Smaller Island States; and five least-developed countries (Kiribati, Samoa, the Solomon Islands, Tuvalu, and Vanuatu). Furthermore, of the four atoll states in the world, three are in the Pacific: Kiribati, the Marshall Islands, and Tuvalu.

The presence of Australia and New Zealand in the PIF has significantly affected the direction of regional integration in the Pacific. In

July 1980, Australia and New Zealand signed the South Pacific Regional Trade and Economic Cooperation Agreement (SPARTECA)—a preferential, non-reciprocal trade agreement similar to the trade chapter of the Lomé Conventions—with the 14 Forum Island Countries (FICs)[21]; the agreement entered into force in January 1981. However, the benefits of SPARTECA were mixed. As the South Pacific Forum noted in its communiqué of August 1984, "while total trade under [SPARTECA] had increased during its three years of operation, ... exports from some smaller island countries had actually decreased".[22] In its communiqué of August 1985, the South Pacific Forum "acknowledged the concerns of Smaller Island Countries that provisions of SPARTECA were not particularly relevant to their needs: their export-oriented base was so small that they could not take advantage of the concessionary terms of trade that were available under the Agreement and special arrangements might be necessary in their case".[23] Then, in 1988, the South Pacific Forum further recognised that "fundamental problems existed with the productive capacity of some Forum Island Countries, especially the Smaller Island Countries".[24] In addition, there were problems related to the rules of origin, in particular the high threshold for local content, cumulation requirements, trade facilitation, and non-tariff barriers. There were, however, some trade benefits for the larger Pacific countries. The textile industry in Fiji, in particular, grew subsequent to SPARTECA, especially after the rules of origin were reformed with the direct aim of developing the industry.

In August 2001, the FICs came together to sign the Pacific Island Countries Trade Agreement (PICTA). This FICs-only free trade area agreement excluded Australia and New Zealand, with the island countries acting collectively to refuse membership in it to the two industrialised economies. However, the FICs gave way to the Pacific Agreement on Closer Economic Relations (PACER)—an economic framework agreement, signed in Nauru in July 2001, between the FICs on the one hand and Australia and New Zealand on the other. PACER, which entered into force in April 2003, envisages the negotiated creation of another free trade area in the Pacific region, but one involving the two industrialised countries in the region, Australia and New Zealand. In particular, Articles 5 and 6 of the agreement include triggers for the start of PACER Plus negotiations for the proposed FTA. Through the mid-2000s, Australia and New Zealand placed increasing pressure on the FICs to start these negotiations. According to PACER, submission of market access offers under an FTA agreement is a sufficient trigger for PACER Plus talks. The submission of such offers by the Pacific ACP countries to Brussels, as part of their negotiations for an economic partnership agreement with the EU, provided the trigger in March–June 2007, with PACER Plus negotiations beginning in August 2009. For Australia and New Zealand in particular, PACER Plus is expected to replace SPARTECA, with the latter seen by them as a preferential, non-reciprocal trade agreement that has outlived its relevance and usefulness.

The proposed PACER Plus FTA is modelled on the concept of the European EPA and, like the latter, is intended to be a developmental tool for the ACP states. In the context of PACER, the "Plus" is the proxy for development. However, as in the EPA talks, the requirement for the agreement to support development in the FICs has been a stumbling block in the PACER Plus negotiations from the outset. There is disunity between the Forum Island Countries, and Australia and New Zealand, on what development should comprise, and how this should be articulated and framed. In addition, there has been dissatisfaction among the FICs about being cajoled into starting negotiations before they had concluded their own national consultations and crafted their respective positions on various issues to take to the negotiations. None of this has augured well for the prospects of PACER Plus. At the time of writing, the PACER Plus negotiations appeared to be floundering on two critical issues for the FICs: the treatment of development resources required for trade restructuring under the agreement, and the treatment of labour mobility.

Implementation of Trade and Economic Cooperation Agreements in the Region

Implementation of trade agreements has been an additional challenge for the development of Pacific regionalism. Execution of the provisions for trade facilitation contained in the Pacific Agreement on Closer Economic Relations (Article 9 and Annex 1), for example, was undermined by disputes on funding arrangements. Under Article 9(4) of the agreement, most of the financial assistance was to be contributed by Australia and New Zealand, but the two industrialised countries argued that other development partners should contribute as well. In the end, additional funding was provided by the EU's Regional Indicative Programme—a key component of the EU-Pacific ACP framework—between 2001 and 2009 to assist with the implementation of the various trade facilitation programmes established under PACER.

The implementation of a trade-in-goods agreement (TGA), under the Pacific Island Countries Trade Agreement, has similarly benefited from programming measures and financial support provided by the EU's regional envelope under the 9th, 10th, and 11th iterations of the European Development Fund (EDF). Even so, several Forum Island Countries, such as the Cook Islands, Kiribati, the Marshall Islands, Nauru, Niue, Palau, and Tuvalu, have been unable to implement the PICTA TGA due mainly to a lack of capacity. At the August 2012 Pacific Islands Forum meeting, held in Rarotonga, Cook Islands, Pacific leaders asked the forum's secretariat and other regional organisations (such as the Secretariat of the Pacific Community) to support the FICs that had not yet implemented the PICTA TGA, thereby underscoring their concern about the issue.[25] The Pacific leaders also welcomed the signing of a trade-in-services (TIS) protocol under PICTA at the same meeting.[26] However, if the implementation of the TGA is any indication, it will be some time before the services protocol is ratified and implemented. At the time of writing, the situation remained broadly unchanged.

Given the delays in implementation, the benefits accruing from PICTA have so far been minimal and unbalanced for the Forum Island Countries, with the free flow of goods and services envisaged under the agreement yet to materialise. The implementation of the Melanesian Spearhead Group (MSG) Trade Agreement (discussed later), however, is well advanced. The EU's regional programme has provided support for the implementation of trade agreements in the region, though the efficiency and efficacy of its delivery has been questioned. Similarly, there have been discussions on the use of Europe's Aid for Trade (AfT) resources, but very little to show for it. That said, national capacity has remained the most critical factor that has hindered the implementation of regional agreements in the Pacific. Despite efforts to align capacity-building resources with development objectives in the Pacific island countries, problems arising from limited human resources and related skills and competence have persisted. This relates directly to the Forum Island Countries' smallness, remoteness, limited resources, and lack of integration into the global economy, which together constitute an overt and overarching constraint on the FICs' development and regional integration efforts.

A similar set of factors has frustrated efforts to develop regional provision of services in the Pacific. The case of the Oceania Customs Organisation (OCO)—established in August 1998 to replace the Customs Heads of Administration Regional Meeting (CHARM)—is an exception. Regional

initiatives to facilitate trade have otherwise not yielded the expected benefits in terms of regional provision of services. These initiatives include the
Pacific Forum Line—as discussed earlier—and Air Pacific, which failed to
become a regional airline due to a corporate structure that did not guarantee protection for the sovereignty of those regional governments not
represented in its governance. In this regard, regional economic integration in the Pacific is still in its infancy.

National Interests

To some extent, the Forum Island Countries' historical relations with the
metropolitan powers in the region have also hindered their commitment
to Pacific regionalism and regional projects.[27] Former colonial powers have
continued to be significant as major sources of much needed resources for
the national development of several FICs. Australia and New Zealand,
together with the EU, are the largest donors and development partners for
the countries of the region. National interests have thus fuelled sensitivity
to any perceived loss of sovereignty to regional projects and initiatives,
limiting the accrual of potential benefits from them. The case of Air Pacific
is a good example.

THE FUTURE OF PACIFIC REGIONALISM

More effective regional arrangements could bring increased benefits—
including a greater flow of goods, capital, skills, and expertise—for the
Pacific island countries. There have been a number of recent developments in the region that could help to create an enabling environment for
a deeper form of Pacific regionalism.

The Development of Sub-Regionalism

Sub-regionalism has been on a growth path in the Pacific. The Melanesian
Spearhead Group was established in March 1988, and the MSG Trade
Agreement—signed in 1993—created the only sub-regional free trade
area thus far (at the time of writing) in the Pacific region.[28] The MSG
Trade Agreement has benefited from the European Union's National
Indicative Programmes (NIPs), under the rubric of the EU-Pacific ACP
framework, in the areas of capacity-building, strengthening of institutions,
and technical assistance. Even so, the FTA has faced several challenges.

The switch from an initial "positive list" approach to the preferred "negative list" approach did not take place as planned.[29] In addition, early in the implementation phase, in the early 2000s, Vanuatu sought to impose an "injury tariff" against Fiji under the MSG Trade Agreement's provision on temporary suspension of obligations, without the prior consultations provided for by the agreement (Article 12[1]). Furthermore, as the Vanuatu-based Pacific Institute of Public Policy (PiPP) noted in 2008: "PNG officials view the MSG-FTA as being largely irrelevant in terms of national economic development, and Solomon Islands and, to a lesser extent, Vanuatu, have questioned the benefits on offer from the agreement."[30] The situation has since improved, with both Papua New Guinea and Vanuatu opening up their markets: Vanuatu has no items on its "negative list", while Papua New Guinea has only three.

The Polynesian Leaders Group (PLG) was created in November 2011, with Samoa providing the interim secretariat.[31] Micronesian leaders have formalised their collaboration through the Micronesian Chief Executives' Summit (MCES), which has met regularly since 2003.[32] In addition, the Smaller Island States group has long existed within the Pacific Islands Forum as a recognised sub-regional grouping. Whether these sub-regional groupings will develop in the same way as the Melanesian Spearhead Group is yet to be determined. Increased sub-regionalism, however, could lead to increased unity and commitments across borders, while fostering greater ownership of cross-country projects. This positive outcome at the sub-regional level could translate into stronger commitment and ownership of regional projects, if the membership and governance of the regional structures were also to be configured to support the same outcome.

The Reconfiguring of Pacific Regionalism

In recent years, regional commentators have pointed to several developments, such as the establishment of the Pacific Islands Development Forum (PIDF) and of the Melanesian Spearhead Group, that indicate reconfigured political dynamics in the Pacific regional project.[33] Dissatisfaction with the dominant role of Australia and New Zealand in regional affairs has been a key driver of this reconfiguration. Perceptions that Canberra and Wellington's leadership has contributed to lethargy and lack of direction in the development of Pacific regionalism has highlighted a growing need to reduce the dependence of regional integration processes on the two industrialised economies. Efforts to reconfigure Pacific regionalism away from reliance on Australia and New Zealand have included the creation of the PIDF in August 2013, the concept for which was endorsed by Pacific leaders at their "Engaging With the Pacific" meeting in August 2012.[34] All Pacific Small Island Developing States (PSIDS), recognised as such by the UN, are entitled to be members of the PIDF, which formally agreed at its inaugural meeting in August 2013 to focus on the implementation of green economic policies in its member states.

The PIDF is thus intended to be a grouping composed only of the Forum Island Countries, free of the influence of Australia and New Zealand, which could in turn nurture greater ownership of decisions and commitment to the PIDF by the FICs. There are hopes in the region that the PIDF could, in due course, deplete the authority of the Australia and New Zealand–dominated Pacific Islands Forum and assume the central role currently played by the PIF in regional affairs. In turn, this could give way to "bilateral" and multilateral cooperation between the PIDF, and Australia and New Zealand, as the basis for a reconfigured Pacific regionalism.[35] By concluding its membership drive to include all PSIDS, and by working towards its corporate plan to achieve solidarity, the PIDF could also help to strengthen the voice of the PSIDS at the UN, where they currently operate without a collective mandate from Pacific leaders.

Reconfigured Pacific regionalism, supported by the growth of sub-regionalism and the emergence of the PIDF, could serve to deepen regional integration in the Pacific. However, to achieve this goal, regional integration initiatives must be creative, bold, and inclusive.[36] As benefits accrue from deeper regionalism, this could in turn encourage the Pacific island states to place the regional agenda above their national interests and nurture a stronger regional identity. In addition, stronger Pacific regionalism, along with close coordination between the PIDF and PSIDS at the UN, could help in raising the profile of the region and leverage its voice in global affairs. In this context, any new initiatives between the EU and the Pacific, in particular the PIDF, are likely to be supported with new vigour and greater strategic vision.

EU-Pacific relations will have to accommodate the reconfiguring of Pacific regionalism before the expiry of the Cotonou Agreement in 2020. This reconfiguration has already begun, and it is in the interest of both sides to accommodate and manage existing, as well as new, EDF programmes so as to avoid dislocation. The task should not be difficult—the Pacific ACP memberships of the new PIDF (excluding Australia and New Zealand) and those of the older PIF are one and the same. Consequently, the process of making the necessary adjustments to EDF programmes and projects, if any, for better fit and compliance, should be smooth, both administratively and politically, while helping to increase the benefits of regional integration for the Pacific ACP countries.

Beyond 2020, the PIDF could develop into a strong regional grouping with competence on a range of global issues, including fisheries, climate change, green economic growth, ocean management, seabed mining, migration, food and energy security, and related issues. However, the achievement of this vision will require strong leadership from Pacific leaders who have the foresight to take charge of their own future and the competence to articulate their positions on global issues of concern to the region, thereby capturing the attention of the international community. Even without the institutional framework of Cotonou, or a new post-2020 ACP-EU framework, reconfigured Pacific regionalism—with a focus on global issues to which the Pacific region is central—could provide a strong basis for EU-Pacific relations, and enjoy support from its constituents on both sides.[37] In this regard, the emergence of global challenges such as climate change—as much as any new energy and vision from changing political dynamics in the region—is likely to shape the future of Pacific regionalism and EU-Pacific ACP relations, and the benefits accruing from them.

EU-Pacific ACP Relations

Negotiations for a comprehensive economic partnership agreement between the European Union and the Pacific island states, as mandated by the Cotonou Agreement of 2000, have been characterised by a general malaise and lethargy that reflects the downside of relations between the EU and the Pacific ACP states. As discussed earlier, several factors have contributed to the situation, including, in particular, the neglect of constraints imposed by the fragmented geography of the Pacific and the weakness of development gains from four decades of ACP-EU cooperation, especially in the area of regional integration.

In the case of trade, the Lomé Conventions benefited only a few Pacific ACP countries, a majority of which had little to no trade with the EU. Fiji has been the sole beneficiary of the Sugar Protocol since 1975. Fiji, as well as other Melanesian Spearhead Group countries, also benefited from the duty-free and quota-free provision for originating agricultural products and from the derogation facility, under the rules of origin for fisheries.

Furthermore, development cooperation did not translate into the provision of effective regional services. In the late 1990s, a Pacific ACP-EU Bureau was established to manage the European Union's Regional Indicative Programme, but the responsibility was subsequently handed back to the PIF secretariat. Even so, the long-standing EU-Pacific ACP development cooperation project should not be abandoned; rather, a more constructive approach should be adopted, drawing on lessons from past and present experiences to craft the strategic future of the relationship.

From the outset, the ongoing negotiations for an economic partnership agreement between the EU and the Pacific states—as in the case of other regions in the ACP (see Akokpari, Carim, Katjavivi, Girvan and Montoute, and Gonzales in this volume)—have struggled, due to differences and lack of clear upfront agreement between the negotiating parties on how development should be conceptualised, approached, and framed. For example, Pacific ACP countries had proposed a separate stand-alone chapter on development, one that could be thorough in its treatment of the issues. The EU, on the other hand, sought for development to be integrated into the text of the agreement. The nub of the problem, however, lay in the lack of both clarity and consensus, from the outset, on a common understanding of development, and what it might entail. The Pacific states, for example, took development to mean having sufficient flexibility in the interpretation of special and differential treatment. The EU, meanwhile, has tended to be guided by the provisions of the World Trade Organisation (WTO). It is highly improbable that that there will be a convergence of views around the issue at this late stage in the EPA negotiations in the Pacific. By 2014, the EPA negotiations had not yet concluded, and commitment to bringing the negotiations on a comprehensive agreement to a close was wearing thin.

The inflexible attitude of the EU in the negotiations has been an additional complicating factor. Brussels has refused to deviate from WTO principles on issues such as special and differential treatment, but at the same time has insisted on negotiating measures—for example, restrictions on export subsidies—that go far beyond WTO requirements. This has been particularly problematic in the case of the Pacific: more than half of the Pacific ACP countries—eight out of 14—are not members of the WTO,[38] and "[o]verall, trade between the EU and the Pacific countries is very small both in absolute and in relative terms".[39] On the contrary, European negotiators have been averse to considering WTO-compatible measures that could advance the development of the Pacific ACP countries. For example, the WTO acknowledges the principle of special and differential treatment as a basis for deviations from its general provisions. However, the EU has been reluctant to apply the principle flexibly, or to frame it in a flexible or creative way that can benefit the Pacific ACP countries. A similar situation prevails in the Doha Round of trade negotiations, which started in 2001 and were yet to conclude at the time of writing. In this regard, the EU has shown selectivity in the multilateral principles it purports to uphold.

A key issue that could have advanced the Pacific's interests in the EPA negotiations related to the temporary movement of natural persons—known as Mode 4 under the General Agreement on Trade in Services (GATS)—and, more specifically, of semi-skilled and unskilled workers, from the Pacific. This could have yielded significant benefits for many Pacific ACP countries that are home to large numbers of underemployed and unemployed persons, who could gain from training opportunities abroad. Initially, the European Commission sought to jettison the issue entirely from the negotiations, claiming technical constraints and lack of WTO compatibility—Mode 4 under the WTO is restricted to treatment of skilled people only. However, it later emerged that the Commission did not have the mandate from EU member countries to negotiate on the matter. The Pacific ACP countries' attempt to lobby European countries on the matter proved futile. There was no appetite in the EU to engage in an issue that was likely to further complicate existing migration challenges in the EU (see Knoll in this volume). For the Pacific ACP countries, the issue was a missed opportunity to enhance their ownership of the overall EPA process.

Another issue on which the Pacific ACP countries could have advanced their interests more effectively was fisheries. The Pacific island countries have a comparative advantage in fisheries,[40] and favoured a regional fisheries agreement with the EU. Brussels initially approved a regional approach to the issue. Thus encouraged, the Pacific ACP countries were later let down when the EU reversed course and rejected a draft regional fisheries partnership agreement put forward by them early on in the negotiations, which had begun in 2004. Brussels opted instead to continue with a bilateral approach to the issue, in the form of its existing bilateral agreements with Kiribati, the Federated States of Micronesia, and the Solomon Islands. In essence, the regional approach that was supposed to underpin the entire EPA process, and that was to a large extent imposed on the ACP group of states by Brussels, was effectively discarded by the EU in favour of its own narrow sectoral interests. The EU could be expected to have the advantage in bilateral negotiations, given its strength in economic size and resources. Thus the EU opted to be divisive and to play the Pacific countries against one another, blithely casting aside a collective approach that Brussels itself had strongly insisted upon, for reasons of expediency.

Ironically, it is a fisheries-related issue—specifically, global sourcing rules of origin for fish—that is likely to scuttle the entire EPA process, and end any hope of concluding a comprehensive economic partnership agreement for the Pacific. In the interim EPA, signed by Fiji and Papua New Guinea in 2009, Brussels granted global sourcing rules of origin for processed (mostly canned) fish. The Pacific ACP countries, as a group, have since proposed to extend the global sourcing provision to chilled and frozen fillets and other fisheries products under the comprehensive EPA, negotiations for which were yet to conclude at the time of writing. The EU, however, has found it difficult to concede on the matter. As in the case of the issue of the temporary movement of semi-skilled and unskilled workers, the extension of global sourcing to more fisheries products could have a significant positive developmental impact in the Pacific ACP countries. However, the EU has found it equally difficult to acquiesce on the issue, due to objections from its own fisheries industry. Yet concessions by the EU on this matter may just be the key to taking the negotiations to their conclusion.

Other contentious issues on which the EU and the Pacific ACP states have diverged, seemingly irreconcilably, include export taxes, infant industry, and non-execution clauses. Disagreement in these areas has not been unique to the Pacific negotiations; EPA processes in Africa have faced the same problem (see Katjavivi in this volume). In the case of the Pacific, the prima facie solution seems simple—it entails getting the EU to accept the solutions and texts that have already been agreed in other regions and to offer the same to the Pacific ACP countries. Indeed, this was a guiding principle to which the negotiating parties had agreed at the all-ACP level back in 2002, before regional negotiations started. However, in 2014, it was still too early to say whether this would, in fact, be adopted as the way forward for the Pacific EPA negotiations.

While pessimism abounded upon the conclusion of a comprehensive economic partnership agreement in the Pacific by 2014, there are many global, non-trade issues—beyond the EPA—such as climate change, seabed mining, ocean health, and the environment, on which the future of EU-Pacific relations can be built.[41] In this respect, it is vital that the EPA negotiations are concluded expeditiously, to enable the EU and the Pacific ACP countries to address the issues of the future. Towards that end, other Pacific ACP countries can choose to join Fiji and Papua New Guinea in the interim EPA or to accept an alternative trading arrangement such as the Generalised System of Preferences (GSP), GSP+, or the Everything But Arms (EBA) initiative offered by the EU. This would be likely to be a very different conclusion to the EPA process compared to that in other ACP regions, for example the Caribbean, which concluded a comprehensive EPA in 2008 (see Girvan and Montoute, and Gonzales in this volume). However, opting for one of the alternative trading arrangements was an outcome that was anticipated from the outset of ACP-EU negotiations. The EU has promoted the interim EPA as the way forward for the region,[42] which may, in any case, bring a halt to negotiations for a (different) comprehensive economic partnership agreement. Once the protracted EPA process has concluded, EU-Pacific relations could then be reconfigured and re-energised based on a more visionary and forward-thinking blueprint for inter-regional cooperation.

The future of EU-Pacific relations should be informed by the lessons and experiences of the past, and translated into concrete action points. The world today faces challenges that will test global resources and human enterprise, but in an era of inter-dependence these problems will also tend to foster an imperative for collective action. The Pacific Ocean region has a critical role to play in ensuring global environmental sustainability.[43] It is also a strategically important region that has already drawn the attention of global powers, in particular China and the US. Against this backdrop, the EU-Pacific relationship must be built on a critical consideration of the changing global environment, with a keener focus on the raison d'être of their development cooperation. In this respect, it is possible that the way forward for EU-Pacific relations could be independent of the wider post-2020 ACP-EU framework, but at the same time inform the direction of that wider process (see Gomes in this volume).

Concluding Reflections

In 2016, the narrative of intra-Pacific regional integration remained one of unrealised potential. Similarly, the relationship between the EU and the Pacific ACP states is yet to achieve its desired objectives after four decades of formalised development cooperation. In this regard, policymakers and decision-makers—both in the EU and in the Pacific—have failed to address creatively and genuinely the challenges stemming from the geography, history, and socio-economic circumstances of the Pacific region. The smallness, remoteness, and limited resources of the Pacific island countries, as well as their lack of full integration into the global economy, have raised questions that, among other things, expose the inadequacy of mainstream economic thought, in particular the restrictions that it places on the use of subsidies as a development tool and on the use of trust funds as a potential means of funding for "special case" countries. Intra-Pacific integration will remain a distant dream unless there are major attitudinal changes in the way more developed and industrialised countries respond to the needs and aspirations of small island and vulnerable states.

This chapter has mapped out a number of potential ways for moving intra-Pacific regional integration and EU-Pacific ACP cooperation forward. While the prospects of Pacific regionalism are likely to depend on changing political dynamics in the region, the future of EU-Pacific relations is related to a broader search for global solutions to global problems such as climate change that will continue to challenge the world's collective resolve in the years ahead.

NOTES

1. Asian Development Bank (ADB) and Commonwealth Secretariat, *Toward a New Pacific Regionalism: An Asian Development Bank–Commonwealth Secretariat Joint Report to the Pacific Islands Forum Secretariat*, Pacific Studies Series (Manila: ADB, 2005), pp. 51–81.
2. ADB and Commonwealth Secretariat, *Toward a New Pacific Regionalism*, p. 52.
3. ADB and Commonwealth Secretariat, *Toward a New Pacific Regionalism*, p. 52.
4. Centre for Conflict Resolution (CCR), "Concept Paper for a Research Policy Seminar on the African, Caribbean, and Pacific [ACP] Group and the European Union [EU]", Cape Town, South Africa, October 2012, p. 8.
5. The Regional Indicative Programme (RIP) for Pacific ACP countries under the European Development Fund (EDF)—part and parcel of the wider EU-ACP development cooperation framework—provides support for regional integration.
6. *See* Lomé I Convention, Article 47, on financial and technical cooperation; and Protocol 2, Article 1, on the application of financial and technical cooperation. *See also* Lomé II Convention, Articles 92 and 133.

7. *See* Lomé III Convention, Title III: Industrial Development, Article 65; and Article 103 on regional cooperation.

8. *See* Lomé IV Convention, Title IX: Development of Services, Articles 114 and 117.

9. *See* Gérard Vernier, "The Lomé IV Mid-Term Review: Main Innovations", *ACP-EU Courier* no. 155 (January–February 1996), p. 13.

10. *See* Articles 1, 17, 29, 35, 37, and 67 of the Cotonou Agreement.

11. Pacific Plan Review, *Report to Pacific Leaders* (Suva, Fiji: Pacific Islands Forum Secretariat, 2013), p. 198.

12. The Smaller Island States (SIS) group comprises seven Forum Island Countries (FICs): the Cook Islands, the Federated States of Micronesia, Kiribati, Nauru, Niue, Palau, and Tuvalu.

13. For a discussion of the vulnerabilities and dependencies of the Pacific island countries, *see* Pacific Plan Review, *Report to Pacific Leaders*, pp. 214–219.

14. ADB and Commonwealth Secretariat, *Toward a New Pacific Regionalism*, p. 79.

15. The United Nations Economic and Social Commission for Asia and the Pacific (UNESCAP), in Resolution 68/1 of 2012, formally recognised the "special case" of the Pacific Small Island Developing States (PSIDS). *See* UNESCAP, *Green Economy in a Blue World: Pacific Perspectives 2012* (Suva: ESCAP Pacific Office, September 2012), p. 16.

16. United Nations (UN) General Assembly, Resolution 66/288, "The Future We Want", UN Doc. A/RES/66/288, adopted 27 July 2012, paras. 178–180.

17. The Pacific Islands Forum (PIF) comprises Australia, the Cook Islands, the Federated States of Micronesia, Fiji, Kiribati, Nauru, New Zealand, Niue, Palau, Papua New Guinea, the Republic of the Marshall Islands, Samoa, the Solomon Islands, Tonga, Tuvalu, and Vanuatu.

18. Technical Team, *Pacific Regional Transport Study*, June 2004, http://www.theprif.org/index.php/resources/document-library/41-pacific-regional-transport-study (accessed 19 June 2015).

19. Tony Hughes, *Strengthening Regional Management: A Review of the Architecture for Regional Cooperation in the Pacific*, August 2005, p. 9, n. 5; and direct communication with the author.

20. *See* What We Can Learn Project, *What We've Learned About Development in Pacific Island Countries*, vol. 2, symposium report, University of the South Pacific, Suva, 6–8 November 2012.

21. The 14 Forum Island Countries are: the Cook Islands, the Federated States of Micronesia, Fiji, Kiribati, Nauru, Niue, Palau, Papua New Guinea, the Republic of the Marshall Islands, Samoa, the Solomon Islands, Tonga, Tuvalu, and Vanuatu. The 14 FICs are also referred to as the Pacific ACP countries in the context of EU-Pacific relations.

22. 15th South Pacific Forum (SPF), Forum Communiqué, Funafuti, Tuvalu, 27–28 August 1984, section on regional trade, http://www.forumsec.org.fj/resources/uploads/attachments/documents/1984%20Communique-Funafuti%2027-28%20Aug.pdf (accessed 19 June 2015).

23. 16th SPF, Forum Communiqué, Rarotonga, Cook Islands, 5–6 August 1985, para. 33, http://www.forumsec.org.fj/resources/uploads/attachments/documents/1985%20Communique-Rarotonga%205-6%20Aug.pdf (accessed 19 June 2015).

24. 19th SPF, Forum Communiqué, Nuku'alofa, Tonga, 20–21 September 1988, para. 8, http://www.forumsec.org.fj/resources/uploads/attachments/documents/1988%20Communique-Tonga%2020-2%20Sept.pdf (accessed 19 June 2015).

25. *See* 43rd PIF, Forum Communiqué, Rarotonga, 28–30 August 2012, para. 35.

26. *See* 43rd PIF, Forum Communiqué, para. 36.

27. The Cook Islands, Samoa, and Niue, as well as Tonga to some extent, are aligned with New Zealand. Papua New Guinea and Nauru are strongly aligned with Australia. The Micronesian states—the Federated States of Micronesia, the Republic of the Marshall Islands, and Palau—have a compact agreement with the United States (US).

28. The Melanesian Spearhead Group (MSG) comprises four FICs: Papua New Guinea, Vanuatu, the Solomon Islands, and Fiji (joined in 1996). The MSG Trade Agreement came into force in September 1993 and has since been reviewed three times.

29. A "positive list" approach is generally preferred in the beginning of implementation, when trading is limited to a small number of goods that can all appear on a list of freely traded products. With growth in trade and in the volume and number of traded goods,

such a list can become too long. The switch is then made to a "negative list", which essentially indicates that any party to the agreement can trade freely in any goods and services except those that appear on the "negative list".

30. Pacific Institute of Public Policy (PiPP), "MSG: Trading on Political Capital and Melanesian Solidarity", Briefing Paper no. 2, July 2008, p. 2. Papua New Guinea's position has since changed. Since October 2012, the country has removed about 400 items from its "negative list" and opened up its markets. Only three items are left in its "negative list": mackerel, salt, and sugar.

31. The Polynesian Leaders Group (PLG) includes five FICs: the Cook Islands, Niue, Samoa, Tonga, and Tuvalu. Overseas territories in the PLG include: American Samoa, French Polynesia, and Tokelau.

32. Micronesia comprises the Federated States of Micronesia, the Republic of the Marshall Islands, and Palau.

33. *See for example* Michael O'Keefe, "PIF at a Crossroad: Setting a Course for 2014 and Beyond", *Island Business*, August 2012, http://www.islandsbusiness.com/2012/8/islands-forum/pif-at-a-crossroad (accessed 18 June 2015); Roman Grynberg, "Healing the Forum Divide: Apathy Towards Regional Body", *Island Business*, August 2012, http://www.islandsbusiness.com/2012/8/islands-forum/healing-the-forum-divide (accessed 18 June 2015); and Kaliopate Tavola, "Mighty Neighbours to East and West: Impact and Opportunities for Economic Growth", presentation, Club de Madrid Symposium, Papeete, Tahiti, 5–6 July 2012.

34. *See* Third Engaging with the Pacific Leaders Meeting, Nadi Communiqué, Nadi, Fiji, 23–24 August 2012, para. 27. The August 2012 meeting, under the theme "Strengthening Partnerships Amongst PSIDS", was attended by 11 FICs (the Cook Islands, the Federated States of Micronesia, Fiji, Kiribati, the Marshall Islands, Nauru, Papua New Guinea, the Solomon Islands, Tonga, Tuvalu, and Vanuatu), two overseas territories (New Caledonia and French Polynesia), and Timor-Leste. The meeting series was started by Fiji in 2010 after its expulsion from the PIF in 2009.

35. As the ADB and Commonwealth Secretariat noted in their 2005 report *Toward a New Pacific Regionalism*: "A final key lesson from economic theory is that for Pacific Regionalism to yield the necessary pool of benefits, Australia and New Zealand must become

meaningful partners in collective institutions with the Pacific countries" (p. 80).

36. A series of independent studies commissioned for the ADB-Commonwealth report identified 13 projects for deeper integration in the region: four aimed at improving "good governance" and nine at economic growth. *See* ADB and Commonwealth Secretariat, *Toward a New Pacific Regionalism*, pp. 83–146.

37. This could happen if the Pacific were to propose regionalising its efforts on non-trade issues of global concern, such as climate change. The benefits from such an initiative would likely accrue well beyond the region's borders and, as such, could elicit strong ownership and commitment from the FICs and beyond. Recent EU initiatives provide support for this proposition. The link between the European Consortium for Pacific Studies (ECOPAS) and the University of the South Pacific's Pacific Centre for Environment and Sustainable Development (PACE-SD), for example, has given rise to the European Society for Oceanists (ESfO), with all three bodies planning major conferences in 2015.

38. The World Trade Organisation (WTO) members among the Pacific ACP states are: Fiji, Papua New Guinea, Samoa, the Solomon Islands, Tonga, and Vanuatu.

39. European Commission, Directorate General for Trade, "Countries and Regions: Pacific", http://ec.europa.eu/trade/policy/countries-and-regions/regions/pacific (accessed 19 June 2015).

40. For example, in a televised panel discussion, hosted by the World Bank, on 23 September 2012, Biman Chand Prasad, a professor and senior economist at the University of the South Pacific, noted that fisheries could play a transformative role in the Pacific, while advocating "weightless exports" (referring to professional services in accountancy, law, engineering, design, editing, and the like, that can be delivered electronically). *See also* Biman Chand Prasad, "Why Fiji Is Not the 'Mauritius' of the Pacific? Lessons for Small Island Nations in the Pacific", Discussion Paper no. 23 (Canberra: Australian National University, Development Policy Centre, September 2012).

41. Email communication from PacTrade, an e-list on regional trade, in September 2012. According to the email, the World Bank's outgoing Pacific Island Countries director in Sydney, Ferid Bethaj, was reported to have said that more thought and money needed to

be put into developing regional integration in the Pacific; and expressed support for regional integration with larger markets to increase global competitiveness. In the subsequent group discussion via email, there was support for focusing regional integration efforts on environmental economics and cooperation, rather than on trade in commodity resources (an area in which the Forum Island Countries will always be disadvantaged). Without an accounting of environmental costs and benefits, the future of the FICs is likely to be unsustainable.

42. Martin Dihm, head of the EU delegation in Papua New Guinea (since 2010), repeatedly argued that the other Pacific ACP countries could conclude an EPA with the EU by signing on to the interim EPA that Brussels had already concluded with Fiji and Papua New Guinea. *See for example* "European Union Welcomes Progress in Pacific Trade Talks", *Pacific Islands News Association* (PINA), 18 October 2012, http://www.pina.com.fj/index.php?p=pacnews&m =read&o=1302742032507f54ce17c01d6e5915 (accessed 18 June 2015).

43. In its 2012 report *Green Economy in a Blue World*, UNESCAP underlined the role that the Pacific will play in ensuring an environmentally sustainable future for the planet: "The Pacific Ocean provides environmental, economic and social benefits to the global community. Thus, there is a need to support the stewardship role of the people of the Pacific through recognizing the unique challenges faced" (p. 4). Also: "Green economy tools and policies, in the context of a blue world, can address many of the structural issues at the heart of these problems—climate change, ocean acidification, vulnerability of islands, lack of capacity, lack of economic performance, and lack of development gains, [thus] helping to inform and advise Pacific nations as the curators of our largest natural global assets—the oceans on which human life itself depends" (p. iv).

PART III

ACP Experiences with the Economic Partnership Agreements

CHAPTER 6

The Economic Partnership Agreements: An African Perspective

Peter H. Katjavivi

Since the turn of the twenty-first century, the European Union (EU) has sought to expand and intensify its political, security, and economic relations with key emerging and developing economies such as China, India, and South Africa in the global South. In Africa, Brussels has also focused on strengthening ties with the African Union (AU) and Africa's regional economic communities (RECs), including the Southern African Development Community (SADC), the Economic Community of West African States (ECOWAS), and the East African Community (EAC).[1] Until the Cotonou Partnership Agreement of 2000, relations between the 28-member EU and the 79-member African, Caribbean, and Pacific (ACP) group of states were governed by the Lomé Conventions, the first of which was signed in 1975—the same year that the Georgetown Agreement brought the ACP group into existence (see Whiteman in this volume).[2] Against a backdrop of rising poverty in the African, Caribbean, and Pacific countries, there was a need to review the ACP-EU trade and aid relationship when Lomé IV expired in 2000.[3] As the European Commission's 1996 green paper on ACP-EU relations noted: "Per capita GDP [gross domestic product] in sub-Saharan Africa grew by an average of only 0.4 % a year between 1960 and 1992, compared with 2.3 % for

P.H. Katjavivi (✉)
National Assembly, Parliament of Namibia, Windhoek, Namibia

© The Author(s) 2017
A. Montoute, K. Virk (eds.), *The ACP Group and the EU Development Partnership*, DOI 10.1007/978-3-319-45492-4_6

developing countries as a whole."[4] The trade preferences granted under the Lomé framework had also become incompatible with the free trade rules of the World Trade Organisation (WTO), created in 1995, and added to the need for a reassessment.[5]

The Cotonou Agreement—signed in June 2000 for a 20-year period—placed greater emphasis on the liberalisation of trade relations between the ACP and the EU, and called for negotiations for economic partnership agreements (EPAs) with six (later seven) EPA regions in Africa, the Caribbean, and the Pacific. Negotiations for these agreements started in September 2002, and have since lain at the heart of the still evolving ACP-EU relationship. The ACP countries, by and large, have held the view that the main objective of the EPAs should be to support their socio-economic development;[6] and towards this end, stressed the importance of policy space and the need for development support measures to complement the agreements. The EU, meanwhile, has focused on trade liberalisation as the pathway to development and stressed the need for the partnership agreements to be compatible with the market-based rules of the WTO.[7]

The ACP countries initially had great expectations of the EPAs as tools for development in the African, Caribbean, and Pacific regions,[8] but the collective bargaining power of the group was lost with the decision to negotiate separate regional agreements. Furthermore, as South African analyst Brendan Vickers has noted, political and economic "asymmetries between the EU and ACP have had an impact on the final negotiated structure and content of the EPAs, which have broadly favoured Brussels' interests (although Southern African states have won some important concessions...)"[9] (see Carim in this volume). The experience has led some within the ACP to fear that the group itself will be weakened and sidelined by the time that the EPA processes are complete, though there are divergent views on the future of the ACP-EU relationship on both sides (see Gomes in this volume). The rise of new powers in the global South—particularly Brazil, Russia, India, China, and South Africa (the BRICS bloc)—and the EU's establishment of strategic partnerships with these emerging powers, have further fuelled uncertainty about the post-2020 prospects of the ACP-EU relationship (see Virk in this volume).

TAKING THE BROAD VIEW: AFRICA AND THE EPAS

In Africa, the EU is negotiating the Cotonou-mandated economic partnership agreements with five sub-regional formations: West Africa, Central Africa, Eastern and Southern Africa, the East African Community, and the

Southern African Development Community EPA group. In West Africa, the EPA negotiations were concluded in February 2014 and the text was initialled in June, with ECOWAS heads of state endorsing the agreement for signature in July the same year. Meanwhile, in Central Africa, only Cameroon has signed an interim EPA with the EU, with the provisional application of the agreement begun in August 2014. In the case of the Eastern and Southern Africa EPA region, by the end of January 2013 the EU had concluded and endorsed a provisional interim EPA with Mauritius, Seychelles, Zimbabwe, and Madagascar. Meanwhile, by October 2014, the EAC and the EU had ironed out differences over their economic partnership agreement and concluded negotiations for the EPA, with signature and ratification processes ongoing at the time of publication.[10] Negotiations for the SADC-EU economic partnership agreement were concluded in July 2014, and the EPA was signed in June 2016.

As this state-of-play indicates for African countries, there have continued to be a number of unresolved concerns about the EPAs with the EU. These concerns—many of them shared by the Caribbean and Pacific ACP countries[11] (see Girvan and Montoute, Gonzales, and Tavola in this volume)—have extended beyond the corridors of trade and finance ministries on the continent, with public protests taking place in some African countries (such as Senegal and Mali) as well as European countries (particularly Belgium and France). In this context, it is worth noting that major meetings—including, for example, the first ACP-EU meeting on the negotiation of EPAs in September 2002—have continued to be characterised by protests by green activists and environmentalists on various issues, including those raised by the EPAs.[12] Yet the EU has pressed hard, forcing the EPA processes forward to its timetable.

Trade Liberalisation and Development

There are important differences in the approaches taken by the ACP and the EU to economic partnership agreements. The ACP group has held the view that, in order to ensure economic growth and sustainable development in the African, Caribbean, and Pacific regions, negotiations for the EPAs should take a coherent and holistic approach, with all parties refraining from discussing trade without considering development at the same time. African countries, in particular, advocate that "institutional and administrative capacity at the national and regional levels needs to be built first before tackling [structural] reforms". The EU, on the other hand, prefers to "negotiate … trade in goods and services" and address "'behind the border measures' such as competition policy and public procurement" as a means to encourage such reforms.[13] The African perspective is based on an assessment that the resources of the European Development Fund (EDF) are insufficient to cover the expected costs of the major adjustments that trade liberalisation under the EPAs will entail in the ACP economies. According to Mikaela Gavas of the London-based Overseas Development Institute (ODI), there are three main critiques against the EDF in this regard: first, that the EDF focuses on middle-income countries at the expense of poor countries in greater need of structural reforms; second, that the EDF is inflexible in its procedures and therefore unable to adapt quickly to changing circumstances, not least of all because it is reviewed only once every six years; and third, that the EDF suffers from weak forecasting and slow disbursement of funds.[14]

African countries have also argued that the economic partnership agreements with the EU should help to provide greater favourable market access for their products into the European common market, and further that trade liberalisation should be curbed lest it facilitate a flood of EU goods into African markets, crippling local industries. These perspectives reflect a broad-based concern that Brussels is trying to promote European competitiveness at the expense of sustainable development in Africa through the EPAs.

The European Union's "Global Europe" strategy of 2005–2006 has added to this concern. The strategy identifies three main priority areas for the EU's trade policy: (1) opening of markets and stronger rules in "new" trade areas considered to be of economic importance, in particular services, intellectual property rights, investment, public procurement, and competition; (2) improving access to resources such as energy, metals, and primary raw materials, including certain agricultural materials, through the removal of developing-country restrictions on resource exports; and (3) reducing non-tariff barriers such as norms and standards, though lessening of tariff barriers also continues to be seen as important to the opening of markets to Europe's industrial and agricultural exports.[15]

In this regard, as British analyst Ronnie Hall has observed, the competitive threat posed by new and fast-growing emerging economies in the global South—such as China and India—has been a key driver of the EU's push towards greater liberalisation in its negotiations with the ACP countries. This has generated acute concern that the EPAs are being used by Brussels to achieve growth and create jobs in Europe, rather than to deliver development in Africa and the other ACP regions.[16] As Nigerian scholar Chukwuma Charles Soludo has argued:

As the old economic powers are largely broke, the emerging economies with cash are roaring. The BRIC [countries—Brazil, Russia, India, and China] are seen as the "new threats". The global economic landscape is unravelling and recoupling in such a manner that would likely alter the economic, military, and geopolitical power in the medium term. With this has [*sic*] emerged new pressures and demand for exhaustible natural resources and markets to sustain national security and prosperity. Since the major powers are no longer able to make use of the WTO as they wish to impose new rules on developing countries, they are now resorting to bilateral and regional policies and agreements to try and get their way.[17]

In this context, Africa, in particular, has once again emerged as a theatre of struggle between old and new powers. There is a perception that China's economic endeavours on the continent form an attempt to weaken the influence of the West in its former African colonies. This has yielded a tendency on the part of Western countries to treat every Chinese move in Africa with suspicion.[18] There is a common assumption that in this context, Europe needs to act quickly to re-establish or consolidate its control, presence, and influence in Africa.

Within the framework of the EPA negotiations, in 2007 the EU went so far as to suggest that African countries should offer the same favourable conditions to EU trading partners as they do to China and others. The most-favoured-nation (MFN) clause in the economic partnership agreements obliges ACP countries to extend to the EU, on a line-by-line basis, any treatment that they might negotiate with third parties. As Brazil argued at the WTO in 2008, this risks severely undermining the prospects of South-South trade by providing a disincentive for African, Caribbean, and Pacific countries to negotiate agreements with other developing countries—agreements that may contain more favourable market access conditions than those enjoyed by the EU under the EPAs. The provision could also "prevent" third-party countries from negotiating free trade agreements with the EPA parties.[19]

Access to Natural Resources

The EU's Raw Materials Initiative (RMI), in particular, has the potential to do significant harm to Africa's development.[20] The EU has strongly pushed ACP countries to open up access to their natural resources in the EPA negotiations through the RMI.

More than ever, Europe needs to import to export. Tackling restrictions on access to resources such as energy, metals and scrap, primary raw materials … must be a high priority. Measures taken by some of our biggest trading partners to restrict access to their supplies of these inputs are causing some EU industries major problems. Unless justified for security or environmental reasons, restrictions on access to resources should be removed … Energy will be a particularly high priority.[21]

As Ronnie Hall argues, Brussels's "Global Europe" policy and its RMI, taken together, are likely to compromise developing countries' sovereign rights over their own natural resources, even though "permanent sovereignty" is enshrined in numerous United Nations (UN) documents, including the UN International Covenant on Economic, Social, and Cultural Rights of 1966, and the Rio Declaration on Environment and Development of 1992. This is because the RMI undermines African countries' efforts to make value additions to their raw materials, a process that could create much-needed jobs on the continent and build stronger African economies. Hall further notes: "The EU is also determined to remove export restrictions that countries use to limit or prohibit exports of unprocessed raw materials … It views these export restrictions as an unfair impediment to its manufacturing industries, implying that Europe should have an equal right to exploit other nations' natural resources."[22] Yet, developing countries need to be able to enact policies that create stable jobs at home, and protect infant industries and services vital to the well-being of their own citizens.

An additional reason for African caution towards the development "solutions" presented by the partnership agreements lies in the multiple ongoing crises—food, energy, financial, and economic—that the world faces, and that starkly show the extent to which the dominant market-based model has failed to deliver development that is equitable and socially, environmentally, and economically sustainable. The EU's aggressive liberalisation strategy and its quest for raw materials—as pursued through the EPAs—ignore the potential "negative social and environmental consequences" of the agreements.[23]

Different Interpretations of the Development Component

According to German scholar Mareike Meyn: "While the ACP countries wanted to tie import liberalisation commitments to development aid, arguing that guaranteed access to long-term funds is crucial to overcoming supply-side constraints and diversifying the productive base of national economies, the European Commission insisted that EPA negotiations and talks on development finance were two separate issues."[24] Reflecting this separation, in 2007 the EPA negotiations were placed by the Commission under its Directorate-General for Trade, while funding for the implementation of EPAs—under the 10th European Development Fund (2007–2013)—was placed under the Directorate-General for Development. Yet African countries, in particular, have continued to feel that the EU funding is limited, given that Africa's own vision for its socio-economic transformation goes beyond trade development to also include infrastructure development, capacity-building, and regional integration. European funding for EPA implementation cannot help in achieving these broader objectives, given its singular emphasis on trade.[25] For ACP countries generally, "it was unacceptable to limit guaranteed funding to 2013, given that the implementation process would extend beyond this date, and that the full effects of major liberalisation and regulatory reform would only be felt thereafter".[26] The EU Commission's response, according to Meyn, was to note that "multilateral and bilateral funds would be made available for the implementation of the EPAs if and when needed".[27] However, even certain key actors within the EU itself, such as the European Parliament and the European Non-Governmental Organisation Confederation for Relief and Development (CONCORD), are not convinced by this assertion.[28]

Policy Space

The economic partnership agreements being promoted by the EU contain commitments that would not only circumscribe African countries' policy space for choosing their own strategies for development, but also limit their ability to respond to economic and financial crises with appropriate regulatory, structural, or macro-economic reforms. The EPAs, in other words, inappropriately lock-in particular economic policy and reform measures, and expose developing countries to risks derived from failures elsewhere in the international economic system, as shown by the global financial crisis of 2008–2009.[29] The EPA provisions on MFN status and rules of origin are the most contentious in this regard. In September 2013, Namibia's minister of trade and industry, Calle Schlettwein, gave an interview in which he captured African concerns on the impact of the EPAs on policy space: "We ... hope that there would be some flexibility on both sides to understand that we, as Namibia, would want to become an industrialised and prosperous nation. If our industrialisation is made more difficult through the erosion of policy space, then the prospects of signing would become small". He added, "If our needs to add value to raw materials and partake in the European market with finished goods in a competitive manner are included in the EPAs, that is a step in the right direction", while noting that "if it is the opposite, it makes things more difficult for us to partake in finished goods, and if we do not have the policy space to start developing finished goods, then it will be difficult to sign".[30]

"WTO Plus" Components

As Mareike Meyn has also argued, most ACP countries do not want to include services, investment, and trade-related aspects (such as competition and public procurement) in the EPA negotiations. In this regard, contrary to the EU's insistence, these countries would prefer to focus on trade facilitation and technical support, with the aim of improving access to higher-value segments of the EU market. There is a strong case to be made that in developing countries, government procurement is a very important part of the economy, and as such, should not be opened to external markets through liberalisation. A government's policy on purchasing goods and services can be a vital development tool for promoting indigenous economic growth. It is also essential for achieving affirmative action objectives such as women's empowerment and the balancing of tensions between vulnerable communities at the national level, or for promoting a green economy and improving employment prospects. Public procurement can be particularly useful as a fiscal stimulus. British scholar Stephen Woolcock notes that "across Africa government procurement averages around 10 % of GDP and can account for anything up to 70 % of public expenditure, as in the case of countries such as Tanzania and Uganda".[31]

Tax Regime

Under the rules of the WTO, least-developed countries (LDCs) are not required to reduce their tariffs; rather, they can decide whether or not to do so. The EPAs that African countries are negotiating with the EU, however, require at least 80 per cent of tariffs be eliminated with no introduction of new tax regimes.[32] Taxes help to meet revenue needs and also provide infant industry protection; therefore, it would be catastrophic for African countries to reduce tariffs without putting new tax regimes in place. For these countries this would also amount to a surrendering of their policy space. Africa is, in effect, being asked to comply with conditions more stringent than those that countries such as Brazil, China, and India are required to meet under WTO rules. The EU, through the EPAs, is thus forcing intrusive and destructive conditionality on African countries that it failed to secure at the WTO—measures that will prevent African governments from deploying the same kind of instruments that all industrialised countries have previously applied to build competitive national economies.[33]

Meanwhile the Everything But Arms (EBA) initiative, under which all imports (with the exception of arms and armaments) to the EU from least-developed countries are duty-free and quota-free, has been contentious. The EBA, which entered into force in March 2001, is part of the EU's Generalised System of Preferences (GSP) and one of the most generous forms of preferential treatment for LDCs globally. However, the rules of origin under the EBA do not fully account for global value chains, and inhibit those imports from LDCs for which all phases of production or value addition have not been fully understood.

Implications for Regional Integration in Africa

The potential impact of the EPAs on regional integration efforts on the continent has been a source of enormous concern throughout the negotiations for the agreements. By 2014, of the 20 African countries that had concluded interim or "stepping stone" agreements covering trade in goods with the EU,[34] only five did so on a regional basis. The fact that some states within a regional grouping have concluded an interim EPA, while others have not and preferred instead to export to the EU under the EBA or standard EU Generalised System of Preferences regime, has naturally become a source of potential tension among members, thereby threatening to undermine the regional integration processes that they are engaged in.[35]

Overlapping regional memberships have posed an additional challenge to African countries. As Nigerian scholar Aniekan Iboro Ukpe has noted: "[M]embership of the EPA negotiating groups is not the same as membership of the AU recognized RECs."[36] For example, six members of the Southern African Development Community—Madagascar, Malawi, Mauritius, Seychelles, Zambia, and Zimbabwe—form part of the Eastern and Southern Africa EPA region, although they normally negotiate in all other matters in international fora as part of SADC. Tanzania, meanwhile, is a member of both the East African Community and SADC, and has negotiated as part of the EAC EPA region (see Carim in this volume). In this regard, the EPAs have risked frustrating African regionalism, and have proven to be a stumbling rather than a building block to regional integration.

The damage being done to regional integration efforts in Africa through the EPA negotiations can be explained, in part, by the EU's neo-liberal agenda in the talks—in particular, its emphasis on removing barriers to trade rather than on creating conditions for advancing Africa's development.[37] It may be the case that larger regional markets can help to reduce economic and political risks and thereby attract greater investments. At a recent meeting of the SADC Parliamentary Forum held in Durban, South Africa, in July 2015, parliamentarians from Namibia, South Africa, and Zambia argued that based on the SADC region's experience of the EPA negotiations, it should in the future speak with a collective voice, rather than negotiate in separate camps, when dealing with issues related to regional development, including but not limited to trade.[38]

CONTENTIOUS PROVISIONS IN THE EPAS

There are difficulties in assessing the implications of the texts of the economic partnership agreements for different African ACP countries. While certain actionable provisions (for example, export bans and intra-regional quantitative restrictions) might not be problematic for some countries, this may not be the case for all countries in the same region. Export bans are a case in point. Used by several African countries (such as Botswana, Namibia, and Swaziland) in case of food emergencies, export bans were prohibited in all interim EPA texts except that of the East African Community. Similarly, intra-regional charges and duties—such as those used by the countries of the Southern African Customs Union (SACU)—were prohibited in the interim agreements, with the economic partnership agreements in Africa envisaging the free circulation of goods within their configurations. Yet, except in the case of the EAC, the EPA configurations do not mirror the memberships of existing joint customs regimes on the continent. This is problematic because it compromises Africa's ability to own its development agenda and policy space, and the continent's flexibility to make decisions that prioritise African concerns.

There may very well be several additional areas in which African ACP countries' existing arrangements and policies are in contradiction to EPA provisions, but of which these countries may not even be aware yet. The EPAs comprise a comprehensive set of commitments that apply not only to EU-ACP trade, but also to intra-regional ACP trade. As such, they are complex documents with far-reaching ramifications, many of which will only be fully understood over time. Civil society campaigners at a meeting of the African Trade Network (ATN)[39] in August 2008 argued, for example, that it was "most unwise and inappropriate for African governments to be entering into far-reaching, long-term, fixed, and highly questionable and contentious agreements with the EU", particularly in the context of the international energy and food crises that are affecting Africa.[40]

In this context, it is imperative that all EPA signatories in Africa undertake country-specific studies, in order to identify the possible implications for them of the agreements, and accordingly to accommodate these implications in the regional EPAs that are still to be finalised. The Caribbean experience is instructive. The Forum of the Caribbean Group of African, Caribbean, and Pacific States (CARIFORUM) undertook a set of studies, covering a wide range of issues, that sought to understand and thereby to ensure that the CARIFORUM-EU economic partnership agreement considered the development objectives, needs, and interests of the region (see Gonzales in this volume).

More generally, one could ask of the EPAs: Who benefits from the policy reforms envisaged by the agreements? If policy reform is to be undertaken, should this not happen within both the ACP countries and the EU? Consider, in particular, the EU's Common Agricultural Policy (CAP), which offers huge agricultural subsidies to European farmers at the expense of those in poorer countries. This means that European agricultural producers have a heavily subsidised comparative advantage and are able to sell cheaply on the international market. It also means that they have the potential to flood the African market with agricultural products at far reduced prices. African farmers are at a distinct disadvantage: without the benefit of similar subsidies, they must try to sell their produce at prices from which they can profit enough to ensure the continuity of their livelihoods. In addition, CAP subsidies have been perceived in Africa to infringe on food security, worsen poverty, and distort trade, and even to harm the environment.[41] (See Akokpari in this volume.) Similarly, the EU imposes tariffs and other restrictions on African imports, and grants preferential trade concessions to European countries that are richer than most

African countries, while asserting that if Africa does the same, it would be in violation of WTO rules.[42]

The EPAs were to have been negotiated by December 2007, when a temporary WTO waiver for the Lomé trade regime expired. However, the Caribbean was the only ACP region to have concluded its negotiations by then. The negotiations elsewhere in the ACP remained incomplete and mired in controversy. Because a total rejection of the EPA process would mean complete exclusion from the EU market, many African countries sought to endorse intermediate or interim EPAs that would allow them to continue trade with the EU while negotiating for a better deal in the final agreements. Each interim EPA was therefore shaped by the negotiating parties' immediate preferences and priorities. Dan Lui and Sanoussi Bilal of the European Centre for Development Policy Management (ECDPM)—an independent Maastricht-based think tank—outlined a selected list of contentious provisions in the interim EPAs, as identified in October 2008 by African Union ministers of trade and finance, and which have been a source of serious concern for many in the African sub-regions:[43]

- *"Substantially all trade" and transition periods for tariff liberalisation*: The World Trade Organisation has never defined "substantially all trade", as a result of which those negotiating the EPAs have had differing interpretations of what is required to comply with the provision. In addition, ACP countries argued for transition periods for tariff liberalisation, given their likely loss of revenue from the dismantling of tariffs and given that European producers would likely have an unfair comparative advantage over their counterparts in the ACP countries.
- *Standstill clauses*: These stipulate that no new tariffs may be introduced, that eliminated tariffs may not be re-imposed, and that existing tariffs may not be increased. This means that under the EPAs, tariffs would be bound at the applied rate. This is different from WTO rules, according to which applied tariff rates are often much lower than the rate at which they are bound. In addition, the standstill obligation is being applied differently in the various EPA regions. For example, in the CARIFORUM region, the SADC EPA region, and the Pacific, the obligation applies only to liberalised products, whereas in the other negotiating regions it applies to all products (including those not liberalised).
- *Export taxes*: The WTO does not prohibit the use of export taxes, although Article XI(1) of the General Agreement on Tariffs and

Trade (GATT) contains a general ban on the use of other forms of export restriction or prohibition. In the case of the EPAs, the European Commission has argued that the elimination of export taxes and restrictions is necessary to meet the GATT Article XXIV requirement for eliminating barriers on "substantially all trade", which covers export as well as import measures. It has also been argued that export taxes are counter-productive, and that ACP countries should take all other measures to increase their exports without undermining their tax regimes.

- *National treatment principle in goods*: This principle—both at the WTO and in the EPA texts—requires parties to treat imported goods no less favourably than goods produced domestically. The aim is to enable equal competition for imported and domestic goods, once within the borders of a country. ACP members of the WTO would hence be unlikely to take issue with the principle in the EPA negotiations; rather the concern has been that exceptions to the principle at the WTO—exceptions that provide flexibility for developing countries—have not been explicitly incorporated into the EPA texts.

- *Free circulation of goods and regional preference*: The clauses on free circulation of goods stipulate that EU goods are only to be taxed once upon entry into an ACP region, while the regional preference clauses specify that any advantage granted to the EU—be it in tariff reductions or in any other area covered—must also be granted to partners within the same region. The latter risks giving the EU (a third party) control over Africa's own regional cooperation and integration processes, and thus undermining their legitimacy and effectiveness.

- *Safeguards and infant-industry provisions*: There is some tension between traditional safeguards for infant industry, which are usually intended to deal with temporary import surges occurring as a result of liberalisation in a related area, and the principle of infant-industry protection, which is a policy choice aimed at protecting a particular local industry for a limited period of time to help it achieve a degree of competitiveness. The EPAs provide for infant-industry protection measures in several instances for temporary durations, while limiting the scope for flexibility in expanding their application.

- *Most-favoured-nation clause*: Once an EPA is in place, should any ACP country or grouping conclude a free trade agreement with another developed country, or any other non-EU country or grouping that is

a major trading economy,[44] then any more favourable treatment provided to the latter must also be extended to the EU. The same applies
in reverse. Notably, the MFN principle applies not only to tariffs, but
also to all measures covered by the chapter in which the MFN clause
is to be found. This has been a concern for ACP countries because
it essentially ensures that they cannot discriminate against the EU in
future agreements, while constraining their ability to pursue independent trade relations with major third countries (thereby infring-
ing on sovereignty). Not surprisingly, the inclusion of the clause has
led some ACP countries to question the EU's motives, given that the
provision seems to centre on EU rather than ACP interests.

- *Non-execution clause*: While economic sanctions are generally incompatible with the trade liberalisation provisions of GATT, economic
sanctions for gross human rights violations may be permitted in excep-
tional circumstances under the EPAs. Exception clauses in the EPAs
preserve the rights of the parties to apply economic sanctions in at least
as broad a range of circumstances as permitted under the WTO. It is
also worth noting that both the ACP and the EU acknowledge the
significance of human rights. However, there seem to be differences
between the two sides in their interpretations of what constitutes a
violation of human rights. (See Akokpari in this volume.)

- *Rules of origin*: These rules are intended to promote the "nationality of goods". This may be relatively simple to do in the case of
raw materials and commodities, but it is more difficult in the case
of goods that have been manufactured using inputs sourced from
more than one country, especially in the case of high-value products (for example, diamonds rings and bracelets made in Belgium
from rough diamonds exported from Namibia). A restrictive rule-
of-origin regime could effectively limit suppliers and investment to
the EU and ACP regions, whereas a relaxed regime could lead to
trans-shipment, whereby almost-finished goods are imported into an
ACP country before undergoing a minimal value-addition and being
exported to the EU as duty-free goods. ACP concerns about the
rule-of-origin regimes under the proposed EPAs include the over-
simplification of text by the EU, the administrative costs of complying with the rules, and the likelihood of a higher value-addition
threshold for EU goods than for ACP goods. Also, most ACP countries have limited capacity and knowledge to challenge the original
status of EU goods accurately.

Other areas of concern for the EU and one or more ACP countries have included administrative cooperation, general exceptions, security exceptions, tax exceptions, incorporation of international instruments, dispute settlement, institutional issues, and monitoring and compliance with objectives.

In May 2008, the EU's General Affairs and External Relations Council (GAERC) formally acknowledged the need for flexibility on these contentious issues:

> Acknowledging concerns expressed by ACP partners and the existence of, in some cases, problematic issues still outstanding in the negotiations, the Council underlines the need for a flexible approach while ensuring adequate progress, and calls on the Commission to use all WTO-compatible flexibility and asymmetry, in order to take account of different needs and levels of development of the ACP countries and regions. The Council emphasizes that ACP countries and regions that so wish could draw, if appropriate, on the provisions agreed by others in their EPA negotiations.[45]

In addition, various EU governments have individually provided a positive response to the need for flexibility, in cognisance of the needs and aspirations in various African countries and regions. Britain's Baroness Catherine Ashton, then EU Trade Commissioner (2008–2009), also made it clear that contentious issues could be re-negotiated in the process of moving towards the final EPAs, noting in February 2009: "All issues tabled during negotiations, contentious or otherwise, are open for discussion. That's why EU and ACP negotiators are regularly re-examining provisions in the interim agreements as well as exploring new areas, such as services, that were not included in the 2007 deals."[46]

Indeed, during Ashton's tenure, the EU acknowledged a need to be flexible. EU and ACP negotiators have since endeavoured to re-examine provisions in the interim agreements regularly and to explore new areas (such as services) that had not been previously included. A more cautious approach to compatibility with international trade rules and the Cotonou Agreement has ensured that, region by region, the EU and ACP have edged closer to full agreements. For example, Isabelle Ramdoo's comparison of the ECOWAS and SADC economic partnership agreements shows that both allow some policy space for African countries to protect their domestic economies in case imports from the EU threaten to destabilise their domestic industries and other sectors of the local economy (including agriculture). Furthermore, according to Ramdoo, the rules of origin in both the ECOWAS and SADC EPAs are quite flexible in that they not only allow countries within the group to cumulate among themselves, but also allow them to cumulate with other EPA signatory states.[47] (On the negotiations for the SADC EPA, see Carim in this volume.)

CONCLUDING REFLECTIONS

The economic partnership agreements between the ACP and the EU are intended to foster sustainable economic and social development in the ACP countries, while promoting their smooth and gradual integration into the world economy, through economic and trade cooperation with the EU that aims to address supply-side constraints, enhance production capacities, improve competitiveness, and attract investment.[48] However, the negotiations for the EPAs have generated disharmony and led to increased tensions between the parties.[49] Although the objectives of the EPAs are clear, the means for achieving them have been disputed by the two sides, making the negotiations difficult.[50] In this regard, EU and ACP positions have often diverged on technical issues as well as on matters of principle. The EU, in particular, has been criticised for adopting an overly aggressive stance, for trying to divide the ACP regions, and for presenting the EPAs as a *fait accompli*. Also, recent changes in the architecture of the European External Action Service (EEAS)—created in 2009—may subordinate the implementation of development cooperation to foreign and security policy interests.

Over the years, most African ACP countries have realised that while they may have achieved political independence, their battles for economic independence and development have yet to be won. There has been enormous dissatisfaction with the negotiations for the EPAs with Europe, which seem to fail to fully comprehend the impact of these agreements on broader issues (beyond trade) such as problems related to globalisation, climate change, sustainable development, and poverty alleviation.[51] Notably, other Africa-EU processes such as the Joint Africa-EU Strategy (JAES) of 2007 appear to have taken greater consideration of these issues than have the EPAs. (See Akokpari in this volume.)

The EU and the ACP need to engage in a joint effort to design mechanisms, strategies, and policies to make international trade policy more transparent and accountable in terms of their sustainable development objectives. For its part, the EU needs to ensure that there is consistency in its internal and external policies, as well as across its international commitments, when it comes to promoting sustainable development.[52] It could be argued that the EPAs, as they stand, are in direct conflict with the European Union's objective of promoting sustainable development and the Sustainable Development Goals (SDGs, which aim to eradicate poverty and hunger, while also supporting environmental sustainability). For their part, the ACP regions—drawing on the experiences of ECOWAS and SADC, as well as the Caribbean, in EPA negotiations—need to ensure that they are guided in their negotiations with the EU by the key concerns, needs, and priorities of their respective regions. In this context, the EU's trade agreements with African and other developing countries in the ACP regions should be subject to an independent development audit, and revised if necessary, as has been advocated by Dan Lui and Sanoussi Bilal, and Charles Soludo, among others.[53]

For the EPAs to garner greater support from African countries, they "need to be broadened through supportive policies that are covered by binding financial commitments", according to Mareike Meyn.[54] Meyn further recommends that investment in African countries needs to be facilitated by generous rules of origin, as well as technical support that can assist African countries to comply with EU standards and thereby take full advantage of duty-free and quota-free market access under the EPA regime.[55] South African scholar Eckart Naumann similarly suggests that if the EU is not comfortable with the quality of goods from the ACP, then the EU should accompany rules of origin with the technical expertise that can enable African, Caribbean, and Pacific countries to produce goods of the standard required by the EU.[56] In addition, discussions on trade in services, competition policies, and intellectual property rights should take place "in a flexible manner with no obligations beyond WTO rules, if they are found to be unacceptable by African governments".[57]

Civil society and analysts have also identified a number of lessons from the still ongoing EPA processes that are important to consider:

- Political will, interest, experience, and capacity are vital for negotiations at the regional and continental levels, given their complexity. To succeed in achieving their objectives, African countries need to have strong regional leadership, as well as champions at the national level, and to craft cohesive and focused regional agendas.[58]
- The relationship between the EPAs and existing regional integration processes—including their timing—warrants greater consideration.[59]
- The EPAs, as well as other free trade agreements, are not just about trade, but also have political aspects that require diplomacy.[60]
- The EPA processes thus far have been characterised by a credibility gap between rhetoric and genuine partnership.[61] They have also been marred by inflexibility.[62]

The EPAs are, first and foremost, a political subject (rather than a technical economic issue). The agreements will have consequences for the strategic relationship between the EU and the ACP that go far beyond the trade arena, and will also have strong repercussions for regional dynamics within the ACP, as well as for the ACP countries' relations with third parties. As the EPA processes continue, it is worth noting the potential, and necessity, for flexibility that exists on contentious issues. Beyond technicalities, both the ACP and the EU will need to demonstrate political will, leadership, and willingness to adapt, in order to shape a solid and more constructive relationship. In this context, the setting of seemingly arbitrary deadlines (first December 2007, then October 2014, and now October 2016)—as the EU has done—cannot be the only strategy. To a significant extent, the first two deadlines were not met because they were not owned by all stakeholders in the process.

Since October 2010, "in the light of the strong resistance from many ACP governments, the EU has slightly softened its position".[63] In June 2013, the European Council publicly stated that it would like to see issues other than trade in goods included in the EPAs, and further that it "fully respects the right of all ACP States and regions to determine the best policies for their development".[64] This indicates the potential that exists for transforming the interim EPAs into final agreements that cover not only trade in goods, but also a limited set of other mutually agreed issues such as export taxes, infant-industry protection, and bilateral safeguard mechanisms.[65]

Occasional concern has been expressed about a "strong decline in common interests and trust" in the EU-ACP trade relationship.[66] This, to some extent, only underlines the significance of broadening the partnership between the two parties to address common emerging challenges such as "climate change and environmental protection, the promotion of good political and economic governance, the fight against terrorism and organised crime and the management of global public goods".[67]

On the whole, the EPA negotiations in Africa have been tough; and for African countries (as well as others in the ACP), they have been all the more difficult given the EU's prominence in setting the agenda for the process. Although African countries have, within their respective negotiating groupings, persisted with their demands for economic partnership agreements that address their needs more effectively, the EU's strategic deal-making has opened fissures within the ACP grouping, which should serve as a lesson to the ACP to approach common problems with strategic unity. The ACP was built on solidarity among African, Caribbean, and Pacific countries, and this needs to continue to define the grouping's approach to common challenges if it is to remain relevant.

NOTES

1. Shada Islam, "The EU and Asia: Lessons for Africa?", in Adekeye Adebajo and Kaye Whiteman (eds.), *The EU and Africa: From Eurafrique to Afro-Europa* (Johannesburg: Wits University Press; and London: Hurst, 2012), p. 153.
2. In a national referendum, held in June 2016, Britain voted to leave the European Union (EU). Official negotiations were yet to begin at the time of writing, but as and when Britain leaves the Union, the membership of the EU will be reduced to 27.
3. European Commission, "Green Paper on Relations Between the European Union and the ACP Countries on the Eve of the 21st Century: Challenges and Options for a New Partnership", Brussels, 20 November 1996, pp. 22–24. *See also* Dieter Frisch, *The European Union's Development Policy: A Personal View of 50 Years of International Cooperation*, Policy Management Report no. 15 (Maastricht: European Centre for Development Policy Management [ECDPM], 2008), http://ecdpm.org/wp-content/uploads/2013/10/PMR-15-European-Union-Development--Policy-International-cooperation-2008.pdf (accessed 27 April 2015).
4. European Commission, "Green Paper", p. 22.
5. *See* European Commission, "Green Paper", pp. 20, 36, 46, 51, 58.
6. James Thuo Gathii, "The Cotonou Agreement and Economic Partnership Agreements", in Navi Pillay (ed.), *Realising the Right to Development: Cooperating for the Right to Development* (New York and Geneva: United Nations Office for the High Commissioner for Human Rights, 2013), p. 217.
7. Dan Lui and Sanoussi Bilal, "Contentious Issues in the Interim EPAs: Potential Flexibility in the Negotiations", Discussion Paper no. 89 (Maastricht: ECDPM, March 2009), p. 38, http://www.folkebevaegelsen.dk/IMG/pdf/ECDPM_Content_issues_EPAs.pdf (accessed 2 April 2009).
8. EcoNews, SEATINI, and Traidcraft, "Economic Partnership Agreements: Building or Shattering African Regional Integration?", Nairobi, Harare, and London, 2007, p. 41.

9. Brendan Vickers, "Between a Rock and a Hard Place: Small States in the EU-SADC EPA Negotiations", *The Round Table* 100, no. 413 (2011), p. 184.

10. *See* European Commission, "Overview of EPA Negotiations", updated October 2016, http://trade.ec.europa.eu/doclib/docs/2009/september/tradoc_144912.pdf (accessed 27 October 2016).

11. *See* Mario Negre, Niels Keijzer, Brecht Lein, and Nicola Tissi, "Towards Renewal or Oblivion? Prospects for Post-2020 Cooperation Between the European Union and the African, Caribbean, and Pacific Group", in Andrew Sherriff (ed.), *The European Union's International Cooperation: Recent Developments and Future Challenges*, Policy and Management Report no. 20 (Maastricht: ECDPM, 2014), p. 207. *See also* Rob de Vos, "Europe, Africa, and Aid: Towards a Genuine Partnership", pp. 105–120; Talitha Bertelsmann-Scott, "South Africa and the EU: Where Lies the Strategic Partnership?", pp. 121–135; Shada Islam, "The EU and Asia: Lessons for Africa?", pp. 153–167; Mareike Meyn, "An Anatomy of the Economic Partnership Agreements", pp. 197–216; Gilbert M. Khadiagala, "Africa and Europe: Ending a Dialogue of the Deaf?", pp. 217–235; and Charles Mutasa, "A Critique of the EU's Common Agricultural Policy", pp. 237–254, all in Adebajo and Whiteman, *The EU and Africa*.

12. Chukwuma Charles Soludo, "Berlin Again? How Europe Is Undermining African Development?" *New African* no. 516 (April 2012), https://groups.yahoo.com/neo/groups/NIgerianWorld Forum/conversations/messages/200700 (accessed 15 June 2015); Chukwuma Charles Soludo, "From Berlin to Brussels: Will Europe Underdevelop Africa Again?", *This Day Live*, 19 March 2012, http://www.thisdaylive.com/articles/from-berlin-to-brussels-will-europe-underdevelop-africa-again-/111757 (accessed 14 July 2015).

13. Meyn, "An Anatomy of the Economic Partnership Agreements", pp. 197–198.

14. Mikaela Gavas, "Reviewing the Evidence: How Well Does the European Development Fund Perform?" (London: Overseas Development Institute [ODI], 2012), p. 3.

15. European Commission, "Global Europe Competing in the World: A Contribution to the EU's Growth and Job Strategy", pp. 6–8, http://trade.ec.europa.eu/doclib/docs/2006/october/tradoc_130376.pdf (accessed 27 April 2015).

16. Ronnie Hall, *Undercutting Africa: Economic Partnership Agreements, Forests, and the European Union's Quest for Africa's Raw Materials* (London: Friends of the Earth, October 2008), pp. v, 9.
17. Soludo, "From Berlin to Brussels".
18. Richard Schiere, Leonce Ndikumana, and Peter Walkenhorst, *China and Africa: An Emerging Partnership for Development* (Tunis: African Development Bank Group, 2011), pp. iii, 1–11.
19. Caribbean Regional Negotiating Machinery (CRNM), "The Cariforum-EC Economic Partnership Agreement: Highlights on the Most-Favoured Nation (MFN) Clause in the EPA", Kingston, Jamaica, and Christ Church, Barbados, 2008, p. 1, http://www. google.com.na/url?sa=t&rct=j&q=&esrc=s&source=web&cd=3& ved=0CCgQFjACahUKEwjE2L7RipzHAhUGiw0KHdenCCc&ur l=http%3A%2F%2Fcafein-online.net%2Fdownload%2Fsummary_ documents_of_provisions_and_issues_of_the_epa%2FBrief_ Addressing_MFN_in_the_EPA_IU.pdf&ei=eVLHVYS4A4aWNtfP orgC&usg=AFQjCNH03bkDcNLFixhXHJK89nH8l5XBsw&bvm =bv.99804247,d.ZGU (accessed 14 July 2015).
20. Tobias Lambert, "The Impact of the European Union's Raw Materials Policies on Poor Countries and Emerging Markets" (Prague: Prague Global Policy Institute [Glopolis], 2011), pp. 14–15; Evert Vermeer Foundation, "The Raw Materials Initiative: The New Scramble for Africa?!", 2011, p. 2.
21. Quoted in Hall, *Undercutting Africa*, p. 9.
22. Hall, *Undercutting Africa*, p. v.
23. Hall, *Undercutting Africa*, p. 9.
24. Meyn, "An Anatomy of the Economic Partnership Agreements", p. 200.
25. European Parliament, "The Implementation of the Joint Africa Europe Strategy: Rebuilding Confidence and Commitments" (Brussels: Directorate-General for External Policies of the Union, Policy Department, 2014), pp. 22–23.
26. Meyn, "An Anatomy of the Economic Partnership Agreements", p. 200.
27. Meyn, "An Anatomy of the Economic Partnership Agreements", p. 200.
28. Meyn, "An Anatomy of the Economic Partnership Agreements", p. 200; European Non-Governmental Organisation Confederation for Relief and Development (CONCORD), "The European Parliament Agrees to Extend the Deadline for ACP Countries to

Conclude EPAs", Brussels, 2015, http://www.concordeurope. org/shaping-development-policy/external-relations/item/41-european-parliament-extend-epa-deadline (accessed 14 July 2015); Europe External Policy Advisors, "European Parliament Urges Caution on EPAs", November 2014, http://www.eurostep. org/wcm/archive-eurostep-weekly/504-european-parliament-urges-caution-on-epas.html (accessed 14 July 2015).

29. Christopher Stevens and Jane Kennan, "ACP Tariff Policy Space in EPAs: The Possibilities for ACP Countries to Exempt Products from Liberalisation Commitments Under Asymmetric EPAs" (London: Overseas Development Institute, 2007), pp. 3, 19–20; Calle Schlettwein, "An Update on the EPA Negotiations and Unilateral Measures Considered by the European Commission to Force the End of the Negotiations" (Windhoek: Namibian Ministry of Trade and Industry, 4 April 2013), pp. 3–7, http://www.namibiaembassy.be/pdf/EPA.pdf (accessed 14 July 2015).

30. Maggy Thomas, "Namibia's Fate on EPAs to Be Decided Soon", *The Namibian*, 23 September 2013, http://www.namibian.com. na/indexx.php?archive_id=114367&page_type=archive_story_ detail&page=1751 (accessed 1 September 2015).

31. Stephen Woolcock, "Public Procurement and the Economic Partnership Agreements: Assessing the Potential Impact on ACP Procurement Policies" (London: London School of Economics, 2008), pp. 2–3.

32. Lui and Bilal, "Contentious Issues in the Interim EPAs", pp. 10, 13–17.

33. Meyn, "An Anatomy of the Economic Partnership Agreements", pp. 215–216.

34. European Commission, "The EU's Common Agricultural Policy: Ensuring the EU's Development and Agricultural Policies Evolve Together" (Luxembourg: Publications Office of the European Union, 2015), http://ec.europa.eu/agriculture/developing-countries/cap/coherence-brochure-2015_en.pdf (accessed 10 August 2015).

35. *See for example* Aniekan Iboro Ukpe, "Will EPAs Foster the Integration of Africa into World Trade?", *Journal of African Law* 54, no. 2 (2010), p. 213.

36. Ukpe, "Will EPAs Foster the Integration of Africa into World Trade?", p. 216.

37. Stephen R. Hurt, "The EU-SADC Economic Partnership Agreement Negotiations: 'Locking in' the Neoliberal Development

Model in Southern Africa?", *Third World Quarterly* 33, no. 3 (2012), p. 499.

38. Personal communication; I attended the meeting.

39. The African Trade Network (ATN) is a major, long-standing network of African social, labour, women's, faith-based, developmental, environmental, farmer, human rights, and other organisations.

40. ATN Declaration, "Standing Firm and Acting Together Against EPAs!", 11th Annual Review and Strategy Meeting of the African Trade Network, Accra, Ghana, 25–28 August 2008, p. 3, http://apps.twnafrica.org/Blog/?c-africa%2-trade%20etwork7p=1 (accessed 28 April 2015).

41. Timothy Josling, *Strengthening the Global Economic System: Rethinking the Rules for Agricultural Subsidies* (Geneva: International Centre for Trade and Sustainable Development [ICTSD] and World Economic Forum, 2015), p. 3.

42. Ricardo Meléndez-Ortiz, Christophe Bellmann, and Jonathan Hepburn, "Agricultural Subsidies in the WTO Green Box: Ensuring Coherence with Sustainable Development Goals", Information Note no. 16 (Geneva: International Centre for Trade and Sustainable Development, September 2009), p. 1.

43. Lui and Bilal, "Contentious Issues in the Interim EPAs", pp. 2–37.

44. A "major trading economy" refers to any industrialised or developed country that accounts for more than 1 per cent of world merchandise exports, or any group of countries that collectively account for more than 1.5 per cent of such exports, in the year before the entry into force of the preferential trade agreement in question; *CARIFORUM-EU Economic Partnership Agreement*, art. 19, para. 4.

45. Council of the European Union, "Conclusions of the Council and Representatives of the Governments of the Member States Meeting Within the Council on Economic Partnership Agreements (EPAs)", 27 May 2008, para. 3, http://www.eu2008.si/si/News_and_Documents/Council_Conclusions/May/0526_GAERC-EPA.pdf (accessed 28 April 2015).

46. "Replace Controversy with Debate, Says Ashton: A TNI Exclusive Interview with Baroness Catherine Ashton", *Trade Negotiations Insights* 8, no. 1 (2 February 2009), http://www.ictsd.org/bridges-news/trade-negotiations-insights/news/replace-controversy-with-debate-says-ashton-a-tni (accessed 15 July 2015).

47. Isabelle Ramdoo, *ECOWAS and SADC Economic Partnership Agreements: A Comparative Analysis*, Discussion Paper no. 165 (Maastricht: ECDPM, September 2014), pp. 7–9, http://ecdpm. org/wp-content/uploads/ecowas-sadc-economic-partnership-agreement-dp-165-september-2014.pdf (accessed 14 July 2015).
48. Meyn, "An Anatomy of the Economic Partnership Agreements", pp. 197–198.
49. Hall, *Undercutting Africa*, p. 11; Lui and Bilal, "Contentious Issues in the Interim EPAs", p. 59.
50. ATN Declaration, "Standing Firm and Acting Together Against EPAs!", pp. 38–39.
51. Hall, *Undercutting Africa*, pp. iv–viii, 31–33.
52. *See for example* European NGO Confederation for Relief and Development, *Spotlight on EU Policy Coherence for Development: The Real Life Impact of EU Policies on the Poor*, Brussels, 2013, p. 11, http://www.concordeurope.org/publications/item/259-spotlight-on-eu-policy-coherence-for-development (accessed 28 April 2015).
53. Lui and Bilal, "Contentious Issues in the Interim EPAs", p. 39; Soludo, "Berlin Again?".
54. Meyn, "An Anatomy of the Economic Partnership Agreements", p. 216. *See also* African Union (AU), "Declaration on the Economic Partnership Agreements", Eighth Ordinary Session of the Conference of AU Ministers of Trade, Addis Ababa, Ethiopia, 21–25 October 2013, pp. 2–4, http://ti.au.int/en/documents/ declaration-economic-partnership-agreements-epas (accessed 14 July 2015); AU, "Report", EPA Negotiations Coordination Meeting, Arusha, Tanzania, 17–18 May 2012, pp. 5–12, http:// www.tralac.org/files/2012/05/Final-EPA-Report-Eng-May2012.pdf (accessed 14 July 2015); AU, "Kigali Declaration on the Economic Partnership Agreement Negotiations", Sixth Ordinary Session of the Conference of AU Ministers of Trade, Kigali, Rwanda, 29 October–2 November 2010, p. 3, http:// www.stopepa.de/img/AU_KIGALI_DECLARATION_ON_ EPAs_101102.pdf (accessed 17 September 2015).
55. Meyn, "An Anatomy of the Economic Partnership Agreements", p. 216.
56. Eckart Naumann, "Rules of Origin in EU-ACP Economic Partnership Agreements", Issue Paper no. 7 (Geneva: International Centre for Trade and Sustainable Development, Programme on EPAs and Regionalism, September 2010), pp. 5, 7, 16–17.

57. Meyn, "An Anatomy of the Economic Partnership Agreements", p. 216.

58. Lui and Bilal, "Contentious Issues in the Interim EPAs", p. 39; ATN Declaration, "Standing Firm and Acting Together Against EPAs!", pp. 1–4.

59. Lui and Bilal, "Contentious Issues in the Interim EPAs", p. 7.

60. AU, "Declaration on the Economic Partnership Agreements".

61. ATN Declaration, "Standing Firm and Acting Together Against EPAs!", pp. 1–4.

62. Lui and Bilal, "Contentious Issues in the Interim EPAs", p. 7.

63. Roberto Bendini, Marika Armanovica, and Willem De Goede, *Economic Partnership Agreements—EU-ACP: Facts and Key Issues*, updated extended edition (Luxembourg: European Parliament, Office for Promotion of Parliamentary Democracy, in cooperation with the Policy Department of DG EXPO [Directorate-General for External Policies], Spring 2012), p. 62, http://www.europarl. europa.eu/pdf/oppd/Page_8/EPAsSpring2012final.pdf (accessed 16 July 2015).

64. Council of the European Union, "2831st Council Meeting: General Affairs and External Relations—External Relations", press release, Brussels, 19–20 November 2007, p. 54, http://www.con-silium.europa.eu/uedocs/cms_data/docs/pressdata/en/gena/97190.pdf (accessed 15 June 2015).

65. Bendini, Armanovica, and De Goede, *Economic Partnership Agreements*", p. 59.

66. Geert Laporte, "What Future for the ACP and the Cotonou Agreement? Preparing for the Next Steps on the Debate", Briefing Note no. 34 (Maastricht: ECDPM, April 2012), p. 3, http:// ecdpm.org/wp-content/uploads/2013/10/BN-34-Future-ACP-and-Cotonou-Agreement-Preparing-debate-2012.pdf (accessed 28 April 2015).

67. James Mackie, Bruce Byiers, Sonia Niznikand, and Geert Laporte, *Global Changes, Emerging Players, and Evolving ACP-EU Relations: Towards a Common Agenda for Action?* Policy and Management Report no. 19 (Maastricht: ECDPM, 2011), p. x, http://ecdpm.org/wp-content/uploads/2013/10/PMR-19-Global-Changes-Emerging-Players-Evolving-ACP-EU-Relations-2011.pdf (accessed 28 April 2015).

CHAPTER 7

South Africa, the EU, and the SADC Group Economic Partnership Agreement: Through the Negotiating Lens

Xavier Carim[1]

South Africa has a wide-ranging relationship with the European Union (EU), which is the country's largest trade and investment partner. These ties are underpinned by the Trade, Development, and Cooperation Agreement (TDCA) of 1999, which also provides for cooperation between the two sides in the economic, political, social, and cultural fields.[2] Launched in 2007, the South Africa-EU strategic partnership further strengthened this engagement, raising it to the level of heads-of-state summits. Between 2008 and 2014, six South Africa-EU summits were held, with the final communiqués of each successive meeting highlighting the scope and depth of cooperation between Tshwane (Pretoria) and Brussels, which now extends to a range of global and regional issues including peace and

X. Carim (✉)
World Trade Organisation (WTO), Geneva, Switzerland

© The Author(s) 2017
A. Montoute, K. Virk (eds.), *The ACP Group and the EU Development Partnership*, DOI 10.1007/978-3-319-45492-4_7

161

security, socio-economic development, and climate change. South Africa's strategic importance for the EU lies in the country's key role in promoting peace, security, and economic development in Africa through its membership of the African Union (AU) and the Southern African Development Community (SADC); and its growing prominence in international affairs, as symbolised by its inclusion in the Group of 20 (G-20) major economies, as well as the emerging BRICS bloc (Brazil, Russia, India, China, and South Africa) (see Virk in this volume). South Africa is one of the EU's ten official strategic partners around the world, and the only African country in the cohort.[3]

Between 2005 and 2014, negotiations for an economic partnership agreement (EPA) between the EU and the SADC EPA group occupied centre stage in the still-evolving relationship between South Africa and the EU. This chapter provides an insider's assessment of South Africa's participation in these talks with the EU. It begins by situating South Africa's trade and investment relationship with the EU in the wider context of changes in the international economy over the past decade, particularly the rise of new economic powers, including China, India, and Brazil, as new sources of economic growth, trade, and investment opportunities,[4] as well as the emergence of African "lions" such as Nigeria, Angola, and Mozambique.[5] This discussion is followed by a brief history of post-apartheid South Africa's bilateral economic ties with the EU, and of the EPA process, highlighting the significance of South Africa's existing trade agreement with the EU for the SADC economic partnership agreement.

The chapter contrasts the different mandates and approaches of the European Commission and South Africa to the EPA negotiations. Following requests from both the EU in 2002 and the SADC EPA group in 2003, South Africa agreed to join the latter group and begin preparations for the negotiations in mid-2004. In broad terms, South Africa's objectives were two-fold: first, to strengthen regional integration by consolidating its international trade arrangements; and second, to improve the country's access to the EU single market. South Africa further argued that any final agreement with the EU should not unduly restrict its development or industrialisation policy space, nor impede its trade diversification efforts. The chapter details pivotal developments in the negotiations for the SADC EPA since 2005, identifies the key dynamics in this process from South Africa's perspective, and reflects briefly on the main challenges that the final agreement—concluded in July 2014 and signed in June 2016—may face during implementation.

I argue that, as for Africa as a whole, South Africa's economic relations with third parties, including the EU, must unambiguously serve the continent's regional integration agenda. These region-building efforts are critical for the structural transformation of African economies, which is necessary, in turn, to achieve sustainable growth and development on the continent over the long term. In the case of a legally binding agreement, such as the SADC EPA, it is essential to move beyond broad declaratory principles and statements, and to assess whether the individual technical and legal provisions of the agreement support Africa's policymaking space for regional integration and sustainable development. I further suggest that such an accord should provide enhanced asymmetrical market access in favour of the smaller economies in the arrangement. These considerations lay at the heart of South Africa's efforts to finalise an economic partnership agreement between the SADC EPA group and the EU.

THE SHIFTING SANDS OF THE GLOBAL ECONOMY

South Africa's trade and economic relationship with the EU has evolved against a background of profound changes in the global economy. The past decade has witnessed the rise of emerging economies within the global South, as well as a marked improvement in Africa's economic and development prospects, leading some to identify the continent as the next major source of global economic growth.[6] Sub-Saharan African economies were forecast by the International Monetary Fund (IMF) to grow by 6.1 per cent in 2014. In comparison, the growth prediction was 2.25 per cent for advanced economies and 5 per cent for emerging and developing economies.[7] Based on these IMF figures, some project that ten of the 20 countries with the highest compounded annual growth rate from 2013 through to 2017 will be from Africa.[8] The continent confronts enormous challenges, including widespread poverty, inadequate healthcare, climate-change-related environmental threats, high commodity export dependence, and under-developed infrastructure. Even so, its rich resource base, favourable demographics, and improved economic governance constitute significant advantages.[9] Africa is already the second-fastest growing continent in the world, and offers among the highest rates of return on investment in any region.[10]

These shifts in the international economy have been reflected in the changing pattern of South Africa's trade flows. While the EU, as a bloc, remains South Africa's main trading partner, its share of South Africa's total trade declined from about 44 per cent in the mid-1990s to 23 per cent in 2013. Starting from a low base, Brazil, India, and China's combined share of South Africa's overall trade meanwhile reached 20 per cent in 2013, with China emerging as the country's single largest bilateral trade partner, accounting for around 14 per cent of South Africa's total trade.[11] Furthermore, since 2009, the Southern African Development Community has grown rapidly in importance as a destination for South Africa's manufacturing exports: in 2013, SADC was South Africa's largest export market after the EU for value-added products.[12]

But the full economic potential of South Africa as well as Africa as a whole are likely to remain unfulfilled if the challenges posed by inadequate infrastructure, small and fragmented markets, and inadequate diversification of industrial output are not addressed.[13] To achieve sustainable growth and development, African countries must move away from an economic path driven by consumption and commodity exports and towards one based on industrial production, economic diversification, and cross-border infrastructure links that can expand intra-African trade. Region-building and regional integration thus lie at the core of Africa's long-term sustainable development agenda.[14] South Africa, in particular, has been active in pursing this agenda in the Southern African Customs Union (SACU) and SADC, as well as through the tripartite free trade area (FTA)—launched in 2011—between the Common Market for Eastern and Southern Africa (COMESA), the East African Community (EAC), and SADC, envisaged in turn as the basis for a continental FTA.

Therefore, in developing its relationship with the EU, South Africa had to consider how to strengthen and consolidate its economic ties with Europe, how to craft a negotiating strategy for the SADC economic partnership agreement that took into account the emerging dynamics in the global economy, and how to support its prioritisation of regional integration and economic development in Africa.

A Brief History of South Africa's Relations with the EU and ACP

Soon after the end of apartheid and South Africa's first democratic elections in 1994, the European Commission approached the South African government with an offer of economic cooperation to support the country's political transition. Following domestic and regional consultations, South Africa responded by requesting full membership in the Lomé Convention, between the EU and the African, Caribbean, and Pacific (ACP) group of states. South Africa reasoned that the arrangement would greatly enhance its access to its largest export market, while ensuring that its trade relations with the EU would be aligned with those of its neighbours. At the time, newly democratic South Africa—the dominant economic force in Southern Africa—was also embarking on efforts to restructure SACU and negotiate a free trade agreement in the sub-region, as apartheid-era dynamics gave way to a more cooperative agenda.

The EU, however, argued that South Africa, with its industrialised, diversified, and competitive economy, was not a typical ACP country, and offered Tshwane a separate free trade agreement instead of full membership in the Lomé Convention. Given that the EU was South Africa's main export market, and that without a preferential trade arrangement the country would remain at a competitive disadvantage vis-à-vis other exporters to the European single market, South Africa acceded to the EU's counter-offer. Importantly, South Africa later proposed that other SACU members should be included in its negotiations with Europe, but the EU rebuffed the idea. The European Commission noted that it had a separate mandate—the Lomé Convention—for engaging with the BLNS countries (Botswana, Lesotho, Namibia, and Swaziland) and, furthermore, that a new SACU agreement (eventually concluded in 2002) was still under negotiation.

In October 1999, South Africa signed the stand-alone Trade, Development, and Cooperation Agreement with the EU. Although Tshwane also joined the ACP, in 1998, its membership in the group is limited. South Africa can participate in ACP-EU political dialogues; the country's exports can partially cumulate with ACP exports to the EU; and its firms can tender for projects in the ACP. However, South Africa can only observe—rather than participate—in development cooperation between the two blocs.

COMPETING PERSPECTIVES: SOUTH AFRICA AND THE EU IN THE SADC EPA NEGOTIATIONS

The origins of the economic partnership agreements lie in the Cotonou Agreement of 2000, between the 79-member ACP group and the 28-member EU (see Whiteman in this volume).[15] More specifically, the EPAs emerged from an EU proposal to replace non-reciprocal trade with the ACP group with an alternative arrangement compatible with the more liberal, free-market prescriptions of the World Trade Organisation (WTO) by 2007, when a legal waiver by the WTO for a system of preferences in ACP-EU trade expired. Negotiations for the EPAs were launched in 2002, with the European Commission making a number of important policy commitments. In various communications, the Commission clearly indicated that no ACP country would be worse off following the EPA negotiations, and that the process would support regional integration and development in the ACP regions. The Commission further clarified that the EU had no mercantilist objectives in the ACP regions, and that the EPAs would provide a platform for enhanced development support for the group's member countries.[16]

Despite these declaratory statements, the actual EPA negotiations revealed concrete elements of a wider and different European trade strategy that was spelled out in the European Commission's 2006 policy document "Global Europe: Competing in the World—A Contribution to the EU's Growth and Jobs Strategy".[17] The strategy called for EU "activism in creating open markets" for European firms in the face of intensifying global competition, particularly from new and emerging economies. The document further clarified that the European Commission no longer considered tariffs as the main barrier to international trade. Rather, it targeted non-tariff measures that impeded access for EU firms, prioritising the opening of markets and drafting of rules in new areas such as services, investment, public procurement, intellectual property, and competition. This disjuncture between the European Commission's stated principles and its actual negotiation ambitions, which went beyond seeking WTO compatibility in the ACP-EU relationship, has since remained at the heart of difficulties faced by the EPA negotiating processes (see Akokpari, Girvan and Montoute, Katjavivi, and Tavola in this volume). By 2014, 12 years after the formal launch of EPA negotiations, the Forum of the Caribbean Group of ACP States (CARIFORUM) was the only regional arrangement to have signed a comprehensive economic partnership agreement with the EU (see Gonzales, and Girvan and Montoute in this volume). Meanwhile, in Africa, West Africa and the SADC EPA group did not conclude agreements until June and July 2014, respectively. Negotiations for a regional EPA between the East African Community and the EU were only concluded in October 2014. As of June 2016, the SADC EPA had been signed, with signature processes ongoing for the other two agreements.

South Africa's decision in 2004 to participate in the SADC EPA group was motivated by a desire to strengthen regional integration in

Southern Africa by consolidating the region's various trading arrangements with the EU. This included, in particular, its own TDCA with the EU, which was due for a mid-term review in 2005. Tshwane's participation in the EPA negotiations was also a response to requests from the ACP group, SADC, and the EU for South Africa to play an active role in the sub-regional process. When South Africa formally joined the ongoing sub-regional consultations on the proposed EPA in 2004, the ACP was divided. The ACP initially held the view that it should negotiate as a bloc with the EU for the EPAs. The EU, however, insisted on negotiating separately with the ACP regions, with further fragmentation in Africa, which has been sub-divided into five negotiating groups: West Africa, Central Africa, Eastern and Southern Africa, the East African Community, and the SADC EPA group. In the case of SADC, its 15 member states are split across four separate negotiating groups,[18] with the existence of South Africa's TDCA with the EU further complicating the process.

The SADC EPA Group Negotiating Framework

South Africa's agreement to join the EPA negotiations in 2004 was followed by an intense process of sub-regional consultations in Southern Africa. Tshwane, together with its Southern African partners, developed a negotiating framework and mandate for talks with the European Union, which was adopted by the SADC EPA group's trade ministers in February 2006.[19] Submitted to the European Commission a month later, this common negotiating position held that:

- First, South Africa's TDCA with the EU should be the basis for the EPA negotiations, so long as the talks also addressed the BLNS countries' concerns about the agreement, notably the impact of tariff liberalisation under the TDCA on sensitive sectors in these countries.
- Second, the three SADC EPA group members that were not part of SACU—Angola, Mozambique, and Tanzania[20]—should continue to receive duty-free and quota-free market access as least-developed countries (LDCs) under the EU's Everything But Arms (EBA) initiative, with the added aim of addressing EU rules of origin that restricted access to the EU market.
- Third, all SADC EPA group states should have duty-free market access to the EU, with the final outcome achieved over a long tran-

sitional period in recognition of Europe's sensitivities on agricultural issues. South Africa further indicated that it would not press the point at the expense of another member of the group.

- Fourth, all "new-generation" trade issues—services, investment, public procurement, intellectual property, competition, labour, and environment—should be subject to non-binding arrangements; and SADC EPA group countries should be allowed time to build their national capacity and to achieve regional convergence in the new areas. The group was willing, however, to consider entering into more concrete negotiations on these issues with the EU at a future but unspecified date.

The European Commission formally responded one year later, in March 2007, and with a negotiating mandate that showed clear areas of divergence from that of the SADC EPA group. While the Commission agreed that South Africa should be included in the EPA negotiations, it insisted that South Africa should continue to be differentiated from the rest of the Southern African sub-region. The European position held that while the TDCA should remain the benchmark for offers on tariffs from the BLNS countries, and that while the EU would consider addressing the sub-region's sensitivities about the TDCA, no new trade protection would be granted to South Africa. The European Commission further argued that the least-developed countries in the SADC EPA group had to offer reciprocal market access. The Commission also insisted that new-generation issues should be included in the final outcome of the EPA negotiations.[21]

The Interim Economic Partnership Agreement

The timing of the European Commission's response to the SADC EPA group's negotiating position left a mere nine months for the conclusion of an agreement between the two sides. With the WTO waiver for trade preferences under the Cotonou Agreement due to expire in December 2007, the short negotiating timeframe placed enormous pressure on the whole process. By August 2007, the Commission was forced to acknowledge that it would not be possible to conclude negotiations on a WTO-compatible agreement on merchandise trade as well as new-generation issues. This gave rise to the notion of an interim EPA: a narrow agreement on trade in goods, but one with a "built-in agenda" for negotiation on new-generation issues after the WTO-imposed deadline in 2007, towards a more comprehensive EPA.

Between March and December 2007, positions within the SADC EPA group also shifted. With the exception of Angola, the least-developed countries in the SADC EPA group agreed to grant the European Commission's demand for reciprocity. In addition, four members of the group—Botswana, Lesotho, Swaziland, and Mozambique—indicated their readiness to negotiate some, if not all, new-generation issues in the EPA.

During the final full negotiating session between the SADC EPA group and the European Commission, in November 2007, there were three sets of issues for South Africa. First, given Brussels's insistence on treating South Africa differently from the rest of the SADC group, Tshwane had to negotiate with the European Commission for a reciprocal exchange of tariff concessions; other members of the SADC EPA group had been offered duty-free and quota-free market access by the Commission.

Second, along with the other members of the SADC EPA group, South Africa had deep concerns about a number of European proposals for the legal provisions relating to national treatment, export taxes, customs administration, quantitative restrictions, infant-industry protection, definition of parties, and more favourable treatment. A number of the clauses, upon which the European Commission continued to insist, prohibited measures that were otherwise permissible under WTO rules. The definition of parties presumed a formal and legally based decision-making structure in the SADC EPA group that did not exist, while the more-favoured nation provision proposed by the Commission would have impeded South Africa's efforts to diversify its trade relations with other major economies, including the dynamic new and emerging economies of the global South.

Third, South Africa was also wary of the built-in agenda on new-generation issues in the interim EPA and was determined to avoid any wording that might legally bind the SADC EPA group to negotiate these issues at a pre-determined future date. However, as mentioned earlier, there were different positions within the SADC EPA group on the European proposal on services, investment, competition, and public procurement. South Africa, though, continued to maintain that a commitment to negotiating the new-generation issues would be likely to lead to new trade policy divisions in the Southern African sub-region, and give EU firms a competitive advantage in areas in which Southern Africa had not yet had an opportunity to build sub-regional markets and provide local firms the opportunity to emerge. Eventually, the European Commission relented, in part by agreeing to exclude Angola, Namibia, and South Africa from the commitment to negotiate new-generation issues.

Overall, the Commission was uncompromising in the final negotiating session in November 2007. Faced with the threat of losing their preferential market access to the EU market, some SADC EPA group members (including Botswana, Lesotho, Swaziland, and Mozambique) felt compelled to initial the interim EPA. South Africa, however, refused to initial it, having failed to reach an agreement with European negotiators on agricultural market access, despite progress on industrial and other tariffs. In the rush to have an arrangement in place before the WTO-imposed December 2007 deadline, the European Commission decided unilaterally to exclude South Africa from the interim EPA. Among other things, this meant that, if implemented by the rest of the group, the agreement with the EU would have applied only to the BLNS countries in SACU, and would have fractured the common external tariff of the world's oldest customs union. Different customs controls would have been required at South Africa's borders with the other SACU countries for the collection of tariffs on EU imports subject to lower tariffs, or different rules of origin, under the interim EPA than under the TDCA. To put it more bluntly, implementing the tariff commitments in the interim EPA (which excluded South Africa) would have led to the break-up of SACU.

More generally, South Africa remained concerned that the benefits of the EPAs would be marginal for ACP countries, while the adjustment costs would be disproportionately higher for them than for the EU. The European Commission had offered all ACP countries—except South Africa—duty-free and quote-free access to its common market for all products, except rice and sugar, which were subject to a transitional period.[22] While impressive in form, the substantive difference between duty- and quota-free access under EPAs, and existing access under the Cotonou Agreement, was marginal. In markets where ACP countries would obtain new access opportunities, their supply-side capacity remained highly constrained. For example, smaller economies in Southern Africa produce and export a narrow range of products to the EU (for instance, sugar, beef, grapes, and fish), beyond which improved market access to the European common market offers little or no benefit.

Moreover, with the ACP accounting for less than three per cent of the EU's total imports, the EU would bear only minor adjustment costs, while aiming to secure new openings for European exports of up to 80 per cent in the markets of the ACP.[23] In this regard, the European Commission's stance in the EPA process needed to be understood in the broader context of multilateral trade negotiations. In the WTO, the EU supported the position that the least-developed countries, and the small and vulnerable economies (SVEs), should make no, or minimal, market access commitments. This meant that while no other WTO member would obtain greater access to the ACP's markets through the multilateral trading system, the EU itself would secure vastly improved access to these markets via the EPA process.

In the end, the December 2007 negotiations pulled the SADC EPA group apart. Taking everything into account, South Africa, along with Angola, decided not to initial the interim EPA. Botswana, Lesotho, Mozambique, and Swaziland initialled the agreement. Namibia joined them in doing so, but issued a declaration that it had serious concerns with many of its provisions, which would have to be addressed before ratification.

Moving Beyond the Interim EPA

After the interim EPA was initialled by the BLNS countries and Mozambique in December 2007, attention turned to signature and ratification. South Africa, Namibia, and Angola continued to argue that all outstanding issues had to be fully addressed before they would consider signing the EPA. In this respect, South Africa's approach was aimed at creating the conditions necessary for the entire SADC EPA group to be able to participate in the final agreement, and for the establishment of a single sub-regional trade arrangement with the EU. The European Commission argued, however, that the initialled interim EPA could not be altered in any substantive way, and that signature was necessary to forestall a WTO challenge. Although the Commission indicated its willingness to consider some of South Africa's concerns during the negotiating process for a full EPA, South Africa held that the Commission's approach served only to strengthen the EU's negotiating leverage for securing the SADC group's participation in negotiations on new-generation issues and for demanding more extensive concessions.

Against the backdrop of a growing chorus of resistance to the EPAs from a number of African governments, as well as civil society groups in Africa and Europe, a somewhat more flexible and constructive approach emerged in the European Commission with the arrival of a new trade commissioner and a new chief negotiator in 2008. This fresh approach was evident at a negotiating session in Swakopmund, Namibia, in March 2009, where the SADC EPA group managed to get the Commission to address its concerns about five provisions in the interim EPA, covering infant-industry protection, free circulation, specific duties on exports, quantitative restrictions, and food security. At the same time, it was clear at the meeting that the EU remained intent on ensuring that those countries that had already initialled the interim EPA should move towards signing and ratifying the agreement. In July 2009, four of the five SADC group countries that had initialled the interim agreement in December 2007 now agreed to sign it; only Namibia held out. This signalled a deepening of divisions within the SADC EPA group.

However, as ratification was considered later in 2009, it became apparent that there were insurmountable practical difficulties to implementing the interim EPA in SACU without the participation of South Africa and Namibia. It was finally recognised by all sides that, if the interim EPA were pursued, a break-up of the customs union would be unavoidable. This realisation marked a critical turning point in intra-SADC group dynamics; and following an intense bout of sub-regional political consultations, there was a re-positioning of the group in its negotiations with the EU.

In a letter to the European Commission in March 2010, SADC EPA group trade ministers proposed moving beyond the divisive interim agreement and towards an inclusive final EPA based on an agenda that focused on: finalising market access negotiations (tariffs); addressing concerns about the legal text of the agreement; and concluding the ongoing services and investment negotiations with the relevant SADC group countries over a longer period. Going forward, this agenda formed the basis of the engagement between the European Commission and the SADC EPA group towards a final agreement, with some progress gradually made on each of the main issues and the only addition being the introduction in September 2011 of a potential bilateral agreement between South Africa and the EU on geographic indications. Otherwise, much of the focus after 2009 was on efforts to address the damage done to the EU's relationship with South Africa and Southern Africa at the time of the initialling and signing of the interim EPA.

An important breakthrough in the SADC EPA negotiations on new-generation issues occurred in November 2011, when both sides agreed that public procurement, intellectual property, and competition policy should be framed in non-binding, cooperative language without pre-judgement of future developments in these areas. Similarly, there was progress on resolving the SADC group's concerns about a number of legal provisions, notably the definition of parties, although others relating to export taxes, customs arrangements, bilateral safeguards, and agricultural safeguards remained outstanding in early 2014.

South Africa, along with the rest of the SADC EPA group, was deeply concerned by the European Commission's decision in mid-2012 to end duty-free and quota-free access to the EU market in October 2014 for those ACP countries that had not yet concluded their EPA negotiations. Within the SADC group, three countries—Botswana, Namibia, and Swaziland—would be affected, losing an important export market at a significant cost to their economies. The Commission's unilateral and arbitrary decision, in effect, set a deadline for finalising the SADC EPA, placing undue pressure on the negotiations.

SOUTH AFRICA AND THE FINAL EPA

Despite the long and tortuous negotiating process and the enormous challenges that confronted the SADC EPA group during it—including the threat to SACU—the group continued to engage the EU in an effort to identify and build on areas of agreement. This commitment paid off, with the SADC EPA negotiating process moving into its final phases between November 2013 and July 2014. The negotiations concluded on 15 July 2014, with agreement reached on a SADC-EU economic partnership agreement that—from a South African perspective—represents an improvement over the terms of the TDCA in several ways. The EU will continue to provide the rest of the SADC EPA group better access to its market than it offers South Africa. Nevertheless, compared with the TDCA, the SADC-EU economic partnership agreement will provide South Africa with improved market access to the EU, as well as more beneficial legal provisions governing its trade relations with Europe. The final agreement also preserves SACU's functional coherence, particularly with respect to maintaining the customs union's common external tariff.

For South Africa, improved access to the EU's single market was a necessary goal in the EPA negotiations. In the area of trade in agriculture, in particular, the EU generally had greater policy space than did South Africa (and SACU). At the end of the TDCA implementation period in 2012, the European Commission would have removed import duties on approximately 61 per cent of the EU's agricultural products from South Africa, while South Africa (and SACU) would have removed import duties on about 81 per cent of agricultural products from the EU. By 2010, 95 per cent of South Africa's and SACU's agricultural imports from the EU received duty-free and quota-free market access in SACU.[24] Furthermore, with the TDCA fully implemented, South Africa (and SACU) retained tariffs on only 112 agricultural lines, whereas the EU retained them on about 615 agricultural lines. South African exporters had also become increasingly concerned about new non-tariff barriers in the EU, particularly new environmental measures (public and private) and labelling standards.

While Tshwane had little to gain in terms of its industrial exports, scope remained to enhance its access to the European agricultural market, especially in agro-processing, which could provide vital support for South Africa's broader industrial policy and job creation objectives. Under the SADC economic partnership agreement, South Africa will have better market access for 32 agricultural products (including flowers, fruit, and fruit products), with a significant improvement in its duty-free access to the large EU market for wine (from 47 million litres to 110 million litres annually), sugar (from no access to 150,000 tonnes annually), and ethanol (from no access to 80,000 tonnes annually).

The EPA's rules of origin are similarly an improvement on the TDCA in that they provide for extensive cumulation, which will facilitate intra-regional trade and industrialisation across Southern and Eastern Africa in particular. The new rules also include a lower "one stage transformation" requirement, which should help in encouraging South African clothing exports to the EU.

Several other restrictive trade rules under the TDCA have been eased under the SADC economic partnership agreement. For example, the EPA provides a greater degree of policy space on export taxes. Under the TDCA, South Africa could impose no new duties on any product after 2000. In contrast, the EPA allows South Africa to impose export taxes on up to eight products at any one time for a period of 12 years, while allowing an exception for the EU for the first six years and imposing only 50 per cent of the tax on it for the subsequent six. In addition, the SADC EPA group was successful in obtaining an agreement from the EU on the elimination of export subsidies on agricultural goods destined for the SACU sub-region.

Similarly, while the standstill clause in the TDCA prohibited South Africa from raising any tariff on EU imports, the EPA allows Tshwane to increase tariffs on several products from the EU that are excluded from full liberalisation. On the whole, the EPA's provisions on safeguard measures to protect against import surges are more comprehensive and effective compared to those under the TDCA. For example, the EPA allows bilateral safeguards for all products subject to trade liberalisation, and covers agricultural products. There is no requirement to prove "injury", but only "disturbances" in the domestic sector, for the introduction of safeguards. Furthermore, a safeguard measure can be imposed for four years and renewed for another four. Notably, the SADC EPA group successfully negotiated for the inclusion of a special agricultural safeguard covering 23 products that can be automatically triggered if imports reach a specified threshold. This particular provision will stay in place for 12 years, and it is the first time that such a provision has been included in any of South Africa's trade agreements.

The SADC EPA furthermore does not establish binding rules in new-generation issue areas such as public procurement, competition policy, intellectual property protection, and sustainable development, but rather provides a basis for cooperation and dialogue on them between the two sides. For the EU, however, it was important to secure a bilateral protocol on geographical indications with South Africa during the course of the EPA negotiations. This protocol was, in essence, seen as "payment" for the improved market access that the EU offered South Africa under the EPA. Geographical indications are a form of trademark protection. Central to the bilateral protocol negotiated between the EU and South Africa is the rule that only products originating in a specific location, and having a quality or reputation that is attributable to this geographical origin, can use the place name to identify the product.

For its part, South Africa agreed to negotiate the protocol on geographical indications, based on its interest in protecting the names of the many South African wines that the country exports to the EU, and a growing interest in similarly protecting specialised South African agricultural products (for example, Karoo lamb). The protocol will not affect product names currently being used by producers in South Africa, and ensures that governments will not be held responsible for private-party transgressions. Notably, it establishes a mechanism to address non-tariff barriers that inhibit trade in wine. Under the protocol, the EU will receive protection for 251 names serving as geographical indications, covering 120 wines, five beers, 20 spirits, and 106 agricultural products (special meats, cheeses, olives, and the like). In return, South Africa will receive protection for 105 geographical indications, comprising 102 wines and three agricultural products (Rooibos, Honeybush, and Karoo lamb). The protocol also includes a provision that will allow another 30 South African names to be protected as geographical indications in the EU, once they are established and protected in South Africa.

The initialling of the SADC EPA by the respective chief negotiators on 15 July 2014, signalling the conclusion of the negotiating process, enabled the EU, in terms of its own internal rules, to initiate a procedure to extend tariff preferences to Botswana, Namibia, and Swaziland until such time that the EPA enters into force. By so doing, these countries averted the risk of losing their preferential market access to the European common market by the October 2014 deadline mentioned earlier. The EPA was signed by the EU and the SADC EPA group in June 2016, paving the way for ratification processes and for its provisional application.

Concluding Reflections

With the conclusion of the SADC EPA negotiations and the signing of the agreement, South Africa can be said to have met its core objectives in the process. The country has obtained significant and improved access to the EU for its agricultural exports, while SACU has managed to retain its functional coherence by preserving its common external tariff. In addition, the EPA contains a range of rules that are an improvement over South Africa's TDCA with Europe, and enables the BLNS countries to set aside many of the concerns that they had with the latter agreement. A key lesson from the EPA negotiations has been that the SADC EPA group countries were best able to obtain a positive outcome by forging and maintaining their unity. The group was at its most vulnerable when divisions opened up between its members, as notably occurred in the negotiations before 2008.

At the same time, the EPA negotiating outcome contains the potential for impacting negatively on Africa's future regional integration prospects. For example, the negotiations on services and investment between the European Commission and only some members of the SADC EPA group, if concluded, will likely create a new set of trade policy divisions within SADC and SACU. This potential for division should be a matter of concern for African countries in other regional groupings that are also negotiating new-generation issues with the EU.

Furthermore, the EU's different policy obligations among different EPA formations will make the search for common African positions on these matters more difficult. The five African EPA arrangements that have been, or are being, negotiated contain varying tariff commitments, phase-down periods, exclusions, and rules of origin, and differ across a range of provisions including those on export taxes and more-favoured-nation status. These variations in African countries' economic relations with, and obligations to, the European Union could pose formidable challenges for the continent's regional and sub-regional integration agendas, including the COMESA-EAC-SADC tripartite FTA and continental free trade area envisaged by the AU. Stronger customs management, for example, will be required to control trans-shipment of EU goods between the different EPA regional groupings. In short, the conclusion of EPAs by groupings that do not correspond to existing sub-regional trade and economic arrangements on the continent could complicate, if not undermine, Africa's wider region-building and regional integration efforts in the years to come. The issue will need dedicated attention.

NOTES

1. I was a senior official of South Africa's negotiating team during the Southern African Development Community's (SADC) negotiations for an economic partnership agreement with the European Union (EU). While the chapter draws on official positions adopted by South Africa, all opinions and judgements expressed here are mine alone and should not be ascribed to the South African government.
2. "Agreement on Trade, Development, and Cooperation Between the European Community and Its Member States, of the One Part, and the Republic of South Africa, of the Other Part", *Official Journal of the European Communities* L 311 (4 December 1999), pp. 3–297, http://www.dfa.gov.za/foreign/saeubilateral/docs/tdcaagreementtext.pdf (accessed 11 June 2014).
3. The other nine countries are Brazil, Canada, China, India, Japan, Mexico, Russia, South Korea, and the United States (US).
4. *See* Jim O'Neill, *Growth Map: Economic Opportunity in the BRICs and Beyond* (London: Penguin, 2011).
5. *See* Charles Roxburgh, Norbert Dörr, Acha Leke, Amine Tazi-Riffi, Arend van Wamelen, Susan Lund, Mutsa Chironga, Tarik

Alatovik, Charles Atkins, Nadia Terfous, and Till Zeino-Mahmalat, *Lions on the Move: The Progress and Potential of African Economies* (New York: McKinsey Global Institute, June 2010), http://www. mckinsey.com/insights/africa/lions_on_the_move (accessed 11 June 2014).

6. *See for example* Roxburgh et al., *Lions on the Move*.

7. International Monetary Fund (IMF), *World Economic Outlook: Hopes, Realities, Risks* (Washington, D.C., 2014), p. xv.

8. These include Côte d'Ivoire, the Democratic Republic of the Congo (DRC), Gambia, Ghana, Guinea, Libya, Mozambique, Rwanda, São Tomé and Príncipe, South Sudan, and Zambia. *See* Lucas Kawa, "The 20 Fastest Growing Economies in the World", *Business Insider*, 24 October 2012, http://www.businessinsider.com/worlds-fastest-economies-2012-10?op=1 (accessed 16 June 2015).

9. Ernst & Young, *Africa Attractiveness Survey 2013: Getting Down to Business*, p. 1, http://www.ey.com/ZA/en/Issues/Business-environment/Africa-Attractiveness-Survey (accessed 27 June 2013).

10. Ernst & Young, *Africa Attractiveness Survey 2014: Executing Growth*, pp. 1–6, http://www.ey.com/ZA/en/Issues/Business-environment/EY-africa-attractiveness-survey-2014 (accessed 16 June 2015).

11. Calculations based on data from South Africa's Department of Trade and Industry (DTI).

12. Calculations based on data from South Africa's DTI.

13. *See* United Nations Conference on Trade and Development (UNCTAD), *Economic Development in Africa Report: Strengthening Regional Economic Integration for Africa's Development* (Geneva, 2009).

14. South Africa's DTI, *South African Trade Policy and Strategy Framework* (Pretoria, 2010), p. 13.

15. In a national referendum, held in June 2016, Britain voted to leave the European Union. Official negotiations were yet to begin at the time of writing, but as and when Britain leaves the Union, the membership of the EU will be reduced to 27.

16. *See for example* Peter Mandelson, "The ACP-EU Relationship in the Global Economy", speech at the ACP-EU ministerial meeting Brussels, Belgium, 1 December 2004, http://trade.ec.europa.eu/doclib/docs/2005/january/tradoc_120436.pdf (accessed 27

June 2013); and also by Mandelson, "Statement to the Development Committee of the European Parliament", Brussels, 17 March 2005, http://trade.ec.europa.eu/doclib/docs/2005/march/tradoc_121920.pdf (accessed 27 June 2013).

17. European Union, "Global Europe: Competing in the World—A Contribution to the EU's Growth and Jobs Strategy", COM (2006) 567, communication from the Commission to the Council, the European Parliament, the European Economic and Social Committee, and the Committee of the Regions, 4 October 2006.

18. The 15-member Southern African Development Community has been split across at least four EPA negotiating regions. First, seven SADC states—Angola, Botswana, Lesotho, Mozambique, Namibia, South Africa, and Swaziland—compose the SADC EPA group, though Angola decided not to join the EPA at the end of the negotiations. Second, Tanzania has negotiated an EPA as a member of the East African Community (EAC). Third, four SADC states—Madagascar, Mauritius, Seychelles, and Zimbabwe—have concluded their EPA negotiations as members of the Eastern and Southern Africa (ESA) grouping. Fourth, at the time of writing, the DRC was expected to negotiate as part of the Central Africa grouping. Additionally, it was not clear whether two SADC states—Zambia and Malawi—would enter into an EPA with the EU.

19. SADC EPA Group, "SADC EPA Negotiating Framework", tabled to the European Community, 7 March 2006.

20. Tanzania was initially a member of the SADC EPA group, but subsequently left it to join the EAC negotiating group.

21. EU Council African, Caribbean, and Pacific (ACP) Working Party, "EPA Negotiations with SADC: EU Response to the SADC EPA Framework", Internal Working Document no. 16090/06, Annex 2, 2 February 2007.

22. European Commission, "EU-ACP Economic Partnership Agreements: Overview of Negotiations and Key Issues", Staff Working Paper no. 2, 16 February 2007, p. 3.

23. European Commission, "EU-ACP Economic Partnership Agreements".

24. Author calculations based on data from South Africa's DTI.

CHAPTER 8

The Caribbean-EU Economic Partnership Agreement: A Caribbean Perspective

Anthony Peter Gonzales

The economic partnership agreement (EPA) between the Forum of the Caribbean Group of African, Caribbean, and Pacific States (CARIFORUM) and the European Union (EU),[1] signed in October 2008, was the first such agreement to be negotiated and implemented between a region in the African, Caribbean and Pacific (ACP) group and the EU. The EPA was concluded in a context of concern and controversy among ACP countries about moving from a non-reciprocity-based trade regime to reciprocal, regionally negotiated, free trade agreements (FTAs) compatible with the rules of the World Trade Organisation (WTO), under the Cotonou Agreement of 2000. This chapter examines the impact and implementation of the CARIFORUM-EU EPA and focuses, in particular, on the issues and challenges that the Caribbean ACP countries have since faced in implementing the agreement. It also identifies lessons from this experience for African and Pacific ACP countries that are still in the process of negotiating or finalising their partnership agreements with the EU.

A.P. Gonzales (✉)
Institute of International Relations, The University of the West Indies (UWI), St Augustine, Trinidad and Tobago

© The Author(s) 2017
A. Montoute, K. Virk (eds.), *The ACP Group and the EU Development Partnership*, DOI 10.1007/978-3-319-45492-4_8

The Caribbean's Approach to the EPA

The CARIFORUM-EU economic partnership agreement seeks essentially to strengthen regional integration in the Caribbean, to facilitate development in the region, and to assist it in responding to the challenges of globalisation. The EPA is an asymmetrical free trade agreement, covering trade in both goods and services. It is also a relatively comprehensive agreement that addresses not only traditional trade policy areas (for example, rules of origin, anti-dumping and countervailing measures, and customs duties), but also new-generation trade-related issues such as competition, public procurement, intellectual property, investment, aspects of sustainable development (including environmental practices and labour standards), development cooperation, and regional integration.

From the outset, the CARIFORUM countries' approach to the EPA process was one of caution and scepticism. The challenge initially was how to negotiate a development-friendly and asymmetrical, but reciprocal, agreement that would yield net welfare benefits greater than those under the best available alternative, the EU's Generalised System of Preferences (GSP). The CARIFORUM countries (except the Dominican Republic) had not before entered into a free trade agreement with a developed country and, generally speaking, could not discern how small developing countries such as themselves could gain from free trade with larger developed European countries positioned at a much higher level of structural competitiveness. Historically, the Caribbean countries had argued for non-reciprocity in trade between developing and developed countries, and even between large and small developing countries. Moving from this traditional position towards a comprehensive economic partnership agreement with the EU was therefore a giant step, one that can only be explained by the asymmetric trade concessions, backed by relevant development cooperation, which the Caribbean obtained in the EPA.[2]

The Caribbean ACP countries' main objectives in the EPA negotiations centred on securing their existing preferences under the Cotonou Agreement of 2000, especially in key traditional export areas (such as sugar, bananas, rice, and rum); achieving full market access to previously uncovered areas for goods (for example, molasses and oranges); obtaining greater flexibility with respect to asymmetry and special and differential treatment; breaking new WTO-plus ground in service areas where the region had capacity, or could quickly develop the required capacity; and obtaining a higher level of development assistance for dealing with the liberalisation that would be demanded by the EPA framework and the WTO's free market-based rules.[3]

Impact of the CARIFORUM-EU EPA on Trade

Trade in Goods: Market Access

Preferential market access is a key component of the economic partnership agreement between CARIFORUM and the EU. Under the Cotonou Agreement, about 97 per cent of exports from the Caribbean Forum countries already enjoyed duty-free market access to the EU. As such, no major expansion in exports of Caribbean goods was expected under the new EPA. Comparison with Cotonou is nonetheless worthwhile, in order to assess the EPA's impact on the margins of CARIFORUM-EU goods trade for new CARIFORUM exports.

In terms of tariffs and other border taxes, the Cotonou Agreement did not cover at least 1,000 combined nomenclature[4] tariff lines out of 14,000 on which the most-favoured-nation (MFN) rate was payable. Furthermore, in the case of the Caribbean, these MFN duties only applied to a small number of traded items, mainly chemical elements and compounds, and a type of methanol. About another 1,200 tariff lines, mainly in agriculture, enjoyed special treatment under Cotonou. Some products (such as bananas and sugar) enjoyed duty-free access within quotas, while others (for example, molasses) benefited from reduced duties. Some were subject to tariff quotas, tariff ceilings or reference quantities, and specific provisions (for example, rice, flowers, oranges, and vegetables). In general, key products subject to these special conditions included essential oils, rum, organic chemicals, tobacco, fish, beer, sauces, cocoa beans, fruits, nuts, arrowroot, sweet potatoes, fresh vegetables, coffee, tea, and spices.

With the provisional application of the EPA in December 2008, all these items—except sugar and rice—had duty-free and quota-free access to the EU market. In the case of sugar and rice, there were short transition periods. CARIFORUM rice exports gained duty-free and quota-free access from 2010 onwards, while sugar exports remained subject to quotas until September 2009.

Furthermore, the EPA addresses non-tariff barriers, which have constituted a major obstacle for exports into the EU, and which were not addressed by the Cotonou Agreement. The economic partnership agreement also identifies the provision of assistance for compliance with technical

standards and sanitary and phyto-sanitary measures as a cooperation priority, while putting in place a monitoring mechanism for certification. These
measures should, in principle, serve as an incentive to export in sectors
where such EU standards had previously inhibited market access. New
provisions on customs and trade facilitation should similarly serve to boost
exports.

With respect to rules of origin, the EPA is not vastly different from
Cotonou, but for a few noteworthy changes that mainly affect the treatment of textiles, clothing, fish, fish products, and certain agricultural
products. These changes relate, among other things, to the definition of
the principle of "wholly obtained", and to the inclusion of a number of
alternative requirements, or derogations, from it. In the case of clothing,
for example, the revised rules reduce the local processing burden to a
"one stage transformation" requirement. This means that under the EPA,
garments can be made from any fabric—local or imported—while fabric
can be produced from imported yarn, whereas previously only the fibre
could be imported. In other words, CARIFORUM producers can now
meet their yarn requirements from any part of the world. With respect
to the fisheries sector, the main changes involve removal of the (local)
crew requirement for vessels, simplification of ownership, introduction
of a specific non-originating (fish) material allowance, changes to leasing
provisions, and expansion of the "wholly obtained" principle to include
maritime products.

Trade in Goods: Export Performance

Total exports from CARIFORUM (the Caribbean Community [CARICOM]
plus the Dominican Republic) to the EU grew by 19.9 per cent in 2013, but
then decreased by 13.8 per cent in 2014. The annual average growth rate
of exports from CARIFORUM to the EU was 1.3 per cent over the period
2010–2014, while the region's market share in the EU declined from 3.8 per
cent over the period 2004–2008 to 2.8 per cent for the period 2010–2014.[5]

Within the CARIFORUM region, the Dominican Republic's exports
to the EU expanded by 7 per cent on average for 2007–2013, against
an overall increase of 31 per cent in its total exports to the world. In
contrast, CARICOM exports to the EU declined by 23 per cent, even
as the Caribbean Community's overall exports to the world increased by
52 per cent over the same period (see Table 8.1).[6] Sugar, rice, bananas,

Table 8.1 CARIFORUM exports to the EU and the world, and EU imports from the world, 2007–2009 and 2011–2013

	Average for 2007–2009 ($ billions)	Average for 2011–2013 ($ billions)	Percentage Change
CARICOM exports to the EU	5.6	4.3	−22.7
CARICOM exports to the world	17.5	26.6	51.7
Dominican Republic exports to the EU	1.2	1.3	6.9
Dominican Republic exports to the world	5.3	7	30.8
EU imports from world	5466	5996	9.7

Source: International Trade Centre (ITC), Trade Map, http://www.trademap.org/Index.aspx (accessed 5 July 2015)

Note: Due to deficiencies in CARICOM data, only the annual average for two years for the periods here (2007 and 2009 in the first three-year period and 2012 and 2013 in the second three-year period) could be calculated

and rum are among the Caribbean ACP's key export commodities to the EU. Again, while the Dominican Republic recorded significant gains—measured in terms of the average value of exports—in bananas and sugar, CARICOM countries registered declines in the case of all four commodities (see Table 8.2). In general, the Dominican Republic's export performance was better than that of the CARICOM region with respect to several Caribbean products that received additional preferential treatment under the EPA, such as bananas, sugar, cocoa beans, and tobacco; footwear; cotton trousers; and certain fruits and vegetables. In the case of CARICOM, export expansion in such products was proportionately much less and limited to a handful of products, in particular cocoa beans, nutmeg, tuna, orange juice, and sauces.

The causes of poor export performance in the EU market vary widely from one CARICOM country to another and from product to product, and an in-depth discussion is beyond the scope of this chapter. In general, however, it appears that CARICOM has been losing ground to its competitors, who have been gaining equal and similar access to the EU market as a result of the erosion of ACP special preferences in that market.[7]

Table 8.2 Traditional CARICOM and Dominican Republic exports to the EU, 2007–2009 and 2011–2013

	CARICOM			Dominican Republic		
	Average for 2007–2009 ($ millions)	Average for 2011–2013 ($ millions)	Percentage Change	Average for 2007–2009 ($ millions)	Average for 2011–2013 ($ millions)	Percentage Change
Bananas	161.2	146.0	–9.4	219	388.7	77.5
Rice	77.2	42.1	–45.0	n/a	n/a	
Rum	241.3	54.4	–77.5	105	96.6	–7.9
Sugar	298.8	226.9	–24.1	0	14.8	

Source: International Trade Centre (ITC), Trade Map, http://www.trademap.org/Index.aspx (accessed 5 July 2015)

Note: Due to deficiencies in CARICOM data, only the annual average for two years for the periods here (2007 and 2009 in the first three-year period and 2012 and 2013 in the second three-year period) could be calculated.

Trade in Services

From a Caribbean perspective, the CARIFORUM-EU EPA seemed to provide an opportunity for increasing and diversifying the region's service exports to the EU, particularly in sectors such as tourism, entertainment, and professional, information, and maritime services with the capacity to expand, and in others such as business services, in which similar capacity could be developed in a relatively short period of time. Under the EPA, the EU's commitments to liberalise trade in services vary by method of delivery, and cover—similar to the WTO's General Agreement on Trade in Services (GATS)—four modes: cross-border supply, consumption abroad, commercial presence, and temporary movement of natural persons. The EU has undertaken to open market access in 94 per cent of the WTO-recognised W120 list of service sectors,[8] ranging widely from business, communication, and financial services, to construction, engineering, and transport, to tourism and recreation.[9] These provisions were to be applicable, once the provisional application of the EPA was begun in 2008, for all EU member states, with the following exceptions: for the ten European countries that joined the EU in 2004—Cyprus, the Czech Republic, Estonia, Hungary, Latvia, Lithuania, Malta, Poland, Slovakia, and Slovenia—the start date was 2011, and for Bulgaria and Romania, which joined in 2007, the start date was 2014.

Additional EPA provisions intended to stimulate CARIFORUM service providers include:

- National treatment, which provides for non-discrimination in treatment of CARIFORUM and EU suppliers for similar services in the EU.
- Mutual recognition, which provides for negotiations on an agreement for mutual recognition of professional requirements, qualifications, licences, and degrees, and, in this regard, for joint development of recommendations in four particular areas: accounting, architecture, engineering, and tourism.
- Elimination of non-discriminatory restrictions on the number of service providers or the operations of any service provider, which effectively abolishes quotas, monopolies, or any other quantitative restrictions except in certain sectors (for example, private operators in the health and social networks) where an economic needs test applies to assess the impact of new entrants on existing suppliers.
- Development cooperation, with support targeted at small service suppliers with a view to assisting them in overcoming their particular constraints.
- A cultural protocol, which provides for the movement of artists and cultural practitioners, collaboration in cultural activities (including audio-visual), and technical assistance to CARIFORUM states for the development of their cultural industries and policies.

Preparatory work for the implementation of the EPA provisions on trade in services has, however, been slow. For example, negotiations for mutual recognition in accounting, architecture, engineering, and tourism were due to start within three years of the EPA's coming into force. Yet the prospects for achieving this goal in the case of engineering and architecture remained distant in 2015, with considerable work still to be done due to the variation in regulations within both CARIFORUM and the EU. Several CARIFORUM countries also continue to lack the necessary regulatory schemes, with EPA progress contingent on their being put into place. In other cases, professional associations and registration bodies still need to be strengthened institutionally. In this regard, CARIFORUM first needs to develop a common regional approach to accreditation, legislation, and regulation in these professions before it can articulate a common negotiating position in relation to the EU. Since 2010, CARIFORUM has targeted an intra-regional mutual recognition agreement in architecture, and to this end consultations have since been held with various national bodies in the region.

The absence in these professions of a CARIFORUM body dealing with accreditation and regulation across the region as a whole has also been a major constraint in talks with the EU, with the latter preferring to negotiate with regional counterparts to its Architects' Council of Europe (ACE) and the European Network for the Accreditation of Engineering Education (ENAEE). On the EU side, a wide divergence in regulation at the national level similarly poses a challenge, though some attempts have been made to harmonise regulations in education, internships, regulated professional practice, compulsory registration, compulsory insurance, and codes of ethics, in order to facilitate the movement of professionals.

More generally, CARIFORUM service providers need to develop a better understanding of the EU's market requirements and to develop more contacts in Europe, in order to exploit the new market access opportunities offered by the EPA. Meanwhile, the absence of change in the EU's labour and immigration regulations, so as to accommodate Caribbean service suppliers and independent professionals, has been a concern. EU member states that have ratified the EPA have not yet begun implementing their commitments to the temporary movement of people under the EPA. As a result, regional service suppliers from the Caribbean have not been able to obtain work or residence permits for entry into the EU. The reasons for the situation are unclear, and the matter requires resolution through the joint institutions that have been created under the EPA.

According to EU data, CARIFORUM service exports to the EU were €4.8 billion both in 2011 and in 2012, up from €4.3 billion in 2010.[10] The impact of the CARIFORUM-EU EPA on the performance of trade in services is difficult to ascertain, and an in-depth evaluation is beyond the scope of this chapter. As a five-year review of the EPA—completed for the European Commission in September 2014—noted, services data have inherent limitations.[11] Based on data from the United Nations Conference on Trade and Development (UNCTAD), the review showed that CARIFORUM exports to the world in nearly all categories declined from 2008 to 2010, as a result of the global financial crisis of 2008–2009; and, furthermore, that certain sectors (for example, travel) had not yet recovered from the impact of the crisis.[12] At the same time, gains continued to be recorded in some travel-related areas, such as personal or cultural services, and in royalty or licence fees, while transport services remained relatively stable. Also, the tourism sector, in particular, was neg-atively affected not only by the global economic downturn, but also by specific measures (such as the air-passenger duty levied by Britain).[13] In the case of investment, the 2014 review noted that in most countries, stakeholders could not provide concrete examples of EU investment after the provisional application of the EPA.[14] The Dominican Republic was an exception, with an observed increase in EU investment, acquisition, and consolidation in certain key industries, including financial services, retail (in particular, supermarkets), beverages (in particular, beer and rum), tourism, telecommunications, and ports. However, in several cases, the investments were in the pipeline prior to the EPA's application.[15]

THE CARIFORUM-EU EPA AND DEVELOPMENT COOPERATION

From the outset, CARIFORUM argued strongly for development assis-tance to support the implementation of the EPA, particularly in the areas of private sector development, competitiveness, capacity-building in regu-lation and compliance, and trade development. More specifically, and in terms of EPA issue-areas, CARIFORUM sought development coopera-tion and assistance to help the region to comply with its immediate com-mitments in areas including public procurement, competition, intellectual property, technical barriers to trade, sanitary and phyto-sanitary measures, and trade facilitation, as well as in the removal of supply-side constraints.

In November 2004, a Regional Preparatory Task Force was created with the aim of coordinating the link between EPA negotiations and devel-opment cooperation. As part of this mandate, the task force undertook a comprehensive set of studies in order to understand the Caribbean's needs better and to translate the final EPA provisions on development coopera-tion into concrete and actionable sectoral programmes—the idea being that this would place the region in a better position to implement its obli-gations under the EPA. The role of the task force was subsequently taken over by the EPA's Joint Trade and Development Committee with the start of the provisional application of the agreement in December 2008.

Two issues have been central in the Caribbean debate on develop-ment cooperation for EPA implementation and adjustment: the adequacy and additionality of European Development Fund (EDF) resources. Additionality, in this case, refers to the incorporation of liberalisation efforts, required under the EPA, into the level of development assistance to be provided under the tenth EDF (2008–2013). The aim, in this regard, was to avoid compromising or diminishing the non-EPA-related assistance provided by the EDF in areas such as health, education, and infrastructure. In other words, the assistance normally provided under Cotonou needed to be supplemented with additional EDF resources to deal with the implementation and adjustment costs of the EPA.

At the same time, it was widely acknowledged that the CARIFORUM countries could not be too strident in their demands, given their middle-income status (with the exception of Haiti). In addition, due to various reasons, including the accumulation of EDF grant sums, the Caribbean's regional allocation under the tenth EDF had more than doubled, and an additional allocation of 25 per cent was made to it in July 2007. Some countries, such as Jamaica, were already using their tenth-EDF national allocations to support EPA-related activities. Several middle-income CARIFORUM countries (for example, Barbados) had, furthermore, been graduated by international lending agencies and were expected to obtain development finance on market or near-market terms from, among others, the European Investment Bank.

CARIFORUM adopted the position that the additional funding demand could be reasonably filled with some increase in the EDF, along with additional funding from the Aid for Trade budgets of the EU and its member states; from the EDF's all-ACP facility; and directly from the general budget of the European Commission. Obtaining resources from other donors also remained a possibility. In a joint declaration on develop-ment cooperation—annexed to the CARIFORUM-EU economic part-nership agreement of 2008—EU member states agreed to ensure that an equitable share of their Aid for Trade commitments would benefit the Caribbean countries, including through the funding of programmes related to the implementation of the EPA. (See Girvan and Montoute in this volume.) In the same declaration, both sides also agreed on the ben-efits of regional development mechanisms, and agreed to consider ways of supporting a regional development fund that could mobilise and channel resources for EPA-related projects from various sources.

Sources of Financing

In general, there are four sources of EU funding available to support Caribbean states in the implementation of the EPA[16]: (1) the National Indicative Programmes (NIPs), (2) the Caribbean Regional Indicative

Programme (CRIP), and (3) the all-ACP facility, all three of which form part of the EDF—the main instrument for development cooperation between the EU and the ACP group of countries; and (4) the Aid for Trade programmes of the European Commission and individual member states.

Under the tenth EDF (2008–2013),[17] according to the European Commission, 12 out of 15 CARIFORUM countries were using the opportunity offered by the fund's national programmes to prepare for the challenges of EPA implementation. This represented a total of €454 million, and 75 per cent of the total national allocations of €600 million.[18]

The CRIP, meanwhile, began providing funding for EPA implementation and adjustment under the ninth EDF (2000–2007). It covered the CARIFORUM-EU EPA preparatory period and concentrated on the priority areas of trade and regional integration. Of the total of €57 million in the regional allocation, approximately 90 per cent of the commitments were linked to trade and integration, including funds for the conduct of EPA negotiations and studies.[19] Then, under the tenth EDF, CARIFORUM countries sought to allocate 30 per cent of the CRIP towards EPA implementation. With the additional allocation of 25 per cent to the original tenth-EDF amount of €132 million, this meant that approximately €73 million (of €165 million) was targeted at EPA implementation as part of the regional programme. The all-ACP facility—about €2.7 billion under the tenth EDF and about €3.6 billion under the eleventh (2014–2020)—represents an additional source of EPA implementation support, particularly with regard to trade-related adjustment and competitiveness. The EU's Aid for Trade programmes are another source of financing for EPA-related costs. In its attempt to increase this funding to €2 billion annually by 2010, the EU committed itself to allocating around 50 per cent of the increase to meet ACP needs.[20]

Challenges of Financing

A major challenge in assessing additionality stems from the difficulty of estimating what amount the tenth EDF would have been in the absence of an economic partnership agreement. To illustrate, the CRIP increased from €57 million under the ninth EDF to €165 million under the tenth. Total allocation for the Caribbean—comprising the regional and national programmes—increased by 109 per cent, from €353.8 million under the ninth EDF to €738.1 million under the tenth. However, it could be argued that the increase merely restored the real value of the eighth EDF (1995–2000), which had seen the CRIP reduced to €90 million from €105 million under the seventh EDF (1990–1995). Following from this, if one assumes that the normal CRIP would have been €132 million under the tenth EDF, then the additionality amounts to €33 million. The question that this would then raise would be whether this additional amount was adequate to safeguard CARIFORUM countries' non-EPA-related development efforts under the indicative programmes against the diversion of funds for EPA implementation and related adjustment.

In September 2006, CARIFORUM initially elaborated on and later developed an implementation programme covering the ninth, tenth, and eleventh EDF periods. This programme focused on developing the Caribbean's institutional capability to honour its EPA commitments, in particular the establishment and operation of EPA implementation units, the operationalisation of a regional development fund, and elaboration of a regional strategy that prioritised the region's needs in relation to the EPA. It also focused on the design and implementation of programmes in several key areas, ranging from fiscal adjustment and customs and trade facilitation, to sanitary and phyto-sanitary measures for fisheries' access to the EU market, to intellectual property and protection of personal data.

Under the tenth EDF, direct support for EPA implementation was allocated, and distributed on a priority basis, in seven key sectors: (1) fiscal reform and adjustment, €4 million; (2) statistics in the Dominican Republic, €0.5 million; (3) sanitary and phyto-sanitary measures, €11.7 million; (4) technical barriers to trade, €7.7 million; (5) services sector, €3.2 million; (6) rum sector, €7.7 million; and (7) institutional support and capacity-building, €10.8 million.[21] Programmes relating to EPA adjustment in areas such as innovation, competitiveness, electronic commerce, investment and business facilitation, and investment promotion came under private sector development, and were funded to the amount of approximately €28.3 million. In practice, therefore, about €74 million under the tenth EDF CRIP was directly spent on EPA implementation and adjustment.

By 2014, CARIFORUM had undertaken and completed 13 feasibility studies in 11 EPA areas: (1) technical barriers to trade; (2) sanitary and phyto-sanitary measures; (3) customs and trade facilitation and risk analysis; (4) investment promotion; (5) investment statistics; (6) trade in services; (7) financial services; (8) taxation; (9) competition policy; (10) intellectual property; and (11) government procurement.[22] On the basis of these studies, an overall rough estimate puts the cost of this programme in excess of €500 million,[23] which implies that the tenth EDF took into account only a small portion of the needs identified in these studies. (See Girvan and Montoute in this volume.)

In view of the shortfall under the tenth EDF, the Caribbean ACP signatories had either to seek non-EDF funding or await the eleventh EDF in several key EPA areas, including customs and trade facilitation, cultural industries, intellectual property, government procurement, environment, protection of personal data, social aspects, competition, and science and technology. In some of these areas—such as public procurement, competition, and intellectual property—projects needed to be implemented in the immediate short term, in order to meet deadlines set for the completion of the CARICOM Single Market and Economy (CSME), upon which progress towards the implementation of the CARIFORUM-EU economic partnership agreement, in turn, depended. For example, in the case of intellectual property, a system of protection of geographical indications had to be established in order for CARIFORUM-EU negotiations on geographical protection to start in January 2014 under Article 145 of the EPA. A regional geographical system was yet to be established as of July 2015, and it remained unclear if CARIFORUM or CARICOM intends to establish one. Negotiations with the EU, nonetheless, started in November 2013.

Yet, under the eleventh EDF, in relative terms, the Caribbean's total indicative allocation—including the regional and national programmes—has declined. Whereas it had increased by 109 per cent in the tenth EDF over the ninth, it only increased by 36 per cent in the eleventh EDF over the tenth (see Table 8.3). This reflects the EU's introduction of a differentiation principle in aid volumes,[24] which has led to smaller national allocations for the middle-income countries of the region.[25] In this context, the EDF's all-ACP facility and the EU's Aid for Trade programmes constitute important alternative sources of funding to cover the costs of EPA implementation and adjustment for the Caribbean.

EU Aid for Trade to the Caribbean region increased from an annual average of €114 million in the period 2006–2008 to an annual average of €273 million for 2009–2011. In total, the Caribbean received €819 million between 2009 and 2011. This development assistance went towards trade policy and regulation, and building productive capacity and trade-related infrastructure, and mainly to three countries: the Dominican Republic, Guyana, and Haiti.[26]

However, as the aforementioned five-year review of the CARIFORUM-EU EPA noted, EU member states, with the exception of Britain and Germany,

Table 8.3 CARIFORUM and ACP ninth, tenth, and eleventh EDF allocations, 2000–2020 (€ millions)

	Ninth EDF allocation (2000–2007)	Tenth EDF allocation (2008–2013)	Eleventh EDF allocation (2014–2020)
Total CARIFORUM indicative allocation (national + regional)	354	738	1,000
CARIFORUM Regional Indicative Programme	57	165	346
Total ACP indicative allocation (national + regional)	10,000	17,766	24,365
All-ACP facility	1,300	2,700	3,590
European Investment Bank allocation	2,200	1,500	1,134
Total ACP allocation	**13,500**	**21,966**	**29,089**

Sources: "EC Internal Agreement", *Official Journal of the European Union* 247/33, Brussels, 9 September 2006, http://ec.europa.eu/europeaid/sites/devco/files/internal-agreement-10edf-2006_en.pdf (accessed 5 July 2015); "EC Internal Agreement", *Official Journal of the European Union* L 210/1, Brussels, 6 August 2013, http://ec.europa.eu/europeaid/sites/devco/files/internal-agreement-11edf-2013-2020_en.pdf (accessed 5 July 2015); European Communities, *The European Development Fund in a Few Words* (Luxembourg: Office for Official Publications of the European Communities, 2002), p. 12, http://www.pedz.uni-mannheim.de/daten/edz-l/gdd/02/fed_en.pdf (accessed 5 July 2015); and European Commission, "EU Announces New Funding for the Caribbean", press release, Brussels, 11 June 2015, http://europa.eu/rapid/press-release_IP-15-5163_en.htm (accessed 5 July 2015)

have largely disappointed the Caribbean countries in terms of their bilateral Aid for Trade support for EPA implementation. In the words of the review, "the shortfall of most EU Member States in actively supporting EPA implementation is particularly unfortunate given that the UK and Germany have shown, during the review period, how bilateral funding can fill the need for more timely, readily accessible and EPA-focused support than that available under the traditional EDF sources".[27] In December 2013, CARICOM countries similarly noted that this lack of support had been a factor affecting the implementation of the EPA since 2008, indicating that "the amount [of Aid for Trade] has fallen far short of what the region had anticipated, as has been [the case with] the number of EU countries providing that aid".[28] (See Girvan and Montoute in this volume.)

According to the European Commission, by 2008, €680 million was allocated to the Caribbean, through the all-ACP facility, in traditional sectors such as rum, rice, sugar, and bananas.[29] However, allocations for direct EPA implementation support made through the all-ACP facility under the tenth EDF are difficult to calculate, because they fall under many different programmes and go to various EU or ACP-EU joint institutions.[30]

Beyond the practical difficulties of calculation, there are a number of problems in assessing the additionality of EPA funding. First, there is no systematic way of tracking and ensuring that EDF resources normally allocated for the regional and national programmes are not diverted for EPA implementation. Moreover, most activities are implemented under the national programme and under "non-EPA" components of the regional programme, and thus are part of a continuous programme of adjustment that would take place even without the EPA. Second, determining the "normal" size of the indicative programmes under the EDF—that is, in the absence of an EPA—is in itself problematic, as this size is essentially established by a decision made by the European Union—one that depends on the prevailing perspectives of the EU, and this is not necessarily related to the needs in the region.

Determining the adequacy of funding is equally complex, and needs to take account of not only the costs of the EPA, but also the availability of additional funds. The global financial crisis of 2008–2009, followed by low economic growth in much of the Caribbean, has deprived most CARIFORUM countries of the fiscal space necessary to achieve an adequate level of EPA implementation and adjustment. Meanwhile, since 2008, recession and slow recovery in the EU have also placed limits on its ability to provide resources for EPA implementation, with several EU member states themselves facing severe difficulties arising from debt, high unemployment, and declining production.

IMPACT OF THE CARIFORUM-EU EPA ON REGIONAL INTEGRATION

The Caribbean Approach to the CARIFORUM-EU EPA and Regional Integration

For the Caribbean side, protecting the integrity of regional integration schemes was central to the EPA negotiations. These projects included the Caribbean Community, established by the Treaty of Chaguaramas of 1973; the CSME, brought into existence by the Revised Treaty of Chaguaramas of 2001; the Organisation of Eastern Caribbean States (OECS), created by the Treaty of Basseterre of 1981; and the CARICOM-Dominican Republic FTA, concluded in 1998. The issues raised were complex, and are beyond the scope of this chapter. The focus here is therefore on the impact of the EPA on the CSME, which includes the OECS and forms the core of Caribbean regional integration.[31] (See also Girvan and Montoute in this volume.)

The main aim of the CSME is to integrate the CARICOM economies into a unified, coordinated, and harmonised market, with free movement of people, goods, services, and capital, and with a common external tariff and trade policy. Progress towards the establishment of the CSME, however, has been slow.[32] Due to delays in policy implementation, the CSME was not formally launched until 2006 and remains incomplete, with CARICOM states still to elaborate protocols on, among other things, government procurement, electronic commerce, treatment of goods produced in free zones and similar jurisdictions, free circulation of goods in the CSME, and rights contingent on establishment. This has, in turn, hindered implementation of the EPA. In particular, CARIFORUM—comprising 14 CARICOM countries and the Dominican Republic—has been unable to take conclusive decisions on several issues, including public procurement (transparency); differentiation in the formulation of liberalisation schedules for goods and services; regional preference; and the free circulation of EU imports in the CARIFORUM region.

Based on a recognition that the Caribbean's regional integration and its EPA implementation efforts are linked, the economic partnership agreement sought to address the weaknesses of the CSME—in particular, its structural, institutional, and financial limitations—through the provision of development support. The challenge was how to accelerate the process without compromising the integrity of the regional integration project. Accordingly, the Caribbean's EPA Implementation Roadmap of 2009 is aligned with the implementation plans of the CSME, OECS, and CARICOM-Dominican Republic FTA: commitments assumed under the economic partnership agreement have been synchronised with, and are subject to implementation of, the Caribbean's regional integration agendas.

Challenges for Regional Integration

However, the EPA addresses trade-related areas—including competition policy, sanitary and phyto-sanitary measures, intellectual property, and public procurement (transparency)—as well as service sectors, in which CARICOM has yet to develop policies and procedures. (See also Girvan and Montoute in this volume.) How the development of the CSME, and the implementation of EPA commitments in these areas, can be sequenced so as to allow CARICOM to establish its regimes first and then determine their relationship with the arrangement with the EU, remains to be seen. The matter is complex. First, under the EPA, the Caribbean's obligations in trade-related areas, as well as in certain service sectors, including finance, telecommunications, and professional services, are time-bound and specific. This is not the case with regard to CARICOM's commitments for the operationalisation of the CSME in these areas, where it has favoured a slower, evolutionary process, one dependent on future policy decisions. Second, in certain areas—for example, competition, technical barriers to trade, and trade facilitation (in particular, customs administration)—the economic partnership agreement goes further than the CSME. The EPA also pushes for recognition and implementation by both parties of environmental standards under a wider range of relevant multilateral environmental agreements—for example, the International Convention for the Protection of New Varieties of Plants, as revised in 1991.

Furthermore, the CARIFORUM-EU EPA includes several WTO-plus commitments in trade-related areas and market access, and in terms of transparency in the financial and telecommunications service sectors in particular. The exceptions are sanitary and phyto-sanitary measures and, to a lesser extent, intellectual property, with respect to which CARICOM's obligations under the EPA are broadly similar to those assumed in the WTO. On the one hand, this poses a challenge for CARICOM, in terms of balancing its commitment to implementing the EPA against its desire to determine the shape and evolution of its own liberalisation and regional integration agenda. On the other hand, the EPA offers an opportunity for CARICOM countries that have lagged to push towards meeting their WTO obligations, and also to develop adequate regional policies, as well as implementation mechanisms, in areas that they have sought to address since the formal establishment of CARICOM in 1973 and the CSME in 2006. For example, by 2014, despite efforts, little to no success had been achieved in terms of establishing a harmonised regime for customs administration; implementation of the CSME remained weak in intellectual property, investment, public procurement, and sanitary and phytosanitary measures. The creation of the CARICOM Regional Organisation for Standards and Quality in February 2002 and Competition Commission in January 2008 constitutes progress, but much still remains to be done in these areas.

Yet, six years into the provisional application of the EPA, only a handful of the commitments assumed in trade-related areas had been met. CARICOM's regional integration and cooperation programme continued to focus on the in-built agenda of the CSME, but the deadline of 2015 for full implementation of the CSME was not met. In this context, focusing effort and resources on trade-related areas, such as customs administration and trade facilitation, intellectual property, and technical barriers to trade, may offer better prospects both for strengthening regional integration and for making progress towards the Caribbean region meeting its commitments under the EPA.

COMPLIANCE AND IMPLEMENTATION CHALLENGES

Deadlines for complying with the obligations assumed under the CARIFORUM-EU economic partnership agreement vary significantly, with due dates ranging from the commencement of provisional application through to stipulated timeframes following the agreement's entry into force. Given this complexity, the Caribbean's EPA Implementation Roadmap of 2009 identifies, in chronological order, the actions that need to be taken at the national and regional levels. Intended to assist the CARIFORUM states in focusing their implementation efforts, the roadmap also identifies several areas—including trade in goods and services, and trade-related issues such as investment, competition, intellectual property, and protection of personal data—that require legislative intervention by the CARIFORUM countries to achieve compliance.

Provisional application of the Caribbean EPA began in December 2008. By August 2014 (the latest data for which information was available at the time of writing), ratification had been implemented by seven (out of 15) CARIFORUM signatories and 16 EU member states.[33] This means that the EPA is yet to enter into force. Even so, certain provisions that have been provisionally applied could stay in place permanently.

Tariff reduction forms a key part of the provisional application of the EPA. However, the pace at which CARIFORUM countries have introduced tariff reduction has been slow and uneven. The first round of cuts, scheduled for January 2011, was implemented by 12 Caribbean countries. Of these, only ten countries then indicated that they had implemented the second round of tariff cuts, due by January 2013.[34] Various factors have accounted for this slow pace, including concern about the impact of the cuts on Caribbean revenues, especially against the backdrop of a global economic downturn since

2008–2009, legislative obstacles, and ongoing talks with the EU to modify the tariff reduction schedule. (See Girvan and Montoute in this volume.)

In the case of obligations assumed under the EPA's services and investment-related provisions, most were due for implementation either upon signing of the agreement (October 2008), upon its provisional application (December 2008), or within six months after the start of provisional application. Progress towards compliance in this area has been difficult to assess with precision and accuracy, due to lack of adequate information, although informal engagements with stakeholders indicate that several obligations have been implemented by CARIFORUM as scheduled.

A debate on the "correct" pace of implementation has ensued in the region following the signing of the EPA, with the value of a slow and cautious approach highlighted by the high costs of implementing the agreement and its negative effects on the CSME. Meanwhile, the case for more rapid implementation has rested on the significance of policy credibility and the need to accelerate the Caribbean's integration into the global economy.[35] On the whole, though, CARIFORUM countries have approached implementation cautiously, given their general scepticism about the benefits of free trade, which has since been compounded by the impact of the global financial crisis of 2008–2009.

EPA Implementation Structures

In line with the requirements of the economic partnership agreement, CARIFORUM established a regional EPA coordinator and national EPA coordinators by 2009. A regional EPA implementation unit was created in February 2009. Furthermore, individual countries have either created a special EPA implementation unit (for example, Antigua and Barbuda, and Barbados), included oversight of EPA implementation among the mandates of existing trade implementation units (for example, the Dominican Republic and Jamaica), or instituted EPA-related focal points (for example, Suriname and Guyana). Implementation was regarded at the outset as critical to achieving compliance, as well as achieving the broader goals of the EPA. It has included liaising with government ministries, regional organisations, private sector actors, and civil society; elaborating national roadmaps; developing monitoring and evaluation systems; monitoring implementation; disseminating information; working with business organisations, in particular, to take advantage of opportunities generated by the EPA; and building knowledge and awareness of the agreement.

The regional EPA implementation unit, in particular, has provided valuable assistance on required legislation and documentation to CARIFORUM member states to help them meet their EPA obligations. However, the unit was short-staffed until 2013, and took several years to produce a work plan and procedures and rules governing EPA implementation. The capacity and resources of the national EPA units, meanwhile, have varied significantly, with staffing levels ranging from two in Grenada to 40 in the Dominican Republic.[36] The most effective units have been those with strong political support and interaction with different government departments (such as in Barbados), and those with greater experience in FTA implementation (such as in the Dominican Republic). The level of resources has generally been considered inadequate to meet implementation challenges. The implementation units, including the regional EPA unit, have been overly reliant on donor funds, which in turn has made them vulnerable to delays in aid programming and left them constantly searching for individual donors and funds for ad hoc activities.[37]

Challenges of EPA Implementation

The CARIFORUM countries are facing several varied implementation challenges, but funding has been the main issue for almost all. Even countries that set about meeting their EPA obligations early on and have been generally compliant with trade agreements, such as Barbados, have experienced financial difficulties in creating their EPA units as a result of the global economic downturn since 2008–2009. Most Caribbean countries, as well as the CARIFORUM Directorate and the CARICOM Secretariat, are reportedly spending an inordinate amount of time writing project proposals in their effort to source needed funding.

Other challenges include inadequate human resources; an absence of awareness and knowledge among stakeholders of implementation requirements; a perceived inability by Caribbean governments to act without development assistance; and inadequate sectoral representation of interests, particularly in services where lack of domestic regulation and key data in certain sectors (such as professional services) have made implementation more difficult. Notwithstanding the existence of the regional 2009 EPA Implementation Roadmap, most countries have taken several years to craft national roadmaps to guide and monitor their implementation efforts.

Furthermore, EPA implementation is highly dependent on the establishment and functioning of joint institutions. These include:

- The Joint CARIFORUM-EU Council, which is the principal ministerial-level institution under the EPA with the power to approve amendments to the agreement and to adopt its own rules of procedure, as well as define those of other joint institutions, and which met for the first time in May 2010.
- The CARIFORUM-EU Trade and Development Committee, which is charged with the proper implementation and operation of the EPA, and which held its first meeting in June 2011.
- Special committees, including the Special Committee on Customs Cooperation and Trade Facilitation, which reports to the Trade and Development Committee and addresses matters related to rules of origin, among other things, and which held its first meeting in December 2011.
- The CARIFORUM-EU Parliamentary Committee, comprising members of the European Parliament and of the legislatures of the CARIFORUM states, which can make recommendations to the Joint CARIFORUM-EU Council, and the Trade and Development Committee, and which met for the first time in June 2011.
- The CARIFORUM-EU Consultative Committee, which is intended to assist the Joint CARIFORUM-EU Council in promoting dialogue and cooperation with civil society, and which held its first meeting in November 2014.

These joint institutions have a key role to play in promoting regular dialogue—a distinguishing feature of the EPA—but are yet to meet expectations. Concern has also been expressed about the scope and quality of the discussions that these bodies have held so far.[38] For example, the Trade and Development Committee has focused mainly on trade and governance issues, while giving inadequate attention to development cooperation. In particular, the committee's decision—taken at its first meeting in June 2011—to create a technical sub-committee on development cooperation, was yet to be fully implemented in May 2015.[39] Meanwhile, the Consultative Committee held its first meeting only in November 2014.[40] As in the case of the implementation units, the creation of these joint institutions has taken a while, and a more conclusive assessment must await the test of time.

On the whole, there have been deficits in implementation of the CARIFORUM-EU economic partnership agreement in key areas, including ratification, tariff reductions, support for EPA implementation units, and establishment and functioning of joint institutions, as well as in the completion of agreements on mutual recognition, aid delivery, and the issuance of visas and work permits for temporary services providers. The EPA is a far-reaching agreement, with deeper commitments than those demanded by the Cotonou framework. As such, the Caribbean's regional and national institutions have struggled to implement the agreement, with most lacking the necessary managerial capacity and resources necessary to accomplish key tasks. Progress towards making the legislative, policy, and administrative changes required by the EPA has been uneven. The process has been further complicated by problems of regional integration, as demonstrated by the challenges faced in implementing the EPA provisions on regional preference and the lengthy negotiations needed for establishing the regional fund. The CARIFORUM states continue to face major resource constraints, and there are fears that the EU's proposed differentiation policy will further reduce bilateral financial assistance to the Caribbean EPA signatories, causing still more delays in implementation of the agreement (see Girvan and Montoute in this volume).

CONCLUDING REFLECTIONS

Against the backdrop of the global economic downturn since 2008, the strength of the CARIFORUM "EPA signal" has been fairly muted.[41] Implementation remains incomplete, and the road ahead remains long, before the impact of the economic partnership agreement on CARIFORUM trade and development can be properly addressed. This does not imply, however, that the EPA has recorded no achievements. On the contrary, positive outcomes include the emergence of some new non-traditional agricultural exports and some free-zone manufactured products (for example, medical supplies and equipment, electrical equipment such as audio alarms and surge protectors or circuit breakers, and textiles and garments) from the Dominican Republic; the forging of new business contacts as a result of trade missions; an increased awareness of market opportunities in the EU; and progress in the area of sanitary and phyto-sanitary standards, as well as changes in policy thinking about accelerating the pace of modernising trade-related areas such as customs harmonisation, competition, and intellectual property in both the public and private arenas.

Ironically, the global economic downturn, which has coincided with implementation of the EPA, has in any case prompted most CARICOM countries to shift into a mode of economic adjustment. Competitiveness, in particular, has emerged high on the Caribbean's agenda, with observable reforms including improvements in the business climate, pursuit of more competitive energy systems, and efforts to control fiscal deficits and to build fiscal buffers. This could facilitate trade and other reforms required by the EPA.

Since the start of provisional application in 2008, the EPA has so far not encountered any visible protests from the private sector, trade unions, or civil society organisations. Even so, it remains vital to bring particular interest groups, especially the private sector, more fully onboard with the EPA and build confidence in the agreement. Training on sanitary and phyto-sanitary measures, along with EDF-funded private sector development programmes, has been helpful in developing capacity.[42] The achievement of key symbolic milestones—notably, the ratification of the EPA by all parties—would help to boost confidence in the agreement. An involved and proactive private sector, with strong ties to the EU market, is vital for the Caribbean to take full advantage of, and benefit from, the opportunities offered by the EPA. Greater time and resources need to be spent on building awareness of the agreement in this respect.

At the same time, there are important lessons to be gained for the Caribbean region from the EPA experience so far, and which may be as relevant for the other ACP regions as they seek to finalise and move towards implementing their own agreements with the EU. First, there is no substitute for competitiveness, as indicated by the performance of key traditional exports such as sugar and bananas under the CARIFORUM-EU EPA. Production has continued to decline in these sectors, even though preferential market access was preserved and, in the case of sugar, improved under the terms of the agreement. The Caribbean needs to find better uses for the resources that it has available, and look beyond its traditional export sectors, which were established on the basis of special non-reciprocal preferences, but have since shown no scope for becoming competitive, as they were never determined by market conditions in the first place.

Second, and related, it is important for the Caribbean not to continue to underestimate the time required to develop new export sectors. The obstacles that the region has faced, and continues to face, in terms of regulatory and organisational weaknesses in its service sectors, and that need to be addressed for the EPA to have its desired impact, serve as a lesson in this regard.

Third, the EPA has shown the possibilities and limitations of inter-regional integration (between the Caribbean ACP and the EU) as a driver of Caribbean regional integration. The EPA sets out commitments with clear timeframes and steps for implementation with a view towards achiev-ing its goals, some of which are also necessary for the attainment of the objectives of the CSME. Competition policy is a good example. At the same time, there are other issue areas (such as geographical indications and regional preference) in which the success of the EPA remains contin-gent upon building regional consensus and the Caribbean's own efforts to progress towards greater regional integration.

Fourth, the CARIFORUM experience illustrates that early mobilisa-tion of resources for the timely establishment and operationalisation of fully equipped regional and national implementation units, working in coordination with each other, is critical. In a fundamental sense, the seam-less movement from negotiation to implementation, with the same or greater technical capacity, cannot be overemphasised.[43] The experience of CARIFORUM suggests that there are benefits in recognising the symbi-otic relationship between implementation and negotiation. The presence of a permanent negotiating team,[44] working alongside an implementation unit, to deal with the complex technical issues that arise in implementa-tion, adds value to the whole process. Similarly, getting started with fore-seeable aspects of implementation during the negotiation phase, as was accomplished through the creation and work of the Caribbean's Regional Preparatory Task Force, helps to facilitate implementation later.

Finally, EPA implementation covers a wide range of areas, and involves significant human and financial resources, which are not necessarily or always available, particularly in a small region such as the Caribbean. In such a context, prioritisation of key areas is essential to achieving progress in implementation of the agreement. Altogether, these are valuable les-sons that the Caribbean can offer to Africa and the Pacific as the latter two regions continue to negotiate their own economic agreements with the EU.

NOTES

1. The economic partnership agreement (EPA), originally signed by 14 countries of the Forum of the Caribbean Group of African, Caribbean, and Pacific States (CARIFOUM), has been provision-ally applied since December 2008; Haiti signed the agreement

later, in December 2009. The CARIFORUM signatories to the EPA include 14 member states of the Caribbean Community (CARICOM)—Antigua and Barbuda, Bahamas, Barbados, Belize, Dominica, Grenada, Guyana, Haiti, Jamaica, St Lucia, St Kitts and Nevis, St Vincent and the Grenadines, Suriname, and Trinidad and Tobago—and the Dominican Republic. Cuba, though a member of the 16-strong Caribbean Forum, is not a signatory to the EPA. The 27 European Union (EU) signatories are Austria, Belgium, Britain, Bulgaria, Cyprus, the Czech Republic, Denmark, Estonia, Finland, France, Germany, Greece, Hungary, Ireland, Italy, Latvia, Lithuania, Luxembourg, Malta, the Netherlands, Poland, Portugal, Romania, Slovakia, Slovenia, Spain, and Sweden. Croatia became the 28th member of the EU in July 2013.

2. Anthony Peter Gonzales, "CARIFORUM's Decision to Sign the EPA", *Trade Negotiations Insights* 7, no. 8 (October 2008), pp. 2–3.

3. Gonzales, "CARIFORUM's Decision to Sign the EPA", p. 3.

4. Combined nomenclature is the customs classification in the EU for goods declared at the border and on which duties and other taxes may be imposed.

5. European Commission, Directorate General for Trade, "European Union, Trade in Goods with ACP—Caribbean Countries", http://trade.ec.europa.eu/doclib/docs/2006/september/tradoc_113476.pdf (accessed 20 April 2015).

6. International Trade Centre (ITC), Trade Map, http://www.trademap.org/Index.aspx (accessed 5 July 2015).

7. For a comparison of CARICOM and Central American Common Market (CACM) countries with regard to products in which they compete directly in the EU market, *see* Anthony Peter Gonzales, "CACM and CARICOM Trade Policy and Competitiveness on the EU market", paper submitted for publication at the Institute of International Relations, University of the West Indies, St Augustine, Trinidad and Tobago, September 2014. The study examines the products in which comparative advantage has been gained or lost on the EU market over two periods: 2007–2009 and 2011–2013. The results show that CARICOM is losing its comparative advantage in the EU market in many of its traditional, sensitive products, while CACM is gaining comparative advantage in many of them.

8. This is a comprehensive list of service sectors and sub-sectors covered under the General Agreement on Trade in Services (GATS).

See World Trade Organisation (WTO), "Note by the Secretariat: Services Sectoral Classification List", MTN.GNS/W/120, Geneva, 10 July 1991.

9. For a more detailed account, *see* Ramesh Chaitoo, "Investment and Trade in Services", in Amerigo Beviglia Zampetti and Junior Lodge (eds.), *The CARIFORUM-EU Economic Partnership Agreement: A Practitioners' Analysis* (Alphen aan den Rijn, Netherlands: Kluwer Law International BV, 2011), pp. 101–128.

10. European Commission, Directorate-General for Trade, "Caribbean", http://ec.europa.eu/trade/policy/countries-and-regions/regions/caribbean (accessed 30 April 2015).

11. Business and Strategies (B&S) Europe and Linpico, *Monitoring the Implementation & Results of the CARIFORUM-EU EPA Agreement*, Final Report, European Commission, Brussels, September 2014, p. 97.

12. B&S Europe and Linpico, *Monitoring the Implementation & Results*, pp. 97–98.

13. The air-passenger duty imposed by Britain made Caribbean destinations more costly than competitive destinations in the United States (US). Note that Britain is used synonymously with the United Kingdom (UK) in this volume.

14. B&S Europe and Linpico, *Monitoring the Implementation & Results*, p. 101.

15. B&S Europe and Linpico, *Monitoring the Implementation & Results*, p. 101.

16. The general budget of the European Commission occasionally can serve as an additional source, but is rarely used and is not addressed here.

17. In 2000, the European Commission decided to move the start of the ninth European Development Fund (EDF) from the date of signing of the agreement (2000) to the date of ratification of the agreement by EU member states and its legal entry into force.

18. CARICOM Secretariat, "Remarks by Louis Michel, EU Commissioner, on the Occasion of the Special Meeting of CARIFORUM Heads of Government on EPA Related Issues, 4 October 2007, Montego Bay, Jamaica", Press Release no. 228/2007, 5 October 2007.

19. B&S Europe and Linpico, *Monitoring the Implementation & Results*, p. 24.

20. Council of the European Union, *EU Strategy on Aid for Trade: Enhancing EU Support for Trade-Related Needs in Developing Countries*, 13070/07 ATR/tk 1DG E II 11, Brussels, October 2007.
21. B&S Europe and Linpico, *Monitoring the Implementation & Results*, p. 23.
22. B&S Europe and Linpico, *Monitoring the Implementation & Results*, p. 12.
23. B&S Europe and Linpico, *Monitoring the Implementation & Results*, p. 12.
24. According to the European Commission, differentiated eligibility for development assistance (that is, graduation) will not apply to the 11th EDF (2014–2020). Instead, the EDF has introduced an increased differentiation of aid volumes. *See* Siân Herbert, *Reassessing Aid to Middle-Income Countries: The Implications of the European Commission's Policy of Differentiation for Developing Countries*, Working Paper no. 349 (London: Overseas Development Institute, 2012).
25. According to one news report, Haiti is expected to receive more than 40 per cent of these funds as a least-developed country (LDC), in line with the European Commission's Agenda for Change—a blueprint to refocus its aid to prioritise those countries and sectors that need it most—with bilateral funding decreasing for some countries. *See* European Commission, "EU to Discuss Future Priorities for Development Cooperation with the Caribbean", press release, *European Union News*, 19 September 2013, http://go.galegroup.com/ps/i.do?id=GALE%7CA34331 4784&v=2.1&u=msu_main&it=r&p=ITOF&sw=w&asid=0c374 d054590bf0e44487af6369a1f6c (accessed 4 July 2015).
26. European Commission, *Aid for Trade: Report 2013*, Staff Working Document, Brussels, 16 July 2013, p. 79.
27. B&S Europe and Linpico, *Monitoring the Implementation & Results*, p. 25.
28. *See* Peter Richards, "CARIFORUM Countries Complain about EU Support for EPA Implementation", *CANA News*, 10 December 2013, http://www.cananews.net/archive/2013/12/ index.24.html (accessed 30 April 2015).
29. CARICOM Secretariat, "Remarks by Louis Michel".
30. There are various all-ACP funds such as STABEX (*Système de Stabilisation des Recettes d'Exportation*); FLEX and V-FLEX (Vulnerability FLEX); ACP-EU project management units, includ-

ing TradeCom, BizClim, and the ACP Multilateral Trading System (MTS) programme; specialised technical assistance centres, such as the Centre for Development of Enterprise (CDE) and the Centre for the Development of Agriculture; as well as sector-specific all-ACP funds for, among other sectors, information and communications technology (ICT), science and technology, fisheries, and cultural industries. *See* B&S and Linpico, *Monitoring the Implementation & Results*, pp. 24, 32–33.

31. The impact of the EPA—in particular, regional preference—on the CARICOM-Dominican Republic free trade agreement is not discussed in this chapter. The EPA requires that all CARIFORUM states also extend to each other any preferential treatment that they have given to the EU (Article 238). This supersedes the provisions of the CARICOM-Dominican Republic free trade agreement, which had granted member countries of the Organisation of Eastern Caribbean States (OECS) non-reciprocal preferential access to the Dominican Republic market. Furthermore, with regard to services, all CARICOM states will now have to negotiate specific commitments with the Dominican Republic, with the EPA's regulatory provisions for liberalisation of trade in services as a guide (Article 64).

32. Though referred to as the CARICOM Single Market and Economy, action on the Single Economy has been either postponed or abandoned.

33. B&S Europe and Linpico, *Monitoring the Implementation & Results*, p. 8.

34. B&S Europe and Linpico, *Monitoring the Implementation & Results*, p. 35.

35. *See* Richard Bernal, "The Challenge of Sustainable Implementation", in Zampetti and Lodge, *The CARIFORUM–EU Economic Partnership Agreement*, pp. 239–259.

36. B&S Europe and Linpico, *Monitoring the Implementation & Results*, p. 10.

37. B&S Europe and Linpico, *Monitoring the Implementation & Results*, p. 11.

38. B&S Europe and Linpico, *Monitoring the Implementation & Results*, p. 12.

39. B&S Europe and Linpico, *Monitoring the Implementation & Results*, p. 13.

40. European Commission, "Overview of EPA Negotiations", updated March 2015, http://trade.ec.europa.eu/doclib/docs/2009/september/tradoc_144912.pdf (accessed 11 June 2015).
41. Sacha Silva, "Implementation Challenges: Insights from the First CARIFORUM-EU EPA Five-Year Review", European Centre for Development Policy Management's (ECDPM) *GREAT Insights* 3, no. 9 (October/November 2014), p. 3, http://ecdpm.org/great-insights/economic-partnership-agreements-beyond/implementation-challenges-insights-first-cariforum-eu-epa-five-year-review (accessed 4 July 2015).
42. This has been an achievement even though the EPA was signed in October 2008, and implementation of the tenth Regional Private Sector Development Programme only began around June 2011, while that of the tenth EDF's EPA capacity-building programme commenced only in the first quarter of 2013.
43. Sacha Silva, "Implementation Challenges", pp. 3–4.
44. The Caribbean Regional Negotiating Machinery, which has been entrusted with the EPA negotiations, was in July 2009 converted into the Office of Trade Negotiations in the CARICOM Secretariat.

PART IV

Other Key Issues in the ACP-EU Relationship

CHAPTER 9

The EU's Security Role in Africa: "The Emperor Has No Clothes"

Adekeye Adebajo

Nineteenth-century Danish author Hans Christian Andersen published his famous fairy tale "The Emperor's New Clothes" in 1837. Building on a medieval Spanish folk tale, the story is about two dishonest weavers who convince an Emperor to buy a new suit of clothes that would be invisible only to anyone who is "hopelessly stupid" or incompetent. As the Emperor does not want to appear to be either, he wears what the weavers pretend are his new clothes and parades through the streets in full view of his subjects. A child in the crowd cries out, "The Emperor is wearing no clothes", and the shout becomes a chorus. The embarrassed Emperor continues to march, but realises he has been conned.

Current efforts by the European Union (EU) to play a security role in Africa contain a similar cautionary tale. The rhetoric from Brussels seeks to portray the institution (which won the Nobel Peace Prize in 2012) as a potential military power and "ethical" force for good in the world, based largely on interventions in the Balkans as well as small and short-term military missions in the Democratic Republic of the Congo (DRC), Chad, the Central African Republic (CAR), Guinea-Bissau, and Somalia. The EU Commission noted in typically grandiose fashion in 2003 that "Europe should be ready to share in the responsibility for global security

A. Adebajo (✉)
Centre for Conflict Resolution (CCR), Cape Town, South Africa

© The Author(s) 2017
A. Montoute, K. Virk (eds.), *The ACP Group and the EU
Development Partnership*, DOI 10.1007/978-3-319-45492-4_9

213

and in building a better world".[1] Scholars have also described the EU as a "normative power", "soft empire", and "metrosexual superpower".[2] However, all the jargon about the EU's "actor-ness" and perennial quest for "coherence" cannot mask the fundamental weakness, inaction, and incoherence of its military capacity. Like the child in Andersen's fairy tale, the African chorus continues to cry out, "The European Emperor has no clothes". Like the Emperor in the story, the EU knows this, but continues to pretend that it is more powerful than it actually is. This tale is a classic one of what British scholar Christopher Hill famously described as the "capabilities-expectations gap".[3]

Debates on the EU's security role in Africa have tended to be dominated by European scholars, most of whom have, to be fair, been critical of the organisation's security role. However, hardly any African voices have been part of these important discourses, and this chapter is partly an effort to correct this glaring imbalance. I will begin by tracing the historical roots of the roles of Europe's three major military powers—France, Britain, and Germany—in Africa, and next outline the evolution of the EU's security role on the continent after 1998. I will then assess case studies of EU interventions in the DRC, Chad, and the CAR, as well as smaller missions in the DRC and Somalia, and, finally, offer some concluding thoughts on the EU's security role on the continent.

A Tale of Three Colonial Powers

Africa's relations with Europe cannot be separated from the century of European colonialism following the infamous Berlin Conference of 1884–1885, at which the rules for the continent's partition effectively were set.[4] Colonialism was, after all, partly justified by European imperialists as a way of providing security and stopping restive African "tribes" from waging war against each other: the restless natives were to be saved from themselves. This history means that any European efforts to justify interventions in Africa as a way of promoting security will often be met with suspicion. It is almost as if the curse of African ancestors on Europe for the "original sin" in Berlin has rendered the EU militarily impotent, unable to rise to the occasion and being doomed to improvise small interventions of limited duration amid political divisions and a lack of military capacity to enforce peace. Though the EU is the largest aid donor in the world, with an economy about the size of the United States (US)—the world's largest—and remains an economic giant, it is a military dwarf.

A brief assessment of the historical roles of Germany, France, and Britain in Africa is essential to explaining the EU's current military role in Africa. After Germany lost its African colonies (Tanzania, Cameroon, Namibia, and Togo) following defeat in the First World War in 1918, it continued to play a limited economic role on the continent for the next century, developing ties in countries such as South Africa, Nigeria, and Namibia. However, Berlin has maintained a historical scepticism of EU military interventionism in Africa, preferring to focus on continental Europe beyond the EU. The Netherlands and Austria share Germany's caution in funding military missions in Africa, while Berlin and the Nordics at first strongly opposed the use of development funds for supporting security efforts on the continent.[5]

After the end of the Second World War in 1945, France and Britain soon lost their empires in Africa, but struggled to find a new role in a world now dominated by two nuclear-armed superpowers: the US and the Soviet Union.[6] The Suez crisis of 1956—when France and Britain invaded Egypt in a bid to reverse Gamal Abdel Nasser's nationalisation of the Suez Canal and were forced to withdraw by American pressure—was a cataclysmic event. France and Britain drew different conclusions from Suez. London decided it would never again launch a military intervention in strategically important parts of the world without the knowledge and support of the US, and largely avoided military interventions in Africa after Suez. This approach lasted until the short-term 800-strong intervention in Sierra Leone to support a crumbling United Nations (UN) mission in 2000. Since 2001, Britain has also sought to develop African peacekeeping capabilities under British Peace Support Teams (BPSTs), and has funded capacity-building projects through its Department for International Development (DFID) under the latter's Africa Conflict Prevention Pool (ACPP).[7]

In stark contrast, after the Suez crisis of 1956, France continued to pursue a *politique de grandeur*, drawing the opposite conclusion to Britain's: that it needed to increase its independence of action from the US. The Gallic power launched over 50 military interventions into its former African colonies, and has pursued a 50-year neo-colonial relationship with Africa known as *Françafrique*. Though all francophone African countries were eventually granted nominal independence by 1963, most signed neo-colonial military and economic pacts that gave France continued influence over their sovereign affairs. Paris maintained military bases across Africa, acting like a "pyromaniac fireman" in intervening to prop up or depose assorted tyrants in countries such as the DRC, Gabon, Togo, and the CAR. An important aspect of French policy was to keep trespassers out of its *chasse gardée* (private hunting-ground), which often frustrated efforts at regional integration in Africa.[8]

France trained and armed the genocidal Hutu-led militias before the Rwandan genocide of 1994, in which 800,000 people were killed, while in neighbouring Zaire (now the DRC), Paris supported a sinking Mobutu Sese Seko long after he had become toxic, even to erstwhile backers: the US and Belgium. More recently, France provided military support to prop up autocratic regimes in Chad and the CAR in 2006, and again in Chad in 2008 and the CAR in 2013. It intervened in Côte d'Ivoire in 2011 and Mali in 2013. In more economically austere times, France is now seeking to "Europeanise" its military interventions to reduce the political and financial costs of past unilateral interventions by convincing its EU partners to share the burden of neo-imperial interventions in pursuit of parochial national interests. As part of this strategy, French-financed, largely francophone troops have been dispatched to Côte d'Ivoire, Guinea-Bissau, and the CAR. As well, a French military project, *Renforcement des Capacités Africaines de Maintien de la Paix* (RECAMP), was transformed into EURORECAMP in a bid to foster collaboration between regional training and operational centres in Africa, in order allegedly to assist the African Union (AU) to deploy peacekeepers to trouble spots on the continent. EURORECAMP is based in Paris and involves personnel from France, Britain, Belgium, Finland, and Italy. One of the key French goals behind the evolving EU military force was to develop an intervention capability that was autonomous of the American-dominated North Atlantic Treaty Organisation (NATO). Britain and Germany, in contrast, have been careful not to develop a force that could weaken NATO.

THE EVOLUTION OF THE EU SECURITY ROLE IN AFRICA

It is against this historical background that one must necessarily assess the EU's evolving security role in Africa. It is also important to note that the sharp decline in European contributions to UN peacekeeping missions in Africa after debacles in Somalia (1993) and Rwanda (1994) resulted in EU members seeking to strengthen the capacity of African peacekeepers to conduct peacekeeping on their own continent as a way of avoiding putting European "boots on the ground". The creation of an EU military force may thus be a way of masking this abdication of international responsibility, and of intervening mainly with a small number of troops in short-term assignments with a clear exit strategy. While large European-led forces were deployed in Bosnia and Kosovo in the 1990s, EU states have offered only small, short-term missions to Africa.

The second pillar of the EU's Amsterdam Treaty of 1997 had called for a Common Foreign and Security Policy (CFSP). Britain and France signed the St Malo agreement in December 1998, which laid the foundation for the creation of a European Security and Defence Policy (ESDP). The policy called for a force with the capacity to take autonomous action during international crises. Four former European colonial powers in Africa—France, Germany, Britain, and Italy—proposed a plan in February 2004 for a 1,500-strong rapid-reaction EU vanguard force that would be deployable within two weeks. These "battle-groups" would intervene to calm conflicts outside the EU (Africa is specifically mentioned) in support of UN-mandated missions.[9] In 2004, the EU adopted the ESDP Action Plan for Africa, which outlined support for the AU and sub-regional bodies. In the same year, an accord on "EU/UN Cooperation in Military Crisis Management Operations" was agreed, in which EU members committed to provide support to UN operations on a national basis, and a multinational EU operation could be launched at the request of the UN under the EU's political control and strategic direction. The document also called for regular political dialogue between the EU rotating Troika in Brussels and the UN Secretariat in New York on broader peacekeeping issues.[10]

The EU Strategy for Africa was adopted in 2005, and the Africa-EU Strategic Partnership in 2007. Both aimed to support the African Peace and Security Architecture (APSA). The European Development Fund (EDF) provided for an African Peace Facility (APF), which was created in 2004. The APF allocated €250 million between 2004 and 2007 to support African security efforts, and was replenished in 2007 for another three years with a further €300 million. The 2007 strategic partnership sought to promote long-term capacity-building, support the evolving African Standby Force (ASF)—which is to consist of five sub-regional brigades—and provide predictable funding for peacekeeping missions in Africa. APF funding of €440 million supported the African Union's capacity-building efforts as well as the AU Mission in Sudan (AMIS), the AU Mission in Somalia (AMISOM), the *Force Multinationale en Centrafrique* (FOMUC), and the AU peace mission in Comoros.[11] By December 2014, the APF had provided €1.4 billion to security efforts in Africa.

As part of its evolving security role, the EU appointed special representatives for the Great Lakes, West Africa's Mano River basin, Sudan, and the Horn of Africa. Brussels sought further to institutionalise its relation-ship with the AU. The EU Commission and AU Commission now meet annually. The EU's Political and Security Council also engages in regular dialogue with the AU's Peace and Security Council. Further, an Africa-EU summit is held every three years, with summits having taken place in Cairo in 2000, Lisbon in 2007, Tripoli in 2010, and Brussels in 2014.

Belgium's Koen Vervaeke was appointed as the first EU ambassa-dor to the AU in December 2007, while a team of EU military advisers assisted AU military capacity-building efforts at its Commission in Addis Ababa. Brussels also funded the AU's Continental Early Warning System (CEWS) and Panel of the Wise, and helped the organisation in its efforts to develop its capacity in the areas of communications, intelligence-gathering, and information analysis. Under a 2008 strategy, the APF was mandated to support the Africa-EU Partnership on Peace and Security. There was much talk in Brussels of a "partnership of equals". However, the fact that the Africa-EU strategy of 2005 had been drawn up entirely by the European Commission, without proper consultation with the AU Commission or African governments (until it was revised by 2007), was a clear sign of the hollowness of this rhetoric. Many in Africa still felt that this remained a partnership—as a former British governor-general had once notoriously noted—between a horse and a rider.[12] (See Akokpari in this volume.)

THE DEMOCRATIC REPUBLIC OF THE CONGO

Operation Artemis

In May 2003, the UN Secretary-General, Ghana's Kofi Annan, called for a troop increase for the United Nations Organisation Mission in the DRC (MONUC) from 4,586 to 10,800, and urged a strengthening of the UN's mandate to enable the mission to contribute more effectively to peacemaking efforts.[13] By November 2003, MONUC had 10,415 troops. But despite some progress on the political front, instability continued in the Kivu region, while the security situation in Bunia (Orientale province, formerly Ituri) deteriorated sharply following the withdrawal of 7,000 Ugandan troops from the north-eastern town in May 2003. The depar-ture of Ugandan soldiers left a security vacuum that ethnic-based militias rushed in to fill, slaughtering hundreds of civilians and threatening the beleaguered UN compound. Bunia had been the battleground for conflicts between Lendu and Hema militias for several years, and Kampala had been accused of supporting both sides at different periods.

With increasing concern about genocide, and following the killing of two UN military observers, Kofi Annan called on the Security Council to deploy a well-equipped peace-enforcement mission to Bunia. In June 2003, France led the 1,000-strong EU Interim Emergency Multinational Force (IEMF) to conduct Operation Artemis, which was mandated to protect 20,000 civilians in and around Bunia, secure the airport, and protect internally displaced persons (IDPs), UN staff, and humanitarian workers. Britain and Sweden were the other main contributors, with Germany and Belgium providing non-combat troops. The EU force was deployed for three months until 2,400 UN peacekeepers took over from it in September 2003. Paris started planning the mission at least a month before the European Council had approved it in June 2003, allowing an impressively rapid deployment.[14]

Operation Artemis, involving a robust force of mainly French marine infantry troops and about 80 Swedish special forces, did secure Bunia and its airport and protect IDPs. France acted as the "framework nation" in leading the mission. An ultimatum in June 2003 by the EU's French force commander, General Jean-Paul Thonier, for the militia to bid farewell to arms or leave Bunia, was largely heeded, but the fighters continued to kill civilians in other parts of Orientale province.[15] Following the departure of the EU force, new massacres occurred in Bunia.[16] Though helpful in saving lives, stabilising the situation, and leading to a strengthened military mandate for MONUC, this force had as much to do with the EU's attempts to find a testing ground for its evolving rapid-reaction force.

EUFOR

Twenty-eight million Congolese voters were registered to take part in the DRC's first polls in 40 years, which cost an estimated $422 million. The EU was the largest funder of the elections, and Aldo Ajello, its blunt-speaking Italian special envoy for the Great Lakes between 1996 and 2007, played an important role in mobilising support for peacebuilding efforts in the DRC.[17] The Congo held historic elections in 2006, supported by MONUC. The EU deployed a small force in Kinshasa—its second in three years—which helped to provide security to the capital during the election period.

The UN approved the 2,000-strong EU force (EUFOR) under a Chapter VII peace-enforcement mandate in December 2005. The mission lasted four months, from July to November 2006, and cost about €100 million. EUFOR's main tasks involved supporting MONUC to provide stability, protecting civilians in and around Kinshasa, securing the airport, and undertaking protection and rescue missions. Amid wrangling between Berlin and Paris, Germany reluctantly agreed to lead the force. Berlin was suspicious of Gallic intentions from its experiences in Operation Artemis, and regarded the evolving EU security force largely as a tool of French and British foreign policy interests.[18] Paris was also hoping to use the mission to strengthen ties with Berlin.[19] Britain complained that its troops were overstretched in US-led missions in Afghanistan and Iraq, and declined to contribute soldiers to EUFOR. These intra-European disagreements constrained effective cooperation with MONUC.

The EU mission deployed eight months after it was mandated, arriving just two weeks before the first round of presidential elections in July 2006. The troops were led by French General Christian Damay, with a backup battalion stationed "over the horizon" in Gabon. Nineteen EU governments contributed troops to the mission, with Germany providing 700 soldiers, though the majority of EUFOR's troops were in Gabon, leading to widespread ridicule.[20] EUFOR's operational headquarters was in Potsdam. Germany, EUFOR's "lead nation", again demonstrated its post-1945 reluctance to project military force abroad when its Bundestag (parliament) attached conditions on the country's deployment that resulted in the dispatch of only 100 German troops to Kinshasa under French command. However, there were also some positive results from EUFOR. Learning from Operation Artemis, the EU and the UN peace-keeping forces improved their coordination.[21]

Fighting between the troops of Congolese President Joseph Kabila and those of his closest rival, Jean-Pierre Bemba, in Kinshasa in August 2006, killed at least 23 people, and rendered the security situation unstable. EUFOR troops were called on by the UN to help defend Bemba's headquarters. Their actions eventually changed some Congolese perceptions about the EU mission's impartiality and the widespread pro-Kabila "neo-colonial" accusations that had preceded its deployment.[22] Though requested to stay longer to help ensure stability in the post-election phase, a surly EUFOR refused.[23] The force's main concern—as expressed by German Defence Minister Franz Josef Jung[24]—appeared to be to get its troops back home by Christmas to be with their families. Fortunately, no serious post-electoral incidents occurred. However, Brussels was widely criticised for being so rigid on its departure date, with its troops leaving at the very moment when stability may have been threatened. As EU Special Representative to the Great Lakes, Aldo Ajello, noted, this approach was "wrong and dangerous, and should never be repeated in the future".[25]

The final incident involving the EU in the DRC was the case of the dog that did not bark: Brussels's non-intervention in the country in 2008. After militia leader Laurent Nkunda—an indictee of the Hague-based International Criminal Court (ICC)—and his Rwandan-backed[26] *Congrès National pour la Défense du Peuple* (CNDP) clashed with the *Forces Armées de la République Démocratique du Congo* (FARDC), claiming to be protecting the rights of the Tutsi minority, the security situation deteriorated. Clashes involving the FARDC, the CNDP, and other groups in North Kivu displaced 150,000 people between August and November 2007.[27] The UN's 17,342 peacekeepers were struggling to keep the peace.

In December 2008, UN Secretary-General Ban Ki-moon requested that the EU deploy a bridging force to calm the situation in Kivu until an additional 3,000 UN troops arrived in eastern Congo. The response to the South Korean diplomat's request revealed the complications behind the Byzantine decision-making processes in Brussels. French Foreign Minister Bernard Kouchner pushed for intervention, a move strongly supported by former colonial power Belgium, which offered 500 troops. The Spanish EU High Representative for the Common Foreign and Security Policy, Javier Solana, flatly rejected the idea. French President Nicolas Sarkozy soon dampened his activist foreign minister's enthusiasm by ruling out any Gallic involvement, and calling instead for African governments to take the lead. Casualty-shy Germany and ambiguous Britain (citing the need to rest its troops for Afghanistan) opposed the intervention. Spain and Italy noted that they were in no position to lead such a mission, while the Netherlands offered funds but no troops.

The EU Nordic contingent of Sweden, Denmark, and Finland called for an urgent response. Having contributed to the under-utilised UN Standby High-Readiness Brigade (SHIRBRIG), the Nordics were keen to put the EU's evolving rapid-reaction force to an early test. However, no consensus could be reached to deploy the force. Sweden and Belgium called the whole idea of the EU's battle-groups into question, with London refusing the Nordics permission to use its headquarters for any operation.[28] Though the improvement of the situation on the ground after an unexpected rapprochement between Kinshasa and Kigali somewhat softened the blow of the EU's refusal to support the UN's peacekeeping efforts, this incident sharply raised the uncomfortable question of the purpose of the EU's rapid-reaction battle-groups if they could not be used in situations where the greatest need existed. The EU's powerful members seemed to prefer relatively risk-free situations in which Brussels could continue to raise its prestige and test its security system.

CHAD AND THE CENTRAL AFRICAN REPUBLIC

France has traditionally played a role in Chad and the CAR, keeping troops in, and intervening in, Chad since the 1960s. France deployed more troops in the country in 1986 as part of its Operation Epervier, and strongly supported the autocratic regime of General Idriss Déby. Paris also helped Chadian rebels to install General François Bozizé in neighbouring CAR in March 2003. The French-supported *Mission de Consolidation de la Paix en Afrique Centrale* (MICOPAX) was deployed in the CAR in 2004, and consisted of 500 soldiers from francophone Central African states. The force's costs of €44.5 million up to 2010 were drawn from the EU's APF.

In 2005, the EU announced that it would no longer fund the AU mission in Darfur, which it had been supporting for a year. Brussels, along with Kofi Annan (and the UN Department of Peacekeeping Operations, led by Frenchman Jean-Marie Guéhenno), then pushed for a UN force to replace AMIS.[29] John Bolton, the US permanent representative to the UN at the time, noted that France was sceptical of a purely UN mission in Darfur, as it feared that such a force would drain resources from more strategic missions for Paris, such as the one in Côte d'Ivoire. Bolton further noted that France's permanent representative to the UN, Jean-Marc de la Sablière, only fully supported the role of the world body in Darfur when the French-backed regime of Idriss Déby was in danger of being toppled by the instability between Sudan and Chad.[30]

The cross-border situation between Sudan and Chad worsened the security situation in Western Darfur, as each side continued to support the rebels of the other. Following a rebel attack on the Chadian capital of N'Djamena that nearly led to the ousting of Déby in April 2006, Chad severed diplomatic relations with Khartoum and subsequently declared itself to be in a state of war with Sudan. Paris provided military support to save Déby's regime. Chadian armed rebels continued to launch attacks into the country from Darfur, which were repelled, with the Chadian army then launching attacks into Sudanese territory in "hot pursuit" of the rebels.

Two EUFOR Missions

In order to maintain stability in Chad, France manipulated the deployment first of an EU bridging force (EUFOR) in the border area of Chad and the CAR between 2008 and 2009. Paris then used its veto-wielding permanent seat on the UN Security Council to ensure the deployment of a self-interested UN force between 2009 and 2010. In both cases, France was effectively "multilateralising" its previously unilateral interventions in Africa, which had become widely discredited after the Rwandan genocide of 1994. Paris was effectively pushing its European partners and the broader international community to subsidise its policies of keeping the autocratic but shaky regime of Déby in power. The Chadian autocrat refused to allow a UN force, and France was instrumental in convincing him to accept EU troops during a visit to N'Djamena by French Foreign Minister Bernard Kouchner in June 2007.

France sent a request to EU member states in March 2007 requesting that they take some action to ameliorate the humanitarian situation in eastern Chad. Germany was reluctant to become involved due to its difficult experiences with French officials during Operation Artemis in the Congo in 2006.[31] Many EU members regarded the EU mission as an ill-disguised effort to support an unsavoury French client.[32] But several European countries, suffering from a guilty conscience at having failed to act decisively to halt the massacres in Darfur, which had by then resulted in over 200,000 deaths, felt that this might be a chance to make amends.[33] The decision to approve the force was taken by the EU Council in October 2007, before a detailed assessment of the conflict or military planning had taken place. When it came time to deploy, most states refused to dispatch troops, while still rhetorically backing the mission.[34]

France had been lobbying for a UN mission in Chad/CAR since the world body effectively agreed to take over the AU mission in Darfur in 2007. UN Secretary-General Kofi Annan, who left office in December 2006, had been opposed to a peacekeeping mission in Chad/CAR due to a lack of a credible political process in both countries. French diplomats, however, falsely sold the force to the UN as a way of securing EU and Western support to strengthen the UN mission in Darfur (UNAMID).[35] The EUFOR mission was mandated by the UN Security Council, in July 2007, to work with a small UN police force to protect refugees and IDPs in camps in the eastern Chad area bordering Darfur, and to act as a bridging force until the UN took over the mission. Even though Brussels has consistently sought to praise EUFOR as its most multinational force,[36] much of the world saw it as a vehicle for promoting French and EU interests in the region. As British analyst Alex Vines noted: "It is probably more accurate to credit this EUFOR operation with increasing European learning and coordination on how to conduct such a bridging exercise successfully than with fulfilling a meaningful humanitarian mandate."[37]

EUFOR Chad/CAR has been the EU's most logistically difficult mission. Most of the military planning was done in Paris, its operational base was in Mont Valérien, and French Foreign Minister Bernard Kouchner at first pushed for 12,000 troops. Other EU members refused, calling for a third of the troops suggested by Kouchner. They even questioned the use of the French operational headquarters. Britain and Germany refused to pay the costs of the operation based on assessed contributions, thus forcing France to bear most of the costs. London and Berlin also argued that EUFOR would take away much-needed resources from the NATO mission in Afghanistan. Finnish diplomats pushed unsuccessfully for the use of the EU's battle-groups.[38]

Just before EUFOR's deployment, the security situation in Western Darfur continued to deteriorate, as tensions between Chad and Sudan heightened. In January 2008, about 2,000 Chadian rebel groups attacked N'Djamena in a bid to topple Déby. French special forces became involved in preventing the rebels from taking over the airport, and helped the Déby government in its military efforts to defend the capital.[39] This was clear evidence to other EUFOR governments, if any were needed, that they were auxiliaries of Gallic foreign policy in Chad. EUFOR's Irish force commander, Patrick Nash, tried hard to distance EUFOR from France's Operation Epervier, but few were convinced. After the rebel attack on N'Djamena, the European Parliament pointedly called for EUFOR to remain neutral and to distinguish itself from the French mission.[40]

EUFOR's deployment by September 2008 had taken six months as a result of these events, raising questions about the EU's touted efficiency. France provided 2,000 of the force's 3,700 troops (though Ireland's Patrick Nash was operation commander, French General Jean-Philippe Ganascia commanded the field headquarters in Chad), again reinforcing the notion that the force was a tool of Paris's foreign policy interests in Chad. About 600 additional troops were kept in Europe. Nineteen EU countries contributed troops, with the largest contingents coming from France, Ireland, Poland, Austria, Italy, and the Netherlands. The mission was mandated to contribute to protecting civilians in danger; to facilitate delivery of humanitarian assistance and the free movement of aid workers; to help protect UN staff and facilities; and to ensure the freedom of movement of both EU and UN personnel.[41]

The mission cost €150 million and conducted 2,500 short-range and 260 long-range patrols in a challenging desert terrain larger than France. EUFOR struggled to obtain additional helicopters, and Russia eventually provided them. Working alongside the European force, the UN Mission in the Central African Republic and Chad (MINURCAT)—with an authorised strength of 300 international police and 50 military liaison officers— trained 418 of Déby's security forces, patrolled refugee camps and IDP sites, and protected UN humanitarian convoys seeking to assist 255,000 refugees and 137,500 IDPs in eastern Chad.[42] Cooperation between EUFOR and MINURCAT was difficult, however, and often hampered the effectiveness of their mandate.[43]

After the completion of the EUFOR mission in July 2009, about 2,000 EU troops from France, Ireland, Austria, Poland, Finland, Portugal, Spain, and Romania were "re-hatted" as UN peacekeepers and joined by European troops from Albania, Croatia, and Russia. Soldiers from Nepal, Ghana, Togo, and Mongolia also joined the mission, which reached a strength of 3,686 by June 2010. MINURCAT II replaced the EU force and was deployed between July 2009 and December 2010.[44]

Though EUFOR was credited with increasing security around refugee camps, its successes were very limited. Banditry and armed robberies continued unabated. Internally, repression increased in Chad even as EUFOR deployed its troops, with the political opposition and press freedom curbed and religious freedom restricted.[45] The CAR government of François Bozizé also continued its autocratic practices. Contrary to French promises, EUFOR did not strengthen UNAMID, nor did it stabilise the region. Regional security, particularly in eastern Chad, which still hosted 290,000 refugees and over 180,000 IDPs, in fact worsened after EUFOR's departure. By July 2009, Chadian government forces were reported to have attacked Sudanese border villages, with soldiers from both countries exchanging fire.[46]

The EU launched its fourth African intervention—a 750-strong mission into the CAR—in April 2014, where 2,000 French and 6,000 Central African troops—re-hatted into an 11,000-strong UN peacekeeping mission—were still seeking in early 2016 to stop religious-fuelled slaughter by militias, even as these armed groups attacked the peacekeepers. About 460,000 CAR refugees spilled into neighbouring countries. Many EU partners considered another intervention in the CAR to be too dangerous, suspected more parochial French interests at play in this mineral-rich country, and were distracted by events closer to home in Ukraine. France's image was badly damaged when its troops were alleged to have sexually abused children in exchange for food or money between December 2013 and June 2014 near the M'Poko IDP camp in Bangui, amid allegations of a cover-up by senior French and UN officials.[47]

EU SECURITY SECTOR REFORM AND PIRACY MISSIONS

In addition to these four small military missions, the EU also provided support to security sector reform (SSR) efforts in the DRC and Guinea-Bissau, and deployed an anti-piracy naval mission off the coast of Somalia.

An EU police mission (EUPOL) was established in the Congolese capital of Kinshasa between February 2005 and June 2007, with 20 police advisers and 29 international staff. Their mandate was to help develop the creation of integrated police forces in the run-up to presidential and parliamentary elections in 2006. The forces contributed to security efforts during the polls. This mission was replaced by EUPOL DRC from 2007, which was mandated to support the restructuring of the Congolese police and went beyond the capital, focusing particularly on North and South Kivu.[48] These projects have, however, been criticised for giving short shrift to Congolese ownership, being badly coordinated with the UN and bilateral donors, and being too small to be effective. There were only 32 staff working for EUPOL DRC in November 2009, covering an infrastructurally dilapidated country the size of Western Europe.[49]

Another such mission in the DRC after June 2005 was the EU Security Sector Reform Mission (EUSEC), which has focused on army integration and developing a rapid-reaction force for the country. The mission was established before the Congo's 2006 election, and its 50 EU officers sought to assist international efforts to unite "reformed" former rebel forces into a single command. Twelve of these 4,000-strong brigades were deployed by the time of the elections in July 2006. EUSEC was at first successful in weeding out "ghost workers" from the Congolese army and introducing a new system of payment for integrated brigades. It developed a biometric record of all soldiers and issued identity cards to 129,394 by December 2008.[50] By this time, the Congolese army had been reduced from 340,000 to 150,000, allowing an increase in their salaries from $5 to $40 a month. But within two years, only a few soldiers received their salaries regularly, and the census had to be re-conducted by the EU.[51]

Both EUSEC and EUPOL were under-staffed and under-resourced, and even EU Special Representative Aldo Ajello described his organisation's contributions to security sector reform efforts in the DRC as "a drop in a vast ocean".[52] EUSEC was also unable to coordinate international donors on the ground effectively, while bilateral actors such as Belgium, Britain, the Netherlands, and Germany were said to have insisted on maintaining their autonomous identity. Furthermore, there was rivalry between the EU and MONUC on the ground, with the UN unwilling to provide security and logistical support to EU officials.[53] The Congolese government of Joseph Kabila must also share some of the blame for the failure of these efforts, as it lacked the political will to tackle corruption within the top brass of the country's armed forces, and to coordinate SSR efforts with its partners.[54]

Despite the "alphabet soup" of acronyms and institutions for which the EU has justifiably gained widespread notoriety, its internal bureaucracy often hampered smooth operations on the ground. Recruitment of staff to field missions was sometimes difficult due to the need for them to be deployed from existing missions or seconded by national governments.[55] As a concrete example, the EU's reconstruction work in the DRC (worth €584 million between 2008 and 2013) was plagued by inter-agency rivalry and lack of cohesiveness between the Commission and the Council, with overlapping mandates affecting the effective delivery of programmes. While the Commission had the resources but lacked a strong mandate, the Council had the mandate but lacked adequate resources.[56] Inter-departmental coordination was poor. Mutual envy and loathing was expressed to independent researchers. The EU mission in eastern Congo was staffed by young and inexperienced personnel with no detailed knowledge of the country or the region.[57] Brussels effectively continued to play its typical bureaucratic game of fiddling while the Congo burned. As Meike Froizheim, Frederik Söderbaum, and Ian Taylor devastatingly concluded: "The EU continues to lack a coherent strategy for the DRC, despite a large budget ... [T]he EU is more concerned with establishing a symbolic presence and a form of representation than with achieving specific goals."[58]

Another EU security sector programme was conducted in Guinea-Bissau between June 2008 and September 2010. The mission had only 27 advisers on a budget of €6 million, and was closed down at the time it was most needed: following an army mutiny in April 2010. The EU programme was mandated to help with the reduction of the country's army. President João Bernardo "Nino" Vieira had been assassinated by the military in March 2009. This mission again underlined Brussels's penchant for small, short-term projects, which often seem designed more to enhance its prestige as a global actor and experiment in uncharted fields than to resolve problems on the ground. Despite this limited and ineffectual role, the EU claimed that its mission had "achieved significant results" and provided "a solid legal framework to start implementing the national SSR strategy".[59] An independent evaluation of the mission in 2010, however, noted that the EU's actors "primarily respond to their own organisational and corporate needs *first*, and to those of Guinea-Bissau *second*".[60] The evaluation also highlighted tensions and competition between the EU mission and the UN Peacebuilding Support Office in Guinea-Bissau (UNOGBIS). It was a Nigerian-led, 750-strong Economic Community of West African States (ECOWAS) mission that helped stabilise the country between 2012 and 2016.

Finally, the naval force (NAVFOR), launched as Operation Atalanta in December 2008, mandated the EU to protect ships and merchant vessels of the UN's World Food Programme (WFP) destined for Somalia. The operational headquarters of the 2,000-strong, 19-nation mission was based in London, and the operation cost €400 million annually to run. NAVFOR again exposed the hollowness of Brussels's rhetoric of an "ethical" power using military tools for humanitarian ends. This was a naked attempt to protect European economic interests from pirates rather than to help suffering Somalis emerge from two decades of conflict. France, Germany, Belgium, and Italy had all contributed to the US-led UN missions in Somalia (UNITAF and UNOSOM II) between 1992 and 1995, which left the country anarchic and leaderless after the Americans abandoned the mission following the deaths of 18 of their peacekeepers in 1993. Despite the presence of the EU operation, piracy attacks continued unabated off the Somali coast after 2009 (though incidents had declined by 2012). This short-term mission, like previous EU deployments, failed to address the root causes of the Somali crisis, which required strategies of state-building rather than pirate-hunting.

Concluding Reflections

It is important to note that the EU has sought to develop a common security role since 1997, and deployed four small military missions to the DRC, Chad, and the CAR. While the two missions in the Congo and the one in the CAR contributed to supporting UN missions, they were of limited duration and appeared to be more about parochial French interests and internal EU needs to establish a global security role than about promoting durable peace in Africa. The results of these interventions are also open to serious question: the DRC's Kivu and Orientale provinces remain conflict-prone; a military coup occurred in Guinea-Bissau in 2012, requiring a military intervention by ECOWAS to re-establish stability; anarchy still reigns on the border between Chad and Sudan; religious-fuelled conflict has failed to abate in the CAR; and pirates continue to roam the waters off the Somali coast.

The areas of the deployment of military missions—the DRC, Chad, and the CAR—have further represented areas of parochial French national interests. Belgium also continues to have a particular interest in its former colony, the DRC. Guinea-Bissau remains an area of French interest, having joined the *Union Économique et Monétaire Ouest Africaine* (UEMOA) in 1997, and become a member of the *Communauté Financière Africaine* (CFA) franc currency zone—now under the euro. France used its permanent presence on the UN Security Council to obtain deployment of the four military missions in the DRC, Chad, and the CAR with strong peace-enforcement mandates. The failure to use the EU's rotating rapid-reaction force in all four conflicts—relying instead on ad hoc deployments—again underlined Gallic efforts to control these missions for political purposes. Sweden, Finland, and Ireland all expressed frustration at the failure to employ these battle-groups.[61] French scholar Catherine Gegout scathingly noted about the EU's security role in Africa: "EU missions are carried out first and foremost to promote the EU as a security actor, not to help civilians in conflicts."[62]

The Anglo-French-led military intervention in Libya that toppled Muammar Qaddafi's 42-year autocracy in 2011 once again raised widespread suspicion of Western interventionism in Africa. Though conducted under the NATO flag rather than that of the EU, it was led by two EU members (Britain and France) and involved mostly EU states, and many felt that the mission had abused a UN Security Council mandate intended to protect civilians by transforming the mission into one of "regime change". The intervention has left Libya embroiled in a bitter civil war, with instability from Libya also spreading to Mali. The third powerful military member of the EU, Germany, not only abstained, as a non-permanent member of the UN Security Council, from supporting the Libya intervention, but also refused to take part and was critical of it.

EU leaders have often shown a failure to demonstrate mature leadership, following public opinion instead. Civil society groups have frequently put pressure on European governments to intervene in humanitarian crises in places such as Somalia, Rwanda, Darfur, and the Congo. But as soon as fatalities occur, rather than making the case to public opinion—as has been done in Afghanistan and the Balkans—of why there is a need to stay the course, and explaining that such missions are rarely casualty-free and that professional soldiers understand the risks entailed—such governments often bow to the pressure of short-term polls. Schizophrenic civic publics, which call for EU interventions and then squirm when soldiers are killed, need to be better led. I end this chapter by adapting the words of the child in Andersen's fairy tale with which I began my own tale. In relation to the EU's security role in Africa, the African chorus should cry out in unison: "Put some clothes on that naked European Emperor. She is not our fairy godmother!"

NOTES

1. Quoted in Meike Froizheim, Frederik Söderbaum, and Ian Taylor, "The Limits of the EU as a Peace and Security Actor in the Democratic Republic of the Congo", *Africa Spectrum* 46, no. 3 (2011), p. 46.
2. Hartmut Meyer, "Europe's Postcolonial Role and Identity", in Adekeye Adebajo and Kaye Whiteman (eds.), *The EU and Africa: From Eurafrique to Afro-Europa* (London: Hurst; New York: Columbia University Press; and Johannesburg: Wits University Press, 2012), p. 446.
3. Christopher Hill, "The Capability-Expectations Gap, or Conceptualizing Europe's International Role", *Journal of Common Market Studies* 31, no. 3 (Summer 1993), pp. 305–328.
4. Adekeye Adebajo, *The Curse of Berlin: Africa After the Cold War* (New York: Columbia University Press; London: Hurst; and Scottsville: University of KwaZulu Natal Press, 2010).
5. Niagalé Bagoyoko and Marie V. Gibert, "The European Union in Africa: The Linkage between Security, Governance, and Development from an Institutional Perspective", Working Paper no. 284 (Sussex: Sussex University, Institute of Development Studies [IDS]), pp. 22–26.
6. This phrase on losing an empire and seeking a new role—used in relation to Britain's post-1945 decline—is credited to former United States' (US) secretary of state Dean Acheson.

7. On Britain's Africa policy, *see* Tom Porteous, *Britain in Africa* (London: Zed, 2008); and Paul D. Williams, "Britain, the EU, and Africa", in Adebajo and Whiteman, *The EU and Africa*, pp. 343–364.

8. *See for example* John Chipman, *French Power in Africa* (Oxford: Blackwell, 1989); Victor T. Le Vine, *Politics in Francophone Africa* (Boulder, Colo.: Lynne Rienner, 2007); and Douglas A. Yates, "France, the EU, and Africa", in Adebajo and Whiteman, *The EU and Africa*, pp. 317–342.

9. Christine Gray, "Peacekeeping and Enforcement Action in Africa: The Role of Europe and the Obligations of Multilateralism", *Review of International Studies* 31 (December 2005), pp. 216–217.

10. Lorenzo Fioramonti, Maxi Schoeman, and Gerrit Olivier, "The EU and Multilateral Crisis Management: Assessing Cooperation and Coordination with the UN", Mercury E-Paper no. 19, April 2012, pp. 10–11.

11. William Asanvo and Christian E.B. Pout, "The European Union: African Peace and Security Environment's Champion?", *Points de Vue*, 27 November 2007, pp. 22–24; Garth le Pere, "AU-EU Security and Governance Cooperation", in Adebajo and Whiteman, *The EU and Africa*, pp. 257–275; and Kenneth Mpyisi, "How EU Support of the African Peace and Security Architecture Impacts Democracy Building and Human Security Enhancement in Africa" (Stockholm: International Institute for Democracy and Electoral Assistance [IDEA], 2009).

12. *See for example* Adebayo Adedeji, "The Travails of Regional Integration in Africa", in Adebajo and Whiteman, *The EU and Africa*, pp. 83–104.

13. United Nations (UN), "Second Special Report of the Secretary-General on the United Nations Organization Mission in the Democratic Republic of the Congo", UN Doc. S/2003/556, 27 May 2003, pp. 9, 28.

14. Per Martin Norheim-Martinsen, "Our Work Here Is Done: European Union Peacekeeping in Africa", *African Security Review* 20, no. 2 (June 2011), p. 19.

15. Norheim-Martinsen, "Our Work Here Is Done", p. 19.

16. Alex Vines, "Rhetoric from Brussels and Reality on the Ground: The EU and Security in Africa", *International Affairs* 86, no. 5 (2010), p. 1094.

17. *See* Aldo Ajello, *Brasiers d'Afrique: Mémoires d'un Émissaire pour la Paix* (Paris: L'Harmattan, 2010). *See also* articles on the UN and EU in the DRC by Denis M. Tull, Catherine Gegout, Gorm Rye Olsen, Claudia Morsut, and Eirin Mobekk in *International Peacekeeping* 16, no. 2 (April 2009).

18. Bagoyoko and Gibert, "The European Union in Africa", pp. 22–26; and Norheim-Martinsen, "Our Work Here is Done", p. 21.

19. Norheim-Martinsen, "Our Work Here Is Done", p. 21.

20. Mary Martin, "A Force for Good? The European Union and Human Security in the Democratic Republic of Congo", *African Security Review* 16, no. 2 (2007), pp. 65, 71.

21. Norheim-Martinsen, "Our Work Here Is Done", p. 22.

22. Aldo Ajello, "The EU Security Role in the Great Lakes Region", in Adebajo and Whiteman, *The EU and Africa*, p. 291; and Martin, "A Force for Good?", pp. 71–73.

23. Fioramonti, Schoeman, and Olivier, "The EU and Multilateral Crisis Management", p. 14.

24. Norheim-Martinsen, "Our Work Here Is Done", p. 22.

25. Ajello, "The EU Security Role in the Great Lakes Region", p. 291.

26. René Lemarchand, *The Dynamics of Violence in Central Africa* (Philadelphia: University of Pennsylvania Press, 2009), p. 277.

27. UN, "Twenty-Fourth Report of the Secretary-General on the UN Organization Mission in the Democratic Republic of the Congo", UN Doc. S/2007/671, 14 November 2007, p. 1.

28. Richard Gowan, "From Rapid Reaction to Delayed Inaction? Congo, the UN, and the EU", *International Peacekeeping* 18, no. 5 (November 2011), pp. 593–611; and Vines, "Rhetoric from Brussels and Reality on the Ground", pp. 1101–1102.

29. John Bolton, *Surrender Is Not an Option: Defending America at the United Nations and Abroad* (New York: Threshold, 2007), p. 350.

30. Bolton, *Surrender Is Not an Option*, p. 350.

31. Giovanna Bono, "The EU's Military Operation in Chad and the Central African Republic: An Operation to Save Lives?", *Journal of Intervention and Statebuilding* 5, no. 1 (March 2011), p. 32.

32. Gowan, "From Rapid Reaction to Delayed Inaction?", p. 599; and Mpyisi, "How EU Support Impacts Democracy Building and Human Security Enhancement", p. 10.

33. Norheim-Martinsen, "Our Work Here Is Done", p. 23.

34. Bono, "The EU's Military Operation in Chad and the Central African Republic", p. 30.
35. Bono, "The EU's Military Operation in Chad and the Central African Republic", p. 33.
36. Norheim-Martinsen, "Our Work Here Is Done", p. 24.
37. Vines, "Rhetoric from Brussels and Reality on the Ground", p. 1096.
38. Bono, "The EU's Military Operation in Chad and the Central African Republic", pp. 34–36.
39. Bono, "The EU's Military Operation in Chad and the Central African Republic", p. 37.
40. Winrich Kühne, "The EU Security Role in Chad and the Central African Republic", in Adebajo and Whiteman, *The EU and Africa*, p. 307.
41. Kühne, "The EU Security Role in Chad and the Central African Republic", p. 300.
42. *See* UN, "Report of the Secretary-General on the UN Mission in the Central African Republic and Chad", UN Doc. S/2010/611, 1 December 2010; UN, "Report of the Secretary-General on the UN Mission in the Central African Republic and Chad", UN Doc. S/2010/529, 14 October 2010; and Amnesty International, *Chad: "We Too Deserve Protection"* (London, July 2010).
43. Kühne, "The EU Security Role in Chad and the Central African Republic", p. 296.
44. Vines, "Rhetoric from Brussels and Reality on the Ground", p. 1096.
45. Mpyisi, "How EU Support Impacts Democracy Building and Human Security Enhancement", p. 11.
46. UN, "Report of the UN Secretary-General on the AU/UN Hybrid Operation in Darfur", UN Doc. S/2009/592, 16 November 2009, p. 3.
47. *See* "Taking Action on Sexual Exploitation and Abuse by Peacekeepers", Report of an Independent Review of Sexual Exploitation and Abuse by International Peacekeeping Forces in the Central African Republic, 17 December 2015.
48. Asanvo and Pout, "The European Union", p. 21.
49. Vines, "Rhetoric from Brussels and Reality on the Ground", p. 1097.

50. Vines, "Rhetoric from Brussels and Reality on the Ground", p. 1097.
51. Ajello, "The EU Security Role in the Great Lakes Region", p. 281.
52. Ajello, "The EU Security Role in the Great Lakes Region", p. 282.
53. Ajello, "The EU Security Role in the Great Lakes Region", p. 284.
54. *See* "The Democratic Republic of the Congo: Taking a Stand on Security Sector Reform", report prepared by 13 local and international organisations, 16 April 2012, http://www.enoughproject. org/files/DRC_SSR-Report_2012_0.pdf (accessed 21 December 2015).
55. Vines, "Rhetoric from Brussels and Reality on the Ground", p. 1098.
56. Ajello, "The EU Security Role in the Great Lakes Region", p. 283.
57. Froizheim, Söderbaum, and Taylor, "The Limits of the EU", pp. 51–56.
58. Froizheim, Söderbaum, and Taylor, "The Limits of the EU", p. 45.
59. Cited in Vines, "Rhetoric from Brussels and Reality on the Ground", p. 1098.
60. Vines, "Rhetoric from Brussels and Reality on the Ground", p. 1098 (emphasis in original).
61. Gowan, "From Rapid Reaction to Delayed Inaction?", pp. 606–607.
62. Quoted in Froizheim, Söderbaum, and Taylor, "The Limits of the EU", p. 65.

CHAPTER 10

ACP-EU Migration Policy

Anna Knoll

In recent years, the global paradigm of international migration has shifted from one of mistrust and polarisation towards a more positive view characterised by broadening understanding and increasing awareness of the links between migration and development. Ongoing global dialogues have highlighted the need to replace security- and control-focused restrictive migration management with improved global governance of migration flows based on partnership and cooperation. Ideas about human mobility have also been slowly changing, with mobility—if governed well—coming to be seen as an important strategy for individuals to increase their choices and capabilities. As a result, and due to the current global refugee crisis, international migration and its interaction with development processes has garnered greater interest and moved up on the international agenda. Notably, consensus exists among policymakers that aspects of migration should be integrated into the post-2015 development agenda.[1]

Migration and mobility offer significant development opportunities, as well as challenges, for the African, Caribbean, and Pacific (ACP) group of states and the European Union (EU), and are set to be a defining feature of future development dynamics in both regions (see Nurse and Ruggeri in this volume). Since 2000, the ACP and the EU have engaged in a

A. Knoll (✉)
European Centre for Development Policy Management (ECDPM),
Maastricht, The Netherlands

© The Author(s) 2017
A. Montoute, K. Virk (eds.), *The ACP Group and the EU
Development Partnership*, DOI 10.1007/978-3-319-45492-4_10

joint dialogue on migration and development, which has opened up new opportunities to discuss cooperation in the governance of migration both within the ACP regions and between the continents in a comprehensive way. At the same time, the ACP-EU relationship has been complicated by tensions over migration management, centring on the issues of readmission and respect for ACP migrants' rights.

This chapter critically explores the relationship between the ACP and the EU as it relates to migration, against the backdrop of an evolving global debate on the links between migrant mobility and development. The chapter first provides an overview of the patterns of international mobility relevant for the ACP-EU relationship. Next, it analyses the dichotomy in this relationship between comprehensive dialogue and development cooperation on South-South migration on the one hand, and disagreement and tensions on the issue of readmission and North-South migration management on the other. Finally, the chapter explores aspects of the future of ACP-EU engagement on migration.

ACP-EU Migration Flows amid Evolving Patterns in International Mobility

Globally, the absolute number of international migrants has grown in recent years, from 175 million in 2000 to 232 million in 2013.[2] Most people moving across borders do so within the region in which they live. In 2010, only about one in three international migrants moved from a developing to an industrialised country.[3]

It is difficult to find reliable data on migration between the 79-member ACP group and the 28-member EU.[4] Eurostat data reveal that ACP countries are not the largest source of migrants for most EU member states, including Germany, Spain, and Britain.[5] Yet, for migrants from ACP countries, Europe remains an important destination for reasons of work and family reunion.

International migration patterns to the EU from Africa, the Caribbean, and the Pacific further vary across the three regions (see Nurse and Ruggeri in this volume). For example, while international migration from the Pacific to the countries of the industrialised North is mostly directed towards Australia, New Zealand, and the United States (US),[6] legal migration of higher-skilled workers from West Africa—though restricted—mainly takes place towards Europe and the US.[7] Often, historical links influence migration patterns between ACP and European countries, with, for example, migrants from the anglophone Caribbean and West African states tending to move to Britain, those from francophone African countries to France, and those from the Dutch Caribbean to the Netherlands.[8]

Although attention has mainly focused on (the effects of) migration between continents, "most international migrants ... reside in the region in which they were born", as indicated earlier.[9] In 2013, South-South[10] migration almost equalled South-North migration in numbers. In 2013, "some 82.3 million international migrants who were born in the global South resided in the global South",[11] whereas about 81.9 million international migrants born in the global South were living in the global North. In most ACP countries, although migration within regions and within the global South is a much more prevalent and significant phenomenon than migration to the industrialised North, it remains a largely unexplored research area.[12]

There are, however, differences across regions and sub-regions within the ACP, with Africa, especially West Africa, having the highest levels of intra-regional migration. For example, in sub-Saharan Africa, the "share of intra-regional migration [was] estimated at 63 [per cent]" in 2010, while in West Africa about 75 per cent of migrants moved within the region in the same year.[13] This is compared with only 24 per cent and 15 per cent in the Pacific and Caribbean regions respectively. Research by the Brussels-based ACP Observatory on Migration has shown that labour migration within regions of the global South, as well as across them, has increased significantly over the past three decades.[14] Yet there seems to be relatively little migration among the three areas of the ACP—Africa, the Caribbean, and the Pacific.[15]

Intra-regional migration poses both challenges and opportunities within the ACP. The large numbers of refugees in the Horn of Africa, for example, have raised challenges of protection and integration in local labour markets for East African states.[16] Kenya, for example, is the main host country for forced migrants in the region, hosting over 370,000 refugees. Though access to work is key for durable solutions, refugee groups in camps, such as Somali refugees, find their freedom of movement and access to labour markets formally restricted. The growing number of urban refugees in Kenya struggle to find livelihood opportunities, as well as access to basic services, while at times facing harassment and physical assault.[17] At the same time, these refugees have adapted in entrepreneurial ways, contributing to small-business creation and economic opportunities, as is the case in the Dadaab camps.[18] In the Caribbean region, the high volume of emigration flows—at times up to 10 per cent of a country's population—have brought a different set of opportunities and challenges for development in the host countries. For example, while remittances sent back from migrants to Guyana supported the decline of the proportion of people living below the poverty rate from 43 per cent in 1992 to 35 per cent in 2002, the country has lost a high proportion of high-skilled workers trained in Guyana, such as teachers, to overseas labour markets (see Nurse and Ruggeri in this volume).[19]

Interestingly, after the global financial crisis of 2008–2009 and the ensuing economic recession in the industrialised North, the phenomenon of North-South labour migration became more prevalent, especially between countries that were culturally or historically familiar and shared the same language. There is a paucity of data on migration figures, yet recent trends in migration from the industrialised North towards countries such as Angola, Brazil, China, and Mozambique exemplify this development. Migration from Europe towards Africa has also increased. For example, the number of emigrants from Spain to Africa increased from 6,000 in 2009 to about 84,000 in 2011.[20] Existing migration trends between Portugal and Angola have similarly changed, with many more migrants now leaving from Portugal to reside in the former colony—a trend known as "reverse migration". In 2012, between 25,000 and 30,000 Portuguese emigrated to Angola, a number about 5,000–10,000 higher than in 2011.[21] Simultaneously, this led to an increase in remittances from Angola to Portugal by 83 per cent, from €147.3 million in 2011 to €270.7 million in 2012.[22] Yet researchers have only just started to examine and observe the implications of North-South movements on development efforts.

INCREASING PRESSURE ON THE MIGRATION-DEVELOPMENT NEXUS

Defining the nexus between migration and development is difficult, although migration is increasingly recognised as a development enabler. Human mobility is induced by, and impacts upon, a variety of socio-economic, environmental, and political factors, with different types of migration (such as economic labour migration, irregular migration, forced migration and displacement, and environmentally induced migration) affecting developments in these areas differently. Whereas safe economic labour migration contributes to poverty reduction through remittances and increased wages, forced migration and displacement require governance approaches to provide protection and integrated long-term solutions of integration in host communities, or return options. The benefits of remittances and diaspora engagement for migrants and their families, as well as the positive effect of migration on the Millennium Development Goals (MDGs), have been widely documented,[23] yet intangible transfers through social remittances and their interaction with human development are issues that have yet to be explored further. These include the transfer and diffusion of ideas, practices, and social values. The view that poverty and under-development are correlated with migration, and that migration flows will decrease with more development, is challenged by evidence[24]—exemplifying the fact that the relationship between migration and development is complex (see Nurse and Ruggeri in this volume).

Yet there is a set of common and significant challenges that cut across different types of international migration, particularly South-South migration. They include the smuggling and trafficking of persons; the integration of newly arrived migrants or of returnees; and the impact of climate change on migration patterns. These challenges are often inadequately addressed by regional or national frameworks within the global South, including the ACP region, and as a result the potential positive benefits of South-South migration are not optimally supported.[25] For example, although several regional cooperation frameworks, such as the African Union (AU), the Intergovernmental Authority on Development (IGAD), and the Economic Community of West African States (ECOWAS), acknowledge environmentally induced migration, they do so mostly indirectly, lack comprehensiveness, and would require increased investment to improve effectiveness.[26] Although greater efforts to govern migration more effectively and to focus on the rights of migrants are being made, ACP countries by and large still need to build up the networks and skills that are needed to manage South-South migration and to benefit from its potential for development.

Research by the ACP Observatory on Migration indicates that future migration trends and patterns will be further influenced by population dynamics. In the global South, economic growth, particularly in Brazil, Russia, India, China, and South Africa (the BRICS bloc) (see Virk in this volume), together with an expanding middle class, is expected to "give rise to an increased demand for migrant workers in these countries".[27] In the cases of China and India in particular, the growth of the middle class, combined with the ageing of their societies, will likely increase their need for both specialised and low-skilled workers, generating greater South-South migration towards these countries.[28]

Against the background of its own ageing society, the EU has indicated an intent to develop—in cooperation with third countries—a new approach to legal migration, in order to attract young migrants with necessary skills.[29] However, EU member states have found it difficult to move beyond a securitised approach to migration management, especially in response to irregular migration to European shores, giving rise to the term "Fortress Europe".[30]

The ACP countries have raised concerns about the treatment and respect for the rights of their nationals resident in EU countries.[31] However, comprehensive solutions to Europe's irregular migration crisis, including an overhaul of migration policies, have remained elusive, and the provision of adequate and effective legal channels for migration has been challenging. While migration has become increasingly necessary for the growth and stability of European labour markets and economies, growing anti-immigration sentiments in EU member states—such as Germany, France, and Britain—may make it even more difficult to improve opportunities for migrants across all skill levels. It is worth noting that mistreatment of migrants and xenophobia are not confined to the EU, but are also issues of concern within ACP countries.

Migration in ACP-EU Politics and Policy

A dichotomy has characterised the discussion on migration between the ACP and the EU. On the one hand, there has been a strong focus on North-South relations in migration management, concerned especially with restrictive EU migration policies and the thorny issue of return/readmission. On the other hand, there have been progressive, though somewhat detached, efforts to integrate migration as a theme in the ACP-EU partnership for development cooperation, based on a broadened understanding of the complexities of migration flows and developments often taking place within the African, Caribbean, and Pacific regions and between individual developing countries.[32]

Furthermore, a longstanding lack of mutual trust in the negotiations on migration has hampered the development and implementation of a comprehensive, common ACP-EU agenda for action. Although migration has increasingly been highlighted in various declarations and agreements by both sides, it has become one of the most contentious aspects of the ACP-EU partnership. The issue of migration was noted in an annex to the Lomé III Convention,[33] signed in December 1984, and garnered a brief reference in the main text of its successor agreement, Lomé IV, signed in December 1989, which governed the relationship between the ACP and the EU until 1999. (See Whiteman in this volume on the history of the ACP-EU relationship.) The Cotonou Partnership Agreement of 2000 included, for the first time, a full article on migration. Yet negotiations for the clause on migration—Article 13—were controversial,[34] and almost derailed the overall process towards Cotonou.[35] Readmission and return were the most contentious issues, with EU justice and home affairs ministers seeking to insert a clause on readmission at the last minute.[36] This clause would have included the duty of ACP countries to admit not only their own nationals but also transiting third-country nationals. The ACP countries resisted, on the grounds that the clause including readmission of non-ACP country nationals or stateless persons would have no basis in international law, but they were open to accepting a provision for the admission of their nationals. The matter was only settled through a compromise in the final round of negotiations: instead of including binding readmission provisions for all ACP countries, Article 13 of Cotonou provides that EU member states can request negotiations with ACP states for bilateral agreements on readmission.[37]

While Article 13 established a dialogue on migration covering the rights of migrants, non-discrimination of legal migrants, and training of ACP nationals abroad, it also placed a strong focus on migration control,[38] and, from the viewpoint of the present, reveals a rather outdated understanding of the complex interrelation between migration, poverty reduction, and development.[39] In particular, the EU's insistence on the readmission clause in Cotonou has since raised questions about the compatibility of the agreement's approach to migration with its overall aim of reducing poverty in the ACP regions.[40]

Against the backdrop of an ongoing global debate on the nexus between migration and development, understanding of the issue has broadened in both the EU and the ACP in the years following the signing of the Cotonou Agreement. Migration has been gradually reframed as an important development issue and enabler in the global debate, as well as in the ACP-EU relationship.

Until the beginning of the 2000s, the EU's policies were focused on addressing the root causes of migration, to reduce outward migration from developing countries, particularly to Europe. Then, in September 2005, the EU Commission's Communication on Migration and Development introduced a more elaborate understanding of the interaction between migration and development, including innovative ideas in the areas of circular migration, remittances, and diaspora involvement. In the same year, the EU's Global Approach to Migration (GAM) was developed. This was replaced in 2011 with an updated Global Approach to Migration and Mobility (GAMM). Together, these policy statements aimed to provide a framework for a more strategic phase of dialogue and cooperation with partner countries, including with the ACP.

Meanwhile, the ACP group's position has been to emphasise the developmental effects of migration, as reflected in its Declaration on Asylum, Migration, and Mobility of 2006, and in the Brussels Resolution on Migration and Development of 2008. The former noted the need for examining the root causes of migration and for taking into account the wider development context when formulating responses to irregular and forced migration. Support for and engagement with the diaspora, as well as the promotion of more efficient and less costly remittance transfer systems, were also highlighted in the 2006 declaration. Its follow-up, the 2008 Brussels declaration, focused more explicitly on the sustainable development dimensions of migration. It pointed to the contributions of migrants and diasporas, the link between migration and the environment, and the relationship between migration and human security, and included the identification of development projects focused on migration.[41] These policy statements were followed by greater engagement by the ACP—through its Brussels-based secretariat—in the global migration debate, and by efforts to highlight the issue of South-South migration in international fora such as the Global Forum on Migration and Development. (See Nurse and Ruggeri in this volume on the role of diasporas in ACP development.)

Despite broadening understanding of migration and growing alignment in ACP and EU policy positions, the revision of the Cotonou Agreement in 2010 did not include any modification of Article 13, with disagreement and tensions re-emerging over the issue of readmission. The initial idea by both sides was to update the migration provisions in a manner that better reflected the forward thinking on development and migration captured in both the European GAM and the ACP's policy declarations, and that took a more positive approach than the focus on restrictive migration management. Accordingly, Article 13 was intended to be retitled "Migration and Development" and to refocus on creating synergies between migration and development.

Yet, once again, the issue of readmission prevented agreement. The EU demanded significant changes that sought to make the provision on readmission binding and operational for all ACP countries, regardless of their specific capacities and conditions, while the ACP countries highlighted their differing capacities and refused to accept the European position. Instead, a joint ACP-EU declaration on migration and development was issued, expressing agreement to strengthen and deepen dialogue and cooperation on the three pillars of the EU's GAM—migration and development, legal migration, and illegal migration. This dialogue was intended to prepare the ground for the next revision of Article 13, in 2015. After a year of productive dialogue, progress had been made on several developmental aspects of migration, such as South-South migration and remittances,[42] and agreement was reached in July 2011 to focus on concrete results in the form of joint reports or Council Conclusions, and to make cooperation more operational in the areas of visas, remittances, and readmission.[43] However, with the 2015 revision not having taken place, these aspects remain to be addressed in discussions on the post-2020 ACP-EU framework.

ACP-EU Relations on Migration in Practice

Despite progress at the level of policy statements, some have described the continuing ACP-EU dialogue on readmission and legal migration as a "dialogue of the deaf".[44] The African, Caribbean, and Pacific countries felt that the EU had compartmentalised issues (such as readmission, visas, and remittances) that needed to be addressed together, and saw the discussions on readmission as taking the form of a "negotiation rather than a dialogue", which was not conducive to building trust. On the other hand, the EU felt that ACP countries had dragged their feet over cooperation on readmission and had failed to live up to their obligations to respond to readmission requests.[45]

It is worth noting that some EU member states saw themselves increasingly under pressure from domestic constituencies to show results on readmission, especially in the context of providing aid to ACP countries. The ACP countries countered that the EU had ignored their inability, due to capacity constraints, to reintegrate returnees adequately, and that forced returns often led to a "revolving door" process, with returned migrants attempting again to reach European shores. Delays in responses to EU requests were explained by the weak capacity of many ACP member states and the complex identification procedures that the nature of irregular migration necessitated. Tensions between the two sides were further fuelled by allegations that some EU member states had breached the non-refoulement principle,[46] as well as by reports of improper treatment of ACP asylum-seekers and degrading return procedures.[47] Enshrined in Article 33 of the Geneva Convention on Refugees, the non-refoulement principle prohibits the expulsion, or return, of a refugee into territories where his or her life or freedom would be threatened on account of race, religion, nationality, or political opinion.

Despite these differences, and after a number of meetings of technical experts in 2011 and 2012, the ACP and the EU, in 2012, adopted a set of joint recommendations on migration-related issues. However, these were once again sparse in terms of detail about specific operational arrangements, instead leaving them open for further dialogue. For example, there was agreement that exchanges should continue (rather than there being specific decisions made) on visa-related legislation and practices and fees, such as the EU Visa Code, to provide a more transparent framework for migration. Both sides also agreed on the need for deeper reflection on how to improve accessibility to visa application procedures in ACP countries, and on how these procedures could be accelerated. On remittances, the 2012 recommendations provided some operational guidance in terms of the particular issues (such as improving the legislative and regulatory framework in sending and receiving countries to promote competition in financial markets, or making data on remittance transfer costs available) that should be pursued at national and regional government and private sector levels. With regard to the thorny issue of readmission, there was agreement that the matter should be considered in a wider framework, and linked with initiatives for legal migration and efforts to promote synergies between migration and development. At the same time, the two sides agreed to continue the dialogue with a view to setting deadlines for responding to readmission requests. However, no breakthrough of concrete commitments was achieved.[48]

Meanwhile, individual ACP and EU countries continued to negotiate bilaterally on migration issues, such as visas, readmission, and asylum.

Impact of ACP-EU Cooperation on Legal Migration Opportunities

At present, ACP-EU migration cooperation includes only a few formal opportunities for legal migration from African, Caribbean, and Pacific countries to the European Union for the purpose of employment. For most EU member states, migration remains a highly politicised issue.

Even though legal migration has been acknowledged as "the best route for individuals seeking to move from their country of origin (as well as) for the receiving country",[49] individual European countries have found it difficult to integrate development considerations into their migration policies and offer more legal routes of entry for migrants from ACP countries. The EU Commission formulated a Policy Plan on Legal Migration in December 2005, following which it issued four new directives focusing on conditions for highly qualified workers, intra-corporate transferees, remunerated trainees, and seasonal workers in subsequent years. The directives set out conditions and a common set of rights for certain types of migrants, while providing the legal framework for their entry into the EU.[50] Most recently, in February 2014, the Commission adopted the Seasonal Workers' Directive, addressing low-skilled migrants.

Yet migration is a shared competence between the EU and its member states, and individual countries have the sovereign prerogative to decide the number of visas that they issue to foreign nationals. Consequently, the reality on the ground has been to restrict migration mostly to higher-skilled individuals, while not increasing opportunities for lower-skilled or unskilled workers—this despite awareness of the potential for lower-skilled migrants to contribute to development in the countries of origin.

In February 2014, the EU agreed to exempt 16 ACP Caribbean and Pacific countries[51] from entry visa requirements through its Visa Code. However, the exemption does not cover long-term legal migration opportunities, and is restricted to certain categories of travellers—in particular, researchers, students, and young persons. Meanwhile, access to EU visas has remained a challenge for applicants in sub-Saharan African countries. There is insufficient consular coverage in several African countries, making it difficult to apply for a visa. The establishment of common visa centres could help to ameliorate the situation.

Some ACP countries had individual agreements with the EU in 2014. Cape Verde was the only ACP country that had entered a mobility partnership with the EU—signed in 2008—which is typically more comprehensive than other bilateral agreements. Such partnerships aim to cover the facilitation of legal migration and integration, short-stay visas, migration and development links, asylum, irregular migration, and return and readmission. Negotiations with Senegal for a similar mobility partnership failed and were suspended in 2009. The EU's primary interest in the negotiations seemed to have been to strengthen Senegal's role as a "gatekeeper" of migratory flows and to regulate return and readmission, rather than to establish legal migration opportunities. The failure to conclude the partnership has been ascribed to its lack of perceived value-added for Senegal compared with its existing bilateral arrangements, notably with France; a belief that the partnership would instate an undesirable level of rigidity to migration cooperation with Europe; legal ambiguity and complexity; as well as incoherencies and the absence of clear leadership in both parties' foreign policies.[52]

In 2012, Ghana and the EU entered discussions on a common agenda regarding migration and mobility, setting out a set of common objectives, though this agenda is less formal than a mobility partnership. A similar, common agenda was signed with Ethiopia in 2015 and with Nigeria in the same year. Meanwhile, the EU and South Africa have also been engaged in a dialogue on migration since 2008, and both sides have voiced an interest in working together on issues related to visa facilitation for the benefit of South African and European nationals.

In sum, despite progress in certain aspects, the legal opportunities for migration between the EU and the ACP countries vary from region to region and country to country. A coherent approach to the issue continues to be lacking. In addition, existing European migration policies have failed so far to integrate development considerations systematically.

EU Development Cooperation with ACP Countries on Migration

Despite tension and disagreement on the issue of readmission and the management of migration from ACP countries to the European Union, ACP-EU cooperation has progressed with a positive impact on the building of migration and development-related capacities in ACP states. Facilitated by the governing framework of the Cotonou Agreement, the support for migration under the European Development Fund (EDF) has placed a strong emphasis on South-South migration. Through its regional, national, and intra-ACP envelopes, the EDF has contributed to supporting a number of beneficial migration-related developmental projects and outcomes. This support is also linked to the recommendations put forward by the ACP-EU dialogue on migration.

In 2009, the Intra-ACP Migration Facility was established, with a view to fostering dialogue within the ACP, and to building capacity and improving policymaking on migration in its member states. ACP-led and EU-funded, the components of the Migration Facility include capacity-building of government institutions and civil society, and an ACP Observatory on Migration to strengthen research on migration issues. The facility's capacity-building and networking activities were slow to get off the ground, with doubts raised about the sustainability of its actions.[53] However, the ACP Observatory has achieved a great deal in terms of advancing research and knowledge on ACP and South-South mobility. It has emerged as the leading research repository on the issue of South-South migration, and its outputs, though the Observatory wrapped up its activities in 2014, continue to provide relevant evidence for migration and development policymaking.

These more positive aspects of the ACP-EU dialogue and joint actions have helped to foster a common understanding on broader migration issues, and established a "common ground for productive exchange and practical programming".[54] The rapprochement was also crucial for the formulation of the joint ACP-EU position that was published ahead of the UN High-Level Dialogue on International Migration and Development in October 2013.

The EU's support for South-South migration has emerged as a general theme in its development cooperation, based on the understanding that "inter- and intra-regional migration in developing regions far exceeds migration to the EU"[55] and, while creating challenges, can also have positive impacts on development. Beyond the intra-ACP envelope of the EDF, migration programmes have also been funded in ACP countries through national as well as regional envelopes. For example, the Economic Community of West African States has received annual support of €26 million, starting in 2012, to implement its Free Movement Protocol of 1979 under the tenth EDF regional envelope for West Africa. In Ethiopia, the eleventh EDF, which covers the period from 2014 to 2020, includes plans to support the Ethiopian government with the reintegration of migrants returning to Ethiopia from crisis-affected Middle Eastern countries. There are numerous such projects supported either by the EU or its member states that focus on better migration governance within ACP countries and regions. For the period 2014–2020, EDF programming will include ACP-EU cooperation on an initiative—to be implemented by the International Organisation for Migration (IOM)—that aims to sustain interest in the phenomenon of migration and to help prepare countries to face the challenges that it brings.[56]

Some analysts have pointed out that the EU, through its development cooperation, has also aimed to reduce migration to Europe by strengthening alternative migration opportunities within the ACP regions.[57] In this context, it is worth noting that the EU has faced continuing pressure from some of its member states to instrumentalise aid funding for its migration policy objectives. In the past, this question centred on whether cooperation on migration—for example, on readmission—could be added as a condition for EU aid programming through the EDF, or if capacity-building should focus narrowly on (restrictive) migration management.[58] However, negative conditionality is not compatible with the legal mandate of EU aid to contribute effectively to poverty reduction. By focusing aid programmes on South-South migration, and identifying and supporting migration-related development issues that matter for poverty reduction within the ACP regions, developmental actors—in particular the European Commission's Directorate-General for International Cooperation and Development—were to some extent able to circumvent the pressures emanating from their home affairs counterparts.

Current ACP-EU development cooperation has also come to be characterised by positive conditionality (or the principle of "more-for-more"), which has emerged through renewed EU efforts to ensure compliance on readmission by ACP countries. In line with this principle, any proposal to negotiate agreements on readmission should be accompanied by an incentive, mostly in the form of aid support through development cooperation on certain migration issues. In June 2014, the Justice and Home Affairs Council, in its conclusions, stressed the need to "strengthen the operational aspects of cooperation on readmission with the ACP countries".[59] In 2014, during the Greek presidency of the EU, deliberations were started within the EU Council on how existing provisions on readmission, such as Article 13 of the 2000 Cotonou Agreement, could be operationalised more effectively, drawing on the example of the principle of "more-for-more". After some EU member states underlined the lack of cooperation on readmission by partner ACP countries, in June 2014 the EU endorsed a pilot project with a proposed focus on two ACP states, Ghana and Nigeria, among others. This project foresees the development of a targeted strategy to increase its leverage on the issue, based on tools to be identified by all the relevant European Commission services—the Directorate-Generals for Migration and Home Affairs; International Cooperation and Development; Trade; and Education and Culture, as well as the EU delegations.

Efforts have also been made by the EU to finance capacity-building in migration management. The EDF and the EU's Development Cooperation Instrument (DCI) are, strictly speaking, not available for financing the external aspects of the EU's migration policy interests if these do not overlap with the development strategies or poverty reduction goals of ACP partner countries. The Asylum, Migration, and Integration Fund (AMIF), created for the period 2014–2020 under the aegis of the EU's Directorate-General for Migration and Home Affairs, aims to finance "cooperation aimed at pursuing the Union's priorities with third countries to reinforce their capacities to adequately manage flows of persons applying for international protection".[60] This includes capacity-building in third countries for the effective implementation of readmission and return policies and reintegration measures, though this focused on non-ACP countries in 2014.[61] With regard to ACP countries, the fund will be used for information campaigns in Niger, Ethiopia, and Sudan, targeting West Africans, Somalis, and Eritreans, with the aim to "raise awareness concerning the … risk and dangers faced by migrants attempting to reach the EU through irregular channels".[62]

The regulations of the AMIF require close cooperation and coherence with the EU's other external instruments and development principles. Yet, as the Office of the United Nations High Commissioner for Refugees (UNHCR) has pointed out, the EU's Directorate-General for Migration and Home Affairs is not a traditional actor in external or development relations. Some of its interventions through AMIF may, however, have implications for development. Accordingly, any such AMIF policy measures should be carried out with a view to the development efforts of the ACP (rather than the objective interests of the EU alone), as is the case with the EU's regional protection programmes in Africa, the Caribbean, and the Pacific. Their complementarity and compliance with development principles thus needs to be monitored for policy coherence with ACP-EU cooperation on migration.[63]

THE FUTURE OF ACP-EU ENGAGEMENT ON MIGRATION

Despite better understanding about the migration-development nexus, the link between legal migration and development has not been made in other relevant areas in the ACP-EU partnership.[64] The negotiations for economic partnership agreements (EPAs) mandated by Cotonou between the EU and the ACP are a prime example (see Akokpari, Carim, Girvan and Montoute, Gonzales, Katjavivi, and Tavola in this volume). There is an acknowledged link between trade and migration flows, yet the ACP-EU discussions on migration and the EPA negotiations have taken place in separate spheres, and there has been only very limited scope for integrating migration aspects into the trade agreements between the ACP and the EU.[65] Although the EPAs include provisions related to the mobility of natural persons (human beings as opposed to legal persons, such as business, governmental, or non-governmental organisations) to varying extents, they seem to be rather restricted, and often only include higher-skilled experts. Overall, legal migration has remained a large "blind spot" in ACP-EU relations, which has meant that significant opportunities to draw positive benefits from the linkages between migration and development and to provide alternatives for irregular migration in joint policies have been foregone.

It is possible that the discussions on migration and development cooperation in other regional dialogue fora, such as the Joint Africa-EU Strategy (JAES) or the Regional Consultative Processes, may outpace those taking place within the framework of the ACP-EU partnership, particularly as the focus strengthens on the future of the ACP group as a whole (see Gomes in this volume). Given that the final five-year revision of Cotonou planned for 2015 did not take place, there is no renewed opportunity to modify the outdated text of Article 13 and to integrate global reflections about the nexus between migration and development into the ACP-EU partnership. The outcomes of the second UN High-Level Dialogue on International Migration and Development, held in October 2013, as well as the debate on the post-2015 development agenda, have provided renewed impetus towards this end. Furthermore, both the EU's and the ACP's own policy frameworks on migration and development, as well as their joint declaration for the UN High-Level Dialogue, provide a basis for a common position on how to broaden the migration partnership formally.

In the longer term, the question about the added value of the ACP group, vis-à-vis other institutional fora, for the EU in dealing with migration issues may come to the fore in the broader context of discussions on the future of the ACP-EU partnership post-2020.[66] For example, under the aforementioned JAES, adopted in 2007, the EU and the AU have issued a number of joint declarations on migration, and pursued an Africa-EU Partnership on Migration, Mobility, and Employment—established under the JAES—that includes the African ACP countries. Though this Africa-EU partnership faces a number of challenges (see Akokpari in this volume), and the dialogue has produced few concrete results thus far, it is more wide-ranging in its scope than Cotonou's provision on migration.

Most recently, following the Lampedusa boat tragedy in October 2013, in which at least 300 migrant lives were lost, the fourth Africa-EU summit, in April 2014, adopted a specific declaration on migration and mobility under the JAES, which aimed to tackle migration and development in a comprehensive way in key areas of the EU's GAMM: human trafficking, irregular migration, the link between migration and development, the relationship between legal migration and mobility, and international protection. From the perspective of EU member states, the Africa-EU partnership has greater strategic value compared with the ACP-EU partnership, as the former includes most of Europe's neighbourhood in the southern Mediterranean. An effective migration partnership with Africa is critically important for the EU, especially one that can help in reducing irregular migration to Europe through both enhanced governance of borders and more effective migration policy cooperation with African countries.[67] The EU does not have a comprehensive partnership similar to the JAES with the Caribbean and Pacific regions in the ACP,[68] which may be due to the lower strategic importance attached to migration flows and relations between the respective regions by both sides. The Joint Caribbean-EU Strategy does not include migration. (See Girvan and Montoute in this volume on the Caribbean-EU relationship.) The EU has also not yet concluded a comprehensive joint strategy with the Pacific, beyond noting skilled labour migration as a key development constraint, and remittances as a substantial part of many Pacific economies, in the 2012 communication on a renewed EU-Pacific development partnership.[69] (See Tavola in this volume on the EU-Pacific relationship.)

Nonetheless, the 79-member ACP group remains a valuable voice in terms of articulating additional perspectives on South-South intercontinental migration and its implications for development. This breadth of perspectives can provide leverage to the grouping, when engaging with its other strategic partners beyond the EU, as well as in global dialogues, on similar migration and development issues. Yet the ACP's internal regional consultations on the future perspectives of the group beyond 2015 and 2020 have not highlighted migration as an agenda item for engaging with new and emerging economies such as the BRICS (see Virk in this volume), or for substantively increasing intra-ACP cooperation going forward. The lack of ownership of the Intra-ACP Migration Facility by ACP member states further indicates that there simply may not be sufficient interest to pursue a strong, common, intra-ACP cooperation agenda on migration.[70]

Ongoing discussions on the future of ACP-EU relations have considered, among other things, a "regionalisation scenario" that would acknowledge the ACP as an umbrella organisation—one based on either the three ACP regions (as presently constituted within the grouping), the regional economic communities (RECs), or the EPA negotiating configurations with the EU (see Gomes in this volume).[71] Indeed, the EU has proposed such a regional approach to the ACP-EU dialogue on the readmission clause of Article 13 of Cotonou: after the adoption of the joint ACP-EU recommendations on migration in 2012, the EU Commission suggested holding regional meetings on readmission. The ACP countries, however, preferred that the discussions take place with the entire grouping, arguing that they would have a stronger negotiating position as a united block.

At the risk of continuing the "dialogue of the deaf", a balance needs to be found between dividing into regional groups for more sensitised and context-specific discussions, and addressing the opportunities and challenges of the migration-development nexus as a global phenomenon.

Concluding Reflections

Migration flows between ACP and EU countries hold much development potential for both regions. The demands for and flows of migration between and within the two groupings have grown, and are unlikely to subside in the coming decades. In the case of Europe, the demands stem from the need to counteract skill shortages and the effects of an ageing population. On the part of the ACP countries, they arise from a need to tap into the positive benefits of the migration-development nexus, which include increased legal labour migration opportunities, remittances and investments, and diaspora engagement. Consequently, migration has emerged as an increasingly prominent issue in the ACP-EU development partnership, becoming progressively more integrated in formal agreements and strategies. However, since 1999, the discussions on migration have also become more contentious, owing to various factors, including reactive politics, pressurised labour markets, and international conflicts. Readmission and return, in particular, have proved to be especially sensitive issues in discussions on ACP-EU policy frameworks since Lomé III. This has hampered the effective integration of developmental aspects into migration policies, as well as the formulation and implementation of plans to operationalise them. As such, both ACP and EU policymaking are exhibiting major lacunas in terms of effectively responding to the demands of both migration and development.

The EU, in particular, has placed too much emphasis on security concerns and the narrow interests of its members. The latter have tended to hold tight to their legal prerogatives on the issue of migration, and have done little to foster its developmental effects in their migration policies. Where the EU has adopted migration policy measures with a view to their developmental impact, these have rarely been legally binding and have entailed weak commitments on the part of the EU, while imposing strict obligations in parallel on third countries. Meanwhile, the ACP has taken little ownership of regional cooperation on migration and development. Despite the large flows of South-South migration among ACP countries, they have shown little appetite for operationalising comprehensive policies on legal migration between the ACP regions. At a time when the very existence of the ACP group is increasingly being questioned, the grouping could find its added value in the contribution it can make to the understanding of migration flows, based on the research generated through the ACP Observatory on Migration, and through the sharing of experiences of integration and return challenges.

In recent years, some progress has been made on integrating the developmental aspects of migration into ACP-EU cooperation. This has mainly focused on support for ACP states to manage the significant South-South migration flows. Within the EU, internal relations between its development actors (primarily the Directorate-General for International Cooperation and Development) and those tasked with migration issues (the Directorate-General for Migration and Home Affairs) have improved, and cooperation is being built. While different interests still come to the fore, recent EU Council Conclusions point towards the intent to integrate development as an explicit component of EU migration policies. Yet, recent unilateral initiatives by the EU to entice particular ACP countries to cooperate more on readmission agreements may lead to renewed tensions. Should both ACP and European leaders want to activate the developmental potential of migration flows within and between their countries, there is much to be gained in terms of forging a more comprehensive vision and cooperation on migration that cuts across different policy areas.

Notes

1. This is most powerfully stated in the outcome document of the 2013 United Nations (UN) High-Level Dialogue on International Migration and Development, and the 2014 proposal of the Open Working Group on Sustainable Development Goals, available at https://sustainabledevelopment.un.org/owg.html (accessed 7 July 2015). However, the recent policy responses of the European Union (EU) to the challenge posed by irregular migration have tended to revert to security- and control-focused restrictive migration management.

2. United Nations, Department of Economic and Social Affairs, Population Division, "Population Facts: The Number of International Migrants Worldwide Reaches 232 Million", New York, United States (US), September 2013, p. 1, http://esa.un.org/unmigration/documents/The_number_of_international_migrants.pdf (accessed 27 February 2015).

3. African, Caribbean, and Pacific (ACP) Observatory on Migration, *Providing the Evidence Base for Policy Development on South-South Migration and Human Development*, report for the tenth Coordination Meeting on International Migration (New York: United Nations, 2012), p. 2, http://www.un.org/en/development/desa/population/events/pdf/10/P2.ACP%20Observatory%20on%20Migration.pdf (accessed 27 February 2015).

4. In a national referendum, held in June 2016, Britain voted to leave the European Union. Official negotiations were yet to begin at the time of writing, but as and when Britain leaves the Union, the membership of the EU will be reduced to 27.

5. Eurostat, "Migration and Migrant Population Statistics", Brussels, Belgium, May 2014, http://ec.europa.eu/eurostat/statistics-explained/index.php/Migration_and_migrant_population_statistics#Foreign_and_foreign-born_population (accessed 19 December 2014). Note that Britain is used synonymously with the United Kingdom (UK) in this volume.

6. ACP Observatory on Migration, "Overview on South-South Migration and Development in the Pacific: Trends and Research

Needs", Regional Overview Paper no. ACPOBS/2011/PUB03 (Brussels, 2011), p. 5.

7. ACP Observatory on Migration, "Overview on South-South Migration and Development in West Africa: Trends and Research Needs", Regional Overview Paper no. ACPOBS/2010/PUB13 (Brussels, 2010), p. 9.

8. Frank Pieke, Nicholas Van Hear, and Anna Lindley, "Synthesis Study: A Part of the Report on Informal Remittances Systems in Africa, Caribbean, and Pacific (ACP) Countries" (Oxford: Centre on Migration, Policy, and Society [COMPAS], University of Oxford, 2005), p. 9.

9. UN, *Report of the Secretary General on International Migration and Development*, UN doc. A/69/207, 30 July 2014, p. 2, para. 5.

10. For the purpose of this chapter, the global "South" refers to low- and middle-income countries and the "North" to high-income countries, as defined by the World Bank.

11. UN Department of Economic and Social Affairs and the Organisation for Economic Cooperation and Development (OECD), *World Migration in Figures* (New York: United Nations, 2013), p. 2.

12. ACP Observatory on Migration, "South-South Migration and Development Conference: Discussing New Evidence from the ACP Observatory on Migration", concept note, Brussels, 3–4 June 2014, p. 1.

13. Jason Gagnon and David Khodour-Casteras, "South-South Migration in West Africa: Addressing the Challenge of Immigrant Integration", Working Paper no. 312 (Paris: OECD, 2012), p. 9.

14. International Organisation for Migration (IOM), "South-South Migration: Partnering Strategically for Development", background paper, 2014 International Dialogue on Migration (IDM), Geneva, Switzerland, 24–25 March 2014, p. 4.

15. Pieke, Van Hear, and Lindley, "Synthesis Study", p. 9.

16. ACP Observatory on Migration, "Overview on South-South Migration and Development in East Africa: Trends and Research Needs", Regional Overview Paper no. ACBOBS/2011/PUB04 (Brussels, 2011), p. 8.

17. Overseas Development Institute (ODI), "Hidden and Exposed: Urban Refugees in Nairobi, Kenya", ODI Event Report, 25 March 2010 (London, 2010), http://www.odi.org/events/2120-hidden-exposed-urban-refugees-nairobi-kenya (accessed 27 February 2015).
18. Alexander Betts, "Put Innovation at the Heart of Protection Work", *The Guardian*, 4 January 2013, http://www.theguardian.com/global-development-professionals-network/2013/jan/04/refugees-camp-innovation-creativity (accessed 27 February 2015).
19. Claremont Kirton and Patsy Lewis, "Guyana Country Case Study", in Wonderful Hope Khonje (ed.), *Migration and Development: Perspectives from Small States* (London: Commonwealth Secretariat, 2015), p. 92.
20. Frank Laczko and Tara Brian, *North-South Migration: A Different Look at the Migration and Development Debate* (Geneva: IOM, 2013), http://www.iom.int/cms/en/sites/iom/home/what-we-do/migration-policy-and-research/migration-policy-1/migration-policy-practice/issues/june-july-2013/northsouth-migration-a-different.html (accessed 27 February 2015).
21. Palash Ghosh, "Portugal's Best and Brightest Escape Hardship in Record Numbers", *International Business Times*, 28 January 2013, http://www.ibtimes.com/portugals-best-brightest-escaping-economic-hardship-record-numbers-1042072 (accessed 27 February 2015).
22. Observatório da Emigração, "Remessas de Emigrantes Portugueses Aumentaram 13 % em 2012", 2013, http://www.observatorioe-migracao.secomunidades.pt/np4/3464.html (accessed 27 February 2015).
23. *See for example* European Union, *Post-2015: Global Action for an Inclusive and Sustainable Future*, European Report on Development (Brussels: ODI, German Development Institute [DIE], and European Centre for Development Policy Management [ECDPM], 2013); and IOM, *The Millennium Development Goals and Migration*, Migration Research Series no. 20 (Geneva, 2005).
24. Hein de Haas, "What Drives Human Migration?" 11 December 2013, http://heindehaas.blogspot.nl/2013/12/what-drives-human-migration.html (accessed 27 February 2015).
25. IOM, "South-South Migration", p. 8.

26. IOM, "South-South Migration", pp. 10–11.
27. ACP Observatory on Migration, *Migration and Development within the South: New Evidence from African, Caribbean, and Pacific Countries*, Migration Research Series no. 46 (Geneva: IOM, 2013), p. 79.
28. ACP Observatory on Migration, *Migration and Development within the South*, p. 79.
29. EU Commission, "Commission Work Programme 2015: A New Start", COM (2014) 910 Final, communication from the Commission to the European Parliament, the Council, the European Economic and Social Committee, and the Committee of the Regions, Brussels, 16 December 2014.
30. Amnesty International, *The Human Costs of Fortress Europe* (London, 2014).
31. Henrike Klavert and Jeske van Seters, "ACP-EU Cooperation on Readmission: Where Does It Stand and Where to Go?" briefing note (Maastricht: ECDPM, April 2012), p. 5.
32. Jonathan Crush, *Between North and South: The EU-ACP Migration Relationship*, Centre for International Governance Innovation (CIGI) Paper no. 16 (Waterloo, Canada: CIGI, April 2013).
33. Annex IX to the Lomé III Convention included a joint declaration on ACP migrant workers and ACP students, noting that "foreign workers shall not be discriminated against and that training of ACP nationals shall be enhanced, in particular with regard to reintegration in their country of origin". *See* Katharina Eisele, *The External Dimension of EU Migration Policy* (Leiden, Netherlands: Koninklijke Brill, 2014), p. 260.
34. Tine Van Criekinge, *The EU-Africa Migration Partnership: A Case Study of the EU's Migration Dialogue with Senegal and Ghana* (Florence: European University Institute, Migration Working Group, March 2010), p. 3, http://www.ies.be/files/VanCriekinge-B2.pdf (accessed 2 March 2015).
35. Glenys Kinnock, "The Devil Is in the Detail: Glenys Kinnock on the New ACP-EU Agreement", *The Courier* no. 180 (April–May 2000), p. 5.
36. The 1999 summit of the European Council in Tampere, Finland, established that readmission clauses would need to be integrated into all subsequent EU partnership agreements with third coun-

tries. *See* "Lomé Convention Used to Impose Repatriation on the World's Poorest Countries", *Statewatch Bulletin* 10, no. 2 (March–May 2000), http://www.statewatch.org/subscriber/protected/sw10n2.pdf (accessed 7 July 2015).

37. Currently, Article 13 commits both parties to cooperation, but complementary bilateral implementing arrangements are needed to make it operational. However, a lack of clarity on the issue remains, with some European Commission officials maintaining that, at least for nationals of ACP countries, the provision made by Article 13 is self-executing. *See* Eleonora Koeb and Henrike Hohmeister, "The Revision of Article 13 on Migration of the Cotonou Partnership Agreement: What's at Stake for the ACP?" working paper (Maastricht: ECDPM, February 2010).

38. Crush, *Between North and South*, p. 9.

39. Koeb and Hohmeister, "The Revision of Article 13", p. 8.

40. Adam Higazi, *Integrating Migration & Development Policies: Challenges for ACP-EU Cooperation*, Discussion Paper no. 62 (Maastricht: ECDPM, 2005), p. 7.

41. ACP Group, *Brussels Resolution on Migration and Development*, Brussels, 30 May 2008.

42. Crush, *Between North and South*, p. 10.

43. ACP Group of States and Council of the European Union, "Report on the Dialogue on Migration and Development", ACP-EU 2115/11, report to the ACP-EU Joint Council, Brussels, 5 July 2011, p. 5, para. 9.

44. Klavert and van Seters, "ACP-EU Cooperation on Readmission", p. 6.

45. Klavert and van Seters, "ACP-EU Cooperation on Readmission", p. 2.

46. Lawrence Chilimboyi, statement at the Global Meeting of Chairs and Secretariats of Regional Consultative Processes on Migration, Gaborone, Botswana, 25–26 October 2011, https://www.iom.int/jahia/webdav/shared/shared/mainsite/microsites/rcps/2011-rcp-global-consultation/day1/ACP-Presentation-Migration-meeting-Botswana-Lawrence-Chilimboyi.pdf (accessed 18 December 2014).

47. Klavert and van Seters, "ACP-EU Cooperation on Readmission", p. 5.

48. ACP Group of States and Council of the European Union, "Report on the 2011–2012 Dialogue on Migration and Development", endorsed by the ACP-EU Council of Ministers at its 37th session, Port Vila, 14 June 2012, p. 7.

49. ACP-EU Joint Parliamentary Assembly, "Resolution on the Human, Economic, and Social Rights of Migrants in ACP and EU countries", 101.674/14/fin, adopted by the 17–19 March 2014 session of the ACP-EU Joint Parliamentary Assembly, p. 5, para. P.

50. This includes the Blue Card Directive for highly qualified immigrant workers; the Directive on the Entry and Stay of Students, Interns, and Volunteers, which provides common rules for their entry; and the Researchers' Directive, which is intended to provide swift admission procedures for researchers. In addition, the Single Permit Directive, the Directive on Family Reunification, and the Directive on Long-Term Residents provide certain harmonised rights and conditions for targeted immigrant groups. Most recently, in February 2014, the Seasonal Workers' Directive was adopted, setting out conditions for legal migration for lower-skilled migrants.

51. These 16 ACP countries are Dominica, Grenada, Kiribati, the Marshall Islands, Micronesia, Nauru, Palau, Samoa, the Solomon Islands, St Lucia, St Vincent and the Grenadines, Timor-Leste, Tonga, Trinidad and Tobago, Tuvalu, and Vanuatu.

52. Meng-Hsuan Chou and Marie Gibert, "The EU-Senegal Mobility Partnership: From Launch to Suspension and Negotiation Failure", *Journal of Contemporary European Research* 8, no. 4 (2012), pp. 408–427.

53. The facility aimed to establish national consultative committees on migration that would identify and prioritise research as well as training needs. Yet, in most cases, these committees did not develop organically, and in many cases the committees are now disintegrating, raising questions about the sustainability of the migration and development dialogue within these countries, as well as between them. *See* Peter Mudungwe, "Major Results of the Capacity-Building Activities of the Intra-ACP Migration Facility", presentation at the conference *South-South Migration and Development: Discussing New Evidence from the ACP Observatory on Migration*, ACP Secretariat House, Brussels, 3–4 June 2014, http://www. acpmigration-obs.org/sites/default/files/Mudungwe%20P.%20 PMU.pdf (accessed 17 December 2014).

54. Crush, *Between North and South*, p. 12.
55. EU Commission, "The Global Approach to Migration and Mobility", COM (2011) 743 Final, communication from the Commission to the European Parliament, the Council, the European Economic and Social Committee, and the Committee of the Regions, Brussels, 18 November 2011.
56. ACP Observatory on Migration, "South-South Migration and Development Conference", p. 7.
57. Crush, *Between North and South*, p. 11.
58. Higazi, *Integrating Migration & Development Policies*, p. 7.
59. EU Justice and Home Affairs Council, "Conclusions on EU Return Policy", CL14-098EN, Brussels, 5 June 2014, http://eu-un.europa.eu/articles/en/article_15108_en.htm (accessed 6 March 2015).
60. EU Commission, "Annex to the Commission Implementing Decision Concerning the Adoption of the Work Programme for 2014 and the Financing for Union Actions and Emergency Assistance Within the Framework of the Asylum, Migration, and Integration Fund", COM (2014) 5652 Final, Brussels, 8 August 2014.
61. In 2014, these countries were Azerbaijan, Morocco, Jordan, and Tunisia. *See* EU Commission, "Annex to the Commission Implementing Decision".
62. EU Commission, "Communication from the Commission to the European Parliament and the Council on the Work of the Task Force Mediterranean", COM (2013) 0869 Final, Brussels, 8 August 2014, p. 8, http://eur-lex.europa.eu/legal-content/en/TXT/?uri=celex:52013DC0869 (accessed 27 February 2015).
63. UN High Commissioner for Refugees (UNHCR), "Funding for International Protection in Europe: UNHCR Comments to the Proposals for Funding in the Area of Home Affairs, 2014–2020", Brussels, 2012, http://www.unhcr.org/50e6e0099.pdf (accessed 6 March 2015).
64. Exemptions include, for example, the Intra-ACP Academic Mobility Scheme, in the area of higher education; and the Erasmus Mundus Strand 2, for ACP countries, in the area of higher-education cooperation.
65. Tine van Criekinge, "The Integration of Migration Issues in the EPAs", in Jan Orbie and Gerrit Faber (eds.), *Beyond Market Access*

for Economic Development: EU-Africa Relations in Transition (London: Routledge, 2009), p. 174.

66. For background on these broader discussions, *see* ECDPM, "The Future of ACP-EU Relations Post-2020" (Maastricht, 2014).

67. Dutch Ministry of Foreign Affairs, "The Netherlands and the European Development Fund: Principles and Practices", Operations Evaluation Department (IOB) evaluation (The Hague, Netherlands, 2013), p. 88.

68. Centre for Conflict Resolution (CCR), *The African, Caribbean, and Pacific (ACP) Group and the European Union (EU)*, seminar report, Cape Town, South Africa, January 2014, p. 33, http://www.ccr.org.za.

69. EU Commission, "Towards a Renewed EU-Pacific Development Partnership", JOIN (2012) 6 Final, joint communication to the European Parliament, the Council, the European Economic and Social Committee, and the Committee of the Regions, Brussels, 21 March 2012.

70. *See* reports and outcome documents of the regional discussions for the future perspectives of the ACP beyond 2015 and 2020, available at http://www.epg.acp.int/documents.

71. James Mackie, Bruce Byiers, Sonia Niznik, and Geert Laporte, *Global Changes, Emerging Players, and Evolving ACP-EU Relations: Towards a Common Agenda for Action?* Policy and Management Report no. 19 (Maastricht: ECDPM, 2011), p. xiii.

CHAPTER 11

Diasporas and Development in the ACP-EU Relationship

Keith Nurse and Ramona Ruggeri

The salience of diasporas to development and to relations between the African, Caribbean, and Pacific (ACP) group of states and the European Union (EU) has grown, and is an expanding area for research and policy development. The growth of global diasporas[1] relates to a new transnationalism and geo-economics of development, in which non-state actors play an increasingly critical role in promoting bilateral trade, entrepreneurship, and social innovation, which in turn impacts on poverty reduction through expanded life capabilities for migrants, their families and communities, as well as home and host nations.

The developmental benefits of diasporas have gained mainstream attention,[2] but public opinion is still often coloured by the negative media images of migrants in receiving countries in the EU. The developmental dimensions of diasporas also remain unmapped, because of the paucity of data and information in both ACP migrant-sending and EU migrant-receiving countries on the roles and linkages of diaspora communities, as well as on the economic flows associated with the diasporic economy.

K. Nurse (✉)
The University of the West Indies (UWI), Cave Hill, Barbados

R. Ruggeri
Independent Researcher, Bologna, Italy

© The Author(s) 2017   263
A. Montoute, K. Virk (eds.), *The ACP Group and the EU Development Partnership*, DOI 10.1007/978-3-319-45492-4_11

This chapter seeks to provide greater insight into contemporary ACP-EU diaspora relations by examining the economic dimensions of migration flows, labour mobility, brain drain, and remittances. Our aim is to highlight the contribution of diasporas and the diasporic economy to both ACP migrant-sending and EU migrant-receiving countries and regions, and thus to identify the ways in which ACP-EU diaspora relations can enhance development prospects, particularly in the ACP region.

DIASPORAS AND DEVELOPMENT IN PERSPECTIVE

The debate on the role of diasporas in development has been dominated by the concerns of the main migrant-receiving countries in the industrialised North, with the focus largely having been on issues of political and social integration, labour market management, and border control. (See Knoll in this volume.) In the context of the EU, this approach has been constructed around the image of "Fortress Europe". Even so, there has been a growing awareness of the wider economic impact of diasporas, and the discourse has moved beyond the narrow confines of migration policy to include matters such as global competitiveness and broader developmental concerns.[3] On the other side of the coin, many developing countries have pursued strategic diaspora engagement programmes with the aim of emulating countries, like China, India, Israel, Mexico, and El Salvador, that have targeted their diaspora communities for trade, investment, technology transfer, collective remittances, and "brain circulation" networks (that is, brain gain).[4]

Based upon this experience, there is increasing recognition that it is important to factor the growth of diaspora communities into the development equations of both migrant-sending and migrant-receiving countries. As analyst Agnieszka Weinar notes: "In European migration policy, the migration and development nexus has been recently promoted as an important area of intervention."[5] Similarly, according to the North-South Centre of the Council of Europe:

> The fact that migration generally has a positive effect on developing home countries has given rise to a conflict between the objectives of development cooperation policy and those on migration policy, which focuses on controlling migration to Europe. In many countries, the migration policy is more about controlling and regulating the flows of migrants rather than development through the migrants already in the country.[6]

The EU's response has been to take a broader approach to the issue, with the EU Commission recognising in 2008 that:

> Migration policies should be incorporated in a structural manner into policies on health, education and human capital, and into social and economic development strategies. Migration and development policies should also focus much more on economic reform and job creation and on improving the working conditions and the socio-economic situation in low-income and middle-income countries, and in regions characterised by high emigration pressures.[7]

Against this backdrop, the question of diasporas and development in ACP-EU relations has been politically sensitive, and vulnerable to rising right-wing populism amid fears about economic stagnation in the Eurozone since the global financial crisis of 2008–2009. It is also worth noting that the main EU member states affected by irregular immigration—in particular, Portugal, Italy, Greece, and Spain—are among the worst-hit economies in the wake of the financial crisis. However, the EU, like most other industrialised economies, has an ageing population and faces an impending labour shortage owing to demographic shifts. Consequently, Europe needs an influx of immigrants to fill gaps in the labour market and maintain adequate numbers of workers, in order to help finance an otherwise looming deficit in social security and pension schemes.

The demographic challenge for the EU is considerable. It is estimated that the old-age dependency ratio (the share of persons aged 65 and older relative to the working-age population in the 15–64 age group) will increase from 17 per cent in 2010 to 30 per cent by 2060. In this context, immigrant labour is expected to be the fastest-growing source of replacement labour. Indeed, according to projections by the Organisation for Economic Cooperation and Development (OECD), without migration the EU's working-age population will decline by 15 million by 2020 and by 84 million by 2050, with significant implications for the region's competitiveness.[8] In particular, this decline would result in labour shortages in key technical skills and areas such as agriculture, science, and information technology, as well as health, education, and personal services.[9]

From the perspective of migrant-sending countries, the developmental impact of emigration also remains a somewhat contested area.[10] On the one hand, emigration creates a culture of dependency on remittances.

It also generates social inequality between families who receive remittances and those who do not, while allowing the brain drain of the tertiary-educated from developing countries to the EU and other OECD countries. On the other hand, emigration tends to ease pressure on labour markets and helps to reduce unemployment and poverty through remittances and the export of surplus labour. Return and circular migrants are also an important source of skills, expertise, and ideas (brain gain) that can serve national and regional development objectives.[11]

Taken together, these views suggest that migration and diaspora relations are a critical new area of interdependence between the ACP and the EU—one that goes beyond the traditional framework of trade and development cooperation as embodied in the Cotonou Agreement of 2000. Since 2000, the ACP and the EU have held a running dialogue on migration and development. The EU also has a migration, mobility, and employment partnership with Africa (see Akokpari in this volume), which serves as the framework for a dialogue on migration between Europe and the continent on the basis of the EU's Global Approach to Migration and Mobility (GAMM). This dialogue covers a broad range of issues, including diasporas, remittances, brain drain, migrant rights, visa issues, smuggling and trafficking of migrants, readmission and return, and refugee protection. (See Knoll in this volume.) Furthermore, in March 2012, diaspora organisations from across Europe gathered for the first African Diaspora Expert Meeting, held in Eschborn, Germany, to share views, discuss strategies, and build alliances for the establishment of a Europe-wide African diaspora platform to contribute to the development of Africa.[12] The second meeting, held in Paris, France, in November 2012, approved the constitution of a legally binding funding document for a diaspora platform, taking a concrete step towards the creation of a sustainable programme for diasporic development cooperation.[13]

These different initiatives and measures are reflective of a broader change in the global discourse about migration that acknowledges its complex relationship with development. As scholar Jonathan Crush has argued:

> By framing their dialogue on international migration as a development rather than security issue, the EU and the ACP have actually made considerable progress since Cotonou. While points of disagreement remain, particularly over revisions to Article 13, the relationship is generally collegial and has defined common ground for productive exchange and practical programming.

This rapprochement would have been inconceivable in the 1990s. The question that arises is how can the development establishment facilitate and give further impetus to the diasporic economy to enhance multiplier effects, boost productive investments and diasporic exports as well as redress the depletion of valuable human resources.[14]

Thus the economic and potential developmental role of diasporas in the ACP-EU relationship requires greater research and analysis, as well as policy and institutional coherence.

LABOUR MOBILITY AND ACP-EU MIGRATION AND DIASPORAS

Globally, the number of people living outside their birth countries grew from 150 million in 2000 to 232 million in 2013, accounting for 3.2 per cent of the world population. Those born in the global South numbered 164 million in 2013, or 71 per cent of the total world-wide foreign-born immigrant population. In terms of distribution and direction of migration, South-South migration flows accounted for 36 per cent, South-North for 35 per cent, North-North for 23 per cent, and North-South for 6 per cent of the total in 2013. Notably, international migrants accounted for a meagre 1.6 per cent share of the population of the global South in 2013, in comparison with 10.8 per cent of the population of the industrialised North.[15]

ACP-EU migration is a sub-set of these global trends. The ACP-EU migration relationship is complex and is shaped by historical, colonial, and linguistic links, which play a significant role in determining the shares of migration and the geographic spread of diasporas. The majority of emigrants from the EU (65 per cent) move within Europe. About 14 per cent of EU emigrants settle in North America, 13 per cent in Asia, 5 per cent in Oceania, 2 per cent in Latin America and the Caribbean, and 1 per cent in Africa (see Fig. 11.1). Although these data are aggregated for regions that do not correspond with the ACP regions, this nonetheless indicates that the flow of migrants from the EU to Africa, the Caribbean, and the Pacific is largely insignificant.

Furthermore, as Fig. 11.2 illustrates, the largest share of migrants to Europe (52 per cent) is European in origin. The next largest source region is Asia, with a 26 per cent share, followed by Africa, with 12 per cent of the total. Latin America and the Caribbean account for 6 per cent, and Oceania

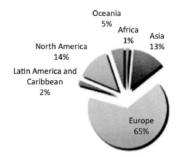

Fig. 11.1 Destination of European migrants, 2013. *Source*: Organisation for Economic Cooperation and Development (OECD) and United Nations Department of Economic and Social Affairs (UN DESA), *World Migration in Figures: A Joint Contribution by UN-DESA and the OECD to the United Nations High-Level Dialogue on Migration and Development, 3–4 October 2013*, http://www.oecd.org/els/mig/World-Migration-in-Figures.pdf (accessed 19 November 2014)

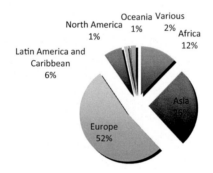

Fig. 11.2 Origins of migrants to Europe, 2013. *Source*: Organisation for Economic Cooperation and Development (OECD) and United Nations Department of Economic and Social Affairs (UN DESA), *World Migration in Figures: A Joint Contribution by UN-DESA and the OECD to the United Nations High-Level Dialogue on Migration and Development, 3–4 October 2013*, http://www.oecd.org/els/mig/World-Migration-in-Figures.pdf (accessed 19 November 2014)

and North America for 1 per cent each, with various other countries contributing the remaining 2 per cent. This overview does not provide a particularly clear picture of ACP migration to the EU, as non-ACP countries are bundled into the African, Latin American and Caribbean, and Oceania regions, and as non-EU countries are included in the European category. However, it nonetheless gives a sense of the scale of ACP migration, and indicates that this is relatively small compared with European and Asian migration flows to Europe.

As mentioned earlier, data on ACP-EU migration and diaspora flows are limited. One of the best available sources for understanding the structure of ACP migration to the EU, though dated, is the University of Sussex's Global Migrant Origins Database (GMOD). According to the GMOD, as of 2007 there were 23 million ACP migrants living outside their countries of birth.[16] Of these, 37 per cent were resident in the industrialised North (Europe, North America, Australia, and New Zealand) and 63 per cent lived in the global South. South-South migration thus represented a significant share of the migration flows from ACP countries. However, the relative importance of South-South migration varied considerably from region to region and from one sub-region to another. South-South migrants made up 78 per cent of total migration in Africa, compared with only 24 per cent in the Pacific and 15 per cent in the Caribbean. Within Africa, there was significant differentiation at the sub-regional level, for example, between West Africa, with South-South migration at a high of 83 per cent of the total, and Southern Africa, with a low of 48 per cent.

Data on South-North emigration from the ACP are similarly scarce. The 2011 ACP Human Mobility Report,[17] which draws on the GMOD, is the best compilation of such data. According to the 2011 ACP Human Mobility Report, the most common destination for Caribbean emigrants is North America (the United States and Canada), which accounted for 70 per cent of total emigration from the region. The exception is Suriname, in which case a large share of emigrants goes to the Netherlands.[18] Meanwhile, Australia and New Zealand are the main destinations for emigrants from the Pacific region, with a 48 per cent share of the total. From Africa, South-North migration accounted for 22 per cent of total emigration, with a 16 per cent share of total emigration going to the EU. The pattern of emigration to the EU differs from one African sub-region to another. An estimated 27 per cent of migrants from Southern Africa went to the EU, compared with 19 per cent of migrants from East Africa, 12 per cent from West Africa, and 19 per cent from Central Africa

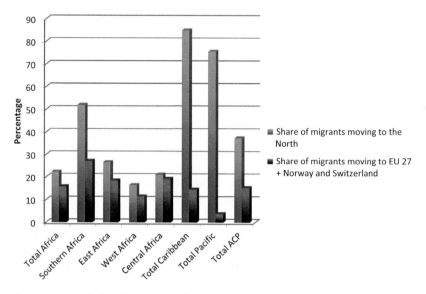

Fig. 11.3 ACP South-North mobility, 2011. *Source*: Andrea Gallina, *Human Mobility Report 2011: Migration and Human Development in African, Caribbean and Pacific Countries* (ACP Secretariat: Brussels, 2010)

(see Fig. 11.3). All told, only 15 per cent of migrants from the ACP went to the EU (regionally, 16 per cent of migrants from Africa, 15 per cent of migrants from the Caribbean, and 4 per cent of migrants from the Pacific went to the EU). Clearly the EU is not the top destination for ACP migrants.

Based on several official datasets, in 2005–2006 (the latest period for which such data are available) there were an estimated two million ACP migrants living in the top eight migrant-receiving EU countries: the United Kingdom (UK), France, the Netherlands, Spain, Germany, Italy, Portugal, and Belgium. Of these migrants, the vast majority (approximately 80 per cent) were living in the United Kingdom, France, the Netherlands, and Spain. Germany and Belgium had the lowest presence of ACP migrants. The average presence of ACP migrants as a share of total resident population of the top eight EU receiving countries was estimated at 0.72 per cent, with the Netherlands having the largest share, at 1.4 per cent (see Table 11.1).

Table 11.1   Number of ACP migrants in selected EU countries, 2005–2006

EU country	Total population	Number of migrants	Number of migrants as percentage of total population
Belgium	10,400,000	25,000	0.24
France	60,600,000	379,000	0.62
Germany	82,500,000	145,000	0.18
Italy	58,500,000	149,000	0.26
Netherlands	16,300,000	228,000	1.40
Portugal	10,500,000	129,000	1.23
Spain	43,000,000	222,000	0.52
United Kingdom	60,000,000	775,000	1.29
Total	**341,800,000**	**2,052,000**	**0.72**

Sources: OECD, *Connecting with Emigrants: A Global Profile of Diasporas,* http://dx.doi. org/10.1787/9789264177949-en (accessed 19 November 2014); Eurostat, *Europe in Figures: Eurostat Yearbook 2006–07,* http://ec.europa.eu/eurostat/documents/3217494/5609869/KS-CD-06-001-01-EN.PDF/ebb28696-2f37-4d37-87c9-e6ac574329c0?version=1.0 (accessed 19 November 2014); and *Where We're From* interactive application hosted by the International Organisation for Migration, http://www.iom.int/cms/en/sites/iom/home/about-migration/world-migration.html (accessed 19 November 2014)

DIASPORAS, BRAIN DRAIN, AND BRAIN CIRCULATION

A key challenge associated with the growth of migration and labour mobility is the problem of brain drain—the migration of the tertiary-educated. The exact impact on ACP brain drain due to emigration to the EU is difficult to determine, given the limited data available. What is known is that "the bulk of the African brain drain is almost evenly split between Europe and the Americas, with less than 10 percent going to Asia/Oceania".[19] For the Caribbean and the Pacific regions, the brain drain rates to the EU are likely to be in line with the broader emigration flows and so would average no more than 15 per cent and 4 per cent respectively of the total brain drain from these regions. The risk of brain drain is acute in countries with small populations and in island states, but it is also critical in more populous countries with high poverty rates.[20] In 2010, close to 90 per cent of highly skilled persons born in Guyana lived in developed economies. Similarly, more tertiary-educated persons from Barbados, Haiti, and Trinidad and Tobago were living outside than within these countries. The emigration rate for highly educated persons was also significant for Jamaica (46 per cent), Tonga (44 per cent), Zimbabwe (43 per cent), Mauritius (41 per cent), the Republic of the Congo (36 per cent), Belize (34 per cent), and Fiji (31 per cent).[21]

For nearly all ACP countries, the emigration rate of the highly skilled exceeds the total emigration rate, reflecting the selectivity of migration by educational attainment. Indeed, this is the case for 137 of 145 countries of origin based on available data. In 2010–2011, for Burundi, Lesotho, Malawi, Mozambique, Namibia, Niger, Papua New Guinea, Tanzania, and Zambia, the emigration rates of the highly skilled were more than 20 times the total emigration rates.[22]

Brain drain is gendered as well, being more pronounced for women than for men. In many countries of origin, the share of tertiary-educated women who live outside their country of birth is higher compared with that of men. This difference reached ten percentage points in 2010–2011 for the Republic of the Congo, Sierra Leone, and Togo.[23] It is estimated that "in about two-thirds of origin countries, the emigration rate of highly educated women is higher than the emigration rate of highly educated men".[24] The gender difference is less pronounced in the Caribbean and the Pacific, but women still outnumber men among highly educated migrants.

The problem of brain drain is particularly significant in key sectors such as health, education, and science and technology. The emigration rate for physicians from small ACP islands, in particular, is alarmingly high. Among Caribbean countries, Dominica and Grenada have an emigration rate of 98 per cent for physicians (as of 2000). The rate is 78 per cent for St Lucia, while for Antigua and Barbuda, and St Kitts and Nevis, the rates are just below 40 per cent. In Africa, Cape Verde has an emigration rate of 51 per cent for physicians born in the country, Mauritius 46 per cent, Comoros 32 per cent, and Seychelles 29 per cent.[25] These rates are comparable with those of countries considered to be among the high-emigration countries for physicians, such as Jamaica (41 per cent physician emigration rate), Ireland (41 per cent), Haiti (35 per cent), Ghana (30 per cent), and Sri Lanka (27 per cent).[26]

The EU, like other OECD economies, is seeking to attract more skilled migrants from the developing world, including the ACP, through initiatives such as the EU Blue Card (see Knoll in this volume).[27] The EU Blue Card seeks to attract highly skilled non-EU nationals by establishing a fast-track admission procedure to provide a secure legal status and a set of guaranteed rights to smooth the process of integration. The provisions include family reunification, a residence permit, equal social security treatment compared with nationals, equal pay, and free movement within the Schengen Area[28] (if in possession of a valid travel document, and if the EU Blue Card is issued by a Schengen member state).[29]

The EU has been mindful of the problem of brain drain. The EU Council's Blue Card Directive of 2009 prohibits active recruitment in developing countries in highly specialised sectors that are already experiencing diminished personnel capacity, while urging ethical recruitment practices. The directive also encourages facilitation of circular and temporary migration, in an attempt to "minimise negative and maximise positive impacts of highly skilled immigration on developing countries in order to turn 'brain drain' into 'brain gain'".[30]

The "brain circulation" argument, which has gained currency in migration and development circles, suggests that temporary outward migration may give the country of origin increased access to newly acquired skills, business contacts, and capital upon the migrants' return.[31] However, the exploitation of the potential development boon of brain circulation cannot be left to chance, and requires a tactical policy response. While there will always be some element of autonomous return, home countries must adopt strategies to improve the attractiveness of return migration. Well-organised returns, which are linked to other aspects of national and regional policy (for example, innovation policy), stand a far greater chance of contributing to the development effort than do sporadic returns.[32] In this context, a strong argument can also be made for the establishment of a mechanism for the governance of diasporic recruitment, which allows migrants to return home and/or participate in the development of the sending countries through the leveraging of intellectual property, the making of investments, or the provision of services.

ACP-EU Remittances and the Diasporic Economy

The European Union as a whole is a net sending region in terms of remittances compared with the ACP, which is a net recipient; although there are several EU economies that are net recipients of remittances, largely from intra-EU flows. In the case of the ACP, non-EU countries account for the largest share of remittance flows. No EU country features in the top ten remittance corridors for the ACP as a whole. This suggests that, from an EU perspective, the flow of remittances to the ACP is relatively small, when compared with intra-EU flows and flows to the rest of Europe and to North Africa.

A closer examination of the remittance flows between the EU and the ACP confirms this view. As Table 11.2 shows, in 2012, total remittances from the EU amounted to $107 billion, of which only 10 per cent

Table 11.2   EU remittance-sending and top ACP receiving countries, 2012

EU country	Total remittance outflow ($ millions)	Total remittances to top ACP countries ($ millions) (%)	Share of ACP remittances in EU country's total remittance outflow (%)	Top ten remittance-receiving countries ($ millions)
Belgium	5,089	102 (0.9)	2	Nigeria (53), Rwanda (16), Senegal (6), Mauritius (6), Dominican Republic (5), South Africa (5), Haiti (3), Kenya (3), Togo (3), Cameroon (2)
France	19,283	735 (6.8)	3.8	Senegal (290), Nigeria (74), Mali (73), Haiti (71), Mauritius (70), Togo (41), Côte d'Ivoire (41), Cameroon (33), Cape Verde (24), Djibouti (18)
Germany	21,031	778 (7.2)	3.7	Nigeria (613), Togo (37), Dominican Republic (26), Kenya (26), Ethiopia (24), Senegal (13), South Africa (11), Sudan (11), Ghana (9), Cameroon (8)
Italy	12,141	1,694 (15.7)	13.9	Nigeria (1,288), Senegal (247), Dominican Republic (78), Mauritius (21), Ethiopia (18), Côte d'Ivoire (12), Ghana (12), Togo (7), Cape Verde (6), Kenya (5)
Netherlands	4,741	244 (2.2)	5.1	Nigeria (151), Dominican Republic (25), South Africa (17), Cape Verde (13), Ethiopia (10), Sudan (9), Kenya (8), Liberia (5), Suriname (3), Senegal (3)

(*continued*)

Table 11.2   (continued)

EU country	Total remittance outflow ($ millions)	Total remittances to top ACP countries ($ millions) (%)	Share of ACP remittances in EU country's total remittance outflow (%)	Top ten remittance-receiving countries ($ millions)
Portugal	2,714	367 (3.4)	13.5	Cape Verde (59), South Africa (20), Guinea-Bissau (16), Mozambique (16), Nigeria (5), São Tomé and Príncipe (4), Senegal (2), Kenya (1)
Spain	18,595	1,619 (14.9)	8.7	Nigeria (934), Dominican Republic (470), Senegal (144), Gambia (28), Mali (21), Cape Verde (5), Kenya (5), Ghana (4), Guinea (4), Guinea-Bissau (4)
United Kingdom	23,601	5,255 (48.6)	22.2	Nigeria (3,842), Kenya (488), Jamaica (328), South Africa (299), Uganda (149), Mauritius (73), Ghana (25), Guyana (22), Tanzania (15), Zambia (14)
Total	107,195	10,794 (10.0)		

Source: World Bank, "Migration and Remittance Flows: Recent Trends and Outlook, 2013–2016", *Migration and Development Brief* no. 21 (2013)

went to ACP countries. The main EU sending countries were the United Kingdom (48.6 per cent), followed by Italy (15.7 per cent) and Spain (14.9 per cent), which together account for approximately 80 per cent of the remittance flows to the ACP, indicating that EU remittance outflows to the ACP are highly concentrated in a few European economies.

When measured as a share of remittances, ACP flows stand above 5 per cent of total flows from five EU countries: the United Kingdom (22.2 per cent), Italy (13.9 per cent), Portugal (13.5 per cent), Spain (8.7 per cent), and the Netherlands (5.1 per cent). Thus the data show that EU economies such as France and Germany, which are the second and third largest remitting countries overall, have a smaller profile in the ACP when compared with other regions such as North Africa and Europe.

From an ACP perspective, remittance flows are similarly concentrated in a few countries. Nigeria is the top recipient country in sub-Saharan Africa, receiving $21 billion in remittances—nearly two-thirds of a total of $33 billion for the region—in 2012.[33] It is also the fifth highest remittance-receiving country in the global South, after India, China, the Philippines, and Mexico. A significant share of the remittances to Nigeria comes from the United Kingdom (55 per cent), followed by Italy (19 per cent), Spain (13 per cent), and Germany (9 per cent). The other top ACP recipient countries in sub-Saharan Africa are Senegal, Kenya, and South Africa.

However, when remittances are expressed as a share of gross domestic product (GDP), the countries that top the list of recipients in sub-Saharan Africa are small, dependent, and land-locked African countries such as Lesotho (24.4 per cent of GDP), Gambia (19.8 per cent), Liberia (18.5 per cent), Senegal (10.7 per cent), Cape Verde (9.3 per cent), Comoros (9 per cent), Togo (7.8 per cent), São Tomé and Príncipe (7.4 per cent), Mali (7.2 per cent), and Guinea-Bissau (5.3 per cent) (see Fig. 11.4).

The importance of remittances to the development equation in sub-Saharan Africa is well illustrated when remittances are compared with other external flows such as official development assistance (ODA), foreign direct investment (FDI), and portfolio investments. As Fig. 11.5 shows, remittances have risen—albeit by a slim margin—to become the largest source of external capital for the region since 2010, ahead of ODA and FDI, with the latter decreasing in the aftermath of the global financial crisis of 2008–2009. Portfolio investments have experienced the widest swings and recoveries since the financial crisis.

Remittances also play a major role in the economies of the Caribbean and Pacific ACP regions. In the case of the Pacific ACP, however, remit-

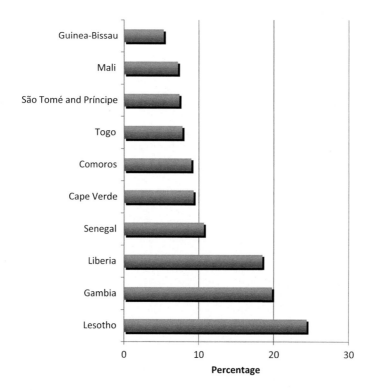

Fig. 11.4 Remittances to selected small states in sub-Saharan Africa as a share of GDP, 2013. *Source*: World Bank, *Migration and Development Brief* no. 23 (October 2014)

tances from the EU are marginal, with the exception of Vanuatu, where they account for approximately 30 per cent of inflows. Vanuatu, with $19 million in 2012, is the fourth largest Pacific ACP recipient of remittances from the EU, after Fiji ($165 million), Samoa ($128 million), and Tonga ($74 million). For the Caribbean (see Table 11.3), EU remittances are second in value after inflows from North America. Among the top recipients of remittances in the Caribbean ACP (as of 2012), the EU accounts for 15.7 per cent of inflows to the Dominican Republic, with Spain and Italy accounting for 75 per cent and 14 per cent respectively; for 15.7 per cent of inflows to Jamaica, with the United Kingdom the dominant source; and for 4.6 per cent to Haiti, with France as the principal source.

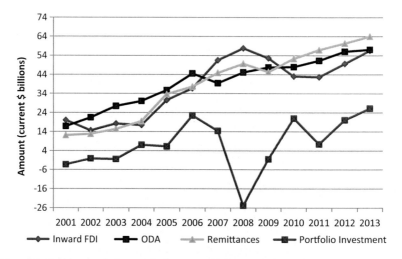

Fig. 11.5 External financial flows to Africa, 2001–2013. *Source*: African Development Bank (AfDB), Organisation for Economic Cooperation and Development (OECD), United Nations Development Programme (UNDP), and United Nations Economic Commission for Africa (UNECA), *African Economic Outlook 2013*, http://www.africaneconomicoutlook.org (accessed 11 December 2015)

Table 11.3 EU remittance inflows to selected ACP Caribbean countries, 2012

ACP country	Total remittances ($ millions)	EU remittances ($ millions)	Share of EU remittances in total remittances (%)	Main EU sending countries ($ millions)
Dominican Republic	3,505	552	15.7	Spain (417), Italy (78), Germany (26), Netherlands (25)
Jamaica	2,158	339	15.7	United Kingdom (328)
Haiti	1,625	75	4.6	France (71)
Guyana	397	24	6	United Kingdom (22), Netherlands (2)
Trinidad and Tobago	95	7	7.4	United Kingdom (7)
Barbados	84	23	27	United Kingdom (23)

Source: World Bank, "Bilateral Remittances Matrix 2012", http://econ.worldbank.org/WBSITE/EXTERNAL/EXTDEC/EXTDECPROSPECTS/0,,contentMDK:22759429~pagePK:64165401~piPK:64165026~theSitePK:476883,00.html (accessed 10 December 2014)

For other Caribbean countries, including Guyana, Trinidad and Tobago, and Barbados, the United Kingdom is the main source of remittances from the EU. However, for these countries, the EU's share of remittances is small, with the exception of Barbados, in which case remittance inflows from the United Kingdom account for 27 per cent of total remittances.

In relative terms, many small ACP states are among the top ten migrant-sending countries (number of emigrants as a percentage of total population) among small states worldwide, with emigrants constituting 40 per cent or more of the locally born population.[34] As such, there is significant potential for growth in the diasporic market if remittances are used as a proxy. Indeed, several small ACP states are among the top ten countries with the highest remittance-to-GDP shares in the global South. Tonga is ranked second, with a remittance-to-GDP ratio of 28 per cent in 2009, while Lesotho is ranked third (25 per cent), Samoa seventh (22 per cent), and Guyana ninth (17 per cent). In the top 30, the other ACP countries are Haiti (15 per cent) and Jamaica (14 per cent), followed by Togo (10 per cent), Guinea-Bissau (9 per cent), Cape Verde (9 per cent), Grenada (9 per cent), Gambia (8 per cent), St Kitts and Nevis (7 per cent), and the Dominican Republic (7 per cent).[35] For these countries, remittances account for a significant share of foreign exchange earnings and thus represent a vital mechanism to stabilise balance of payments and currency markets, and to securitise external debt. In addition, remittances and other economic flows have played a critical role in terms of poverty reduction and bilateral trade.

The notion that migrant remittances have positive short- and long-term development implications for the migrant-sending households and communities has been widely accepted.[36] The consensus in policymaking circles is that remittances are an effective way of addressing the root causes of migration, as they reduce poverty and ultimately dampen pressures for outward migration beyond a certain threshold. As Crush has noted:

> States in the North and South not only agree that remittances are a positive outcome of international migration, but moreover, that their impact on development can be maximized by reducing, for example, transaction costs for migrants through more formal and accessible remitting channels, and by introducing policies that promote the development "multiplier effects" of remittances, such as a growth in savings, investment, employment and productive activity.[37]

Indeed, reducing transaction costs is crucial to leveraging the development potential of remittances. High rates are mainly due to the oligopolistic structure of the remittance market. Remittance flows rely on money-transfer organisations that now include banking financial institutions, non-banking financial institutions, credit unions, post offices, and, increasingly, internet-based operators and mobile-phone providers. Companies like Western Union, MoneyGram, and Ria control a sizable share of the remittance market in the ACP regions.[38] A notable exception is the case of Suriname, where 80 per cent of the remittance market is controlled by a Surinamese diaspora-owned firm called Surichange.[39] It is on this basis that policymakers in the ACP regions have called for increased competition and regulation of the remittance business.

Financial remittances are a key aspect of the transnational relationship that overseas migrants have with the countries to which they emigrate. However, the diasporic economy is much wider than financial transfers from remittances. It includes trade in service sectors such as telecommunications, tourism, and transportation; and trade in goods often defined as nostalgic, ethnic, speciality, or niche goods.[40] It further includes the monetisation of intellectual property through copyrights in the media and creative industries.[41] Countries also benefit from diasporas by tapping into networks of diasporic trade as well as scientific and professional diasporic communities. These economic flows also facilitate investment by diaspora communities, and encourage brain circulation (for example, return migration and mobility of professional services), which redresses the problems associated with brain drain.

CONCLUDING REFLECTIONS

Both the ACP group of states and the EU have much to gain from strengthening their partnership in migration and cooperation on diaspora relations, given the development and demographic challenges they face (see Knoll in this volume). In particular, a strategic approach to improving the development prospects of labour-exporting ACP countries should be adopted, one that addresses the problems of labour mobility and brain drain. At the same time, the growth of the diasporic economy—particularly in terms of remittances and diasporic trade—has presented new opportunities for rethinking and diversifying ACP economies, while also enhancing the competitiveness of EU countries. The question then becomes one of facilitating and further stimulating the growth of the diasporic economy in ways that enhance its positive multiplier effects and boost its productivity, while redressing the depletion of human resources in ACP home countries.

In this context, securing the rights of migrants is vitally important. Restrictive migration policies encourage irregular and unstable migration, impeding stable labour market integration and diaspora community settlement.[42] Migrants are exposed to exploitation in the workplace and discriminatory practices, and are often used as political scapegoats for a range of social ills such as crime, disease, and high unemployment. In this regard, both ACP and EU countries should adopt the International Labour Organisation's (ILO) Multilateral Framework on Labour Migration (MFLM).[43] Though non-binding, it is a rights-based tool that incorporates the key principles and guidelines, as well as a selection of best practices, for effective labour migration governance and policies. Policy coherence could further be achieved by adopting the International Organisation for Migration's (IOM) handbook *Mainstreaming Migration into Development*, which contains recommendations for policymakers on how to use migration as a development tool and aims to "promote the wider application of all relevant international and regional instruments and norms relating to migration, and ... the adoption of more coherent, comprehensive and better coordinated approaches to the issue of international migration".[44]

Widening and strengthening a range of initiatives to improve diasporic flows (for example, diasporic exports and tourism), while lowering the transaction costs of remittances, is equally key. This includes "banking the unbanked" by using, for instance, mobile technologies for financial transactions to provide "unbanked" consumers a way to store and access money digitally.[45] Similarly, there is scope for expanding the involvement of companies based in the ACP migrant-sending countries in the business of remittance transfers, which is largely dominated by transnational companies such as Western Union, MoneyGram, and Ria. In addition, the majority of ACP countries have yet to conceive a diasporic export strategy as a viable means of diversifying their economies and generating new exports, employment, and forms of entrepreneurship.[46] Although there is an emerging consensus that diaspora communities can make vital contributions to bridging the development gap, most ACP countries and EU development agencies have yet to maximise this potential through appropriate human development schemes and/or trade facilitation measures.

Finally, the development of a permanent institutional capacity to monitor and inform ACP-EU migration and diaspora relations is absolutely essential. In this regard, the 2010 establishment of the ACP Observatory on Migration, under the aegis of the Intra-ACP Migration Facility, was an important step (see Knoll in this volume). This project, however, has focused on intra-regional migration from a South-South perspective. A corresponding investment to facilitate greater understanding of South-North migration and diaspora relations is now required to improve evidence-based policymaking and institutional coherence. In the absence of such investment, data on diaspora communities in both the EU and ACP countries remain limited, with analysis constrained by the use of different datasets (from different years in particular) and mismatched regional categories.

Diasporas represent an untapped potential in ACP-EU development cooperation. However, both sides need to move further away from immigration-centred approaches and towards more diaspora-focused development policymaking, and integrate diaspora communities and institutions as critical stakeholders in the design and implementation of ACP-EU cooperation, to their mutual benefit.

NOTES

1. *See* Robin Cohen, *Global Diasporas: An Introduction*, 2nd ed. (London and New York: Routledge, 2008).
2. "The Magic of Diasporas", *The Economist*, 19 November 2011.
3. Jonathan Crush, *Between North and South: The EU-ACP Migration Relationship*, Centre for International Governance Innovation (CIGI) Paper no. 16 (Waterloo, Canada: CIGI, April 2013); Keith Nurse, *Diaspora, Migration, and Development in the Caribbean* (Ottawa: Canadian Foundation for the Americas [FOCAL], 2004); Sonia Plaza and Dilip Ratha (eds.), *Diaspora for Development in Africa* (Washington, D.C.: World Bank, 2011); Alumita Durutalo, "Pacific Islands Diaspora Groups and Foreign Policy", in James Headley, Andreas Reitzig, and Joe Burton (eds.), *Public Participation in Foreign Policy* (Basingstoke: Palgrave Macmillan, 2012), pp. 213–233.
4. Yevgeny Kuznetsov (ed.), *Diaspora Networks and the International Migration of Skills: How Countries Can Draw on Their Talent Abroad* (Washington, D.C.: World Bank, 2006), http://siteresources.worldbank.org/KFDLP/Resources/461197-1122319506554/DiasporaIntro.pdf (accessed 17 December 2014).

5. Agnieszka Weinar, "Instrumentalising Diasporas for Development: International and European Policy Discourses", in Rainer Bauböck and Thomas Faist (eds.), *Diaspora and Transnationalism: Concepts, Theories, and Methods*, (Amsterdam: Amsterdam University Press, 2007), p. 86.

6. North-South Centre of the Council of Europe, *Social Remittances of the African Diasporas in Europe: Case Studies—Netherlands and Portugal* (Lisbon, 2006), p. 29.

7. European Union (EU), "Strengthening the Global Approach to Migration: Increasing Coordination, Coherence, and Synergies", COM (2008) 0611 Final, communication from the Commission to the European Parliament, the Council, the European Economic and Social Committee, and the Committee of the Regions, Brussels, Belgium, 8 October 2008.

8. Jason Gagnon, "Demographic Change and the Future of the Labour Force in the EU27, Other OECD Countries, and Selected Large Emerging Economies", in Organisation for Economic Cooperation and Development (OECD) and EU, *Matching Economic Migration with Labour Market Needs* (Paris, 2014), pp. 37–65.

9. OECD, *The Looming Crisis in the Health Workforce: How Can OECD Countries Respond?* (Paris, 2008).

10. For a review of the literature, *see* Manuel Orozco, B. Lindsay Lowell, Micah Bump, and Rachel Fedewa, "Transnational Engagement, Remittances, and Their Relationship to Development in Latin America and the Caribbean" (Washington, D.C.: Institute for the Study of International Migration, Georgetown University, 2005); Dilip Ratha and Sonia Plaza, "Harnessing Diasporas: Africa Can Tap Some of Its Millions of Emigrants to Help Development Efforts", *Finance & Development* 48, no. 3 (September 2011), pp. 48–51; Charles W. Stahl, "Labor Emigration and Economic Development", *International Migration Review* 16, no. 4 (1982), pp. 869–899; Peter Stalker, "The Impact of Migration in Countries of Origin", in *The Link Between Migration, Globalization, and Development*, Novib Expert Meeting Report (Noordwijk A/D Zee, Netherlands, 2003), pp. 62–78; Jon Swanson, *Emigration and Economic Development: The Case of the Yemen Arab Republic* (Boulder, Colo.: Westview, 1979).

11. Kevin Hjortshøj O'Rourke, "The Era of Migration: Lessons for Today" (London: Centre for Economic Policy Research, July 2004), http://www.cepr.org/active/publications/discussion_papers/dp.php?dpno=4498 (accessed 7 November 2014).

12. *See* Africa-Europe Platform, "Report of the 1st African Diaspora Expert Meeting", Eschborn (Frankfurt am Main), Germany, 5–7 March 2012, http://www.icmpd.org/fileadmin/ICMPD-Website/ICMPD-Website_2011/Capacity_building/Migration_and_Development/Report_1st_EM_Final_June12.pdf (accessed 2 July 2015).

13. *See* Africa-EU Partnership, "A Platform for African Diaspora Organisations in Europe: Scaling-Up and Joining-Up Cooperation", 6 February 2013, http://www.africa-eu-partnership.org/newsroom/all-news/platform-african-diaspora-organisations-europe-scaling-and-joining-cooperation (accessed 2 July 2015).

14. Crush, *Between North and South*, p. 12.

15. OECD and United Nations Department of Economic and Social Affairs (UN DESA), *World Migration in Figures: A Joint Contribution by UN-DESA and the OECD to the United Nations High-Level Dialogue on Migration and Development, 3–4 October 2013*, October 2013, http://www.oecd.org/els/mig/World-Migration-in-Figures.pdf (accessed 19 November 2014).

16. The Global Migrant Origins Database (GMOD), which was last updated in March 2007, extends the basic stock data on international migration that are published by the United Nations (UN), and is subject to the weaknesses that characterise all stock data derived from censuses. *See* http://www.un.org/esa/population/publications/migstock/2003TrendsMigstock.pdf (accessed 19 November 2014).

17. Andrea Gallina, *Human Mobility Report 2011: Migration and Human Development in African, Caribbean and Pacific Countries* (Brussels: ACP Secretariat, 2010).

18. For further details and analysis, *see* Keith Nurse, "Diasporic Tourism and Investment in Suriname", *Canadian Foreign Policy Journal* 17, no. 2 (2011), pp. 142–154.

19. William Easterly and Yaw Nyarko, "Is the Brain Drain Good for Africa?" Global Economy and Development Working Paper no. 19 (Washington, D.C.: Brookings Institution, March 2008), p. 6.

20. OECD and UN DESA, *World Migration in Figures.*
21. OECD and UN DESA, *World Migration in Figures.*
22. OECD and UN DESA, "Key Statistics on Migration in OECD Countries", 2013, http://www.oecd.org/els/mig/keystat.htm (accessed 19 November 2014).
23. OECD and UN DESA, *World Migration in Figures.*
24. OECD, *Connecting with Emigrants: A Global Profile of Diasporas* (Paris, 2012), p. 27.
25. World Bank, *Migration and Remittances Factbook 2011* (Washington, D.C.: International Bank for Reconstruction and Development [IBRD], 2011), p. 11.
26. Fitzhugh Mullan, "The Metrics of the Physician Brain Drain", *New England Journal of Medicine* no. 353 (2005), pp. 1810–1818.
27. Keith Nurse and Jessica Jones, "Brain Drain and Caribbean-EU Labor Mobility", paper commissioned by *Observatorio de las Relaciones Unión Europea—América Latina (OBREAL)* for the Building Relationships and Improving Dialogues Geared Towards Erasmus Mundus Goals—Latin American and Caribbean (BRIDGES-LAC) project, 2009, http://www.sknweb.com/wp-content/uploads/2011/10/6.2-Brain-Drain-and-Caribbean--EU-Mobility-UWI.pdf (accessed 23 December 2014). The EU "Blue Card" entitles the holder (third-country national) to settlement and to employment with a certain employer in the territory of an EU member state.
28. The Schengen Area includes 26 European countries that are signatories to the Schengen Convention of 1985, which abolished internal border controls and established a common visa policy. For further details, *see* http://ec.europa.eu/dgs/home-affairs/what-we-do/policies/borders-and-visas/index_en.htm (accessed 31 July 2015).
29. Silvia Mosneaga, "Building a More Attractive Europe: The Blue Card Experience", in Lars Klein and Martin Tamcke (eds.), *Europeans In-between: Identities in a (Trans-) Cultural Space*, selected texts presented at the European Studies Intensive Programme, Georg-August-University Göttingen, 2011, http://irs.ub.rug.nl/ppn/352878479 (accessed 9 December 2014).
30. Council of the European Union, "Council Directive 2009/50/EC of 25 May 2009 on the Conditions of Entry and Residence of Third-Country Nationals for the Purposes of Highly Qualified Employment", *Official Journal of the European Union*, (2009).

31. Laura Thompson, "A World on the Move: The Benefits of Migration", speech, International Organisation for Migration (IOM), Brussels, 25 September 2014, http://www.iom.int/cms/en/sites/iom/home/news-and-views/speeches/speech-listing/a-world-on-the-move-the-benefits.html (accessed 5 December 2014).

32. *See* Yiagadeesen Samy (ed.), "Strategic Opportunities in Caribbean Migration: Brain Circulation, Diasporic Tourism, and Investment", special issue of *Canadian Foreign Policy Journal* 17, no. 2 (2011). *See also* Godfrey Baldacchino, "The Brain Rotation and Brain Diffusion Strategies of Small Islanders: Considering 'Movement' in lieu of 'Place'", *Globalisation, Societies, and Education* 4, no. 1 (2006), pp. 143–154.

33. Data from World Bank, "World Bank Launches Initiative on Migration, Releases New Projections on Remittance Flows", press release, Washington, D.C., 19 April 2013, http://www.worldbank.org/en/news/press-release/2013/04/19/world-bank-launches-initiative-on-migration-releases-new-projections-on-remittance-flows (accessed 17 November 2014).

34. World Bank, *Migration and Remittances Factbook 2011*, p. 4.

35. Data from World Bank, *Migration and Remittances Factbook 2011*.

36. *See* Crush, *Between North and South*; Devesh Kapur, "Remittances: The New Development Mantra?", G-24 Discussion Paper no. 29 (New York and Geneva: United Nations Conference on Trade and Development [UNCTAD], April 2004); Eleonora Koeb and Henrike Hohmeister, "The Revision of Article 13 on Migration of the Cotonou Partnership Agreement: What's at Stake for the ACP?", briefing note (Maastricht: European Centre for Development Policy Management [ECDPM], 2010); Faruk Balli and Hatice Ozer Balli, "Income and Consumption Smoothing and Welfare Gains Across Pacific Island Countries: The Role of Remittances and Foreign Aid", *Economic Modelling* 28, no. 4 (2011), pp. 1642–1649; Sanjeev Gupta, Catherine Pattillo, and Smita Wagh, "Effect of Remittances on Poverty and Financial Development in Sub-Saharan Africa", *World Development* 37, no. 1 (2009), pp. 104–115; B. Gabriela Mundaca, "Remittances, Financial Market Development, and Economic Growth: The Case of Latin America and the Caribbean", *Review of Development Economics* 13, no. 2 (2009), pp. 288–303; Dilip Ratha, Sanket

Mohapatra, Caglar Ozden, Sonia Plaza, William Shaw, and Abebe Shimeles, *Leveraging Migration for Africa: Remittances, Skills, and Investments* (Washington, D.C.: World Bank, 2011).

37. Crush, *Between North and South*, p. 6.

38. Manuel Orozco, *The Market for Money Transfers: Ranking of Remittance Service Providers in Latin America and the Caribbean*, Inter-American Dialogue, 2012, http://www.thedialogue.org/PublicationFiles/LatAm_Final_120612.pdf (accessed 8 December 2014).

39. For further details, *see* Nurse, "Diasporic Tourism and Investment in Suriname", pp. 142–154.

40. *See* Orozco et al., "Transnational Engagement".

41. *See* Keith Nurse, "Migration, Diaspora, and Development in Latin America and the Caribbean", *International Politics and Society* 2 (2004), pp. 107–126.

42. Weinar, "Instrumentalising Diasporas for Development".

43. International Labour Office (ILO), International Migration Programme, *ILO's Multilateral Framework on Labour Migration: Non-Binding Principles and Guidelines for a Rights-Based Approach to Labour Migration* (Geneva, 2006).

44. Global Migration Group (GMG), *Mainstreaming Migration into Development: A Handbook for Policy-Makers and Practitioners* (Geneva: IOM, 2010), p. 2.

45. "Unbanked" consumers refers to those who do not use banks or banking institutions.

46. *See* Samy, "Strategic Opportunities in Caribbean Migration". *See also* Baldacchino, "The Brain Rotation and Brain Diffusion Strategies", pp. 143–154.

PART V

Looking Ahead

CHAPTER 12

The ACP Ambassadorial Working Group on Future Perspectives of the ACP Group

Patrick Gomes

In November 2010, the African, Caribbean, and Pacific (ACP) Council of Ministers decided to establish the Ambassadorial Working Group on Future Perspectives of the ACP Group. The Council mandated the working group to consider ways "to maintain and strengthen unity and solidarity within the ACP Group".[1] This mandate was set to expire in 2014, ahead of the third and final five-yearly review of the 20-year Cotonou Partnership Agreement of 2000, then scheduled to take place in 2015.[2] By then, it was expected that the 79-member ACP group of states would have not only crafted the contours of a meaningful vision for its future in the twenty-first century, but also reflected critically on the shape and form that it should give to its privileged partnership with the 28-member European Union (EU).[3] Should the ACP seek a successor agreement to Cotonou that enhances continuity, but with special and fundamentally different dimensions from those of its predecessor?

In this chapter, I outline the context in which the ACP Ambassadorial Working Group was conceptualised. The chapter also explains the approach and methodology that the working group used to gather and analyse data, and discusses the substantive issues and questions that have arisen from its work. In concluding the chapter, I reflect on the prospects of the ACP

P. Gomes (✉)
ACP Group, Brussels, Belgium

© The Author(s) 2017
A. Montoute, K. Virk (eds.), *The ACP Group and the EU Development Partnership*, DOI 10.1007/978-3-319-45492-4_12

group and on the future of its relationship with the EU, as the end of the Cotonou Agreement approaches in 2020.

The Historical and Contemporary Context

From the outset, the ACP Ambassadorial Working Group was guided by the objective of "transforming the ACP Group while managing change and continuity in a spirit of unity and solidarity".[4] This aim indicated recognition by the ACP group that it needed to identify and assess critically its geo-strategic relevance in a rapidly evolving global political and economic environment, and to formulate a coherent response to the changes being wrought by the rise of new powers in the global South.

The principles of unity and solidarity are deeply embedded in the Georgetown Agreement of 1975, which established the then 46-member ACP group, comprising 37 countries from sub-Saharan Africa, six from the Caribbean, and three from the Pacific (see Whiteman in this volume). Twenty-five years later, in June 2000, 77 ACP countries[5] signed the Cotonou Partnership Agreement with the European Community. The preamble to the Georgetown Agreement—amended in 2003 after the signing of Cotonou—explicitly avers that the ACP group is "desirous of contributing through continuous and concerted endeavours to the *reinforcement of the process of solidarity of developing countries*", and further "resolved to establish the African, Caribbean and Pacific Group of States to achieve common objectives so as to *contribute towards the realization of a new, fairer and more equitable world order*".[6] ACP unity and solidarity, thus, are further seen to have a global role. The Cotonou Agreement identifies this role—in terms of achieving the eradication of poverty and sustainable development through the "smooth and gradual integration of ACP States into the world economy".[7] These objectives are clear, straightforward, and complementary, and they have been supported with firm commitment and resolve by ACP governments since 1975 and endorsed at six ACP summits of heads of state and government between 1997 and 2008.[8]

Since 2008, however, global political and economic developments have impacted on the ACP group, the EU, and their "privileged" relationship. Trade and economic patterns in the global South have faced upheaval caused by broad geo-political changes, with the international economy going through a period of protracted stagnation in the wake of the global financial crisis of 2008–2009. According to the International Monetary Fund (IMF), global growth was forecast to be 3.5 per cent in

2015, but remain uneven and vulnerable to a range of complex factors, including weakened expectations and "crisis legacies" such as high debt.[9] Meanwhile, gross inequalities have come to compose a common thread in societies—developed and developing—across the world. Research by the Organisation for Economic Cooperation and Development (OECD), for example, shows a long-term and broad rise in income inequality, with the Gini coefficient[10] having risen in OECD countries from 0.29 in the mid-1980s to 0.32 in 2011–2012.[11] In the words of noted British historian Eric Hobsbawm: "This surge of inequality, especially in the conditions of extreme economic instability such as those created by the global free market in the 1990s, is at the roots of the major social and political tensions of the new century."[12] The financial crisis, for example, negatively impacted the ability of the majority of ACP countries to achieve the Millennium Development Goals (MDGs)—set by the United Nations (UN) in 2000—by the deadline of 2015.[13]

Furthermore, since 2005, changes to the EU's architecture and its approach to economic and trade relations with the ACP countries suggest that Brussels is reconsidering the exclusive and privileged nature of its trade and development partnership with the ACP group as a unified entity. For example, the European Council's initiative to create joint strategies— beginning with Africa in December 2005 and then with the Caribbean in March 2006, followed by the Pacific in May 2006—is indicative of a desire to pursue separate regional processes with the three ACP regions. This shift towards regionalism was heralded at an elaborate Africa-EU summit held in December 2007 in Lisbon, Portugal, that endorsed a Joint Africa-EU Strategy (JAES) and action plan. In addition, the now seven (previously six) region-based negotiating processes for economic partnership agreements (EPAs) with the EU—as mandated by Cotonou—have the potential to fragment the ACP group. Concerns and questions also remain about the benefits for ACP development of the trade liberalisation model being pursued through the EPAs (see Akokpari, Katjavivi, Girvan and Montoute, Gonzales, and Tavola in this volume). Taken together, these developments have encouraged serious reflection in various quarters about the future of ACP-EU relations beyond Cotonou.

In this context, it is also worth noting that the EU's Treaty on the Functioning of the Union, adopted in Lisbon in 2007, which entered into force in December 2009, makes no reference to the Cotonou Agreement as constituting a legally binding accord in the external relations of the EU. For some commentators, the omission pointed to the diminishing importance attributed to the ACP group. However, others have viewed the Lisbon Treaty as an internal EU accord on how it intended to reorganise its operational structures. This reordering was realised at the organisational level with the establishment of the European External Action Service (EEAS) in 2009. Notably, the EEAS has divided the ACP countries across three separate geographic departments—Africa, Asia, and the Americas—with the managing director of the Africa department assigned responsibility for intra-ACP affairs.

These developments on the EU side signal, to some extent, Europe's unease about its own future, or what German intellectual Jürgen Habermas has referred to as "the faltering project",[14] against a backdrop of wider changes by the global geo-political environment. Since the end of the Cold War by 1990, new powers have emerged in the global South to disrupt established trade patterns and political relations. This has been reflected in the emphasis placed on the Group of 20 (G-20) major industrialised and developing economies, and the growing prominence of Brazil, Russia, India, China, and South Africa (the BRICS bloc) (see Virk in this volume). Taken together, the shifting global dynamics and the changes within the EU offered compelling reasons for the ACP to adopt a proactive stance towards its own prospects. The growth of South-South cooperation was an additional factor in prompting the ACP group into a comprehensive stocktaking. India, Brazil, and South Africa (IBSA), for example, have undertaken tangible initiatives—such as the establishment of the IBSA Facility for Poverty and Hunger Alleviation (IBSA Fund) in 2004—in the struggle against poverty in other developing and emerging countries.

Bearing all of this in mind, the ACP had a multidimensional task: (1) to deepen and strengthen the unity and solidarity of the ACP group through a process of internal self-reflection; (2) to prepare for more effective engagement with its long-standing partners in the industrialised North, with a view to enhancing commonality of interests; and (3) to diversify and build stronger South-South collaborative arrangements. This then is the overarching context in which the ACP Ambassadorial Working Group set about trying to reinvent and transform the ACP group for the twenty-first century.

ENGAGING STAKEHOLDERS IN A CONSULTATIVE PROCESS

The ACP Ambassadorial Working Group on Future Perspectives— launched in January 2011—was composed of representatives from each of the four regions of sub-Saharan Africa (West, Central, East, and Southern), the Caribbean, and the Pacific, and also included two representatives from the ACP Secretariat's Staff Association and its senior management. The eight-member Ambassadorial Working Group was supported in its work by a rapporteur (a staff member of the ACP Secretariat).

Between January 2011 and September 2014, the working group convened 37 regular meetings and various activities with a view towards raising awareness among ACP member states, civil society groups, and regional organisations about the changing and fluid geo-political context in which the ACP group functioned. Discussions and hearings were held in Brussels, at the Commonwealth Secretariat, and in the ACP regions to encourage serious questioning about how the ACP saw itself; about the extent to which the group had lived up to the objectives of the Georgetown Agreement of 1975; and about the rights, obligations, and benefits of the Cotonou Partnership Agreement with Europe. More importantly, perhaps, the Ambassadorial Working Group also sought views on how the ACP group was perceived by others in terms of its relevance, achievements, shortcomings, and areas for greater effectiveness.

In early 2012, the Ambassadorial Working Group created an ad hoc group—as a sub-committee of the whole—on the "structure and functions of the organs of the ACP", to help, as the name indicates, with in-depth analysis of matters concerning the ACP's internal structures, organs, and decision-making processes. The working group also considered it valuable to scrutinise the strategic impact made by European Development Fund (EDF)–managed programmes and projects on intra-ACP development cooperation. Consequently, a second ad hoc group was formed in May 2012 to examine this area of work; some €300 million is annually committed to this group under the EDF, subject to an annual action plan approved by the ACP Committee of Ambassadors. Through this division of labour, the Ambassadorial Working Group sought to gain a holistic understanding of the complex dynamics that define the ACP group; and, through critical reflection and questioning, craft substantive themes for the 79-member grouping to take forward on its journey of transformation.

Over the course of its deliberations, the Ambassadorial Working Group benefited from presentations by a number of key organisations, including the European Centre for Development Policy Management (ECDPM),[15] the European Non-Governmental Organisation Confederation for Relief and Development (CONCORD), the *Organisation Internationale de la Francophonie* (OIF), and the United Nations Development Programme (UNDP) office in Brussels. Three key consultations are highlighted here.

ACP Retreat of March 2012

A two-day retreat, involving the ACP Secretariat's senior management, its Staff Association, and core members of the Ambassadorial Working Group, was held on 30 and 31 March 2012 in Limlette, Belgium. The meeting provided an opportunity for frank and open exchanges that restored a strong sense of common purpose and a shared commitment to change among the attendees. At the time, the ACP Secretariat itself had just completed a lengthy exercise for a strategic management plan for 2011–2014 that it was in the midst of operationalising. Organisationally, since 2005 the ACP Secretariat has seen itself become more grounded in knowledge management; more proactive in preparing working papers on key issues; and more involved in creative implementation of the principle of "comanagement"[16] that underlies its relations with the European Commission, in accordance with the Cotonou Agreement of 2000. This is particularly relevant with respect to EDF allocations for multiannual intra-ACP programmes and projects, which require mid-term and end-of-term reviews by the technical services of both the ACP Secretariat and the European Commission.

A key outcome of the retreat was to confirm the importance of the two ad hoc groups established as sub-committees of the Ambassadorial Working Group: first, to provide more in-depth analysis of the structure and functions of the organs of the ACP; and second, to provide a critique of intra-ACP development cooperation. While the former addressed matters internal to the ACP group, the latter entailed looking at priority-setting; negotiations for development funding; complex project management; and "partnership exchanges" with the labyrinthine directorates of the European Commission, as well its equally complicated procedures and processes. At the same time, there was an awareness at the retreat that although these and other activities of the ACP Ambassadorial Working Group were useful avenues of reflection, they ought not to lose sight of a key objective of the Cotonou Agreement: "reducing and eventually eradicating poverty consistent with the objectives of sustainable development and the gradual integration of the ACP countries into the world economy".[17]

Commonwealth Secretariat Consultation of April 2012

On 16 and 17 April 2012, the Commonwealth Secretariat convened a consultation on future perspectives for the ACP group of states. The two-day meeting brought together about 20 key stakeholders, including officials from African, Caribbean, and Pacific public and private sector agencies dealing with ACP-related trade, finance, and political issues, and academics and consultants with expertise on strategic management, trade in services, and law. A number of useful suggestions emerged from the consultative exercise. With reference to ACP-EU relations, they included the following. (1) Whatever agreement or arrangement followed Cotonou, it should be premised on the ACP group's goals and objectives, and on the pursuit of benefits for the group as a whole. The debate, in other words, had to be from the standpoint of the ACP and its interests. (2) In charting its way forward, the ACP had to appreciate the changing global environment, particularly within the EU, including the serious impacts of the global financial crisis of 2008–2009 in the Eurozone. (3) The tradition of ACP solidarity could be built upon through concentration on key priority areas that addressed the main challenges facing the ACP group as a whole and the specific issues confronting its regional configurations. (4) The relationship between the ACP and the EU had essentially been one of donor and recipient, even though it was intended to be predominantly about trade and development cooperation. ACP-EU engagement was deserving of expansion to include a broader range of political issues of mutual interest—for example, climate change and the struggle against terrorism—particularly in multilateral fora. (5) The asymmetrical relationship implied that the ACP group had weak bargaining power in the negotiations on trade and aid with the EU, but the group had political leverage in other areas and fora, based on its numerical strength in, for example, the UN, as well as the Group of 77 (G-77) together with China, that it could bring to the negotiating table.

The consultation also yielded useful recommendations towards making the organisation of the ACP group more "fit for purpose". These included:

- Restructuring the ACP based on a model of functional cooperation involving networking around key themes. In particular, the ACP Secretariat could draw "best practice" lessons from other organisations, such as the IBSA forum, the South Centre, and various UN specialised agencies, and strengthen its knowledge-base through access to expertise in specialised areas of interest. This could equip the ACP group to respond more effectively to future challenges in an increasingly complex, multilateral, global arena.

- Rationalising the division of labour between the ACP group as a collective platform, and various regional organisations and regional economic communities (RECs), to avoid overlapping mandates and to achieve complementarity.[18]
- Reconsidering the monochromatic focus on the ACP-EU relationship—a historical North-South construct—and exploring the benefits of South-South and triangular cooperation with new and emerging actors such as the BRICS bloc and the CIVETS group comprising Colombia, Indonesia, Vietnam, Egypt, Turkey, and South Africa.

The Commonwealth consultation further concluded that, generally speaking, the ACP group could be of increasing relevance globally, for a number of reasons. First, there was growing competition for access to, and trade in, the vast natural resources of ACP member states. Second, the ACP group as a whole, including through its regional groupings, has the potential to wield significant geo-political influence through its membership in multilateral organisations such as the World Trade Organisation (WTO). Moreover, the group's relatively long record of over three decades of development finance cooperation could also position it as a credible partner and critical assessor in leveraging development cooperation support, on behalf of its members, in crafting a global partnership for effective development cooperation (as envisaged by MDG Eight). Third, the ACP's ability to interface with larger third-party countries (such as Indonesia, Brazil, and Australia) in areas such as natural resource development, particularly mining and the management of mineral resources, could be critical for ensuring value-added enterprise development in ACP countries that are otherwise overly dependent on primary commodity exports.

However, the Commonwealth meeting also noted the need for the ACP group to document these advantages and achievements, in order to be able to explain clearly to its stakeholders why it was essential for the group's 79 member countries to work together and, in so doing, to specify where and how ACP-wide approaches could offer outcomes superior to those that could be achieved from purely national or regional efforts.

Van Reisen Report of April 2012

The April 2012 UNDP-funded study by Mirjam van Reisen of Tilburg University in the Netherlands was of particular importance to the Ambassadorial Working Group's efforts to increase awareness about the challenges facing the ACP group. The terms of reference for the study were ambitious in scope, and aimed to gather views in seven key areas: (1) the ACP group's relevance and achievements, as well as the functioning of its organs; (2) its relationship and cooperation with the EU; (3) the group's comparative advantage in trade negotiations on behalf of its member states; (4) its relations with regional organisations in Africa, the Caribbean, and the Pacific; (5) the scope for (greater) integration through intra-ACP cooperation; (6) the feasibility of ACP enlargement; and (7) options and scenarios in view of the impending expiry of the Cotonou Agreement in 2020.

The approach and methodology adopted by the study involved a baseline, panoramic assessment of the achievements and challenges of the ACP group as a self-financing inter-governmental entity, based on which five possible scenarios for the future prospects of the group were delineated and proposed to respondents: (1) maintaining the status quo; (2) winding up the ACP; (3) regionalisation; (4) decreasing membership, limiting it to least-developed countries (LDCs); and (5) creating an autonomous, independent, and self-financing inter-governmental body with multiple sets of relations.

The final report[19]—discussed at a stakeholders' workshop convened in May 2012 in Brussels—offered a synthesis of current thinking among 60 key respondents, which mainly included those whom one might call "ACP insiders". More than 80 per cent of the people interviewed for the study were ambassadors or representatives of the 66 ACP missions based in Brussels.[20] Admittedly, this created the possibility of some bias based on the self-interest of the respondents. Further, it could be argued that the Brussels-based ambassadors interviewed for the van Reisen report lacked adequate distance from the ongoing business of the ACP-EU relationship to be sufficiently critical of the organisation. They were, at the same time, also perceived by some as too removed from the impact of ACP programmes at the national and regional levels.

Even so, ACP ambassadors are key to implementation of the ACP-EU relationship, and their views represent an important source of knowledge. Not only do they serve as crucial links between the ACP capitals and Brussels, but they are also vital sources of intelligence, expertise, insights, beliefs, and concerns, which together can, and do, inform political decision-making on the relevance and effectiveness of the ACP group. The ACP Committee of Ambassadors exercises policy oversight over the work programmes of the ACP group, monitoring the implementation of the ACP-EU Partnership Agreement, as stipulated in Article 19 of the

Georgetown Agreement of 1975 (amended in 2003). These programmes entail a broad range of activities that encompass trade and sustainable economic development; development finance; and political, cultural, and educational relations among and between the ACP's 79 members, various RECs and regional integration organisations, as well as the finance and administration sections of the ACP Secretariat.

Notwithstanding its limitations, the van Reisen report provided several insights for deeper reflection by the ACP Ambassadorial Working Group. First, it was clear that maintaining the status quo was not an option: a majority of respondents in the study supported the demand, and a need, for the ACP group to undertake structural and operational changes, which were required to reinforce the relevance and effectiveness of the impact of the ACP's programmes at the global, regional, and national levels. The point was closely related to the visibility and identity of the ACP group. The potential represented by the group's numerical strength, accumulated experience, in-house expertise, and negotiating capacity on trade and commodity issues, development finance, migration, and parliamentary democracy, for example, has remained largely unrealised in a sufficiently cohesive and coherent manner.

Second, it was equally clear that the long-standing ACP-EU relationship was not immune to the rapid changes and turbulence affecting the global political and economic environment. As the van Reisen report noted: "From the interviews, it emerges that the ACP-EU relationship is seen as fundamentally changing. This change could not be illustrated in a better way than that Portugal is now receiving financial aid from Angola. Portuguese people such as nurses, engineers and architects, are now seeking employment possibilities in oil-rich Angola, Mozambique as well as Brazil."[21] Admittedly, the global order is still evolving and the full impact of ongoing changes (such as the increasing demand for energy and the volatility of food prices) has not been fully determined. Even so, the upheaval has manifested itself in various food, financial, and climate-related crises, as well as in the contrasting economic growth performances and prospects of emerging economies, such as the BRICS countries and several ACP member states (such as Mauritius, Papua New Guinea, and Suriname) on the one hand, and those of major European economies on the other, which have become characterised by stagnation, austerity policies, and persistent structural unemployment.

Third, in response to these changing conditions, the interviewees in the van Reisen study explicitly recognised that the underlying basis and rationale of the ACP-EU relationship are being questioned in many quarters in Europe, as well as by the ACP. This recognition arose not merely from the Lisbon Treaty's omission of any reference to the Cotonou Agreement of 2000, but also, and more significantly, from mixed signals from Brussels about what Europe aims to be in an increasingly competitive global marketplace. In March 2011, the European Commission introduced a new economic strategy—known as Europe 2020—to prepare the EU's market economy for the decade ahead, in particular to help it become knowledge-based and more resource-efficient, with a focus on fighting poverty within Europe.[22] This strategy supposes that the EU's commercial interests will be better served by deeper relations primarily within EU member states and regions and, if at all, with individual ACP regions through the mechanism of "joint strategies", or through free trade agreements (FTAs), and by increasing preferential market access bilaterally to countries such as Pakistan and regionally to areas such as the Western Balkans. Yet the EU has remained silent about how such measures might further erode its economic relations with the ACP group, even though Article 12 of the Cotonou Agreement requires Brussels to provide the ACP with full information about any measures that might impact the objectives of their partnership.

For the ACP, meanwhile, the growth in demand for its natural and mineral resources from competing powers in both the industrialised North and the emerging global South has opened up new possibilities, when negotiating conditions for investment and access to these primary materials, and has drawn attention to policies that promote mineral beneficiation and value-added processes. The benefits of the latter have been evident in the transformation of the diamond industry in Botswana and of the cane industry in Mauritius. In addition, concern about the ACP's exclusion from key global institutions, such as the United Nations Security Council, has stimulated debate for a post-Cotonou arrangement with the EU that is based on a deeper shared understanding of mutual interdependence. At the same time, there is awareness that the ACP must also look beyond Europe to the possibilities that have arisen for the ACP to be a voice for the global South, working through the BRICS and other emerging regional groupings. This will entail diversifying the ACP group's partnership agreements, as has been effectively done in the WTO with the formation of the Group of 90 (G-90). At other times, it may involve taking on a leadership role, as in the case of the group of small, vulnerable economies (SVEs) on issues pertaining to trade facilitation.

Fourth, in defining its strategic objectives over the medium and long term, the ACP's comparative advantage in the negotiation of trade agreements, the design and implementation of development cooperation policies, and the facilitation of knowledge exchanges through South-South and triangular cooperation must be given greater prominence. This advantage refers to the tricontinental ties that bind the group's 79-strong membership, and further link it with North Africa, the Asia-Pacific region, and the Americas; this is in addition to its formal accord with Europe. The challenge that the ACP faces relates to how it can effectively deploy to its benefit the political, organisational, commercial, and cultural capital that these linkages offer. In this context, the ACP group needs to give greater and more systematic attention to the expanding scope of South-South and triangular cooperation—an area in which it can potentially carve a leadership role.

Fifth, political support and demonstrable commitment at the highest level to a recrafted vision and mission for the ACP are essential prerequisites for renewing the impact, relevance, and effectiveness of the group as a global player. In this regard, the Sipopo Declaration—the outcome document of the seventh ACP summit of heads of state and government, held in December 2012 in Malabo, Equatorial Guinea—provides an unequivocal statement of political commitment to the ACP's future.[23]

Sixth, with respect to the five scenarios for the ACP "towards 2020 and beyond" provided by the van Reisen report, a majority of respondents supported the idea of "an independent ACP with multiple sets of relations".[24] Interpreting the concept of "independence", however, has given rise to much internal debate within the ACP, particularly over the concern that the responsibility for financial sustainability of the group (primarily the operational costs of its secretariat) needs to be increasingly assumed by its members. In the ACP Secretariat's annual budget, 50 per cent of projected income is composed of assessed contributions from member states and 37 per cent of a contribution from the EDF, with the remaining 13 per cent drawn from staff taxes and expected arrears from member states with outstanding contributions. In this regard, unexplored options include the creation of trust funds and income generation from the ACP Secretariat's project management services. As the van Reisen report noted: "[T]here is also a significant majority in favour of a Secretariat core that is financed by the ACP countries themselves and reflects the political commitment to the ACP Group".[25]

Financial independence for the ACP does not preclude a special relationship with the EU on the basis of mutual respect for human rights, democratic governance, and the rule of law. Rather, in keeping with UNDP's 2011 *Human Development Report*,[26] equity becomes a fundamental principle, with the ACP's future perspectives able to embrace enhanced and diversified partnerships. These and related aspects of the van Reisen report were discussed at the May 2012 Brussels stakeholders' workshop, in which much attention was given to exploring further the synergies between the option of "regionalization" and that of an "independent ACP with multiple sets of relations".[27]

Beyond the van Reisen report, another study, by the Bonn-based German Development Institute (DIE) and the Maastricht-based ECDPM, was able to solicit views from a wider cross-section of stakeholders on how they envisioned a future for the ACP with the expected conclusion of the Cotonou Agreement in 2020. According to this study: "ACP-country ambassadors in Brussels, as well as others working within the current framework, indicate broad support for upgrading the Agreement. However, most stakeholders in ACP countries see no reason to maintain the ACP structure or the CPA [Cotonou Partnership Agreement]: they opt for letting Cotonou expire, regionalising relations with the EU, and possibly maintaining a scaled-down ACP."[28]

PRELIMINARY THEMES UNDER CONSIDERATION FOR A RENEWED ACP GROUP

Beyond the processes and issues addressed by the ACP Ambassadorial Working Group, three substantives themes or ideas have emerged in the debate on the ACP's reform efforts that merit consideration here: (1) an ACP free trade area; (2) an ACP trade and investment bank; and (3) South-South and triangular cooperation in the context of developments since the High-Level Forum on Aid Effectiveness, held in Busan, South Korea, in November–December 2011.

Feasibility of Establishing an ACP Free Trade Area

The decision to undertake a feasibility study for an ACP free trade area was taken at the sixth ACP summit of heads of state and government, held in Accra, Ghana, in October 2008. However, with attention mainly centred on the EPA processes and their potentially negative effects on regional trade and integration, little to no systematic effort was made towards implementation of the 2008 summit decision. The creation of the ACP Ambassadorial Working Group, with its mandate to strengthen group unity and solidarity, provided an opportunity, and a logical space, to explore the feasibility of an ACP free trade area. The intention, in this regard, was to search for ways of advancing trade in general and among ACP countries in particular for the promotion of economic growth and development, employment creation, and poverty reduction, in the context of high population growth rates in the African, Caribbean, and Pacific regions and recession in the industrialised countries of the North.

The ACP Sub-Committee on Trade and Commodities—a permanent structure within the ACP Secretariat for dealing with trade policy matters—was identified by the ACP Committee of Ambassadors as the logically appropriate organisational locale for providing the necessary technical inputs in this thematic area. This helped to avoid duplication with the tripartite free trade area being pursued by the Common Market for Eastern and Southern Africa (COMESA), the East African Community (EAC), and the Southern African Development Community (SADC) (see Carim in this volume). The matter was discussed at the April 2012 Commonwealth consultation mentioned earlier, with the Commonwealth Secretariat offering to provide technical assistance in the form of a pre-feasibility study. This study was subsequently undertaken with the aim of assessing: (1) current intra-ACP trade flows and patterns; (2) the potential for increased trade among ACP countries associated with an ACP free trade area; (3) barriers and constraints to intra-ACP trade; (4) the state of regional economic integration and cooperation in intra-ACP trade relations; and (5) appropriate policy and other measures to promote intra-ACP trade and integration.

A joint report by the UN Conference on Trade and Development (UNCTAD) and the ACP Secretariat, published in 2013, indicated that:

> [While] intra-ACP merchandise trade in value terms increased strongly to about US$40.5 billion in 2009 from about US$17.8 billion in 1995 ... [t]he share intra-ACP merchandise exports occupies in total ACP merchandise exports to the world ... has significantly declined over this 15-year period from 20 to 15 per cent. This denotes that intra-ACP trade is becoming relatively less important to ACP States ... Intra-ACP trade is ... increasingly dominated by trade in primary commodities.[29]

Another report, for the Commonwealth Secretariat, prepared in 2012, found that existing preferential trade arrangements in the African, Caribbean, and Pacific regions hindered the expansion of intra-regional

ACP trade. Additional barriers to increased intra-regional ACP trade, especially between Africa and the Pacific, Africa and the Caribbean, and the Pacific and Caribbean regions, include geographical distances and the limited volume and range of tradable goods and services.[30] The report thus indicated that, rather than focusing on an inter-regional FTA, the ACP might be better served by focusing on reducing non-tariff trade barriers to greater inter-regional trade, such as weak infrastructure, poor quality and regulatory standards, and other restrictive non-tariff measures, while supporting regional initiatives aimed at reducing tariffs, such as the proposed tripartite FTA between COMESA, the EAC, and SADC.

In addition, the ACP's Sub-Committee on Trade and Commodities has proposed further ideas for consideration, including a need to pay greater attention to trade in services; to the identification of niche areas in which the ACP has a comparative advantage; and to partial scope agreements in key areas of cooperation such as trade in agricultural commodities and staple food products. It is worth noting that while some ACP countries (such as Togo) have recorded surplus production of certain foods (including grains and vegetables), others (for example, Haiti and Zambia) face food deficits and are net food importers. The ACP's efforts to increase inter- and intra-regional trade are still a work in progress, and going forward are intended to place an emphasis on value-addition, diversification, and industrial transformation.

This approach was discussed comprehensively at an ACP forum in Brussels on 18 November 2014 on the theme of a new integrated and sustainable approach to the ACP's commodity sector. The meeting brought together Brussels-based diplomats and international commodity specialists, as well as representatives of various development agencies, including the African Development Bank (AfDB), the Common Fund for Commodities (CFC), West Africa's Ecobank, and UN agencies such as the Food and Agriculture Organisation (FAO), UNCTAD, and UNDP. The forum extensively reviewed a report, titled "Commodity Policy Review: Toward an Holistic Commodity-Based Development", that was commissioned by the ACP and undertaken by UNCTAD, with the discussion forming the basis of a set of concrete recommendations. These focused, among other things, on reducing the impact of commodity price volatility on ACP producers, with stabilisation policy instruments for guaranteed prices and income; reducing the vulnerability of ACP states to global shocks, through policy measures to reinforce regional commodity markets; decreasing ACP states' excessive dependence on primary products;

and strengthening governance structures, particularly in non-renewable commodity sectors such as mining and minerals. The forum also strongly recommended encouraging and reinforcing farmers' organisations and agricultural cooperatives, through policy measures and legislation aimed at providing security for small producers, particularly women, in order to enable and sustain their active participation in commodity value chains. These and other recommendations generated at the November 2014 forum in Brussels are intended to form the basis of the ACP Secretariat's programme of work under the senior management team that took office in March 2015.

Exploring Options for an ACP Trade and Investment Bank

The idea for an ACP bank goes as far back as July 1980, when an extraordinary session of the ACP Council of Ministers in Montego Bay, Jamaica, took the decision that a group of experts should draw up a framework for the creation of such a bank.[31] Though visionary, there was not enough follow-up and the idea languished. The Council of Ministers then revisited the idea in May 2011, when it decided to establish a trade and development bank, mandating the ACP Secretariat to prepare a report by its next meeting in December 2011. A draft concept note[32] for the proposed ACP bank was presented to the Ambassadorial Working Group by Obadiah Mailafia, Chef de Cabinet of the ACP Secretariat, in April 2012, and, subsequently, also to the ACP Committee of Ambassadors in May 2012 and the ACP Council of Ministers in June 2012. A summarised version of the concept note was also presented to the Committee of Ambassadors in October 2012.[33] In 2013, a comprehensive gap analysis and market feasibility study were undertaken, with the outcome document—prepared by February 2014—distributed for comments thereafter to ACP finance, planning, and development ministries and central banks, as well as to prospective investment agencies.

The justifications for an ACP trade and investment bank are many. The first relates to the ACP group's high level of economic vulnerability, much of which arises from member countries' dependence on commodity exports, small size, low levels of income, and varied geographical challenges. While the population of the ACP group was an estimated 932 million in 2012, amounting to 13 per cent of the global total, its share of global gross domestic product (GDP) was a mere 2 per cent, compared with the EU's 28 per cent and China's 7 per cent, in the same year.[34]

Second, since the global financial crisis of 2008–2009, several funding sources, particularly short-term trade finance, have dried up for many low-income countries. As a recent study on small and medium enterprises (SMEs) in ACP countries noted, many such organisations have been starved of the lifeblood of capital, with the result that their "ability to invest in new technology, expand production and marketing and grow their businesses, even when opportunities exist, is constrained".[35]

It is envisaged that the proposed ACP bank will have a strong private sector orientation, with a focus on niche areas that do not compete with the work of existing multilateral banks. Its operations will focus on key areas such as mining and natural resource development, manufacturing, SMEs, and regional projects and infrastructure. In this regard, the ACP Roadmap and Action Plan on Mineral Resources, adopted by the first ACP ministerial meeting on mineral resources, held in December 2010 in Brussels, is an important framework for identifying the needs to be financed by the proposed bank, with a view to enhancing beneficiation and value-addition in the extractive industries sector in ACP states.[36]

As a trade finance instrument, the planned ACP bank is intended to complement existing efforts to consolidate and deepen ACP-wide trade—a major lacuna in the ongoing EPA processes at both the negotiation and implementation levels. Initial ideas for sources of capital for the proposed bank include: share capital from member states, capital market borrowing, bond issuance, trust funds from bilateral sources, and sovereign wealth funds. These and other fundamental dimensions of the bank were to have been rigorously analysed in the aforementioned pre-feasibility study on the ACP investment bank project, which has since been circulated for comments from ACP member states and prospective investors. Furthermore, a decision has since been taken to undertake a feasibility study on the establishment of an endowment and trust fund. An ACP private sector development strategy, with a focus on SMEs, has also been adopted.

Promoting South-South and Triangular Cooperation

International debates on development finance cooperation and aid effectiveness have assumed greater importance and garnered increasing attention among donors and recipients alike through the Rome Forum of 2003, the Paris Principles of 2005, the Accra Agenda for Action of 2008, and more recently, the High-Level Forum on Aid Effectiveness held in

Busan in November–December 2011. The ACP group's experience of development cooperation—accumulated through its partnership with the EU—spans about four decades, going back to the group's creation in 1975. Negotiation of programmes, rules and procedures, and timeliness of disbursements, together with resistance of conditionalities, have been key elements of this experience. In addition, the Paris Principles, covering country ownership, alignment, harmonisation, results-based management, and mutual accountability, have been accepted by ACP countries as desirable for improved aid effectiveness.

However, a number of factors have led the ACP Secretariat to support a fundamental rethink of "effectiveness" as a process, rather than a technical issue related to the measurement and management of external outputs. These factors include: the ACP group's own experience of development finance programming and implementation under the EDF since 1976; wider debates on official development assistance (ODA), including during the 2010 review of the MDGs; and in particular, the unlikelihood of the ACP's traditional donors among the Group of Eight (G-8) achieving their target of committing 0.7 per cent of gross national income (GNI) to ODA by 2015.

Shifting from "aid effectiveness" to "development effectiveness" further emphasises a holistic approach, one in which aid has a catalytic role and, though significant, is of less importance than an understanding of how both internal and external factors interact to promote development. Focusing on process in this manner means that the stated objectives of development can be targeted, whether at local or sectoral levels, while avoiding a "one size fits all" approach. Within this framework of thinking, South-South cooperation, in particular, has gained greater relevance as a means of utilising specialised knowledge and enhancing the management experiences of developing countries through the sharing of best practices among them.

The ACP group's commitment to South-South cooperation has been highlighted by a series of events since 2010. A major symposium on the topic was held by the ACP Secretariat, in collaboration with the *Organisation Internationale de la Francophonie*, in January 2011 in Brussels. The meeting included participation from the development cooperation agencies of Brazil and India, as well as from those of Cuba, Nigeria, and South Africa, and entailed presentations based on case study research that demonstrated the long-standing experience of, and thematic areas successfully addressed by, ACP member states in the area of South-South cooperation. Contributions were also made by the European Commission, the Commonwealth Secretariat, and the Lusophone

Development Cooperation Organisation (CPLP), highlighting the scope of and interest in collaborating with the ACP in South-South cooperation and triangular cooperation initiatives.[37] Later, in April 2011, on the sidelines of the UN Conference on Least Developed Countries in Istanbul, Turkey, the ACP and the OIF also cohosted a roundtable discussion on the "Cotton Four"—Burkina Faso, Benin, Mali, and Chad. This strongly enhanced the role of the ACP as an advocate for LDCs. Thirty-nine out of the world's 48 least-developed countries are members of the ACP group.

Since the High-Level Forum on Aid Effectiveness held in Busan in 2011, the ACP has emerged as a coordinator of the Building Block on South-South and Triangular Cooperation, and in the formulation of a medium-term action plan as part of the Busan recommendation for "horizontal partnerships for better development outcomes".[38] The recommendation calls for collaborative and joint programmes to be undertaken by two or more development agencies involving the public sector, private sector, or civil society organisations. South-South and triangular cooperation offer great promise, through deeper and expanded partnerships, for the ACP to meet its goal of eradicating poverty in its member states, and for the global South as a whole. At the same time, the ACP has continued throughout, and repeatedly, to stress that South-South and triangular cooperation are not substitutes for, but are complementary to, ODA resources and modalities. As the outcome document of the Busan forum explicitly recognises, "many countries engaged in South-South Cooperation both provide and receive diverse resources and expertise at the same time, and ... this should enrich cooperation without affecting a country's eligibility to receive assistance from others".[39]

CONCLUDING REFLECTIONS

The final report of the Ambassadorial Working Group on Future Perspectives of the ACP Group, "Transforming the ACP Group of States into an Effective Global Player", was unanimously adopted by the ACP Council of Ministers at its 100th meeting, held in December 2014.[40] The report argues for the repositioning and transformation of the ACP group into a dynamic inter-governmental organisation fully responsive to the global challenges of an unsettled and multipolar twenty-first century. It also puts forward an all-ACP strategic policy framework with five focus areas for a transformed ACP group: global justice and human security; rule of law and democratic governance; trade, enterprise development, and regional integration; building sustainable, resilient, and creative economies; and financing for development.

The conclusions and recommendations of the report further provide a roadmap and outline of an action plan through 2030 that identifies priority actions for the short, medium, and long term in phased sequences. These address issues such as the matter of amendments to the Georgetown Agreement; the introduction of measures for structured relations between RECs and regional integration organisations through an Inter-Regional Organisations Coordinating Committee (IROCC); and the provision of support for the ACP as a facilitator and hub of South-South and triangular cooperation. A key emphasis of the ACP's annual action plan will be on intra-ACP cooperation through specific activities in the five strategic policy domains in ways that are mutually reinforcing and that avail of partnership arrangements with the EU, multilateral organisations, and groupings such as the BRICS bloc as well as the G-77 together with China, as appropriate.

Meanwhile, the Eminent Persons Group submitted its final report at the eighth ACP summit of heads of state and government, held in May–June 2016. Ahead of the summit, the report of the Ambassadorial Working Group was shared with the Eminent Persons Group with a view to helping identify synergies between the two undertakings, while fully respecting the independent views of both. ACP declarations and decisions, based on deliberations at the 2016 summit, have further enriched the process of transformation that the group has undertaken to confront the demands and challenges of the twenty-first century.

In retrospect, the extensive stakeholder consultations and vigorous debates that characterised the work of the Ambassadorial Working Group reconfirmed the ACP's foundational principles of unity and solidarity, but at the same time showed that they were in need of a fundamental rethink. To some extent, this is self-evident, given the vastly different socio-economic and political conditions that exist today compared with those that prevailed during the Cold War and heyday of the Non-Aligned Movement (NAM). The ACP's membership has grown from 46 in 1975 to 79 in 2015, and encompasses a variegated group of high-, middle-, and low-income economies across three continents. These countries are further engaged in navigating a complex international environment, while seeking to resist the legacies of colonialism and neo-colonialism and remaining wary of the threats to their security interests posed by ethnic, tribal, religious, and class differences.

Against this backdrop, the Ambassadorial Working Group's vision for the ACP has sought to demonstrate the ACP's unity and solidarity, while explicitly addressing a need to build greater complementarity and coherence actively between national, regional, and continental ACP policies through partnerships aimed at poverty eradication and sustainable development. To translate this thinking into concrete action, the ACP Secretariat's working methods, service delivery, and financial sustainability will require serious attention between 2015 and 2020, ahead of Cotonou's expiry.

In this regard, a major challenge that the ACP Secretariat administration (under the senior management that took office in March 2015) will face relates to active consultations with key EU institutions, in particular the Council, Commission, and Parliament. An exchange of negotiating memoranda and policy papers will be the basis for shaping a mutually beneficial relationship that addresses the two sides' common commitment to global justice, peace, security, and poverty eradication, while conserving public goods for future generations. Going forward, the ACP should strongly advocate for a legally binding arrangement with the EU, rather than strategies of best endeavour, to be the foundation of their post-Cotonou relationship.

Thus, it would be reasonable for the ACP group to approach post-2020 ACP-EU relations from a perspective that aims to deepen intra-ACP cooperation; to consolidate the gains acquired over four decades of trade, development cooperation, and political dialogue with Europe; and to diversify the group's relations with emerging economies of the global South. This is an exciting era of challenges and opportunities, and the Ambassadorial Working Group has sought through its work to provide the ACP's member states and other stakeholders with interesting insights and principles for innovative thought and action that can help the ACP become an effective global advocate and catalyst for the benefit of all developing countries.

NOTES

1. Council of Ministers of the African, Caribbean, and Pacific (ACP) Group of States, Decision no. 4/XC11/10, 92nd Session, November 2010, p. 5.
2. The ACP group and the European Commission agreed that there were no immediate issues to warrant a revision to the Cotonou

Agreement in 2015, and that the next revision would take place in 2020, with a view to determining a successor agreement to Cotonou.

3. In a national referendum, held in June 2016, Britain voted to leave the European Union (EU). Official negotiations were yet to begin at the time of writing, but as and when Britain leaves the Union, the membership of the EU will be reduced to 27.

4. "Terms of Reference of the Ambassadorial Working Group on Future Perspectives of the ACP Group", 18 October 2010, p. 1.

5. Of the 79 members of the ACP group, Cuba and South Africa are not signatories to the Cotonou Agreement. In addition, though South Africa is a signatory to the Georgetown Agreement, the country does not benefit from the European Development Fund (EDF) in light of its stand-alone Trade, Development, and Cooperation Agreement (TDCA) of 1999 with the European Union—see Carim in this volume.

6. The Georgetown Agreement, as revised in November 2003, is available at http://www.dfa.gov.za/eumaltilateral/docs/Georgetown%20Agreement/the_georgetown_agreement_en.pdf (accessed 30 June 2015) (emphasis added).

7. Cotonou Partnership Agreement of 2000 (revised in 2005 and 2010), chap. 1, art. 34, para. 1.

8. The summits were held in Liberville, Gabon, in 1997; Santo Domingo, Dominican Republic, in 1999; Nadi, Fiji, in 2002; Maputo, Mozambique, in 2004; Khartoum, Sudan, in 2006; and Accra, Ghana, in 2008.

9. International Monetary Fund (IMF), *World Economic Outlook: Uneven Growth—Short- and Long-Term Factors* (Washington, D.C., April 2015), p. xv, http://www.imf.org/external/pubs/ft/weo/2015/01/pdf/text.pdf (accessed 30 June 2015).

10. The Gini coefficient is a commonly used broad measure of inequality, which ranges from 0 (complete equality) to 1 (complete inequality).

11. Organisation for Economic Cooperation and Development (OECD), "Does Income Inequality Hurt Economic Growth?" *Focus on Inequality and Growth*, December 2014, p. 1, http://www.oecd.org/els/soc/Focus-Inequality-and-Growth-2014.pdf (accessed 20 June 2015).

12. Eric J. Hobsbawm, *Globalisation, Democracy, and Terrorism* (London: Abacus, 2007), p. 3.

13. *See* "ACP-EU Joint Resolution on the Economic and Financial Crisis", Brussels, Belgium, 28–29 May 2009, http://eu-un.europa. eu/articles/en/article_8762_en.htm (accessed 30 June 2015).
14. Jürgen Habermas, *Europe: The Faltering Project* (Cambridge: Polity, 2009).
15. *See* James Mackie, Bruce Byiers, Sonia Niznik, and Geert Laporte (eds.), *Global Changes, Emerging Players, and Evolving ACP-EU Relations: Towards a Common Agenda for Action?* European Centre for Development Policy Management (ECDPM), 25th Anniversary Seminar, Policy Management Report no. 19 (Maastricht: ECDPM, September 2011), http://www.ecdpm. org/pmr19 (accessed 5 October 2012).
16. "Comanagement" refers to collaboration between the ACP Secretariat and European Commission services in the planning, implementation, and review of joint projects.
17. *See* Cotonou Partnership Agreement, pt. 1, title 1, art. 1.
18. The creation of the ACP Inter-Regional Organisations Coordination Committee (IROCC) in 2012 constitutes an important step in this direction. IROCC held its inaugural meeting in October 2011, and is intended to meet annually, with the Secretary-General of the ACP as permanent chair and with a co-chair designated from among the regional organisations on a rotating basis. ACP Secretariat, "Rules of Procedure for ACP Inter-Regional Organisations Coordination Committee", ACP/61/050/11 Rev. 4, Brussels, 2012.
19. Mirjam van Reisen, "ACP 3D: Future Perspectives of the ACP Group", report prepared for the ACP Group and the United Nations Development Programme (UNDP), Brussels, 2012, p. 80. The study comprised desk-based research; SWOT (strengths, weaknesses, opportunities, and threats) analysis; and triangulation of quantitative and qualitative data from interviews with 60 participants, including ACP government ministers, ACP ambassadors and officials based in Brussels, and key personnel from EU agencies and relevant civil society organisations. A stakeholders' workshop to discuss the findings and recommendations of the study was held on 21 May 2012 at ACP House in Brussels, Belgium.
20. For an interesting discussion on the scope of the administrative apparatus of the ACP group, *see* Obadiah Mailafia, "*Pax Europaea* Revisited: The ACP-EU Partnership in the Emerging Global

Order—A Briefing Memorandum Prepared for Members of Parliament of the Royal Kingdom of the Netherlands", ACP Secretariat, Brussels, April 2012, p. 16.

21. van Reisen, "ACP 3D", p. 33.
22. Communication from the European Commission, "Europe 2020: A Strategy for Smart, Sustainable, and Inclusive Growth", COM (2010) 2020 Final, Brussels, March 2010, http://eur-lex.europa.eu/LexUriServ/LexUriServ.do?uri=COM:2010:2020:FIN:EN:PDF (accessed 30 June 2015).
23. Sipopo Declaration, Seventh Summit of ACP Heads of State and Government, Sipopo, Equatorial Guinea, 13–14 December 2012, paras. 64–65.
24. van Reisen, "ACP 3D", p. 15.
25. van Reisen, "ACP 3D", p. 15.
26. United Nations Development Programme, *Human Development Report 2011: Sustainability and Equity—A Better Future for All* (New York, 2011).
27. van Reisen, "ACP 3D", pp. 15, 45.
28. Mario Negre, Niels Keijzer, Brecht Lein, and Nicola Tissi, "Towards Renewal or Oblivion? Prospects for Post-2020 Cooperation between the European Union and the Africa, Caribbean, and Pacific Group", Discussion Paper no. 9 (Bonn and Maastricht: German Development Institute [DIE] and ECDPM, 2013), http://ecdpm.org/wp-content/uploads/2013/10/DP-9-Post-2020-Cooperation-EU-Africa-Caribbean-Pacific.pdf (accessed 5 January 2015).
29. United Nations Conference on Trade and Development (UNCTAD) and ACP Secretariat, *Participation of African, Caribbean, and Pacific States in International Trade* (New York and Geneva, 2013), p. 31, http://unctad.org/en/Publications Library/webditctncd2011d2_en.pdf (accessed 5 January 2015).
30. Chris Milner, "Review of the Feasibility and Scope for Deepening Commercial Linkages Among ACP Members and Expanding Intra-ACP Trade and Economic Cooperation", Interim Report to the Commonwealth Secretariat, London, July 2012.
31. *See* ACP Secretariat, "Rapporteur's Report Containing List of Resolutions Adopted at the Extraordinary Session of the ACP Council of Ministers at Montego Bay", Jamaica, 7–10 July 1980 (report issued 22 July 1980). The remarks in this section rely heav-

ily on Obadiah Mailafia, "Concept Note on the Establishment of the ACP Bank for International Trade and Investment", ACP Secretariat, Brussels, May 2012.

32. Mailafia, "Concept Note".

33. ACP Secretariat, "Summary Concept Note on the ACP Investment Bank Project", ACP/11/003/12, Brussels, October 2012.

34. UNCTAD and ACP Secretariat, *Participation of African, Caribbean, and Pacific States*, p. 5.

35. ACP Secretariat, "ACP-EU Joint Cooperation Framework for Private Sector Development Support in ACP Countries", ACP/85/012/14 Final, Brussels, 11 June 2014, p. 4, para. 10.

36. Mailafia, "Concept Note".

37. I define triangular cooperation as a demand-driven mechanism whereby assistance is provided to a developing country by three or more countries, agencies, or organisations working together to address a specific need identified by the developing country concerned.

38. Members of the Building Block on South-South and Triangular Cooperation include developing countries such as Bangladesh, Bolivia, Cambodia, Chile, Costa Rica, El Salvador, Ghana, Honduras, Indonesia, Malawi, and Peru. Member states of the Organisation for Economic Cooperation and Development include Germany, Japan, Korea, Mexico, and Spain; the OECD also includes the European Union, the Asian Development Bank (ADB), the Caribbean Community Secretariat, the Inter-American Development Bank (IADB), the *Organisation Internationale de la Francophonie*, the Organisation of American States (OAS), the New Partnership for Africa's Development (NEPAD), the Pacific Islands Forum (PIF), the Pan-American Health Organisation (PAHO), the United Nations Development Programme, the World Bank, the ACP Group, and the Islamic Development Bank.

39. Busan Partnership for Effective Development Cooperation, Fourth High-Level Forum on Aid Effectiveness, Busan, South Korea, 29 November–1 December 2011, para. 31, http://www.oecd.org/dac/effectiveness/49650173.pdf (accessed 20 September 2012).

40. ACP Secretariat, "Transforming the ACP Group of States into an Effective Global Player", Final Report of the Ambassorial Working Group on Future Perspectives of the ACP Group of States, ACP/27/022/14 Rev. 4, Brussels, 2 December 2014.

CHAPTER 13

The ACP, the EU, and the BRICS: Opportunities on the Horizon or Just a Mirage?

Kudrat Virk

The rise of the global South, led by China's economic takeoff, has been one of the major developments of the past two decades and has excited a great deal of comment on its potential for reshaping the international order into something unrecognisable from the vantage point of the early twentieth century.[1] In the ensuing turbulence, traditional relationships such as the development partnership between the African, Caribbean, and Pacific (ACP) group of states and the European Union (EU) have come under stress, with small and large countries alike, at varying stages of development, confronting changing patterns of global production, consumption, trade, and investment. However, even as economic power is diffusing from the industrialised West to the rest, in particular to (re-) emerging powers such as Brazil, Russia, India, China, and South Africa (the BRICS bloc), neither the process nor its implications can be taken as a given. In 2015, China's economy continued to slow down, with overall growth in emerging and developing economies projected to decline

K. Virk (✉)
Centre for Conflict Resolution (CCR), Cape Town, South Africa

© The Author(s) 2017
A. Montoute, K. Virk (eds.), *The ACP Group and the EU
Development Partnership*, DOI 10.1007/978-3-319-45492-4_13

further from about 6.3 per cent in 2011 to 4 per cent.[2] The progressive potential of the political dynamics playing out is similarly far from certain. Questions persist about the motivations and goals of the BRICS bloc, which has sought to position itself in the vanguard of the global South's quest for a more just and sustainable world. Furthermore, the ties that bind the five emerging powers are fragile, with doubts frequently cast over the prospects of the new bloc's role as an agenda-setter. Against that backdrop, in this chapter I reflect on the opportunities and challenges posed by the emergence of the BRICS—the most prominent focus of interest in the new powers—for the ACP group and its relationship with the EU.

NEW PLAYERS: THE RISE OF THE BRICS—WHY AND HOW THEY MATTER

Deep-seated political, social, and economic changes, combined with technological innovation, are driving a global rebalancing, decreasing the concentration of relative wealth in the West, while lifting many countries across the global South up the ladder of development.[3] The 2008–2009 global financial crisis accelerated this long-term process. In particular, it challenged the ability of key Western powers such as the United States (US) Germany, Britain,[4] and France to formulate an effective response to the turmoil in international financial markets, while bringing the Group of 20 (G-20) major industrialised and emerging economies—including the five BRICS countries—to the fore as the main forum for international economic policy coordination. Perceptions of Western decline were further heightened by the European sovereign debt crisis that followed. In contrast, Brazil, Russia, India, and China led global recovery from the 2008–2009 financial crisis, which also served as a stimulus for strengthening intra-BRIC cooperation: the first BRIC summit was held in Yekaterinburg, Russia, in June 2009.[5] (South Africa acceded to the group later, in 2011.)

The BRICS together account for about 22 per cent of the world economy and host more than 40 per cent of the global population,[6] and their growing importance has been reflected in changing international trade and investment flows. The BRICS' share of world exports, for example, was 19 per cent in 2014, up from 8 per cent in 2000.[7] Similarly, outward foreign direct investment (FDI) from the five emerging economies surged from $7 billion in 2000 to $126 billion in 2012, rising from less than 1 per cent to 9 per cent of the world total.[8] Despite recent signs of internal weaknesses, the structural drivers of change (for example, demographic trends) in the global South are such that some, if not all, of the BRICS will continue to be important players on the international stage. According to United Nations' (UN) projections, by 2050 Brazil, China, and India will collectively produce 40 per cent of world economic output, exceeding the combined production of major industrialised Western countries—specifically the US, Germany, Britain, France, Italy, and Canada.[9]

This rise of the BRICS has been accompanied by an increase in expectations of them. In the context of weak-to-modest growth in most industrialised economies and the persistence of Europe's debt crisis, the original four BRIC countries, in particular, have become the main drivers of economic growth in poor and marginalised countries,[10] of which a majority belong to the ACP group (see Montoute in this volume). According to a study by the International Monetary Fund (IMF), "growth [in low-income countries] would have been 0.3 percentage point to 1.1 percentage points lower during the [2008–2009 global financial] crisis if BRICs' GDP [gross domestic product] growth had declined at the same pace as [that of] advanced economies".[11] Since 2000, the emerging powers have indeed expanded their engagement with African, Caribbean, and Pacific countries. As in the case of the EU, Africa has attracted the greatest interest (see Akokpari, Carim, and Katjavivi in this volume).

Of the five BRICS, China is the indisputable giant, constituting over 60 per cent of the bloc's total GDP, and is the dominant player on the African continent, with large-scale Chinese-built and Chinese-financed infrastructure projects—such as the $850 million Abuja-Kaduna railroad in Nigeria and the $622 million Bui Dam in Ghana—serving as concrete displays of its commercial presence. Trade between China and Africa grew in leaps and bounds from $10 billion in 2000 to $220 billion in 2014,[12] with China surpassing the US in 2009 as Africa's largest bilateral trading partner. India's and Brazil's trade ties with Africa, though dwarfed by those of China, have also expanded. India-Africa trade stood at $72 billion in 2014, up from $5.3 billion in 2001.[13] Similarly, trade between Brazil and Africa increased six-fold, from $4.3 billion in 2000 to $26.5 billion in 2012.[14] Although the US and Europe have remained the main sources of FDI in Africa, the BRICS' share of the continent's FDI stocks and inflows has increased, with South Africa, China, India, and Russia being among the 20 largest holders of FDI in Africa.[15]

The BRICS' interest in Africa has further been reflected in their dip-lomatic outreach and summitry.[16] The triennial Forum on China-Africa Cooperation (FOCAC), inaugurated in 2000, has become a key platform for promoting dialogue and strengthening economic cooperation between the two sides. Against the backdrop of China's cooling economy, South Africa's financial capital, Johannesburg, hosted the sixth FOCAC meeting in December 2015, at which Chinese President Xi Jinping tripled Beijing's financial pledges to Africa to $60 billion from $20 billion in 2012,[17] while proposing to elevate the relationship to a comprehensive strategic coop-erative partnership. India followed suit, launching the India-Africa Forum Summit (IAFS) in 2008, with 41 African heads of state and government in attendance at the third IAFS meeting, held in October 2015 in New Delhi. Brazilian outreach to Africa also gathered pace under the leader-ship of Luíz Inácio "Lula" da Silva, though it has since lost its vigour somewhat under the beleaguered presidency of Lula's successor, Dilma Rousseff. Between 2003 and 2010, Lula visited 29 African countries on 12 separate visits, while the number of Brazilian embassies on the conti-nent more than doubled, from 18 to 37.[18] Russia's interest and diplomacy have lagged behind those of the rest of the BRICS, though there have been signs of "new dynamism", particularly after the bloc's fifth sum-mit—held in Durban, South Africa, in March 2013—which focused on BRICS-Africa cooperation.[19]

In general, the Caribbean and Pacific regions have featured less promi-nently in the BRICS' expanding global economic footprint. Even so, China, in particular, has gained in importance as a trade and investment partner for both regions, hand-in-hand with its rise as the world's sec-ond largest economy. In 2014, trade between China and the Caribbean Community (CARICOM) stood at $2.7 billion, up from less than $1 bil-lion in 2004,[20] although this was still meagre compared with China-Africa trade worth $220 billion in the same year. CARICOM's commercial rela-tions with Brazil, albeit in the shadow of China, have also grown, with total trade worth $3.7 billion in 2014.[21] Both Beijing and Brasília have set up institutional arrangements to strengthen cooperation with the region: the China-Caribbean Economic and Trade Cooperation Forum, and the CARICOM-Brazil Summit, respectively. (See Girvan and Montoute in this volume.) Similarly, China's economic presence in the Pacific has expanded. According to Australian analyst Jenny Hayward-Jones, "China's trade with Papua New Guinea alone increased tenfold between 2001 and 2011 to US$1.265 billion".[22] However, China's trade with the Pacific island countries is dwarfed by that of Australia, which has remained by far the largest trading partner and aid donor. Between 2006 and 2013, Beijing disbursed economic assistance worth $1.1 billion to the Pacific island countries, the lion's share of which went to Papua New Guinea and Fiji. In comparison, Canberra provided aid worth $6.8 billion over the same period.[23] (See Tavola in this volume.)

Beyond economic imperatives such as the search for natural resources and consumer markets, the BRICS' interest in the African, Caribbean, and Pacific regions is driven by varied political and strategic calculations. This interest manifests itself, at least in part, in their desire for greater influence in the international system. Brazil, India, and South Africa, for example, need the support of ACP countries—a significant voting bloc—to achieve their aspirations for permanent membership in a reformed UN Security Council. China's conflict with Taiwan over the latter's international status has remained a factor in its economic diplomacy. Of the 22 countries that had formal diplomatic relations with Taiwan in 2015, 14 were members of the ACP group.[24] The Pacific island ACP countries, furthermore, constitute an arena of potential geo-strategic competition between China and Russia, and the US. Though opinions have remained divided on the region's importance for China, Beijing's expanded relations with the Pacific island countries has generated unease in Washington, as well as Canberra.[25]

Finally, the BRICS' economic diplomacy has been the most noted, though not the only, aspect of their engagement in the ACP regions.[26] With the limited exception of Russia, the emerging powers are playing an important role in maintaining international peace and security by putting their "boots on the ground" in conflict zones. In October 2015, there were 16 UN peacekeeping operations, of which half were in ACP countries—specifically, the Central African Republic (CAR), Côte d'Ivoire, the Democratic Republic of the Congo (DRC), Liberia, Mali, and Sudan's Darfur and Abyei regions in Africa; and Haiti in the Caribbean. Among the BRICS, India has long been one of the largest troop-contributing countries to UN missions, and in October 2015 ranked third, with over 7,700 troops deployed to nine peacekeeping operations, including in Abyei, Côte d'Ivoire, the DRC, Liberia, and Haiti.[27] China has moved into the ranks of top troop-contributors since 2000, with a twenty-fold increase in deployments to UN missions, from fewer than 100 peacekeepers to over 3,000 in 2015.[28] South Africa similarly belongs to a generation of new contributors, with a peacekeeping presence concentrated in Africa, while Brazil has ramped up its participation in UN operations and had over 1,200 troops deployed in October 2015, the bulk of them in Haiti.[29] Alone among the BRICS, Russia seems to have preferred to act as a "regional peacekeeper" outside the UN umbrella, such as in Georgia,[30] and had fewer than 100 police and military personnel deployed to nine UN missions in October 2015. However, the rest of the BRICS—unlike Britain and France—have deployed their soldiers mainly as blue helmets (see Adebajo in this volume).

Opening Up New Horizons: the BRICS and the ACP-EU Relationship

Since the signing of the first Lomé Convention in 1975, the ACP-EU relationship has been a mainstay of Europe's trade and development policy. For the African, Caribbean, and Pacific regions, it has similarly been a defining feature of their economic engagement with the world and an integral part of their efforts to achieve poverty reduction, sustainable development, and integration into the global economy. In 2000, the Lomé regime gave way to the 20-year Cotonou Partnership Agreement. As Cotonou's expiry in 2020 nears, this historic partnership has come under pressure for several reasons, including the difficult and protracted negotiations for economic partnership agreements (EPAs) between the EU and seven regional groupings within the ACP (see Akokpari, Carim, Gonzales, Katjavivi, and Tavola in this volume). The process has led many on both sides, some more nervously than others, to question the contribution of the ACP-EU relationship towards increasing the competitiveness and growth prospects of the developing countries.

The arrival on the scene of the BRICS has added to the tension in this relationship. On the one hand, the new bloc has provided the EU with competition for the ACP's resources and markets. China, in particular, depended heavily on an export-focused model to fuel its economic climb in the 2000s, though it has begun a transition to more domestic consumption-led growth since 2011. According to the IMF's Kai Guo and Papa N'Diaye, "During 2001–2008, net exports and the investment which is predominantly linked to building capacity in tradable sectors … accounted for over 60 percent of China's growth, up from 40 percent in the 1990s."[31] At the same time, for the ACP group's membership, the BRICS represent new opportunities for economic diversification and for potentially reducing its dependence on Europe as a source of trade, aid, and investment.

Brazil, India, and China have—as mentioned earlier—actively courted Africa, in particular, as "a continent of opportunity".[32] Since the Cold War, Africa has experienced a significant geographic shift in its trade patterns: between 1990 and 2008, Europe's share of Africa's trade shrank from 51 per cent to 28 per cent, while Asia's share of the same doubled.[33] The continent further experienced accelerated growth after 2000, with its collective GDP increasing to $1.6 trillion in 2008—roughly the same as that of Brazil or Russia, according to the McKinsey Global Institute (MGI).[34] The MGI research does not claim a direct link between the role of the BRICS and the African growth story, nor attribute more than one-third of the latter to the commodities boom generated by surging demand from China (and to a lesser extent India) during the 2000s. Yet it points to a brighter future that is a far cry from the "lost decade"[35] of the 1980s, buoying up a sense of optimism about greater engagement with the BRICS, while sharpening existing dissatisfaction with four decades of aid-focused ACP-EU development cooperation. Between 2001 and 2010, African countries occupied six spots in the top ten economies by annual average GDP growth[36]; and in 2015, the continent was projected to remain one of the world's fastest-growing regions, behind only Asia.

For many across Africa, the Caribbean, and the Pacific, the BRICS are thus a source of inspiration—"an example of what ACP countries can achieve".[37] Their development stories are individually different, and the five emerging powers can provide valuable lessons for the ACP's diverse membership, given that their individual successes have already begun "reshaping ideas about how to attain human development", while challenging "the notion of 'right' policies".[38] In this regard, China stands out, having lifted more than 500 million people out of poverty and transformed itself into an economic powerhouse in a span of less than two decades.[39]

The BRICS, at least in their rhetoric, have further sought to distinguish themselves from established Western powers by holding out the prospect of socio-economic advancement through genuine partnership, pointing to their shared experience of and solidarity against (neo-)colonialism to underscore that their offer of economic cooperation is different. For example, in July 2012, Chinese President Hu Jintao, in his opening address at the fifth FOCAC meeting, affirmed Beijing's commitment to "give genuine support to African countries' independent choice of development paths and genuinely help African countries strengthen capacity for self-development", identifying China as "a good friend, good partner and good brother of the African people".[40] The 2015 FOCAC Johannesburg Declaration described China-Africa relations as a "model manifestation" of South-South cooperation.[41] Similarly, at the second IAFS meeting, held in May 2011 in Addis Ababa, Indian Prime Minister Manmohan Singh characterised New Delhi's partnership with Africa as "unique", noting its origins in a "common struggle against colonialism, apartheid, poverty, disease, illiteracy and hunger" and calling on the need for "a new spirit of solidarity among developing countries".[42]

Meanwhile, there have been signs of ambivalence from the EU about its extant relationship with the ACP, as Brussels also tries to craft its own response to the rise of the BRICS and to remain relevant in a changing world. The 2007 Treaty of Lisbon set out the EU's foreign policy principles and introduced a number of institutional changes, including the creation of the European External Action Service (EEAS), with a view towards providing greater clarity and coherence to its external engagements. However, the treaty mentions neither the ACP group nor its privileged relationship with the EU. In a similar vein, the administrative setup of the new EEAS does not have an ACP division, nor does it recognise "the special status of the European Development Fund (EDF)"—the main instrument through which the EU channels aid to the ACP group.[43] Furthermore, since 2003, Brussels has established several "strategic partnerships" with advanced and emerging economies—including the BRICS—in an attempt to boost its global profile. To make matters more complicated, the EU also has a "strategic partnership" with the African Union (AU), a "joint partnership" with the Caribbean, and a "strategy" for its relations with the Pacific. How this arguably ill-defined range of new instruments relates to the older ACP-EU development cooperation framework is still unclear. More understandably, these developments have provoked concern within the ACP about the grouping's diminishing importance for Europe, and in turn have prompted the ACP group to reassess its own strategic options as a bloc. (See Montoute, and Gomes in this volume.)

NEW OPPORTUNITIES, BUT WITH NEW CHALLENGES

At first blush, the rise of the BRICS is a "clear and present" opportunity for the ACP group to diversify and grow economically, to learn from the development stories of the new powers, and to use the BRICS' interest in partnering with the group's members as negotiating leverage in relations with the rest of the world, including the EU. However, the nature of the BRICS' engagement with the ACP—mainly based on the experience of Africa with China and India—gives reason for optimism and caution in equal parts.

The emerging powers are not complete newcomers in the ACP regions. The bonds that Brazil, India, and China have with Africa and the Caribbean, for example, go back centuries. Close to 50 per cent of Brazil's population identified as African-Brazilian in the country's 2010 census,[44] with "[m]ore slaves ... brought to Brazil than to any other country in the Western Hemisphere, including the United States" between the sixteenth and nineteenth centuries.[45] Similarly, after the end of slavery, large numbers of indentured labourers from China and India came to the Caribbean, which is home to diaspora communities of considerable size from both Asian countries. During the Cold War, China provided support to liberation struggles in Africa (for example, in Angola, Mozambique, and Zambia), while India was one of the earliest, most vocal, and most consistent critics of the apartheid regime in South Africa. Afro-Asian solidarity and anti-colonialism were similarly key planks of Soviet engagement in the so-called Third World. In other words, except South Africa with its apartheid legacy, the BRICS—unlike major European powers such as Britain and France—do not have an imperial past in the ACP regions, but can instead draw on a well of "positive" history to contextualise their current engagement.

However, notwithstanding rhetoric, unsentimental strategic and economic imperatives lie at the heart of the BRICS' present-day efforts to renew and strengthen their ties with various ACP countries and regions. Of the five BRICS, China and India are the leading importers,[46] and both are energy-hungry giants. Growth imperatives have created a strategic need for a variety of natural resources, ranging from oil and timber to minerals and grains, with energy security a critical concern for both. China—the world's largest energy consumer—is expected to consume almost 70 per cent more energy than the US in 2035, while energy consumption in India and Brazil is projected to grow yet faster.[47] The ACP includes resource-rich countries—from Angola and Nigeria (oil), to Trinidad and Tobago (natural gas), to Papua New Guinea (timber)—that have lured the emerging powers. Africa, in particular, is home to 10 per cent of the world's oil reserves, 40 per cent of its gold, and 80–90 per cent of chromium and platinum-group metals,[48] as well as large deposits of bauxite, cobalt, copper, and diamond. Unsurprisingly, this demand-and-supply match-up has generated concern, as well as a vigorous debate on the extent to which the BRICS are, in fact, different from Africa's traditional partners. Much of the discussion has dwelt on China, the heavyweight in the cohort of emerging powers, and Africa, the primary focus of Beijing's interest. One of the principal fault-lines in this conversation separates those who have tended to see the Chinese engagement as a new "scramble for Africa" that marks a continuity in the continent's exploitation by mercantilist outsiders,[49] and those who have been prone to dismiss the criticism as "alarmism" and instead embrace Beijing's proposal of a "win-win partnership".[50]

Cutting through this often emotionally charged rhetoric is important, but the exercise is difficult. This is due, in part, to the nature of the BRICS' economic approach, in which aid, trade, development finance, and FDI are often bound up in complex package deals lacking transparency, and in part to the unavailability of robust data. As one study noted in 2012: "Not all BRICS are publishing respective statistics [on outward FDI to low-income countries]."[51] Bearing these limitations in mind, the balance of evidence is somewhat mixed. In terms of trade alone, there are reasons for concern. According to South African scholar Maxi Schoeman, the pattern of interaction between Africa and the BRICS is "reminiscent of colonial and post-colonial trade relations with the developed world". Based on 2008 data from the UN Conference on Trade and Development (UNCTAD), Schoeman points out that about 90 per cent of Africa's exports to non-African developing countries consist of primary products, which "is very similar to … the continent's exports to developed countries, with primary products accounting for 92 percent of exports to the US and 75 percent to the EU".[52] The trade relationship between China and the Caribbean is similar: it is "based on the importation of manufactured products from China and the exportation of raw materials from the Caribbean" and, in the words of St Lucian academic Annita Montoute, "holds the danger of replicating [the relationship] of the Caribbean with traditional partners".[53] Furthermore, scholars have noted that in both Africa and the Caribbean, growth in trade with China and Beijing's investments has not been accompanied by significant skills development or technology transfers.[54]

On the other hand, China's commercial interaction in Africa, involving state-owned and private enterprises, has been more diversified. While Chinese FDI is concentrated in the energy, mining, infrastructure, and communication sectors and in resource-rich countries such as Angola,

Sudan, Nigeria, and South Africa, "private companies are focusing on manufacturing and service sectors."[55] As the London-based Africa Research Institute (ARI) has noted, the idea that China's interest in Africa is solely driven by its need to access energy and raw materials rests on the assumption that the Chinese state exercises "central control over Chinese concerns operating overseas". This neglects the idea that "[p]rovincial administrations and private companies attracted by the margins attainable in Africa have forged their own presence in resource extraction, infrastructure construction and consumer markets—accounting for a quarter of Chinese investment in the continent by 2007. Chinese traders independently seek new markets for exports and low-cost production".[56] Furthermore, there is significant competition for business projects, even among state-owned enterprises. In the words of Aubrey Hruby, "One of the great misconceptions about the China-Africa business relationship is that there's some smoke-filled room in Beijing where all the [state-owned enterprises] sit around and divvy up the projects. This doesn't exist."[57]

In the case of democratic Brazil and India, the state has even less control over commercial interaction, which, in the broader context of an increasingly open international economy, is becoming a more organic process with investment following opportunity.[58] With governments in each of the BRICS trying to encourage their domestic companies to venture abroad and become competitive globally, the new game in Africa is thus not reducible to exploitation.

Moreover, while there may be some truth in the assertion that "[w]ithout China, the BRICS are a toothless tiger",[59] China is not synonymous with the BRICS. These emerging powers do not have a common approach to Africa or, for that matter, to the Caribbean and the Pacific. While all five may attach priority to Africa, and to some extent "talk the same talk" about South-South cooperation, their engagements differ in a number of ways. For example, both China and India are driven by a search for energy and food security; but while China has tended to focus on large state-to-state deals and on extractive industries and infrastructure development, "the Indian presence in Africa is largely commercially driven, private, and facilitated by the Export-Import Bank of India and the Confederation of Indian Industries" and has been more concentrated in the information and communications, manufacturing, and pharmaceutical sectors.[60] Furthermore, there are dynamics of cooperation and competition between the two emerging Asian powers that are important to consider. India's Oil and Natural Gas Corporation Videsh (OVL) and the China National

Petroleum Corporation (CNPC), for instance, are partners in the Greater Nile Petroleum Project in Sudan (though the two have also been competitors for oil contracts elsewhere). At the same time, India has also concentrated on distinguishing itself from China by drawing attention to its capacity-building, education, and training activities in Africa, and projecting itself as a "genuine" developmental partner that offers "a middle ground between China's profit-maximising and largely statist approach and the much resented intrusive conditionalities associated with western policies".[61] India has not been alone in this respect: as Oliver Stuenkel observes, "Brazilian companies in Africa have sought to [similarly] distinguish themselves from their Chinese counterparts—for example by hiring and training local workers".[62]

This intra-BRICS competition raises two important points. First, reputation clearly matters. China, since its aggressive penetration of Africa, has faced criticism, resentment, and popular discontent in several countries, including Botswana, Malawi, Uganda, and Zambia. For example, in Zambia, Chinese investments have been a highly sensitive issue, with companies accused of exploitative working conditions, poor health and safety standards, and wage disparities between Chinese and African workers.[63] The quality of Chinese imports into Africa has also come under scrutiny, prompting demands for greater regulation and forcing the Chinese government to respond for fear of "reputational damage".[64] There have been similar protests against the Chinese presence in Guyana in the Caribbean. This then forms part of the context in which India, Brazil, and others have sought to set themselves apart from China.

Second, as one BRICS country tries to capitalise on another's discomfiture (mainly China's) and identify its own "unique selling point", with reputation as an important currency, this gives African—as well as Caribbean and Pacific—countries leverage and greater bargaining power in their interactions with the emerging powers. This in turn places the onus on ACP and other developing countries for ensuring that the relationships they forge with the BRICS are advantageous to their long-term interests. The emerging powers are not acting out of pure altruism in building new bonds within the global South, but are each pursuing their own interests: greater security, growth, development, and influence. It is up to African, Caribbean, and Pacific policymakers to identify and demand, to the greatest extent possible, the terms of their (continuing) engagement with the BRICS and others. As Schoeman writes, while the emerging powers may not be very different from traditional powers in scrambling for the continent, "on the part of Africa there is a difference, or ought to be: in contrast to the colonial and post colonial/Cold War period, this time round the continent is engaging with the BRICs with [its] eyes wide open ... It is up to Africa to ensure that [its] relations with the new emerging markets do not plunge the continent into neo-colonialism in which Africa is, once again, the only loser".[65] In other words, African countries must take greater ownership of their present and future. And the same could easily be said of their Caribbean and Pacific peers.

CONCLUDING REFLECTIONS

Is an ACP-BRICS "partnership" possible? Could—even should—the ACP broaden its traditional focus on the EU to leverage cooperation with the BRICS in the collective interests of its membership? A good case can be made that it should. From the perspective of the ACP countries, the advantages of greater formalised cooperation with the BRICS are, to some extent, clear—the new players offer a tangible opportunity to diversify economic relations, reduce dependence on aid, integrate into the international economy through partnerships with its rising stars, and gain greater leverage on the international stage.

For the ACP group (as an organisation), its strength—most obviously— lies in its numbers. Despite the growth surge since 2000, the vast majority of African, Caribbean, and Pacific countries remain economically weak, and the smallest among them have little to no bargaining power individually. These countries would benefit from engaging collectively with the BRICS and working together to exploit the competition among the emerging powers, as much as their competition with traditional European powers, thereby setting the agenda in their new relationships and taking greater ownership of their own development paths. The BRICS also offer an option to the small and historically marginalised countries of the ACP, as well as other developing countries, to gain a greater say in key international decision-making structures. As Dutch analyst Mirjam van Reisen argues: "The ACP could expand its influence at the international level by demanding a political voice in the G-20, where the BRICs have secured a privileged position of decision making on finance and economic policy with the G-8, which also affects the poorest countries."[66] One could even argue that it may not be a choice, if the group is to maintain its relevance, given the growing significance of the BRICS' accelerating commercial and economic ties with the ACP regions.

There are, however, several tasks that the ACP group must undertake to lay a solid foundation for, and to benefit from, any future strategic partnership with the BRICS. First, a key issue for the ACP is the need to establish a coherent consensus and formulate a strategy with buy-in from all its members on how to deal with the BRICS, and not forget the other emerging powers such as South Korea and Turkey that are following in their wake. Turkey's Africa policy, for example, has gained momentum over the past decade, with the launch of the first Turkey-Africa Cooperation Summit in 2008, while South Korea has been referred to as "Africa's unsung Asian partner".[67] Building and maintaining internal unity, however, has been a challenge for the ACP group in recent years, even in its relations with the EU.[68] The task is further rendered difficult by the disproportionate attention that Africa has received, as well as the varied levels of interest from different actors in the African, Caribbean, and Pacific regions. Yet, as a report by the Maastricht-based European Centre for Policy Development Management (ECPDM) points out: from a strategic point of view, "[a] coherent ACP Group that managed to profile itself better in the world would also be of much greater diplomatic interest to the EU (which might need its longstanding privileged partner to help it realise its ambitions of becoming a more prominent global player)".[69]

Second, an additional and related task for the ACP will be to build any new partnerships in a manner that does not undermine its relationship with the EU, which as a whole remains its dominant partner and the largest provider of official development assistance in the world, and that enhances complementarities, as opposed to strategic competition, among its old and new partners. The task is particularly vital in a still-evolving world order, where old hierarchies have been disrupted while uncertainty surrounds the future, and which is awash in a sea of shifting, mostly issue-based alliances that cut across traditional North-South categories and are breaking down dichotomous ways of thinking. Also, the BRICS, notwithstanding their rhetoric, and bearing in mind the caveats of generalisation, are guided mainly by pragmatism and the pursuit of their own national interests, rather than by any particular ideology that prioritises South-South cooperation or solidarity in its own right. In this regard, systematically considering the prospects of and mobilising interest in trilateral cooperation may offer a useful way forward (see Gomes in this volume). Brazil and South Africa, for example, have partnered with Germany in trilateral development projects in Africa. The EU and Brazil have also sought to strengthen their strategic partnership through exploring the prospects of trilateral cooperation in third countries, though these efforts have not yet resulted in concrete projects.[70]

Third, the role of South Africa—the only country with membership in both the ACP group and the BRICS—is an important consideration, and the ACP needs to strategise about using South Africa as a potential bridge towards more concrete relations with the BRICS, or at the very least as a "channel for [conveying] ACP concerns" to the BRICS—an idea mooted by van Reisen.[71] At first glance, this is an obvious opportunity for the group to leverage one of its own. While question marks continue to be raised about the inclusion of South Africa in the BRICS bloc in terms of its economic credentials, the other BRICS seem to have clearly accepted it as a "gateway partner" into Africa.[72] Beyond South Africa's potential role "as an ally and as a guide on economic development opportunities, into the Southern African region and the broader African continent",[73] its inclusion in the group is an important plank in the BRICS' claim to legitimacy as representing the global South in international fora. Most of the world's marginalised countries belong to the ACP group. However, the ability of the ACP to leverage South Africa's membership in both groupings depends on the country's ability and willingness to play that role. While Tshwane (Pretoria) has asserted its objective of enhancing the African agenda and sustainable development through its BRICS membership, it has not claimed to represent the continent, let alone the ACP. Far from it. In the words of South Africa's Deputy Minister of International Relations and Cooperation, Ebrahim Ismail Ebrahim, in May 2011: "We wish to state that, we have no mandate nor have we asked for one from the African Union (AU) to represent them within the BRICS Mechanism."[74] Furthermore, questions remain about the extent to which South Africa's interests converge with those of the rest of Africa, as was made evident during the EPA process in the Southern African Development Community (SADC) region, with divergence becoming apparent between the interests of South Africa and its smaller neighbours (see Carim in this volume).[75]

Fourth, the ACP needs to work towards making itself attractive to the "other side"—that is, to engage with the BRICS in terms of their willingness to work with the ACP as a whole. At an individual level, the BRICS countries have shown a preference for bilateral relations. For example, whereas FOCAC conferences have produced joint declarations and plans of action intended to inform China-Africa relations, and provided a platform to outline overall commitments, in practice China has shown a strong preference for signing trade and investment agreements and project contracts bilaterally with individual African governments.[76] Beijing has signed agreements with regional organisations—such as the East African Community (EAC) in 2011—and, at the fifth FOCAC meeting, held in Beijing in July 2012, "outlined new measures to negotiate infrastructure projects directly with Africa's regional institutions".[77] But multilateral agreements are not the norm in China-Africa relations. Similarly, according to Montoute, China's participation in the China-Caribbean Economic and Trade Cooperation Forum "represents a pseudo regional approach".[78] Thus, while it may be to the ACP group's advantage to deal multilaterally, there is little to indicate that China might be motivated to engage with the group as the EU has, let alone sign an instrument such as the 2000 Cotonou Agreement and cede its bargaining power.[79] A coordinating role may, in this context, be the way forward for the ACP.

Furthermore, the BRICS bloc is a relatively new political grouping and remains very much a work in progress. Notwithstanding the growing significance of India and China as rising economic and political giants, considerable doubts remain in many quarters about whether the bloc can develop from a loose and informal alliance pursuing often disparate or competing interests, into an agenda-setting actor with a unified, coordinated approach to issues and policies.[80] On the one hand, there is general consensus among the BRICS that developing countries are underrepresented in international institutions; however, they do not necessarily agree on how these institutions—for example, the UN Security Council—should be reformed. India, Brazil, and South Africa are liberal democracies, which neither Russia nor China can claim to be. Brazil and Russia are primarily exporters of commodities, while China and India are leading importers of natural resources. Furthermore, bilateral relations within the grouping have been fraught with tension, distrust, and rivalry. For example, India and China, in addition to their strategic competition in Africa, are rivals for influence in the Indian Ocean and in Asia, and share a disputed border over which they went to war in 1962.

That said, the BRICS, in July 2014 at their sixth summit meeting—held in Fortaleza/Brasília—agreed to establish a New Development Bank (NDB), with a view to providing financing for "infrastructure and sustainable development projects in BRICS and other emerging and developing economies".[81] This represents a concrete effort to institutionalise the bloc's agenda, and the NDB could be a vital resource for funding the infrastructure gap in the African, Caribbean, and Pacific regions. With an initial subscribed capital of $50 billion, there are doubts about the potential impact of the bank as a source of finance, although its "usefulness …

extends beyond the provision of capital and includes knowledge-sharing about innovative ways to meet the demands of development".[82] Be that as it may, the larger point is this: even if one accepts that the BRICS can come together as a collective agency, the bloc will continue to lack, for some time to come, an institutional structure into which external actors, such as the ACP, can plug. As one opinion-editorial in South Africa's *Mail & Guardian* put it: "[I]t will take time [for the BRICS] to build a minimum common agenda, much as it took the G7 decades to achieve relative coherence. It can be expected that significant time and resources will be spent on the internal agenda of the [BRICS] in the short to medium term."[83] To whom, or how, then can the ACP present any agenda that it is able to formulate, and in a way that could convince the BRICS—be it individually—to move away from their preference for engagement through summits and bilateral agreements and towards the ACP group as a preferred partner for South-South cooperation?

Notes

1. I would like to thank Margaret Struthers, former Librarian of the Centre for Conflict Resolution (CCR) Peace Library, Cape Town, South Africa, for her invaluable time and assistance in finding research resources for the writing of this chapter.
2. International Monetary Fund (IMF), *World Economic Outlook: Adjusting to Lower Commodity Prices* (Washington, D.C., 2015), p. 11.
3. National Intelligence Council (NIC), *Global Trends 2025: A Transformed World* (Washington, D.C., 2008), p. 7; United Nations Development Programme (UNDP), *Human Development Report 2013—The Rise of the South: Human Progress in a Diverse World* (New York, 2013), pp. 1, 11.
4. Britain is used synonymously with the United Kingdom (UK) in this volume.
5. Oliver Stuenkel, "The Financial Crisis, Contested Legitimacy, and the Genesis of Intra-BRICS Cooperation", *Global Governance* 19, vol. 4 (2013), pp. 611–630.
6. Data from the World Bank, http://wdi.worldbank.org/table/4.2 (accessed 19 December 2015); and Rosstat, *BRICS Joint Statistical Publication: 2015* (Moscow, 2015), p. 17.
7. World Trade Organisation (WTO), *International Trade Statistics 2015* (Geneva, 2015), p. 28.

8. United Nations Conference on Trade and Development (UNCTAD), "The Rise of BRICS FDI and Africa", *Global Investment Trends Monitor*, special edition, 25 March 2013, pp. 1, 3, http://unctad.org/en/PublicationsLibrary/webdiaeia2013 d6_en.pdf (accessed 19 December 2015).

9. UNDP, *Human Development Report 2013*, p. 13.

10. *See* IMF, "New Growth Drivers for Low-Income Countries: The Role of BRICs", 12 January 2011, http://www.imf.org/external/np/pp/eng/2011/011211.pdf (accessed 1 October 2012).

11. IMF, "New Growth Drivers for Low-Income Countries", p. 31.

12. "China-Africa Trade Approaches $300 Billion in 2015", *China Daily*, 10 November 2015, http://www.chinadaily.com.cn/business/2015-11/10/content_22417707.htm (accessed 19 December 2015).

13. Miko Brown, "India-Africa: A Partnership of Pragmatism and Potential", *Africa at LSE*, 5 November 2015, http://blogs.lse.ac.uk/africaatlse/2015/11/05/india-africa-a-partnership-of-pragmatism-and-potential (accessed 19 December 2015); Confederation of Indian Industry (CII) and WTO, *India-Africa: South-South Trade and Investment for Development* (New Delhi and Geneva, 2013), p. 15.

14. Ana Cristina Alves, "Brazil in Africa: Achievements and Challenges", in Nicholas Kitchen (ed.), *Emerging Powers in Africa*, LSE Ideas Special Report no. SR016 (London: London School of Economics and Political Science [LSE], June 2013), p. 39, http://www.lse.ac.uk/IDEAS/publications/reports/SR016.aspx (accessed 3 July 2014).

15. UNCTAD, "The Rise of BRICS FDI and Africa", pp. 1, 7.

16. Timothy M. Shaw, Andrew F. Cooper, and Gregory T. Chin, "Emerging Powers and Africa: Implications for/from Global Governance?", *Politikon: South African Journal of Political Studies* 36, no. 1 (2009), pp. 29–31.

17. Yun Sun, "Xi and the 6th Forum on China-Africa Cooperation: Major Commitments, but with Questions", *Africa in Focus*, 7 December 2015, http://www.brookings.edu/blogs/africa-in-focus/posts/2015/12/07-china-africa-focac-investment-economy-sun (accessed 20 December 2015).

18. Robert Muggah, "What Is Brazil Really Doing in Africa?", *Huffington Post*, 1 April 2015, http://www.huffingtonpost.com/robert-muggah/what-is-brazil-really-doi_b_6413568.html

(accessed 20 December 2015). *See also* Christina Stolte, "Brazil in Africa: Just Another BRICS Country Seeking Resources?", briefing paper (London: Chatham House, November 2012).

19. Alexandra Arkhangelskaya and Vladimir Shubin, "Is Russia Back? Realities of Russian Engagement in Africa", in Kitchen, *Emerging Powers in Africa*, p. 27.

20. Data from the National Bureau of Statistics of China, http://www.stats.gov.cn/tjsj/ndsj/2014/indexeh.htm (accessed 20 December 2015); and Richard L. Bernal, "The Dragon in the Caribbean: China-CARICOM Economic Relations", *Round Table* 99, no. 408 (2010), pp. 286, 288.

21. Based on data from World Integrated Trade Solution (WITS), "Brazil Trade Statistics", http://wits.worldbank.org/CountryProfile/en/BRA (accessed 20 December 2015).

22. Jenny Hayward-Jones, "Big Enough for Us All: Geo-Strategic Competition in the Pacific Islands" (Sydney: Lowy Institute for International Policy, May 2013), p. 7, http://www.lowyinstitute.org/publications/big-enough-all-us-geo-strategic-competition-pacific-islands (accessed 20 December 2015).

23. Philippa Brant, "Chinese Aid in the Pacific" (Sydney: Lowy Institute for International Policy, February 2015), http://www.lowyinstitute.org/files/chinese_aid:in_the_pacific_regional_snapshot_0.pdf and http://www.lowyinstitute.org/chinese-aid-map (both accessed 20 December 2015).

24. These 14 ACP countries are: Burkina Faso, São Tomé and Príncipe, and Swaziland in Africa; Belize, Haiti, St Kitts and Nevis, St Lucia, and St Vincent and the Grenadines in the Caribbean; and Kiribati, Nauru, Palau, the Marshall Islands, the Solomon Islands, and Tuvalu in the Pacific.

25. Jenny Hayward-Jones, "China in the Pacific Islands: Competition Not Dominance", *The Diplomat*, 22 May 2013, http://thediplomat.com/2013/05/china-in-the-pacific-islands-competition-not-dominance (accessed 22 December 2015).

26. This paragraph is drawn in part from Kudrat Virk, "South Africa and the BRICS: Progress, Problems, and Prospects", concept note (Cape Town: CCR, July 2014).

27. Data from the UN Department of Peacekeeping Operations, http://www.un.org/en/peacekeeping/resources/statistics/contributors.shtml (accessed 20 December 2015).

28. Chin-Hao Huang, "Peacekeeping Contributor Profile: The People's Republic of China", *Providing for Peacekeeping*, September 2013, http://www.providingforpeacekeeping.org/2014/04/03/contributor-profile-china (accessed 20 December 2015).
29. Data from the UN Department of Peacekeeping Operations.
30. Sharon Wiharta, Neil Melvin, and Xenia Avezov, *The New Geopolitics of Peace Operations: Mapping the Emerging Landscape*" (Stockholm: Stockholm International Peace Research Institute [SIPRI], 2012), p. 14.
31. Kai Guo and Papa N'Diaye, "Is China's Export-Oriented Growth Sustainable?", Working Paper no. WP/09/172 (Washington, D.C.: IMF, August 2009), p. 4, https://www.imf.org/external/pubs/ft/wp/2009/wp09172.pdf (accessed 21 December 2015).
32. James Mackie, Bruce Byiers, Sonia Niznikand, and Geert Laporte (eds.), *Global Changes, Emerging Players, and Evolving ACP-EU Relations: Towards a Common Agenda for Action?*, Policy and Management Report no. 19 (Maastricht: European Centre for Development Policy Management [ECDPM], 2011), p. viii, http://ecdpm.org/wp-content/uploads/2013/10/PMR-19-Global-Changes-Emerging-Players-Evolving-ACP-EU-Relations-2011.pdf (accessed 27 October 2012).
33. Maxi Schoeman, "Of BRICs and Mortar: The Growing Relations between Africa and the Global South", *International Spectator* 46, no. 1 (2011), p. 39.
34. Acha Leke, Susan Lund, Charles Roxburgh, and Arend van Wamelen, "What's Driving Africa's Growth", *McKinsey Quarterly*, June 2010, http://www.mckinseyquarterly.com/Whats_driving_Africas_growth_2601 (accessed 27 October 2012).
35. This term was coined by Adebayo Adedeji, former executive secretary of the UN Economic Commission for Africa (UNECA).
36. The six African countries were: Angola, Nigeria, Ethiopia, Chad, Mozambique, and Rwanda. "Africa's Impressive Growth", *The Economist*, 6 January 2011, http://www.economist.com/blogs/dailychart/2011/01/daily_chart (accessed 20 December 2015).
37. Mirjam van Reisen, "The ACP's Position in the World: Laying the BRICs for a Better Future", *The Broker* no. 25 (June/July 2011), p. 12.
38. UNDP, *Human Development Report 2013*, p. 2.

39. UNDP, *Human Development Report 2013*, p. 26; Nick Bisley, "Global Power Shift: The Decline of the West and the Rise of the Rest?", in Mark Beeson and Nick Bisley (eds.), *Issues in 21st Century World Politics* (Basingstoke: Palgrave Macmillan, 2010), p. 69.

40. "Chinese President's Speech at Opening Ceremony of Fifth Ministerial Conference of Forum on China-Africa Cooperation", *Xinhua*, 19 July 2012, http://news.xinhuanet.com/english/china/2012-07/19/c_131725637.htm (accessed 27 October 2012).

41. Sixth FOCAC, *Declaration of the Johannesburg Summit of the Forum on China-Africa Cooperation*, combined draft version of Africa and China, http://www.dirco.gov.za/docs/2015/focac_declaration.pdf (accessed 21 December 2015).

42. Press Information Bureau, Government of India, Prime Minister's Office, "Address by the Prime Minister Dr. Manmohan Singh at the Plenary Session of the 2nd Africa-India Forum Summit", Addis Ababa, 24 May 2011, http://pib.nic.in/newsite/PrintRelease.aspx?relid=72281 (accessed 27 October 2012).

43. Mirjam van Reisen, "The Future of the ACP-EU Relationship: The Old Man and the Seas", *The Broker*, no. 25 (June/July 2011), p. 6.

44. Tom Phillips, "Brazil Census Shows African-Brazilians in the Majority for the First Time", *The Guardian*, 17 November 2011, http://www.guardian.co.uk/world/2011/nov/17/brazil-census-african-brazilians-majority (accessed 27 October 2012).

45. Oliver Stuenkel, "Brazil in Africa: Bridging the Atlantic?", 15 January 2012, http://www.postwesternworld.com/2012/01/15/brazil-in-africa-bridging-the-atlantic (accessed 27 October 2012).

46. WTO, *International Trade Statistics 2015*, pp. 44–47.

47. International Energy Agency (IEA), "World Energy Outlook 2011: Executive Summary", http://www.worldenergyoutlook.org (accessed 13 September 2012).

48. Leke et al., "What's Driving Africa's Growth".

49. *See for example* Patrick Bond (ed.), *BRICS in Africa: Anti-Imperialist, Sub-Imperialist, or In Between? A Reader for the Durban Summit*, March 2013, http://ccs.ukzn.ac.za/files/

Bond%20CCS%20Brics%20booklet%2022%20March%202013.pdf (accessed 19 November 2014).

50. *See* Garth Shelton and Farhana Paruk, *The Forum on China-Africa Cooperation: A Strategic Opportunity*, Monograph no. 156 (Tshwane [Pretoria]: Institute for Security Studies [ISS], December 2008).

51. European Union (EU), *The Role of BRICS in the Developing World* (Brussels, April 2012), p. 20, http://www.ecologic.eu/4738 (accessed 27 October 2012).

52. Schoeman, "Of BRICs and Mortar", pp. 38–39.

53. Annita Montoute, "Caribbean-China Economic Relations: What Are the Implications?", *Caribbean Journal of International Relations and Diplomacy* 1, no. 1 (February 2013), p. 122.

54. Africa Research Institute, "Between Extremes: China and Africa", Briefing Note no. 1202, October 2012, http://www.africaresearchinstitute.org (accessed 24 October 2012); Montoute, "Caribbean-China Economic Relations", p. 122.

55. EU, *The Role of BRICS in the Developing World*, p. 21.

56. Africa Research Institute, "Between Extremes".

57. Quoted in "China's Investments in Africa: What's the Real Story?", *Knowledge@Wharton*, 19 January 2016, http://knowledge.wharton.upenn.edu/article/chinas-investments-in-africa-whats-the-real-story/ (accessed 21 January 2016).

58. *See* Liam Halligan, "Global Africa: The Last Investment Frontier", in Adekeye Adebajo and Kaye Whiteman (eds.), *The EU and Africa: From Eurafrique to Afro-Europa* (London: Hurst; New York: Columbia University Press; and Johannesburg: Wits University Press, 2012), pp. 171–196.

59. EU, *The Role of BRICS in the Developing World*, p. 13.

60. Ian Taylor, "India's Rise in Africa", *International Affairs* 88, no. 4 (2012), p. 780.

61. Taylor, "India's Rise in Africa", p. 793.

62. Stuenkel, "Brazil in Africa".

63. Fredrick Mutesa, "China and Zambia: Between Development and Politics", in Fantu Cheru and Cyril Obi (eds.), *The Rise of China and India in Africa: Challenges, Opportunities, and Critical Interventions* (London and New York: Zed, 2010), pp. 171–178.

64. Africa Research Institute, "Between Extremes".

65. Schoeman, "Of BRICs and Mortar", p. 49.

66. van Reisen, "The ACP's Position in the World", p. 13. Created in 1999, the Group of 20 (G-20) major industrialised and emerging countries comprises Argentina, Australia, Brazil, Britain, Canada, China, France, Germany, India, Indonesia, Italy, Japan, Mexico, Russia, Saudi Arabia, South Africa, South Korea, Turkey, the United States (US), and the EU. The Group of Eight (G-8) indus-trialised economies – the Group of Seven, since the suspension of Russia in 2014 – is an older and smaller group, comprising Britain, Canada, France, Germany, Italy, Japan, and the US.

67. Eleanor Whitehead, "South Korea: Africa's Unsung Asian Partner", *This Is Africa*, 26 February 2013, http://www.thisisafricaonline.com/Countries/Africa/South-Korea-Africa-s-unsung-Asian-partner?ct=true (accessed 20 January 2016).

68. Mackie et al., *Global Changes, Emerging Players, and Evolving ACP-EU Relations*, p. 34.

68. Mackie et al., *Global Changes, Emerging Players, and Evolving ACP-EU Relations*, p. 33.

70. Lidia Cabral, "The EU-Brazil Partnership on Development: A Lukewarm Affair", Policy Brief no. 10 (Madrid: Fundación par las Relaciones Internacionales y el Diálogo Exterior [FRIDE], June 2014), pp. 5–6.

71. van Reisen, "The ACP's Position in the World", p. 12.

72. Maite Nkoana Mashabane, "South Africa's Role in BRICS, and Its Benefits to Job Creation and the Infrastructure Drive in South Africa", speech, Johannesburg, South Africa, 11 September 2012, http://www.dfa.gov.za/docs/speeches/2012/mash0911a.html (accessed 27 October 2012).

73. Ebrahim I. Ebrahim, keynote address, BRICS Roundtable Discussion hosted by the International Marketing Council (IMC) of South Africa and the *Financial Times*, 11 May 2011, http://www.dfa.gov.za/docs/speeches/2011/ebra0511.html (accessed 27 October 2012).

74. Ebrahim, keynote address.

75. *See* Brendan Vickers, "Between a Rock and a Hard Place: Small States in the EU-SADC EPA Negotiations", *The Roundtable: The Commonwealth Journal of International Affairs* 100, no. 413 (2011), pp. 183–197.

76. Dot Keet, "South-South Strategic Bases for Africa to Engage China", in Cheru and Obi, *The Rise of China and India in Africa*, p. 22.

77. Africa Research Institute, "Between Extremes".
78. Montoute, "Caribbean-China Economic Relations", p. 114.
79. Mackie et al., *Global Changes, Emerging Players, and Evolving ACP-EU Relations*, p. 34.
80. Walter Ladwig, "An Artificial Bloc Built on a Catchphrase", *New York Times*, 26 March 2012, http://www.nytimes.com/2012/03/27/opinion/an-artificial-bloc-built-on-a-catchphrase.html?_r=0 (accessed 18 October 2012).
81. Sixth BRICS Summit, *Fortaleza Declaration*, 15 July 2014, http://brics6.itamaraty.gov.br/media2/press-releases/214-sixth-brics-summit-fortaleza-declaration (accessed 8 October 2014). *See also* CCR, *South Africa and the BRICS: Progress, Problems, and Prospects*, seminar report, Tshwane, November 2014.
82. CCR, *South Africa and the BRICS*, p. 10.
83. Peter Draper and Catherine Grant, "SA Must Be Pragmatic About Brics", *Mail & Guardian* (South Africa), 26 October–1 November 2012, p. 12.

CHAPTER 14

Conclusion

Kudrat Virk

Development cooperation in the 21st century is compelled to move beyond the simplistic paradigm of transferring funds from the developed North to the developing South. With the global endorsement of Agenda 2030, including new modes of development finance, the proliferation of actors, and the rise of emerging economies, the traditional "donor–recipient" aid paradigm needs to be buried.

—Patrick Gomes[1]
Secretary-General of the African, Caribbean, and Pacific Group

We should not be asking whether our cooperation and partnership is still important. Because it is—more so than ever. Instead, we should be asking how we can best equip our cooperation for the future, so that it delivers maximum benefits.... We also believe that in a world of partnership and ownership, development cooperation should be about more than donors and recipients. It should be about mutual benefit. All of which opens up development cooperation in a range of other policy areas.

—Neven Mimica[2]
European Commissioner for International Cooperation and Development

K. Virk (✉)
Centre for Conflict Resolution (CCR), Cape Town, South Africa

© The Author(s) 2017   341
A. Montoute, K. Virk (eds.), *The ACP Group and the EU
Development Partnership*, DOI 10.1007/978-3-319-45492-4_14

Since its birth in Lomé in 1975, the development partnership between the African, Caribbean, and Pacific (ACP) group of states and the European Union (EU) has endured a great deal—from the dissipation of the "almost beatific euphoria" that marked its origins to the "doldrums of the 1980s" and the uncertainties of the first post-Cold-War decade (see Whiteman in this volume). But over the past 15 years, under the neo-liberal "spirit of Cotonou", the relationship has seemed to reach a nadir that has shrouded its future in doubt, with questions openly asked of its continued value and benefits beyond 2020, when the 20-year Cotonou Partnership Agreement that currently governs the relationship is due to expire. Against the backdrop of an unsettled global order, this uncertainty has been further exacerbated by difficult and divisive negotiations for economic partnership agreements (EPAs), mandated by Cotonou, between the EU and seven (initially six) regional groupings within the ACP group.[3] Especially for the ACP, as St Lucian academic Annita Montoute emphasises in her introduction to this volume, the issue is existential, given the group's origins in, and focus on, cooperation with the EU—a crisis-stricken economic power that itself is struggling to hold together and stay relevant in a changing world. In this context, "the demands for fundamental renewal and transformation", as ACP heads of state and government declared in December 2012, "are no longer mere options but unavoidable imperatives for strategic change".[4]

With official negotiations for a successor agreement due to start no later than 2018, both sides have been engaged in ongoing processes of reflection on their post-Cotonou future. The ACP Eminent Persons Group—launched in March 2013—presented its recommendations on the future purposes and practices of the organisation to the eighth summit of ACP heads of state and government in Port Moresby, Papua New Guinea, in May–June 2016, with the summit mandating the ACP Council of Ministers "to put in place implementation modalities for [the] recommendations ... by the end of 2016".[5] In Europe, meanwhile, the debate has gathered momentum since the appointment in October 2014 of the European Commission for 2014–2019, headed by Luxembourg's Jean-Claude Juncker. Notably, from October to December 2015, the EU undertook a 12-week public consultation process, intended to form part of an in-depth analysis in 2016 by the Commission of the strengths of, and prospects for, the ACP-EU partnership. With a view to contributing to these continuing deliberations, this edited volume has in part been an analysis of the history and political economy of the ACP-EU relationship, and in part a deliberation—from the perspective of the ACP in particular—on the challenges of renewing the partnership and making it fit for purpose in the twenty-first century. Moreover, how the future unfolds for the ACP and the EU, after their unique four-decade experience in international cooperation, is likely to be a barometer for the changing nature of, and prospects for, North-South efforts at large to bridge the socio-economic divides that separate them.

The task that these two long-standing development partners face is daunting and complex, not to forget emotionally charged, in view of the colonial roots of their association. It is also an imperative, in view of their shared commitment to the 2030 Agenda for Sustainable Development—comprising 17 Sustainable Development Goals (SDGs)—and the agenda's vision of "a world free of poverty, hunger, disease and want",[6] with over half of the ACP's membership still among the world's poorest.[7] In tackling these challenges, the ACP group and the EU must inevitably—as the diverse, mostly Southern voices in this volume make plain—build on their experiences of the past four decades, address the damaging impact of the EPA processes on the partnership, and adapt to the strengthening of regionalism both in the ACP and in EU policies, while responding to the rise of new players such as the BRICS bloc (Brazil, Russia, India, China, and South Africa). The 2016 Port Moresby Declaration, adopted by the ACP at its eighth summit of heads of state and government, notes "in particular the role and place of South-South and Triangular Cooperation and innovative financing in the implementation of the SDGs", while recognising the SDGs as being "vital to poverty eradication, reducing inequalities, and achieving growth and sustainable development".[8] Thus for the ACP, as the group's Guyanese Secretary-General, Patrick Gomes, contends in this volume, the way forward includes not only shoring up its partnership with the EU through a legally binding post-Cotonou agreement, but also looking beyond Europe for diversified partnerships and, in so doing, moving beyond the traditional North-South debate.

AN ENDURING BUT TROUBLED RELATIONSHIP SHAPED BY ASYMMETRY

Looking back, Lomé I, when it was signed in February 1975, was unique: a comprehensive North-South agreement, based on the twin principles of trade preferences and development aid. British analyst Kaye Whiteman, in his chapter on the political history of ACP-EU relations, notes that the first Lomé Convention was further promoted as a partnership among equals, and as such was welcomed by many as a pioneering model of North-South economic cooperation. However, within a few short years, disillusionment had set in. Far from being an exemplar of jointly managed partnership, the Lomé Conventions (1975–2000) replicated a mainly donor-recipient relationship, driven by the resources of the European Development Fund (EDF) and marred by European paternalism.[9] In recounting the African, Caribbean, and Pacific stories of the ACP-EU relationship in this volume, Ghanaian academic John Akokpari, Jamaican scholar Norman Girvan and St Lucian academic Annita Montoute, and Fijian diplomat Kaliopate Tavola note the benefits of preferential access to the European market under Lomé, but for the most part describe a history of disappointment with its lack of success in stimulating trade expansion and diversification and in stemming the marginalisation of ACP countries in the global economy. Yet as others have noted, Lomé alone could not have transformed or alleviated the structural weaknesses of African, Caribbean, and Pacific economies.[10] For Tavola in this volume, the poor record of both ACP-EU cooperation and intra-Pacific regional integration is attributable to the failure of Pacific leaders as much as to EU decision-makers, who failed to "creatively and genuinely address the challenges stemming from the geography, history, and socio-economic circumstances of the Pacific region".

Cotonou, which replaced Lomé in 2000, marked a major shift in the nature of the ACP-EU relationship, but at the same time continued to reflect the predominant perspectives and interests of the EU. It contained several European-driven innovations, of which two have been of particular note in shaping the current and future course of the ACP-EU relationship. The first comprised economic partnership agreements, a mainstay of Cotonou's new trade pillar and championed by the European Commission as "an innovative type of accord, which will combine trade and development issues in ways tailored to national and regional conditions" in ACP countries.[11] The reality, as several of the chapters in this volume show, has been quite different. From the outset, the EPAs have been a source of acrimonious contention and have generated grave disquiet about European intentions towards the ACP, while rendering bare the ACP-EU relationship—in Akokpari's words in this volume—as "a partnership between unequals". The second innovative feature of Cotonou was the deepening and broadening of the political dimensions of the ACP-EU partnership, with an emphasis on human rights, democratic principles, rule of law, and "good governance"—once again a reflection of European rather than ACP preferences, in this case for "value-driven cooperation" and for a more encompassing partnership.[12]

ECONOMIC PARTNERSHIP AGREEMENTS: THE LITMUS TEST OF AN UNEQUAL RELATIONSHIP

The economic partnership agreements—negotiated, at the EU's insistence, on a regional basis—constitute a dismantling of the Lomé system of preferences in favour of reciprocal trade. Though justified on the need for compliance with the free-market-based rules of the World Trade Organisation (WTO), the EPAs reflect, fundamentally, the EU's neo-liberal approach to development. This, as several contributors to this volume have noted, has privileged trade liberalisation over the emphasis on complementary development finance and adjustment support in African, Caribbean, and Pacific perspectives. Namibian scholar-diplomat Peter Katjavivi, in his chapter on African perspectives on the EPAs, further contends that in the case of Africa in particular, the European push for liberalisation through the new partnership agreements has also been aimed at securing access to the continent's natural resources, as well as its markets, in the face of rising competition from China and other emerging powers. The experience of negotiating the EPAs has inevitably varied across Africa, the Caribbean, and the Pacific, but there is one clear point on which disagreement within the ACP, and on the pages of this volume, is scarce: the structure and content of the EPAs, as well as the negotiating processes for them, have been driven primarily by the agendas of the EU, which has imposed deadlines and compelled agreement, often without due care and attention for the views and needs of its ACP partners.[13] The Europeans have in turn complained about the slow responsiveness of their ACP interlocutors during the EPA negotiations.

By 2015, the Caribbean was the only region to have started implementing a comprehensive EPA with the EU. In his chapter on the Caribbean EPA, Trinidadian scholar Anthony Gonzales acknowledges several positive outcomes of the agreement, which was signed in a context of "concern and controversy among ACP countries", but overall charts the region's struggle to implement it. Girvan and Montoute, in their chapter, sketch a similar picture of a slow and onerous process beset by challenges, and going further, argue that the region "needs to prioritise healing its [fractured] relationship with the African, Caribbean, and Pacific group". In their view: "Both CARICOM [the Caribbean Community] and CARIFORUM [the Forum of the Caribbean Group of ACP States] will ... need ACP support in resolving their differences with the EU over the implementation of the Caribbean EPA—differences that are bound to multiply in the future as the full implications of the agreement become manifest."

By 2015, three negotiating processes for regional EPAs had also been concluded in Africa—with the Southern African Development Community (SADC) EPA group, West Africa, and the East African Community (EAC)—but with serious criticisms continuing to abound among stakeholders about the failure of the EU-driven EPA processes to take African concerns into account fully. These concerns have covered the full gamut, from the restriction of policy space and flexibility, to the adequacy of adjustment support, and are detailed at length in this volume by Akokpari and Katjavivi, both of whom are trenchant in their criticisms of the proposed agreements for being detrimental for African development and region-building efforts. The break-up of the African ACP, in particular, into five regional groupings, further fragmenting the continent's "spaghetti bowl"[14] of multiple and overlapping memberships, could, as Xavier Carim, one of South Africa's most senior trade multilateralists and its ambassador at the WTO, concludes in his in-depth chapter on the SADC EPA, "complicate, if not undermine, Africa's wider region-building and regional integration efforts in the years to come". Meanwhile, the outcome of the protracted negotiations for an EU-Pacific EPA remains uncertain.

This state of play, along with the lack of a systematic review of Cotonou by either the EU or the ACP,[15] makes it difficult to assess conclusively the consequences of the EPAs. That being said, their potential to impact negatively on the prospects of ACP development and regional integration efforts, while serving the interests of the EU, is a key cross-cutting theme to emerge from the chapters in this volume. How the episode plays out up to and after 2020 will be important for the ACP-EU partnership. As Katjavivi notes, the adoption of a more flexible approach from 2008 onwards by the EU played a vital role in moving the negotiating processes forward in Africa. This was evident, as Carim shows in his chapter, in the negotiations for the final SADC EPA, which were concluded in July 2014, with the agreement subsequently signed in June 2016. For Carim, another key lesson from the SADC experience related to the importance of "forging and maintaining ... unity". The Southern African experience further indicates that African ACP countries have gained valuable lessons that may have helped them, by and large, in negotiating seemingly better deals. For example, West Africa's EPA with the EU—concluded in February 2014—allows for a partial and more gradual opening of the West African market to EU exports; for some policy space to protect sensitive products (including in the agricultural sector); and for relatively flexible rules of origin. In addition, West African countries were able to negotiate a development support assistance package, expected to complement and assist in the implementation of the EPA, with the EU confirming the availability of at least €6.5 billion for 2015–2020.[16]

For several contributors to this volume, the onus remains on the ACP to be the master of its own present and future, and based on their analysis of the EPA processes, two broad recommendations emerge. The first focuses on the individual need for Africa and the Caribbean and Pacific regions to strengthen their region-building and regional integration efforts.[17] For Girvan and Montoute, in their chapter on Caribbean-EU relations, this means that first, the Caribbean needs to define, for itself, a clear strategic agenda that prioritises "sustainable human development for the region and … supportive strategic international engagements"; and that, second, it must put in place "an appropriate set of political and institutional arrangements among Caribbean states enabling the region to provide a coherent, united front in dealings with the EU". Tavola, in his chapter on the Pacific ACP, urges "creative, bold, and inclusive" initiatives for stronger and deeper regional integration as the foundation of EU-Pacific relations. In a similar vein, Carim points to a need for "dedicated attention" on the part of African countries to the trade policy divisions created by the patchwork of EPAs in Africa. The second recommendation advocates greater ACP unity. In Katjavivi's words, "the EU's strategic deal-making has opened fissures within the ACP grouping, which should serve as a lesson to the ACP to approach common problems with strategic unity. The ACP was built on solidarity among African, Caribbean, and Pacific countries, and this needs to continue to define the grouping's approach to common challenges if it is to remain relevant". At the 2016 Port Moresby summit, ACP heads of state and government re-committed themselves to "strengthening coordination and dialogue" within the group.[18]

Looking ahead, how the economic partnership agreements fit into the post-Cotonou framework will be a key issue for the ACP as it reflects on and forges its common negotiating position ahead of 2018. The EPAs have not only strengthened the regionalisation of Europe's relations with the ACP, but have also "outsourced" the trade pillar of the partnership.[19]

This does not necessarily mean that trade will be decoupled from the formal ACP-EU relationship after Cotonou's expiry in 2020, not least of all because the EPAs are, as Mauritian analyst Isabelle Ramdoo points out, "partial agreements" limited in scope—with the exception of the Caribbean EPA, which also covers services, investment, and trade-related issues—to trade in goods[20]; have weak development components; lack adequate financing support; and are, in Africa, a patchwork of deals negotiated under immense pressure that have generated divisions within and between countries.[21] Furthermore, not all ACP countries have opted for an EPA. For the ACP, it will thus be important to ensure that the architecture of a post-Cotonou framework is based on more broad-based trade cooperation. This would be in keeping with the emphasis that the ACP group has historically placed on the trade and economic dimensions of cooperation with Europe, not to forget that the EU as a whole continues to be the group's largest trading partner, accounting for about a quarter of its total trade with the world in 2014.[22] More importantly, without a strong trade dimension that serves ACP interests, this relationship with the EU runs a genuine risk of becoming—to borrow a metaphor for Cotonou—"an unstable house built on two pillars"[23]: development aid, and political dialogue and conditionality. This, in turn, would be a backward step towards a more donor-recipient relationship, given the importance attached by Brussels to value-based cooperation and the potential for divergences in values between the ACP and the EU.[24]

The Political Dialogue Pillar: a European Initiative with Weak ACP Ownership

Cotonou institutionalised political cooperation as a separate pillar—alongside trade and economic relations, and development cooperation—and in so doing, formalised regular political dialogue between the EU and ACP countries in an expanded range of cooperation areas including the environment, gender, and migration. Importantly, the agreement identifies respect for human rights, democratic principles, and the rule of law as essential elements, and "good governance" as a fundamental element of the ACP-EU partnership. The agreement further contains non-execution clauses that allow for the suspension of development cooperation as a last resort, in the event that these elements are violated and consultations fail to yield a mutually acceptable solution.[25] Yet this shift from "neutrality and non-interference" towards shared values and political conditionality—

begun under Lomé III and IV but strengthened under Cotonou—was "strongly driven by the EU", and ultimately, reflects the donor-recipient nature of the ACP-EU relationship.[26] The use of conditionality under Article 96, in particular, is based on the assumption of leverage, which lies squarely with the EU in this relationship, and the resultant imbalance is reflected in the reality that "it has only been used unilaterally by the EU" (over, for example, governance issues in Guinea and Zimbabwe).[27] In addition, there has been inconsistency and selectivity in practice, with "significant variation in the willingness of the EU to invoke Article 96 in ACP countries" based on several factors, including its own strategic, security, and economic interests.[28] Meanwhile, the ACP, for its part, has been inclined to view the consultations under this article as a "punitive and cumbersome process".[29]

Similarly, and unsurprisingly, given the ACP's initial resistance to this dimension of the relationship, its members have asserted, at best, limited ownership of the political dialogue under Cotonou, which has tended to be experienced by them as a "periodic obligation", or as a "one-sided performance review rather than an open discussion of issues of mutual concern".[30] There is little masking the reality that there are, in fact, deeper divergences between the EU and the ACP—Africa, in particular—on the content of the fundamental values of their partnership, which have been manifest in disagreements over gender equality; lesbian, gay, bisexual, transgender, and intersex (LGBTI) rights; migrant rights; and the role of the International Criminal Court (ICC).[31] Yet for several European countries, political dialogue remains a "crucial element" for inclusion in any post-Cotonou framework, with the main challenge being to improve its effectiveness.[32] For the ACP, on the other hand, given the lack of prioritisation that many of its members have attached to Cotonou's political pillar, the challenge in this context will be to mobilise interest in, and forge and sustain consensus within the group on, a common position in what are likely to be tense and difficult negotiations about its post-2020 relations with the EU. In this context, it is worth noting that the 2016 Port Moresby Declaration "encourage[s] a more systematic implementation of the Framework and General Principles for enhanced Intra-ACP Political Dialogue" (adopted in 2002).[33]

The political pillar of Cotonou further placed cooperation in peace-building; conflict resolution and management; and in-depth dialogue on migration within the framework of the partnership. In practice, however, Africa—rather than the ACP as a whole—has been the primary focus of

EU interest in cooperation on peace and security, as well as on migration issues, with relatively low levels of engagement with the Caribbean and Pacific, "reflecting the marginal status of both small regions for Europe or the emergence of alternative political groupings with more political traction" in these areas, such as the Community of Latin American and Caribbean States (CELAC).[34] The EU's security role in Africa has—as Nigerian scholar Adekeye Adebajo demonstrates in his chapter in this volume—evolved and expanded, with the creation of the EDF-funded African Peace Facility (APF) in 2004 and the emergence of a parallel dialogue with the African Union (AU) under the 2007 Joint Africa-EU Strategy (JAES), though, in his view, the EU's military interventions on the continent have "appeared to be more about parochial French interests and internal EU needs to establish a global security role than about promoting durable peace in Africa".

The trend towards the regionalisation of Cotonou's political elements has included migration, which is covered under the Joint Africa-EU Strategy. As German analyst Anna Knoll notes in her chapter on ACP-EU migration policy: "From the perspective of EU member states, the Africa-EU partnership has greater strategic value compared with the ACP-EU partnership, as the former includes most of Europe's neighbourhood in the southern Mediterranean." Neither the Joint Caribbean-EU Strategy nor the EU's strategy towards the Pacific focuses on migration as a key area for cooperation. In this respect, the greater importance attached to Africa may reflect the emphasis placed by the EU on security concerns in its approach to migration, which has, on the whole, been "one of the most contentious aspects of the ACP-EU partnership".[35] In the absence of a more concerted effort by the ACP to build internal cooperation, consensus, and ownership of migration as an agenda item, regional fora such as the Joint Africa-EU Strategy, as Knoll suggests, may further gain in importance and contribute to a further diminution of the ACP as a partner for the EU. For many, the Valletta Summit on Migration between EU and African countries, held in Malta in November 2015, has been significant in this regard—the ACP group, through its secretariat, was neither present at the summit, nor consulted in preparations for the EDF-funded Emergency Trust Fund launched at the meeting.[36]

Yet there is a need for the ACP to take greater initiative and ownership of this debate, given the growing importance—also highlighted in this volume by Trinidadian academic Keith Nurse and Italian scholar Ramona Ruggeri—of migration and diaspora relations as a "critical new area of interdependence between the ACP and the EU" and of its actual and potential developmental role. For Nurse and Ruggeri, "the development of a permanent institutional capacity to monitor and inform ACP-EU migration and diaspora relations is absolutely essential". They further stress the need for the ACP, as well as the EU, "to move further away from immigration-centred approaches and towards more diaspora-focused development policymaking". This will be no small challenge in negotiations for a post-Cotonou framework, in view of the current nature of the debate on migration in Europe, which has focused on security and terrorism concerns and sharpened the idea of "migration as threat".[37] Beyond the ACP-EU framework and the European discourse, Nurse and Ruggeri are critical of ACP countries, by and large, for their failure to "conceive a diasporic export strategy as a viable means" of economic diversification and export expansion. This finds an echo in Knoll's emphasis on the lack of interest shown by the ACP in harnessing the potential of large South-South migration flows and in "operationalising comprehensive policies on legal migration between the ACP regions". For her, this is a critical area in which the ACP group could form a niche and be of added value to its members in shaping and coordinating development cooperation with Europe and beyond.

THE CHALLENGE FOR THE ACP OF STAYING RELEVANT IN CHANGING TIMES

The context in which the post-Cotonou prospects of the ACP-EU development partnership are decided is, and will continue to be, vastly different from 2000, when Cotonou was finalised—even more so from the Lomé period when its foundations were laid. As Canadian scholar John Ravenhill wrote of the conception of Lomé in 1985: "Weakness constrains choice. ACP countries, among the weakest in the world, have few viable options available to them in their efforts to overcome the constraints imposed by their economic weakness. Collaboration with their most important partner, the EEC [European Economic Community], was a rational response to their predicament."[38] Thirty years on, the ACP is marked by diversity, but its members remain, by and large, weak states with weak economies characterised by a lack of diversification, dependence on raw material and agricultural exports, and poor integration into the world economy. On the one hand, sub-Saharan Africa was among the world's fastest-growing regions between 2001 and 2014, with three African ACP countries projected to be among the fastest-expanding economies in the world in 2016: Côte d'Ivoire, Tanzania, and Senegal.[39] However, at the same time, 39 of the world's 48 least-developed countries are members of the ACP group, the vast majority in Africa.[40] The Caribbean, though it comprises mainly middle-income countries, is experiencing decelerating growth, while the Pacific ACP includes among it the world's smallest and most remote island economies. However, there has been one key change in their predicament: the EU is no longer the only, or single most important, partner for the ACP. The emergence of new powers in the global South—in particular the BRICS bloc—has created space and opportunities for the ACP to forge a diverse and dynamic set of relationships, while providing it with a source of leverage in its partnership with the EU.

Regardless of the post-Cotonou structure of the ACP-EU relationship, the EU—as the world's largest aid donor—will remain relevant and important for African, Caribbean, and Pacific countries. The challenge for the ACP lies, to a significant extent, in ensuring its relevance for the EU, as Europe itself focuses on adjusting to changing production patterns and trade flows with the rise of new and emerging powers such as Brazil, China, and India in the global South—beyond the African, Caribbean, and Pacific regions. Faced with economic crises that have diminished its resources, the EU comprises a more diverse membership since Cotonou and includes, in particular, new members from Eastern and Central Europe that have no historical ties with the ACP and "object to a too generous funding of the ACP, which they see as competing with their own development needs".[41] At the same time, in the face of rising competition from China, in particular, the EU is also seeking to remain relevant to, and protects its traditional interests in, the ACP.

The numerical strength of the ACP has often been seen and cited as a source of diplomatic support and leverage for the EU in multilateral fora. This has, for the most part, remained a potential, though there is recent evidence of such cooperation with Europe. The ACP and the EU, for example, defined common positions at the 2012 United Nations (UN) Conference on Sustainable Development (Rio+20) and in discussions, held in 2014, on the then emerging post-2015 SDGs.[42] However, critics point out that these positions, "drafted and negotiated" in the so-called Brussels bubble, had little to no influence on the outcomes of the two fora.[43] The presence and identity of the ACP, in particular, have thus far been weak in the international arena, and if it is to realise its potential beyond Cotonou, this will require, first and foremost, greater investment in building convergence within the ACP, strengthening its institutions, as well as broadening and engaging with its constituency in the ACP regions. Finding national and regional anchors within the ACP—countries, as well as leaders, that can champion its relevance and value-added—could be vital to rooting the group's inter-regional cooperation project.

Furthermore, in preserving and renewing its long-standing, and for the most part valuable, partnership with the EU, it will be critical for the ACP to guard against any further loss of policy space and flexibility that might impede its efforts to collaborate and partner with new powers in the global South. At the same time, as I suggest in my chapter on the emerging powers, the BRICS, in particular, are an uncertain prospect, with neither the institutional and policy coherence nor the interest (thus far) to pursue comprehensive, inter-regional cooperation. This does not by definition pose a difficulty for individual African, Caribbean, and Pacific countries or regions that have attracted the interest of the emerging powers. However, for the ACP as a grouping, it presents a more complex and challenging situation. The ongoing shift and diffusion of power at the global level has contributed to the regionalisation of EU policies, as Brussels has itself sought to adjust to these changes, and to the singling out of Africa within the ACP, with the continent emerging as an arena for competition between traditional and emerging powers. Though China's footprint has grown across the ACP, the BRICS—not unlike Europe—have focused mainly on Africa, followed by the Caribbean, with the Pacific on the margins of their interest. This sets up a problematic, potentially centrifugal, dynamic—one of several, in fact—within the ACP. The group's 48 African members lie at the core of its numerical strength, which has in turn given the ACP political heft. From the perspective of these African countries, however, the 54-strong AU is a more inclusive grouping, and since its birth in 2002 has become the focus of a continental drive towards development and regional integration. Similarly, as Girvan and Montoute note in this volume, "Caribbean states have forged their own institutions of regional integration and are building closer ties with their Latin American neighbours". Meanwhile, efforts to reconfigure Pacific regionalism have also been under way, and as Tavola notes, these will have to be accommodated in EU-Pacific relations, as well as in a post-Cotonou framework. This strengthening regionalism, on the face of it, has diluted ACP identity, while providing alternative and arguably easier entry points for the EU—as well as emerging powers—to engage individually with the ACP regions, and has formed the basis of a parallel diplomacy, particularly on political and security issues, outside the Cotonou framework.

For the formal ACP group, the resultant challenge is at least two-fold. First, how can the group accommodate this growth in regional architecture into its *modus operandi* as well as into a post-Cotonou framework? Both the EU and the AU are multilayered regional processes based on principles of subsidiarity and complementarity, which have been considered as a means of organising the roles of still-evolving African, Caribbean, and Pacific regional institutions and processes under an all-ACP umbrella. This would have the added advantage of creating space for the diversity that exists within the ACP to flourish. However, the ACP will need to root such inter-regional collaboration in a common vision, based in turn on common interests and values, which can attract the commitment and resources of its members. Regional projects in the ACP regions themselves remain works in progress, and as the experience of the AU and Africa's regional economic communities (RECs) shows, it is far from easy to garner acceptance for and implement subsidiarity in reality.[44] Second, as the ACP seeks to go beyond the binary North-South divide, what is the vision around which its diverse membership, from three disparate continental regions with different interests beyond Cotonou, can cohere? In its ongoing efforts to reposition itself globally, to move beyond aid-dependency, and to define a common set of interests around which solidarity can be built, the ACP had by December 2014 identified five strategic areas to form the core of its future work—rule of law and "good governance"; global justice and human security; building sustainable, resilient, and creative economies; intra-ACP trade, industrialisation, and regional integration; and financing for development.[45] These reflect the 2030 Agenda for Sustainable Development, and in this respect provide the basis for moving beyond aid in the ACP-EU relationship, given the prioritisation of the SDG agenda by the EU. The SDG framework, though, seeks also to move beyond the North-South divide, and the 2016 Port Moresby Declaration identifies it as an anchor for the future of the ACP. What remains to be seen is how the ACP can reconstruct itself to become, in the words of Gomes in this volume, "an effective global advocate and catalyst for the benefit of all developing countries".

NOTES

1. Patrick I. Gomes, "Viewpoint: EU-ACP—A Force for South-South & Triangular Cooperation", 5 April 2016, http://www.acp.int/content/viewpoint-eu-acp-force-south-south-triangular-cooperation (accessed 3 May 2016).

2. Statement by the European Commissioner for International Cooperation and Development, Neven Mimica, 28th ACP-EU Joint Parliamentary Assembly, Strasbourg, France, 2 December 2014, http://www.acp.int/content/statement-european-development-commissioner-28th-acp-eu-joint-parliamentary-assembly-mr-neve (accessed 4 May 2016).

3. These are: West Africa, Central Africa, Eastern and Southern Africa (ESA), the East African Community (EAC), the Southern African Development Community (SADC) economic partnership agreement (EPA) group, the Caribbean, and the Pacific.

4. Quoted in Mark Paterson and Kudrat Virk, "EU Challenged to Renew Its Duty to a Fairer World Order", *Business Day*, 15 February 2013, http://www.bdlive.co.za/opinion/2013/02/15/eu-challenged-to-renew-its-duty-to-a-fairer-world-order (accessed 2 May 2016). *See* African, Caribbean, and Pacific (ACP) Group of States, "The Future of the ACP Group in a Changing World: Challenges and Opportunities", Sipopo Declaration, ACP/28/065/12 (Final), Seventh Summit of ACP Heads of State and Government, Sipopo, Equatorial Guinea, 13–14 December 2012.

5. Decision of the Eighth Summit of ACP Heads of State and Government on the Report of the ACP Eminent Persons Group (EPG), Port Moresby, Papua New Guinea, 31 May–1 June 2016, para. 2.

6. United Nations (UN) General Assembly, "Transforming Our World: The 2030 Agenda for Sustainable Development", UN Doc. A/RES/70/1, 25 September 2015, para. 7.

7. Centre for Conflict Resolution (CCR), *The African, Caribbean, and Pacific (ACP) Group and the European Union (EU)*, seminar report, Cape Town, South Africa, January 2014, p. 11, http://www.ccr.org.za.

8. Port Moresby Declaration, ACP/28/005/16 Final, Eighth Summit of ACP Heads of State and Government, "Repositioning the ACP Group to Respond to the Challenges of Sustainable Development", Port Moresby, 31 May–1 June 2016, preambular para. J and para. 2.

9. *See* John Ravenhill, *Collective Clientelism: The Lomé Conventions and North-South Relations* (New York: Columbia University Press, 1985).

10. Ravenhill, *Collective Clientelism*, p. 2.
11. European Commission, "European Commission Sets Out Negotiating Strategy for New Economic Partnership Agreements with African, Caribbean and Pacific Countries", Brussels, 9 April 2002, http://europa.eu/rapid/press-release_IP-02-527_en.htm (accessed 30 April 2016).
12. Jean Bossuyt, Niels Keijzer, Alfonso Medinilla, and Marc De Tollenaere, *The Future of ACP-EU Relations: A Political Economy Analysis*, Policy and Management Report no. 21 (Maastricht: European Centre for Development Policy Management [ECDPM], 2016), p. 59.
13. Port Moresby Declaration, para. 58.
14. Peter Draper, Durrel Halleson, and Philip Alves, *SACU, Regional Integration and the Overlap Issue in Southern Africa: From Spaghetti to Cannelloni?*, Trade Policy Report no. 15 (Johannesburg: South African Institute of International Affairs [SAIIA], 2007), p. 7.
15. Tina Tindemans and Dirk Brems, "Post-Cotonou: Preliminary Positions of EU Member States", Briefing Note no. 87 (Maastricht: ECDPM, 2016), p. 2.
16. European Commission, "West African Leaders Back Economic Partnership Agreement with EU", Brussels, 11 July 2014; Isabelle Ramdoo, "Economic Partnership Agreements: What Has Africa Gained and What Can It Lose?", *Bridges Africa* 4, no. 7 (September 2015), p. 11.
17. *See* Daniel H. Levine and Dawn Nagar (eds.), *Region-Building in Africa: Political and Economic Challenges* (New York: Palgrave Macmillan 2016); Chris Saunders, Gwinyayi A. Dzinesa, and Dawn Nagar (eds.), *Region-Building in Southern Africa: Progress, Problems, and Prospects* (London and New York: Zed, 2012); Adekeye Adebajo and Kaye Whiteman (eds.), *The EU and Africa: From Eurafrique to Afro-Europa* (London: Hurst; New York: Columbia University Press; and Johannesburg: Wits University Press, 2012).
18. Port Moresby Declaration, para. 63.
19. Tindemans and Brems, "Post-Cotonou", p. 10.
20. Ramdoo, "Economic Partnership Agreements", p. 11.
21. Alan Beattie and Andrew Bounds, "How Europe's Trade Talk with Poor Former Colonies Became Mired in Mistrust", *Financial Times*, 12 December 2007, http://www.ft.com/intl/cms/s/0/2ae09950-a8e3-11dc-ad9e-0000779fd2ac.

html#axzz47TPwRPLR (accessed 1 May 2016); European Parliament, "African, Caribbean and Pacific (ACP) Countries' Position on Economic Partnership Agreements" (Brussels: Directorate-General for External Policies of the Union, Policy Department, 2014).

22. European Commission, "European Union, Trade in Goods with ACP Total (African Caribbean and Pacific Countries)", Directorate-General for Trade, Brussels, 14 April 2016, p. 8.

23. ECDPM, *The Cotonou Agreement: A User's Guide for Non-State Actors* (Brussels: ACP Secretariat, 2003), p. 14, https://ec.europa.eu/europeaid/sites/devco/files/methodology-the-cotonou-agreement-user-guide-for-non-state-actors-200311_en_2.pdf (accessed 1 May 2016).

24. Tindemans and Brems, "Post-Cotonou", pp. 6–7, 9–10.

25. *See* Articles 8–9 and 96–97 of the Cotonou Partnership Agreement.

26. Niels Keijzer, Mark Furness, Christine Hackenesch, and Svea Koch, "Towards a New Partnership between the European Union and the African, Caribbean, and Pacific Countries After 2020" (Bonn: German Development Institute/Deutsche Institut für Entwicklungspolitik [DIE], December 2015), p. 3.

27. Bossuyt et al., *The Future of ACP-EU Relations*, pp. 62, 64–65.

28. Bossuyt et al., *The Future of ACP-EU Relations*, p. 63. *See also* Jean Bossuyt, Camilla Rocca, and Brecht Lein, *Political Dialogue on Human Rights Under Article 8 of the Cotonou Agreement* (Brussels: EU, 2014), pp. 13–14.

29. Bossuyt et al., *The Future of ACP-EU Relations*, p. 63.

30. Bossuyt et al., *The Future of ACP-EU Relations*, p. 61. *See also* Keijzer et al., "Towards a New Partnership", pp. 3–4.

31. Tindemans and Brems, "Post-Cotonou", p. 6; Bossuyt et al., *The Future of ACP-EU Relations*, pp. xiii, 70–71.

32. Tindemans and Brems, "Post-Cotonou", p. 6.

33. Port Moresby Declaration, para. 9.

34. Bossuyt et al., *The Future of ACP-EU Relations*, pp. 37–38.

35. Bossuyt et al., *The Future of ACP-EU Relations*, p. 96.

36. Keijzer et al., "Towards a New Partnership", p. 9.

37. Jonathan Crush, "Between North and South: The EU-ACP Migration Relationship", Centre for International Governance Innovation (CIGI) Paper no. 16 (Waterloo, Canada: CIGI, April 2013), p. 6.

38. Ravenhill, *Collective Clientelism*, p. 3.
39. Joe Myers, "Which Are the World's Fastest Growing Economies?", 18 April 2016, https://www.weforum.org/agenda/2016/04/worlds-fastest-growing-economies (accessed 1 May 2016). *See also* International Monetary Fund (IMF) DataMapper, http://www.imf.org/external/datamapper/mobileipad/index.html (accessed 9 May 2016).
40. UN Department of Economic and Social Affairs, "List of Least Developed Countries" (as of 16 February 2016), http://www.un.org/en/development/desa/policy/cdp/ldc/ldc_list.pdf (accessed 1 May 2016).
41. CCR, *The African, Caribbean, and Pacific (ACP) Group and the European Union (EU)*, p. 2.
42. Adekeye Adebajo, "Towards a Post-Cotonou ACP/EU Partnership for Sustainable Development", presentation at the ACP roundtable seminar *Enhancing Inter-Regional Cooperation on Agenda 2030*, Brussels, 31 March 2016.
43. Bossuyt et al., *The Future of ACP-EU Relations*, p. 38.
44. Adebajo, "Towards a Post-Cotonou ACP/EU Partnership".
45. Patrick Gomes, "The ACP at 40—Repositioning As a Global Player", *Inter Press Service*, 28 June 2015, http://www.ipsnews.net/2015/06/opinion-the-acp-at-40-repositioning-as-a-global-player (accessed 5 May 2016).

NOTES ON CONTRIBUTORS

Adekeye Adebajo has been Executive Director of the Centre for Conflict Resolution (CCR) in Cape Town, South Africa, since 2003. He obtained his doctorate from the University of Oxford in England, where he studied as a Rhodes Scholar. Dr Adebajo served on United Nations (UN) missions in South Africa, Western Sahara, and Iraq. He is the author of five books: *Thabo Mbeki: Africa's Philosopher-King*; *Building Peace in West Africa*; *Liberia's Civil War*; *The Curse of Berlin: Africa After the Cold War*; and *UN Peacekeeping in Africa: From the Suez Crisis to the Sudan Conflicts.* He is co-editor or editor of eight books, on managing global conflicts, the United Nations, the European Union (EU), West African security, South Africa's and Nigeria's foreign policies in Africa, and Nobel peace laureates of African descent. Dr Adebajo is a Visiting Professor at the University of Johannesburg in South Africa.

John Akokpari is an Associate Professor in the Department of Political Studies at the University of Cape Town, South Africa. He obtained his doctorate from Dalhousie University in Halifax, Canada. Professor Akokpari has previously taught and researched at Dalhousie University and St Mary's University, both in Canada; and at the National University of Lesotho. In 2007 he was a Visiting Research Fellow at the Japan External Trade Organisation's (JETRO) Institute of Developing Economies in Chiba, Japan. Professor Akokpari has published in reputable international journals and has also contributed chapters to a number of books on a wide variety of topics on African politics and development. He is co-editor

© The Author(s) 2017
A. Montoute, K. Virk (eds.), *The ACP Group and the EU
Development Partnership*, DOI 10.1007/978-3-319-45492-4

of *The African Union and Its Institutions* and *Africa's Evolving Human Rights Architecture*. His current research focuses on, among other things, civil society; democratisation; development; foreign policy; globalisation; international migration; conflicts; and regionalism in Africa.

Xavier Carim is South Africa's Permanent Representative to the World Trade Organisation (WTO) in Geneva, Switzerland. He had previously been South Africa's representative to the WTO from 1998 to 2002. Prior to his current appointment, he was the Deputy Director-General for International Trade and Economic Development at the South African Department of Trade and Industry (DTI), responsible for managing South Africa's trade and investment policy development and for leading the country's international negotiations in these areas. Before joining the DTI, between 1992 and 1995, he was a Research Fellow at the Centre for Southern African Studies and a Lecturer in International Studies at the University of the Western Cape, South Africa. Ambassador Carim holds a bachelor's with specialist honours in international relations, economics, and political studies from the University of Toronto, Canada; and a master's in international relations from Rhodes University in Grahamstown, South Africa.

Norman Girvan was Professor Emeritus of the University of the West Indies (UWI) and Professorial Research Fellow at the UWI Graduate Institute of International Relations in Trinidad and Tobago. He had previously served as the Secretary-General of the Association of Caribbean States (ACS); as Professor of Development Studies and Director of the Sir Arthur Lewis Institute of Social and Economic Studies at the University of the West Indies; and as Head of the National Planning Agency of the government of Jamaica. In 2010 he was appointed the UN Secretary-General's Personal Representative on the Guyana-Venezuela Border Controversy. He obtained his doctorate in economics from the London School of Economics and Political Science. He published extensively on the political economy of development in the Caribbean and the global South, and was the recipient of several honours and awards. Professor Girvan passed away in April 2014.

Patrick Gomes is the Secretary-General of the African, Caribbean, and Pacific (ACP) group of states. He previously served as Guyana's Ambassador to the EU and as Guyana's representative to the WTO, the Food and Agriculture Organisation (FAO), and the International Fund for Agricultural Development (IFAD). Ambassador Gomes has held various key positions in the ACP system, including Chair of the Working

Group on Future Perspectives of the ACP Group and Dean of ACP Ambassadors in Brussels. He previously headed the Caribbean Centre for Development Administration for ten years. Ambassador Gomes has also worked as a Senior Adviser in Human Resources Development at the UN's Economic Commission for Latin America and the Caribbean (ECLAC). He has authored several publications on issues related to development and social policy analysis, and also served as Chairperson of the Board of Governors of the Maastricht-based European Centre for Development Policy Management (ECDPM).

Anthony Peter Gonzales is former Director of the Institute of International Relations at the University of the West Indies, where he previously taught international trade and development. Dr Gonzales worked as an Expert at the ACP Secretariat in Brussels between 1977 and 1982, and actively participated in the negotiations for the second Lomé Convention. During the period 2000–2003, he served as Director of the Institute of International Relations at the University of the West Indies in St Augustine. He also served as Vice-Chair of the Smaller Economies Consultative Group in the Free Trade Area of the Americas (FTAA), as well as Chairman of the ACP Trade Advisory Group. From 2004 to 2007, Dr Gonzales held the position of Director and WTO Representative at the Caribbean Regional Negotiating Machinery (CRNM) and represented the CRNM in the Doha Round of trade negotiations between 2005 and 2007.

Peter H. Katjavivi is a Member of Parliament and Speaker of the National Assembly of Namibia, prior to which he was the Government Chief Whip from 2010 until 2015. He previously served as Namibia's Ambassador to the EU and Belgium, Netherlands, and Luxembourg between 2003 and 2006; and was the country's Ambassador to Germany from 2006 to 2008. Upon returning to Namibia, he served as Director-General of the National Planning Commission from 2008 to 2010. Professor Katjavivi, who obtained his doctorate from the University of Oxford, was the founding Vice-Chancellor of the University of Namibia from 1992 to 2003. He is the author of *A History of Resistance in Namibia* and has written on a variety of topics including Namibia's bilateral relations with Germany and the liberation struggle in Southern Africa. He has also served on the boards of various organisations including the European Centre for Development Policy Management.

Anna Knoll is a Policy Officer in the Strengthening European External Action Programme at the European Centre for Development Policy

Management in Maastricht, Netherlands. Before joining the ECDPM, she worked as a *stagiaire* at the European Commission in the Trade and Development Unit of the Directorate-General for Trade. Her current work focuses on development cooperation in the context of the post-2015 global framework for development, specifically the role of the European Union; the EU's migration and development policies; and the European External Action Service (EEAS) in peace mediation and conflict resolution. Ms Knoll holds a master's in international political economy from the London School of Economics and Political Science.

Annita Montoute is a Lecturer at the Institute of International Relations at the University of the West Indies, from which she obtained her doctorate in international relations in 2009. Her doctoral thesis focused on the role of civil society in trade policy formulation, which has since led her to engage with a variety of non-governmental organisations (NGOs) on trade, as well as security-related issues. In 2012 she was a Research Fellow at the European Centre for Development Policy Management. Dr Montoute has written widely on a variety of topics related to the Caribbean's economic and external relations, including development cooperation between the ACP and the EU; civil society participation in the Caribbean's economic partnership agreement (EPA) with the EU; and the region's relations with China and other emerging powers.

Keith Nurse is Senior Fellow at the Sir Arthur Lewis Institute for Social and Economic Studies and the World Trade Organisation Chair at the University of the West Indies. He is also a member of the executive bureau of the UN Committee for Development Policy and an Expert Member of the Economic Development Advisory Board of the government of Trinidad and Tobago. He is the former Executive Director of UWI Consulting Inc.; former Director of the Shridath Ramphal Centre at the UWI Cave Hill Campus, Barbados; and former president of the Association of Caribbean Economists. Dr Nurse is one of the founding members of the World Economics Association; and has served on advisory boards for international organisations, including the WTO, the International Organisation for Migration (IOM), and the ACP. He is on the editorial board of several academic journals, as well as the Anthem Press *Other Canon Series*.

Ramona Ruggeri is an independent researcher based in Bologna, Italy, where she also works for a local non-profit organisation, planning and implementing language learning and educational activities for migrants in public schools and reception centres for unaccompanied refugee minors.

In 2014 she worked as a junior researcher at the ACP Observatory on Migration in Brussels and conducted an impact study on the academic value of the Observatory's activities that highlighted its role in promoting networking of academic scholars, fostering knowledge-sharing processes, and serving as a platform for dialogue with governmental actors. Dr Ruggeri holds a post-graduate degree in intercultural cooperation for development from the University of Trieste in Italy, as well as a master's in language, ethnicity, and education from King's College London. Her research interests lie in issues related to migration and development cooperation, and in the fields of language contact, teaching, and intercultural communication.

Kaliopate Tavola is a trade and development expert, and a member of the ACP Eminent Persons Group. From 2001 to 2006 he was Fiji's Minister for Foreign Affairs and External Trade. Ambassador Tavola also served as the Chief Negotiator for the Pacific ACP States in negotiations for an economic partnership agreement with the EU. He was previously Fiji's Ambassador to the EU and Belgium, Netherlands, and Luxembourg from 1988 to 1998, during which time he was also the ACP Spokesperson for Least-Developed, Landlocked, and Island Countries in negotiations for the fourth Lomé Convention. Additionally, Ambassador Tavola served as Chief Negotiator for the ACP Sugar Group in the negotiations on additional preferential sugar access to the EU, which led to the signing of the Special Preferential Sugar Agreement in 1995. Ambassador Tavola holds a master's in agricultural development economics from Australian National University.

Kudrat Virk is a Senior Researcher at the Centre for Conflict Resolution in Cape Town. She completed her doctorate in international relations from the University of Oxford, where her research examined the perspectives of the global South on the principle and practice of humanitarian intervention after the Cold War, with an in-depth focus on India and Argentina. Dr Virk has contributed chapters on Indian foreign policy to several books, including, most recently, *The Oxford Handbook of Indian Foreign Policy* on India's relations with South Africa. Her work has previously been published in the journals *International Review of the Red Cross* and *Global Responsibility to Protect*. Her current research interests include international peace and security; the responsibility to protect (R2P); peacekeeping and the protection of civilians; and emerging powers, in particular the BRICS bloc (Brazil, Russia, India, China, and South Africa).

Kaye Whiteman was a journalist and writer on African affairs. Based in London, he was an editorial advisor to *Business Day* (Nigeria) and also wrote for other publications such as *Africa Today*, *The Annual Register*, and *Geopolitique Africaine*. Prior to that, he was based at *Business Day* in Lagos; served as Director of Information and Public Affairs at the Commonwealth Secretariat in London; and was Editor-in-Chief, General Manager, and Managing Editor of the London-based weekly magazine *West Africa*. Between 1973 and 1982, he was a senior Information Official at the European Commission in Brussels, working on development issues. He was the author of *Lagos: A Cultural and Historical Companion*, and held a master's in history from the University of Oxford. He wrote extensively on West African affairs, Europe-Africa relations, and the Commonwealth. Mr Whiteman passed away in May 2014.

Index

Note: Page numbers followed by "n" denote notes.

© The Author(s) 2017
A. Montoute, K. Virk (eds.), *The ACP Group and the EU
Development Partnership*, DOI 10.1007/978-3-319-45492-4